Women, Modernism and British Poetry, 1910–1939

Resisting femininity

D0088366

JANE DOWSON
De Montfort University, Leicester

Ashgate

Published by
Ashgate Publishing Limited
Gower House
Croft Road
Aldershot
Hants GU11 3HR
England

Ashgate Publishing Company
131 Main Street
Burlington, VT 05401-5600 USA

Ashgate website: http://www.ashgate.com

British Library Cataloguing in Publication Data
Dowson, Jane
Women, modernism and British poetry, 1910-1939 : resisting
femininity
1. English poetry - 20th century - History and criticism
2. English poetry - Women authors - History and criticism
3. Modernism (Literature) 4. Femininity in literature
I. Title
821.9'12'099287

Library of Congress Cataloging-in-Publication Data
Dowson, Jane
Women, modernism and British poetry, 1910-1939 : resisting femininity / Jane Dowson.
p. cm.
ISBN 0-7546-0463-2 (alk. paper)
1. English poetry--Women authors--History and criticism. 2. Feminism and literature--Great Britain--History--20th century. 3. Women and literature--Great Britain--History--20th century. 4. English poetry--20th century--History and criticism. 5. Feminist poetry--History and criticism. 6. Modernism (Literature)--Great Britain. 7. Sex role in literature. I. Title.

PR605.W6 D69 2002
821'.912099287--dc21
2001053715

ISBN 0 7546 0463 2

Printed and bound by Athenaeum Press, Ltd.,
Gateshead, Tyne & Wear.

Contents

Preface

Although late twentieth-century cultural histories of modernism have aimed to be inclusive, they still overlook women poets, largely due to the scarcity of their books or the absence of literary criticism. My intention here is to put the records straight and evaluate their work in relation to literary modernism, or rather modernism*s*, in Britain. In a climate of new rights and opportunities, early twentieth-century women became a significant presence as public poets and literary figures; they ran printing presses and bookshops, edited magazines and wrote criticism. I also assess how their work registered and influenced the cultural shifts relating to the First World War, women's suffrage, the development of psychoanalysis and the growth of popular culture in the years 1910–1939.

Modernism as a period consists of progressive and reactionary cultural cross-currents. Under the umbrella of 'rear-guard modernism' I explore poetry which is not formally adventurous but which represents a 'conservative modernity', that is women's simultaneous internalisation and rejection of contemporary idealisations of femininity. It includes poems of the First World War and poets associated with the so-called 'Georgians', Frances Cornford and Vita Sackville-West. Their writing often registers an official public discourse in conflict with an unarticulated, non-symbolised, resistance to the literary and social formations of the feminine, particularly with reference to the idealised maternal function.

In the remaining sections I argue for women's participation in modernist innovation through radical aesthetics, radical perspectives or radical subject matter. In 'The British Avant-Garde', the most significant experimentalist is Edith Sitwell, but the less well-known work of Nancy Cunard, Iris Tree and Helen Rootham is also historically significant. 'The Anglo-American Avant-Garde' incorporates Mina Loy who was British but settled in the United States and American women who lived in Britain or who were indirectly influential through the network of writers in London, Paris and New York: H.D., Amy Lowell, Gertrude Stein, Laura Riding and Marianne Moore. The group of 'Female Modernists', Charlotte Mew, May Sinclair, Edna St Vincent Millay, Anna Wickham and Sylvia Townsend Warner, project a feminist consciousness in negotiation with poetic formalism. Some of their poems dramatise the assured voice of the 'New Woman'. In the chapter on the 1930s I concentrate on the political poetry of Sylvia Townsend Warner, Valentine Ackland, Nancy Cunard, Winifred Holtby, Naomi Mitchison and Stevie Smith.

By segregating women, I have inevitably confronted the difficulty of defining a specifically female practice. I have concluded that the cohering aesthetic is in women's problematic relationship with both male and female traditions. In the context of a male-dominated literary environment, most of these writers aimed to align themselves with a masculine tradition which excluded them and insisted upon their difference. They also constructed themselves antithetically to the mythologised poetess of the nineteenth century and popular verse. Women developed strategies for disguising their gender through indeterminate pronouns or anti-realist syntactical manoeuvres. Only the 'Female Modernists' wrote woman-centred poetry and subverted or parodied conventional femininity through fictional dramatisations. These writers particularly indicate women's progress towards an emancipated and self-asserting aesthetic.

Acknowledgements

I particularly wish to thank Nick Everett for his generosity with his time, continuing enthusiasm and constructive discussions. I am grateful to De Montfort University for granting me a sabbatical and to my colleagues who covered for me, particularly Caroline Daly, Clare Walsh, Sue Panter, Maureen Little and Alistair Walker. Thanks to Alison Light, Joanne Shattock and Judy Simons for their valued comments on the first draft. I have, as ever, appreciated the tolerance and partnership of Mark Dowson, along with the blessing and interest of my parents and friends.

Permissions

I have tried to clear rights on all the poetry extracts but some are hard to trace when books are out of print or publishers have merged or ceased to be. Permission has kindly been granted as follows. May Wedderburn Cannan: Major James Cannan Slater. Frances Cornford: from *Selected Poems*, Stephen Stuart Smith at Enitharmon Press. Nancy Cunard: by A.R.A. Hobson as representative of her heirs. H.D. Doolittle, from *Collected Poems, 1912–1944*, copyright 1982 by the Estate of Hilda Doolittle. Reprinted by permission of New Directions Publishing Corp. Winifred Holtby: with the cooperation of Marion Shaw. *The Lost Lunar Baedeker* by Mina Loy: Carcanet Press. *Collected Poems and Prose* by Charlotte Mew: Carcanet Press. Laura Riding: Alan J. Clark for the Literary Board of Management of Laura Riding. Vita Sackville-West: Nigel Nicolson. *Selected Poems* by Edna St Vincent Millay: Carcanet Press. Marianne Moore, from *The Complete Poems of Marianne Moore*, Faber and Faber. May Sinclair: reproduced with permission of Curtis Brown Group Ltd, London on behalf of the estate of May Sinclair; copyright May Sinclair. Edith Sitwell: David Higham Associates. From *Me Again: the Uncollected Writings of Stevie Smith:* by Virago/Little Brown. *Collected Poems* by Sylvia Townsend Warner: Carcanet Press. Anna Wickham: by Margaret and George Hepburn; I am also grateful for their time, hospitality and information.

Chronology of Poetry Publications and Enterprises by Women, 1910–1939

1910
Frances Cornford, *Poems*, London.

1911
The Freewoman: A Weekly Feminist Review, ed. Dora Marsden, London. 23 November 1911–10 October 1912.
Winifred Holtby, *My Garden and Other Poems*, Scarborough.
Katherine Tynan, *New Poems*, London.
Anna Wickham (pseudonym 'John Oland'), *Songs*, London.

1912
Frances Cornford, *Death and the Princess: A Morality*, Cambridge.
Amy Lowell, *A Dome of Many Coloured Glass*, Boston.
Poetry: A Magazine of Verse, ed. Harriet Monroe, Chicago, 1912–35.
Lady Margaret Sackville becomes the first President of the Poetry Society in London.

1913
Alice Meynell, *Collected Poems*, Boston.
The New Freewoman (formerly *The Freewoman*), ed. Dora Marsden, London.

1914
The Egoist (formerly *The New Freewoman*), ed. Harriet Shaw Weaver, assisted by Richard Aldington and Dora Marsden, London, 1914–18.
The Little Review, ed. Margaret Anderson, Chicago, New York; Paris, 1914–29.
Amy Lowell, *Sword Blades and Poppy Seed*, Boston.
Gertrude Stein, *Tender Buttons*, New York.

1915
Djuna Barnes, *The Book of Repulsive Women: 8 Rhythms and 5 Drawings*, New York.
Frances Cornford, *Spring Morning*, London.
Amy Lowell (ed.), *Some Imagist Poets*, Boston.
Amy Lowell, *Six French Poets: Studies in Contemporary Literature*, London; New York.
Alice Meynell, *Ten Poems 1913–1915*, London.
Jessie Pope, *Jessie Pope's War Poems*, London.
May Sinclair, *A Journal of Impressions in Belgium*, London; New York.
Katherine Tynan, *Flower of Youth: Poems in War Time*, London.
Anna Wickham, *The Contemplative Quarry*, London.

1916
Vera Brittain, *Verses of a VAD*, London.

H.D., *Sea Garden*, London.
Amy Lowell, *Men, Women and Ghosts*, Boston.
Amy Lowell (ed.), *Some Imagist Poets*, Vol. II, Boston.
Sylvia Lynd, *The Thrush and the Jay: Poems and Prose Sketches*, London.
Charlotte Mew, *The Farmer's Bride*, London.
Charlotte Mew, *The Rambling Sailor*, London.
Jessie Pope, *Simple Rhymes for Stirring Times*, London.
Lady Margaret Sackville, *The Pageant of War*, London.
Katherine Tynan, *The Holy War*, London.
Edith Sitwell and Nancy Cunard (eds), *Wheels: First Cycle*, Oxford.
Anna Wickham, *The Man with a Hammer*, London.

1917

May Wedderburn Cannan, *In War Time*, London.
Elizabeth Bridges (Daryush), *Verses*, Oxford.
Amy Lowell, *Tendencies in Modern American Poetry*, Boston.
Amy Lowell (ed.), *Some Imagist Poets*, Vol. III, Boston.
Amy Lowell (ed. with Louis Untermeyer), *A Miscellany of American Poetry*, New York.
Alice Meynell, *A Father of Women and Other Poems*, London.
Edna St Vincent Millay, *Renascence and Other Poems*, New York.
Vita Sackville-West, *Poems of West and East*, London.
Edith Sitwell (ed.), *Wheels: Second Cycle*, Oxford.
Katherine Tynan, *Late Songs*, London.

1918

Eva Gore-Booth, *Broken Glory*, London.
Margaret Cole, *Poems*, London.
Amy Lowell, *Can Grande's Castle*, London; New York.
Amy Lowell (ed.), *A Miscellany of American Poetry*, Vol. II, New York.
Edith Sitwell, *Clowns' Houses*, Oxford.
Edith Sitwell, *Mother and Other Poems*, Oxford.
Edith Sitwell (ed.), *Wheels: Third Cycle*, Oxford.

1919

The Egoist becomes Egoist Press, London.
Amy Lowell, *Pictures of the Floating World*, Boston.
Rose Macaulay, *Three Days*, London.
Edith Sitwell (ed.), *Wheels: Fourth Cycle*, Oxford.

1920

Sylvia Lynd, *The Goldfinches: Poem*, London.
Edna St Vincent Millay, *A Few Figs from Thistles: Poems and Sonnets*, New York; London.
Edna St Vincent Millay, *Second April*, New York (3 reprints in 1921).
Ruth Pitter, *First Poems*, London.
Jessie Pope, *Hits and Misses*, London.
Edith Sitwell, *The Wooden Pegasus*, Oxford.
Edith Sitwell (ed.), *Wheels: Fifth Cycle*, Oxford.

Time and Tide (1920–76) started by Lady Margaret Rhondda, London.
Iris Tree, *Poems*, London; New York.
Dorothy Wellesley, *Poems*, London.

1921

Nancy Cunard, *Outlaws*, London.
Elizabeth Bridges (Daryush), *Sonnets from Hafaz and Other Verses*, London.
H.D., *Hymen*, London; New York.
Charlotte Mew, *The Farmer's Bride* (new edition with 11 new poems), London.
Marianne Moore, *Poems*, London.
Vita Sackville-West, *Orchard and Vineyard*, London.
Edith Sitwell (ed.), *Wheels: Sixth Cycle*, Oxford.
Anna Wickham, *The Little Old House*, London.
Elinor Wylie, *Nets to catch the Wind*, New York.

1922

Amy Lowell, *Fir-Flower Tablets*, poems translated from the Chinese, New York; London.
Edna St Vincent Millay, *The Ballad of the Harp Weaver*, New York; London.
Edith Sitwell, 'Readers & Writers', *The New Age* new series, weekly column, July–August, Vol. 31, Nos 14–21, London.

1923

Louise Bogan, *Body of this Death: Poems*, New York.
May Wedderburn Cannan, *The House of Hope*, London.
Nancy Cunard, *Sublunary*, London.
Mina Loy, *Lunar Baedecker* [sic], Paris.
Alice Meynell, *Last Poems*, London.
Edna St Vincent Millay, *The Harp Weaver and Other Poems*, New York; London.
Edna St Vincent Millay, *Poems*, London.
Edith Sitwell, *Bucolic Comedies*, London.

1924

H.D., *Heliodora and Other Poems*, London. Boston.
Marianne Moore, *Observations*, New York.
May Sinclair, *The Dark Night*, London. New York.
Edith Sitwell, *The Sleeping Beauty*, London.

1925

Eva Gore-Booth, *The Shepherd of Eternity and Other Poems*, London.
Nancy Cunard, *Parallax*, London.
H.D., *Collected Poems of H.D.*, New York.
Amy Lowell, *What's O'Clock?*, Boston.
Amy Lowell, *John Keats*, Boston.
Mina Loy, *Lunar Baedecker* [sic], Paris.
Marianne Moore becomes editor of *The Dial* (1920–29), New York.
Edna St Vincent Millay, *Renascence and Other Poems*, New York.
Edith Sitwell, *Troy Park*, London.

Edith Sitwell, *Poetry and Criticism*, London.
Gertrude Stein, *The Making of Americans*, Paris.
Sylvia Townsend Warner, *The Espalier*, London.

1926

Amy Lowell, *East Wind*, London.
Harriet Monroe, *Poets and their Art*, New York.
Dorothy Parker, *Enough Rope*, New York.
Laura (Riding) Jackson, *The Close Chaplet*, London; New York.
Vita Sackville-West, *The Land*, London.
Dorothy Wellesley, *Genesis: An Impression*, London.

1927

Ruth Pitter, *First and Second Poems*, London.
Amy Lowell, *Ballads for Sale*, Boston.
Laura Riding and Robert Graves start the Seizin Press (1927–39), Mallorca; London.
Laura Riding and Robert Graves, *A Survey of Modernist Poetry*, London.
Edith Sitwell, *Rustic Elegies*, London.
Elinor Wylie, *Black Armour: A Book of Poems*, Martin Secker.

1928

Djuna Barnes, *Ladies Almanack*, New York.
Frances Cornford, *Different Days*, London.
Nancy Cunard starts The Hours Press (1928–31), Paris.
Sylvia Lynd, *Selected Poems*, London.
Amy Lowell, *Selected Poems*, Boston.
Edna St Vincent Millay, *The Buck in the Snow and Other Poems*, New York; London.
Dorothy Parker, *Sunset Gun*, New York.
Laura (Riding) Jackson, *Contemporaries and Snobs*, Frome; London.
Laura (Riding) Jackson with Robert Graves, *A Pamphlet against Anthologies*, London.
Sylvia Townsend Warner, *Time Importuned*, London.
Elinor Wylie, *Trivial Breath*, New York.

1929

Eva Gore-Booth, *Poems*, London.
Vita Sackville-West, *The King's Daughter*, London.
Edith Sitwell, *Gold Coast Customs*, London.
Elinor Wylie, *Angels and Earthly Creatures*, New York.

1930

Nancy Cunard, *Poems (Two)*, 1925, London.
Elizabeth Daryush, *Verses*, Oxford.
Laura (Riding) Jackson, *Poems: A Joking Word*, London.
Laura (Riding) Jackson, *Twenty Poems Less*, Paris.
Laura (Riding) Jackson, *Though Gently*, Deya.
Edith Sitwell, *Collected Poems*, London.
Katherine Tynan, *Collected Poems*, London.

Dorothy Wellesley, *Deserted House: A Poem Sequence*, London.
Amy Lowell, *Poets and Poetry* (essays), Boston.

1931

Sylvia Lynd, *The Yellow Placard: Poems*, London.
Edna St Vincent Millay, *Fatal Interview: Sonnets*, New York and London.
Marianne Moore, *Predilections*, (critical writings), New York.
Dorothy Parker, *Death of Taxes and other Poems*, New York.
Ruth Pitter, *Persephone in Hades*, privately printed.
Laura (Riding) Jackson, *Laura and Francisca*, Deya.
Vita Sackville-West, *Sissinghurst*, London.
Vita Sackville-West, *Invitation to Cast out Care*, London.
Vita Sackville-West, *Rilke* (translations), London.
Sylvia Townsend Warner, *Opus 7*, London.
Katherine Tynan (ed.), *Augustan Books of Poetry*, London.

1932

Elizabeth Daryush, *Verses: Second Book*, Oxford.
Sylvia Townsend Warner, *Rainbow*, New York.
Sitwell, Edith, *The Pleasure of Poetry* (3 vols, Vol. 3), London.
Elinor Wylie, *Collected Poems*, New York.

1933

Valentine Ackland with Sylvia Townsend Warner, *Whether a Dove or a Seagull*, New York; London.
Elizabeth Daryush, *Verses: Third Book*, Oxford.
Eva Gore-Booth, *Selected Poems*, London.
Naomi Mitchison, *The Delicate Fire: Short Stories and Poems*, London.
Lady Margaret Rhondda, *This Was My World*, London.
Laura (Riding) Jackson, *Poet: A Lying Word*, London.
Laura (Riding) Jackson, *The Life of the Dead*, London.
Vita Sackville-West, *Collected Poems*, London.
Edith Sitwell, *Five Variations on a Theme*, London.
Edith Sitwell, *The English Eccentrics*, London.

1934

Lilian Bowes Lyon, *The White Hare and Other Poems*, London.
Vera Britain, *Poems of the War and After*, Frances Cornford (illustrated by Gwen Raverat), *Mountains and Molehills*, Cambridge
Nancy Cunard (ed.), *Negro: An Anthology*, London; New York.
Elizabeth Daryush, *Verses: Fourth Book*, Oxford.
Sylvia Lynd, *The Enemies: Poems*, London.
Edna St Vincent Millay, *Wine from these Grapes*, London; New York.
Ruth Pitter, *A Mad Lady's Garland*, London; New York.
Laura (Riding) Jackson, *Americans*, Los Angeles.
Edith Sitwell, *Aspects of Modern Poetry*, London.
Dorothy Wellesley, *Poems of Ten Years*, London.

1935

Elizabeth Daryush, *Poems*, London.
Winifred Holtby, *The Frozen Earth and Other Poems*, London.
Harriet Monroe, *Chosen Poems: A Selection from My Books of Verse*, New York.
Marianne Moore, *Selected Poems* (introduced by T.S. Eliot), New York; London.

1936

Lilian Bowes Lyon, *Bright Feather Fading*, London.
Elizabeth Daryush, *The Last Man and Other Verses*, Oxford.
Marianne Moore, *The Pangolin and Other Verse*, London.
Ruth Pitter, *A Trophy of Arms: Poems 1926–1935*, London; New York.
Edith Sitwell, *Selected Poems*, London.
Dorothy Wellesley, *Selections from the Poems of Dorothy Wellesley*, London.
Anna Wickham, *Anna Wickham: Richards Shilling Selections*, London.
Edna St Vincent Millay, translation of *Fleurs du Mal*, Baudelaire.

1937

Winifred Holtby, *Letters to a Friend*, London.
Dorothy Parker, *Not so Deep as a Well: Collected Poems of Dorothy Parker*, London.
Stevie Smith, *A Good Time Was Had By All*, London.
Edna St Vincent Millay. *Conversation at Midnight*, New York; London.

1938

Elizabeth Daryush, *Verses: Sixth Book*, Oxford.
Laura (Riding) Jackson, *Collected Poems*, London; New York.
Harriet Monroe, *A Poet's Life: Seventy Years in a Changing World*, New York.
Vita Sackville-West, *Solitude*, London.
Stevie Smith, *Tender Only to One*, London.

1939

Naomi Mitchison, *The Alban Goes Out* (poem; wood engravings by Gertrude Hermes), Harrow.
Ruth Pitter, *The Spirit Watches*, London; New York.
Anne Ridler, *Poems*, Oxford.
Edna St Vincent Millay, *Huntsman, What Quarry?*, New York; London.
Edna St Vincent Millay, *Collected Lyrics 5th edition*, New York; London.

Chapter One

Introduction

(You seldom get the impression of femininity from a woman's book.)[1]

My vision for this book was to restore the reputations which literary women gained and lost while also reassessing their significance to a pluralised modernism*s*. One central strategy is to unsettle the binary concepts which falsely sever 'experiment' from 'tradition' and which support a hierarchical model of modernist poetics. The omission of women from histories of literary modernism is particularly invidious because of its elevated status and metonymical 'intellectuality'. It assigns women to modernism's antithetical ground of the 'popular' or 'sentimental'. Since, however, the dominance of high modernist principles partly accounts for the exclusion of much poetry from twentieth-century literary canons, there have to be reservations about endorsing the principles of selection which have undermined women. Some feminist histories have also colluded with the exclusivity of the so-called avant-garde and discounted non-experimentalists, partly because they seem old-fashioned and partly because they appear to support patriarchal structures by adopting verse forms associated with a male-dominated tradition. In privileging the formally adventurous, however, feminist critics have often missed women's negotiations with literary conventions; they have not always recognised the cultural constraints which meant that many women in the early years of the century were writing as men in order to publish at all. Their textual practice was complicated by their uncomfortable relationship with their literary foremothers – the nineteenth-century 'poetesses', caricatured as imitative and genteel personifications of sentimentality – particularly in this period when both the impersonal poetics of modernism and the emergent social realism of orthodox thirties poetry were exceptionally hostile to the sentimental. Consequently, they disguised their gender, often literally by using pseudonyms or initials or by male speakers and male-associated verse forms and metres. Some used anti-realist strategies to evade gender identification altogether. The 'avant-garde' poets, however, subverted the male-associated

---

1   Richard Aldington, 'New Poetry', review of *The Contemplative Quarry*, by Anna Wickham (London: The Poetry Bookshop, 1915) *Egoist* II, 1 June 1915: 89–90.

traditions through innovative syntax or by breaking conventional boundaries of genre. Others were formally cautious but occupied with sex and class politics. Common to all poets was a negotiation with stereotyped femininity, by denial, rejection, avoidance, parody or transgressive representations.

I concentrate on the poetry scene in Britain because most of the feminist revisionary histories have come from the American academy and have tended to overlook British women and the contribution of American women to poetry in Britain. I include some American women's involvement in the international network of writers which was significant to the production and promotion of modern poetry in Britain. Although Amy Lowell, Marianne Moore, Gertrude Stein and H.D. are frequently canonised in the United States, they have yet to be integrated into British anthologies or academic syllabuses of women's writing. Laura Riding, an American who lived in Britain on and off during the 1920s, and Mina Loy, who was English but lived in the United States, have not been properly reassessed in relation to Anglo-American, modernist or women's poetry.

Most of the work was written or published between 1910 and 1939 and therefore follows on from the revisionary studies of women's poetry of the nineteenth century.[2] Modernism's inauguration is cited variously between 1890 and 1919. I have chosen 1910 as a suitable starting point, since the death of Edward VII and accession of George V that year were marked by the new 'Georgian' poetry. Additionally, the Post-Impressionist exhibition stimulated interest in new modes of formalism in art and writing.[3] For Virginia Woolf, 'in or about 1910' heralded the arrival of modernity when 'human character changed': 'All human relations have shifted – those between masters and servants, husbands and wives, parents and children, and when human relations change there is at the same time a change in religion, conduct, politics, and literature.'[4] The years 1910 to 1939 were a period of social upheaval dominated by the First World War and changes in legislation concerning the rights of women. Women's poems contribute to a more comprehensive cultural representation of modernism and demand a revision of the narrowly language-centred model of literary criticism.

---

2   See, for example, Angela Leighton, *Victorian Women Poets: Writing Against the Heart* (Hemel Hempstead: Harvester Wheatsheaf, 1992).

3   The post-impressionist exhibition in 1910, organised by Roger Fry, was seen by about 25,000 artists and writers. See Peter Stansky, *In or about December 1910: studies in cultural history* (Cambridge, Massachusetts: Harvard University Press), 1996.

4   Virginia Woolf, 'Mr Bennett and Mrs Brown', in Woolf (1924), *A Woman's Essays* (Harmondsworth: Penguin, 1992), 70–1.

In order to destabilise its hegemony, feminist critics can find themselves wanting to place women within modernism, to discredit it as a meaningful term, to claim it as a feminine aesthetic, to identify a distinctly female modernism or to locate it as an international female movement. There is a convincing case for redefining modernism as a cultural crisis associated with feminist activity at the beginning of this century. The persistent supremacy of formal experiment in the rhetoric of literary criticism also means that women must be counted among the experimentalists if they are not to be perceived as perpetually conservative and irrelevant. While experimental modernism continues to be associated only with male poets in Britain, the conceptual association of 'women' and 'sentimental' – because modernism defined itself in opposition to the 'sentimental' – is able to persist. Modernism needs to be pluralised for historical accuracy. Celeste Schenck argues for opening up modernism to 'anything written between 1910 and 1940', judging that the loss of 'a certain stylistic designation' is less than the gain of 'all other modernisms against which a single strain of white male, international modernism has achieved such relief'. Although not going as far as 'anything written', I use Celeste Schenck's distinction between 'avant-garde' and 'rear-guard' modernisms:

> If Mew's case is to be heard and the annals of poetic 'modernism' duly revised, we must attend more carefully to the differences between rear-guard and avant-garde modernism. If we listen to the more traditional meters of Anna Wickham, Charlotte Mew, Sylvia Townsend Warner, Alice Meynell, and Edith Sitwell (not to mention the five hundred or so British women who wrote strong war poetry during the years around 1914) as attentively as we now hear the daring verbal experiments of H.D., Gertrude Stein, and Mina Loy, we must renounce, salutarily, any hope for a unitary totalising theory of female poetic modernism. The situation of marginalised modernists such as Mew, Wickham, Townsend Warner, Meynell and Sitwell has much to tell us, not only about the dispersive underside of the 'Modernist' monolith but also about inadvertent feminist participation in the politics of canonicity.[5]

There have to be reservations about even Schenck's division – between avant-garde and rear-guard modernisms – since it suggests a point at which an 'avant-garde' modernist crosses the 'rear-guard' line. In separating 'avant-garde' from 'rear-guard' and 'female' modernisms, I do not intend to endorse the superiority of stylistic innovation or to entrench clear-cut categorisation. On the contrary,

---

5   Celeste M. Schenck in Bonnie Kime Scott (ed.), *The Gender of Modernism* (Indianapolis: Indiana University Press, 1990), 317.

my difficulty in classifying the poems indicates that the line is only ever arbitrary. My chapter titles, 'Between Georgian and Bloomsbury', 'The Anglo-American Avant-garde' and 'Female Modernists', emerged from the textual and contextual complexities which necessitated cross-classification and new groupings. Stylistically radical poetry is often not as anti-realist as it would appear and a poet like Charlotte Mew runs across all the groups. I use 'rear-guard' to describe a stylistic reserve which is associated with the psychological conflict between embracing and rejecting modernity with its implications for newly defined gender roles.

Collectively, the diversity and ingenuity of the poets demonstrate that it is fruitless to approach the period with a binary model of modernist or non-modernist art. As Suzanne Clark puts it, 'modernism is both caught in and stabilised by a system of gendered binaries: male/female, serious/sentimental, critical/popular. Upsetting the system – as women do – introduces an instability and reveals the contradictions'.[6] A binary model is also inappropriate since literary histories have exaggerated the schism between 'tradition' and 'experiment'.

The radical and reactionary forces of modernism co-exist in parallel or in competition. The cross-currents of literary practices which considered themselves 'modern' mean that there are no grounds for the exclusion of poetry which was not stylistically extreme. For a start, the long shadow of W.B. Yeats casts doubt over any attempt to divide the 'old' from the 'new' in poets or poetry. T.S. Eliot reckoned that modern poetry was recognisable but unclassifiable: it was 'perceived by the sensibility, but not defined in words'.[7]

The contemporary debate recognised that the sense of modern could not be divorced from a sense of tradition and wrestled with whether 'modern' meant a clean break from, a reaction to, or a continuation of the past. In his influential anthology, *The Faber Book of Modern Verse* (1936), Michael Roberts cited Hart Crane's dismissal of the myths of a radical modernity: 'The deliberate program then, of a "break" with the past or tradition seems to me to be a sentimental fallacy.'[8]

If form and metre are used as registers of the simultaneous tugs of the 'old' and 'new', poets variously used the short lyric, the narrative poem or

---

6   Suzanne Clark, *Sentimental Modernism: Women Writers and The Revolution Of The Word* (Bloomington and Indianapolis: Indiana University Press, 1991), 8.

7   T.S. Eliot (1934) (ed.), *The Little Book of Modern Verse*, new edition edited by Anne Ridler (London: Faber, 1941), 8.

8   Hart Crane, cited in Michael Roberts (ed.) (1936), *The Faber Book of Modern Verse* (London: Faber, 1954), 26.

ballad of the English tradition – that is nineteenth-century Romanticism – and the ignominious *vers libre*. For some, the revival of older forms, notably Elizabethan and classical, was an attempt to connect with a more distant past than the previous century.

Formalist structure, by itself, does not signify the measure of modernity in a poem. It is more discernible in the collapse of formal rhetoric and preference for contemporary idioms. Modernity was most palpably registered in a change of subject matter, from the rural to the urban and from romance to desire. It was also registered in a psychological alienation from the modern world and its counterpoint condition of retreat, through myth, fantasy and dream.

The continuing respect for traditional forms in the literary papers contradicts the myth that all literary practice was avant-garde. The equation between radical form and potential anarchism originated in the reception to *vers libre* by a conservative literary establishment whose approval women needed to be taken seriously. To some extent the war deflated the revolutionary ideals associated with imagism and vorticism. Although the General Strike in 1926 and two minority Labour governments in 1924 and 1929 sharpened the socialist awareness of intellectuals, which developed through the 1930s, it was mitigated by their reaction against mass culture. As John Lucas observes, 'The radical impulse in poetry of the 1920s is, therefore, a complex matter ... [English poetry] was a great deal more various and more accomplished than is usually allowed.'[9] He contests the myths that all the best English poets before Auden were killed in action, leaving poetry to the foreigners, Yeats, Pound and Eliot, and recognises the number of women writers: 'If the 1920s sees the emergence of a new generation of women prose writers – Woolf, Rhys, Bowen, for example – it is also remarkable for the number of women poets who begin to publish.'[10] However, the poets named – Anna Wickham, Charlotte Mew, H.D., Sylvia Townsend Warner, Elizabeth Daryush – are 'not worth making a fuss over', except for Laura Riding, 'a poet of real worth, though the nature of that worth is very difficult to pin down and deserves an essay in itself'. The difficulty of 'pinning down' women's poetry is one reason why it is dropped from literary records and why I aim to restore women's place in literary movements. At the same time, their poetry presses upon the boundaries of these established groups and unsettles the binary oppositions between conservative and progressive or between sentimental and experimental.

---

9   John Lucas, *The Radical Twenties* (Nottingham: Five Leaves, 1997), 176.
10   John Lucas, 'Making the 1920s New', *Poetry Review* (Winter 1993/4), 26.

In 'The Literary Context' I outline women's achievements in a cultural environment which demeaned them. In a climate of new opportunities, many women became public literary figures but they found that the literary establishment had the ethos of the exclusive male club. Consequently, in their writing, women masked their womanly identity which was detrimental to their status. The section on 'Rear-guard modernism' includes poetry of the First World War which documents women's differing responses to the models of femininity projected through the powerful government recruiting propaganda. Some poems appear to be complicit with the official responses for women, as maternal nurturers of the country, while others resisted them through direct or implicit protest. Some poetry can be placed alongside canonical anti-war poems whereas others are obviously separated by the gender specific experiences of the war at home or medical aid abroad. Some women seemed to unconsciously enter into male activity and others paraded as the paradigms of feminine self-sacrifice, but a covert disjunction between the discourse and the unarticulated subjectivity of the poet often provides textual ambiguity and energy. Women's poems are vital to the cultural records of the War, but also demonstrate that war poetry was contiguous with, not parallel to, the fluctuations of modernist innovation. The grouping, 'Between the Georgians and Bloomsbury', blurs the reductive binaries of 'tradition' and 'experiment'. It was difficult to classify any poets as simply 'Georgian', partly because it has become a term of ready contempt in literary criticism and partly because Frances Cornford and Vita Sackville-West do not conform to either Georgian stereotype – the country gentleman or the demure poetess.

The poets counting as 'modernist' were difficult to arrange because they traverse the experimental/traditional and expressive/impersonal fences. The radical experimentalists are grouped as 'avant-garde' while the 'female modernists' are less stylistically ground-breaking but more radical in their class and gender politics. It is striking that there were technical links between women who were in closer contact with the avant-garde communities in Paris and New York. Just as Ezra Pound and T.S. Eliot were native Americans, so the majority of avant-garde women were American. It can be hypothesised that non-British writers were less constricted by the reservations of British literary critics about *vers libre*. In 'The British Avant-garde' chapter, Edith Sitwell is the luminary, but I include Nancy Cunard, Iris Tree and Helen Rootham because of their common social backgrounds and collaborative work on the *Wheels* anthologies. Like Sitwell, they lived as independent women in reaction against the cultural complacency of their families and were as sensitive to class as to gender divisions. One of their concerns was how to express a social conscience according to modernism's principles of impersonality, and their poetry negotiates between anti-realism and psychologically realist representation. Writing in opposition to the idealised 'feminine', they avoided gendered identity in their writing and offered new models of the woman poet. These women have not, however, been recognised in feminist histories, probably because they do not overtly articulate feminist protest.

Like Edith Sitwell, the women in the next part, 'The Anglo-American Avant-garde', hold their own in the orthodox terms of high modernist experimentation. Although the poetry is rarely woman-centred, its subversions of traditional syntax and forms are feminist strategies for breaking and entering the traditions from which women had been excluded. The poetry and criticism of H.D., Amy Lowell, Mina Loy, Marianne Moore, Laura Riding and Gertrude Stein indicate how women gave impetus to formal innovation. They influenced literary developments in Britain through spending time with the intellectuals in London, through personal connections, through their publications and through the new literary journals. It is also notable that non-Americans, Anna Wickham, Charlotte Mew, May Sinclair and Sylvia Townsend Warner, have featured sparsely in feminist revisions of modernism. These poets, along with Edna St Vincent Millay, are the 'Female Modernists' in the following section. Female modernists were clearly interested in the politics of language but in conjunction with the representation of social and gender issues.

Radical content, such as coded lesbian eroticism, feminist polemics or other challenges to dominant ideologies can take both innovative and traditional verse forms. Poets like Gertrude Stein, Charlotte Mew, H.D., Mina Loy and Amy Lowell can be classified as both 'avant-garde' and 'female' modernists. Charlotte Mew exemplifies the ways in which orthodox categories are limiting. The unclassifiability of Mew's works means that she tends to accrue a variety of labels, namely 'Victorian', 'Edwardian', 'Georgian' and 'high' or 'lesbian' modernist. In accruing these labels, women alter the male-associated assumptions of literary conventions and groupings.

Classifying women's poems requires a critical vocabulary which can investigate a specifically female aesthetic. In the context of the modernist period, it was formulated in reaction to the feminising of a generic 'women's poetry'. The frequency of their allusions to Sappho, Elizabeth Barrett Browning and Christina Rossetti indicate that they had a concept of a woman's tradition, but related to it negatively. In 'The Sisters', Amy Lowell imagines meeting Sappho, Elizabeth Barrett Browning and Emily Dickinson, three different kinds of predecessor, with whom she cannot identify:

Taking us by and large, we're a queer lot
We women who write poetry. And when you think
How few of us there've been it's queerer still.
I wonder what it is that makes us do it,
Singles us out to scribble down, man-wise,
The fragments of ourselves.
  …
Strange trio of my sisters, most diverse,
And how extraordinarily unlike
Each is to me, and which way shall I go?
  …
I cannot write like you, I cannot think
In terms of Pagan or of Christian now.
I only hope that possibly some day
Some other woman with an itch for writing
May turn to me as I have turned to you
And chat with me a brief few minutes.
  …
Although you leave me sad and self-distrustful,
For older sisters are very sobering things.
Put on your cloaks, my dears, the motor's waiting.
No, you have not seemed strange to me, but near,
Frightfully near and rather terrifying.[11]

The sense that the poetess was 'frightfully near and rather terrifying', impelled women to define themselves antithetically to the feminine.

Women poets lived and wrote in opposition to iconographies of the poetess, whose validity critics reinforced by reviewing women together and by attributing feminine features to their work. In 1848, Frederic Rowton, in his forward-looking anthology of women's poetry, concluded that 'such a word as "poetess" should be struck from the vocabulary' because it was responsible for the occlusion of woman's intellect in poetry.[12] However, the epithet 'poetess', was a continuum in the language of twentieth-century criticism. In 1921, when modernist experimentation was at its most acclaimed,[13] the

---

11 Amy Lowell (1925), 'The Sisters', *What's O'Clock, Complete Poetical Works* (Boston: Houghton Mifflin, 1955), 459–61.

12 Frederic Rowton, cited in *Victorian Women Poets: An anthology*, ed. Angela Leighton and Margaret Reynolds (Oxford: Blackwell, 1985), xxxiii.

13 1922 is considered the *annus mirabilis* of modernism, with the publication of T.S. Eliot's *The Waste Land*, James Joyce's *Ulysses* and Virginia Woolf's *Jacob's Room*.

publication of *An Anthology of Women's Verse*, edited by J.C. Squire, revived the 'old controversy ... Has Woman any really poetic talent?'[14] The response to the anthology embodies the way in which the weakest women's poems were publicised and universalised as the generic 'Women's Poetry' from which literary women dissociated themselves. In *The Bookman*, Rebecca West observed that it was 'a remarkably thin volume and a remarkably poor one', and advised that 'feminist societies should buy up all copies of this book and suppress them.'[15] Squire's anthology provoked a long article in the *Times Literary Supplement*, headed 'Poetesses'. The reviewer admitted that civilisation is only 'partial, one-sided, while the expression of its meaning and purpose is in the hands of one sex', but embellished the mythologies of the 'eternal feminine': 'sincere women's poetry will have the warmth, the wholeness, the grace, the allurement, the tenderness, or the mockery of the feminine mind.'[16] He further idealised the female muse: 'The root of the impulse of poetry is love and woman is the object of man's love.' Since woman's proper place was to inspire not write poetry, the reviewer took issue with Squire's proposal that 'Even though we may not expect it, we should be only mildly surprised if a female Plato or Shakespeare were to appear, and a second of the sort would cause no surprise at all' to assert that, 'our surprise would be immense', because:

> We know that the difficulties of artistic creation for women are far greater than for men, that their temperament is reflective rather than imaginative, and that the chance of any work of the widest scope being given to the world by a woman is remote, since Nature has irretrievably weighted the scale against them.

The final excoriation was the personal/public opposition:

> Does not the poetry of women tend to be about themselves? Man, it would appear, in the intellectual as in the practical sphere, excels in the power to go forth and enlarge his life by what he finds and makes; woman excels in her power of attachment and assimilation, so that that alone is real to her which she includes, which she has brought home.

14 E. Macbeam, 'Poetry and the Woman: the creative power', review of *An Anthology of Women's Verse* (Oxford: Clarendon, 1921), ed. J.C. Squire, *Time and Tide* 9 June 1922, 545.

15 Rebecca West, 'Women Poets', review of *An Anthology of Women's Verse*, ed. J.C. Squire. *Bookman* May 1921, 92–3.

16 'Poetesses', review of *A Book of Women's Verse*, ed. J.C. Squire, *TLS* 24 November 1921, 267.

Literary women had to resist the relentless mythologies of femininity in order to construct themselves as credible poets. In distancing themselves from 'women's poetry', they sought to be on equal terms with men who accentuated gender difference. In America, in 'The Poet as Woman', John Crowe Ransom confessed his difficulty in evaluating Edna St Vincent Millay, a poet who 'is also a woman':

> No poet evur registered herself more deliberately in that light. She therefore fascinates the male reviewer but at the same time horrifies him a little too. He will probably swing between attachment and antipathy, which may be the very attitudes provoked in him by generic woman in the flesh, as well as by the literary remains of Emily Dickinson, Elizabeth Barrett Browning, Christina Rossetti, and doubtless, if we only had enough of her, Sappho herself.[17]

Amy Lowell's narrative poem, 'A Critical Fable', articulates women's troublesome relations with one another which were aggravated by the scepticism of their male contemporaries. It takes the form of a dialogue about changing fashions in poetry between the poet and a male critic who expresses his doubts about women's talent:

> Then seeing me shrug, he observed, 'I am human,
> And hardly can bear to allow that a woman
> Is ever quite equal to man in the arts;
> The two sexes cannot be ranked counterparts.
> …
> But have you no women whom you must hate too?
> I shall think all the better of you if you do,
> And of them, I may add.' I assured him, 'A few.
> But I scarcely think man feels the same contradictory
> Desire to love them and shear them of victory?'
> 'You think wrong, my young friend,' he declared with a frown,
> 'Man will always love woman and always pull down
> What she does.'[18]

The dialogue dramatises what Gilbert and Gubar describe as the anxious male reaction to women's progress which in turn aggravates the 'female affiliation complex' in women. I have found their theory to be enduringly convincing in

---

17   John Crowe Ransom, 'The Poet as Woman', *The World's Body* (Ransom, 1938) (New York: Kennikat Press, 1964), 76–7. John Crowe Ransom (1888–1974) was a member of the American 'Fugitive poets'.

18   Amy Lowell, 'A Critical Fable', *Complete Poetical Works*, 409.

exploring the connection between cultural politics, psycho-sexual relations to language and literary practice. They account for women's competing desires to both identify with and be separate from a segregated female tradition in Freudian terms of the pre-Oedipal mother-daughter relationship and the castration complex.[19] Freud describes three lines of psychosexual development for a girl: either renunciation of sexuality altogether, or a 'masculinity complex', or 'normal' femininity where she takes her father as the love object. Translated into literary development, these alternatives are: either aesthetic frigidity, or assuming a masculine identity, or identifying herself as feminine. The last way involves post-Oedipal envy for the male pen, the symbol of woman's missing phallus, and the attendant repression of her pre-Oedipal attachment to her mother. Consequently, as Gilbert and Gubar put it, 'women writers oscillate[e] between their matrilineage and their patrilineage in an arduous process of self-definition'.[20] This oscillation is indicated in Amy Lowell's dramatised love/hate relationship with other women in 'The Sisters' and 'A Critical Fable'. However, Freud's diagnosis commits women to an inevitably negative access to the symbolic order of social and public discourse and prescribes an *essential* hostility towards their literary foremothers. In addressing the problem of women's entry into male literary traditions, Cora Kaplan stresses the *social* construction of women's alienation and she recommends that women identify their entry into language as different rather than negative.[21] In attempting to replace the negative mythologies of women's poetry with positive role models, I emphasise the poets' negotiations with the cultural injunctions of gender so that Freud's Oedipal stage will be understood to be a means of rationalising the social oppression of women writers.

In evidence that they were up against cultural, rather than essentialised, prohibitions to their creativity, most women recorded that writing poetry was a process of liberation; it was the absence of a proper critical reception which damaged them. The common aesthetic of modernist women poets is their attempt to demonstrate their competence with the conventions of British poetry without blindly conforming to them. It is this *negotiation with*, but not wholesale *repudiation of*, tradition which characterises poets as diverse as Vita Sackville-West, Edith Sitwell, Anna Wickham and Charlotte Mew. In

---

19 Sandra Gilbert and Susan Gubar, *No Man's Land: The place of the woman writer in the twentieth century. Vol. 1. The War of the Words* (New Haven: Yale University Press, 1988), 168.

20 Gilbert and Gubar, *The War of the Words*, 169.

21 Cora Kaplan, 'Language and Gender', in Deborah Cameron (ed.), *Feminist Critique of Language* (London: Routledge, 1990), 58–62.

their resistance to the feminine tropes which were propagated by the literary and popular presses, the 'rear-guard' women appropriated and occasionally eschewed the male traditions with which they had been educated. Their woman-consciousness is mostly manifested in its denial. The avant-garde writers escaped the masculine/feminine dyad by destabilising conventional systems of representation. Marianne Moore defied all gender imperatives through her male and animal impersonations. The dramatisations or *logopoeia* of H.D., Edith Sitwell, Gertrude Stein or Mina Loy subverted 'masculine' language. In the section on the 1930s, I look at how the political poetry of Valentine Ackland, Sylvia Townsend Warner and Naomi Mitchison avoided gendered identification and was more preoccupied with achieving realist observations which avoided propaganda. However, their socialism and feminism were intersecting drives towards their ideals of democracy.

In their woman-centred poetry, however, the thirties poets, along with the female modernists, identified themselves as women and articulated feminist concerns. They rework conventional representations of women. The unashamed depictions of female identities by Edna St Vincent Millay and Anna Wickham, particularly indicate a new aesthetic freedom for women. Through fictionalised personae they satirised gender stereotypes, substituted sexual desire or female autonomy for idealised romance and explored female psychology. In not displaying signs of either a masculinity complex or the female affiliation complex, they refute Freud's prescriptions of femininity. They culminate a narrative of women's progress towards an aesthetic freedom which is characterised by self-dramatisation.

Chapter Two

The Literary Context

Introduction

The dominance of high modernist criticism and the omission of women from modernist histories have tended to perpetuate a conceptual binary opposition between experiment and women's poetry. If all modern poetry is a reaction against the 'genteel' tradition and 'genteel' is associated with the feminine, there is a need to contest that association: the dominance of formal experiment has been exaggerated and many women became significant producers and promoters of new writing. There was a complex nexus of a predominantly male conservative literary establishment and the cultural changes which created both obstacles and new opportunities for women's personal and professional lives.

The First World War, the influence of America through film, the radio and magazines, the impact of psychoanalysis, the first wave of feminism, the development of literary criticism and a large literate public were significant influences on cultural formations, particularly in relation to the concepts of nationalism and gender.[1]

The beginning of the twentieth century was a period of intense suffragette activity. In 1900, married women were allowed to vote in Local County Council elections (London County Council Act, 1899); the Private Members Suffrage Bill in 1908 was carried in its second reading and in 1910, the All Party Conciliation Bill for women's suffrage passed its second reading but was quashed by the Government front bench. In all, the Women's Suffrage Bill went through eighteen parliamentary debates but the slow process provoked hunger striking which began in 1909. The 'Cat and Mouse' Act of 1913 (The Prisoners' Temporary Discharge for Ill-Health Act) epitomises the impasse whereby there was no progress for, and no yielding by, women. The subsequent militancy of the suffragettes alienated the temperamentally and politically

---

1   See, for example, Herbert Read, 'Psycho-analysis and the critic', *Criterion* III, 10 January 1925: 214–230. Sigmund Freud's (1856–1939) *Interpretation of Dreams* (1900) was translated into English in 1913. Carl Jung (1875–61) influenced literary practice with his theories of the collective unconscious, myth and the role of the artist. Key works included *The Theory of Psychoanalysis* (1912), *Psychology of the Unconscious* (1916) and *Psychological Types* (1923).

liberal who were in sympathy with the goal of equal rights and equal votes but not with violence. In 1913 suffragism became divided with the founding of the East London Federation for working class suffragettes by Sylvia Pankhurst who was asked to leave the WSPU (Women's Social and Political Union). The non-violent National Union of Women's Suffrage Societies also started in 1913. It was in this climate of unachieved goals, divisions between the militant and non-militant, and between the working and middle or upper classes, that the First World War began. Women took over men's work and by 1918 all married women over thirty who were on the local government electoral register were granted the vote. In 1919 Nancy Astor was the first woman MP to take her seat in the House of Commons,[2] and the Sex Disqualification Act removed barriers to women becoming barristers, solicitors, magistrates and other positions of power or learning.

Legislation in favour of women's rights continued throughout the 1920s and 1930s. Oxford and Cambridge agreed to confer degrees on women (1920, 1921), all women over twenty one were allowed the vote (1928) and there were alterations in law concerning divorce and inheritance (Matrimonial Causes Act, 1937; Inheritance Act, 1938). Changes in law were both causes and effects of altered ideas about domestic gender roles. In 1918, Marie Stopes (1880–1958) published *Married Love* and *Wise Parenthood* which emphasised changing attitudes towards marriage, the nuclear family and women's sexuality. Her *Contraception* in 1923 registered women's advances towards sexual autonomy. Stopes started Britain's first birth control clinic in 1921, the same year that the American Birth Control League was founded.[3] (Women in America had been granted the vote in 1920.)

Their participation in literary production registers the emerging psychological, sexual and economic independence of women.[4] However, antagonism towards pre-war suffragism and towards women's public roles during and their new rights after the War spilled over into the reception to their poems. The model of reviewing set by the *Times Literary Supplement* (*TLS*) was particularly influential in establishing an atmosphere of the male club; it not only excluded women from its echelon but also from 'Poetry' by feminising their writing.

---

2   Countess Marckiewicz was elected to parliament in 1918 but Nancy Astor was the first woman MP to take her seat in 1919.

3   Margaret Sanger had opened the first American birth control clinic in 1916.

4   See correspondence about the sexual needs of women. *Egoist* I, 2 and 16 March 1914: 98–9, 120.

Escaping the Feminine

In the post-war climate of new equalities, women developed confidence in publishing their work and presenting themselves as public literary figures. The number of women publishing provoked anxiety about their encroachment on to the male-dominated terrain. In his introduction to *A Book of Women's Verse* in 1921, J.C. Squire observed the phenomenon of women's public presence:

> Today we scarcely bother about the distinction between male and female writers. With thousands of women writing, with women's verses in every magazine and women represented in every newspaper office, when literary women congregate in clubs, and robust women novelists haggle with editors and discuss royalties with their male rivals, we take composition for granted as a feminine occupation.[5]

It is significant, however, that most of Squire's poets were dead. E. Macbeam's review of Squire's anthology in *Time and Tide* illustrates the anxious male reaction to the proliferation of women's poems:

> What can we say in 'defence'? Women *do* write verse, far more of it than men do; a great deal of it gets into print in the *Poetry Review*, the prize page of *The Bookman*, and in minor publications. Women do not, however, always excepting the 'star' names, produce great or lasting poetry. And yet the creative talent is not lacking ... novels written by women are in greater demand than novels written by men.

'The Poetry of Women', a review of three new books of poetry in the *Times Literary Supplement* in 1920, also indicates the ways in which men's anxiety about women's new freedoms was projected on to the reception of their poems:

> Literature which answers to every change in the social life of a people, has already begun to register the fact of woman's emancipation. The ideal of self-expression, which has supplanted self-sacrifice as the aim of the modern woman,

---

5   J.C. Squire (ed.), *A Book of Women's Verse* (Oxford: Clarendon, 1921). J.C. Squire was literary editor of the *New Statesman*, chief literary critic of the *Observer* and founded the *London Mercury* in 1919, which he edited until 1934. He was reputedly a congenial personality and championed the 'common man' but was treated with condescension in the *TLS*. Edith Sitwell coined the term 'Squirearchy' to represent the artistic complacency which he was purported to represent. Consequently, 'Squirearchy' became polarised to Bloomsbury. See John Pearson, *Facades: Edith, Osbert and Sacheverell Sitwell* (Basingstoke: Macmillan, 1978), 146–150.

has possibly brought with it as many abuses as it has banished ... Certainly, the result in literature may not at first seem very happy. As we contemplate the profusion of modern fiction with women's names on the title page, we may reasonably fear for the welfare of art smothered between the smatterings of science and the anarchy of instincts ... But though we allow the novel to be abused in the interests of sex propaganda, lyrical poetry, by the very strict limits of its constitution, will permit no such transgression.[6]

The phrase, 'The ideal of self-expression, which has supplanted self-sacrifice as the aim of the modern woman', exemplifies my central argument that women were intent on discarding the mythologies of poetesshood which men wanted to sustain. The reviewer's resistance to professional women writers was partly a nostalgia for the pre-war ideals of femininity (and presumably of masculinity):

> The poetry of women, then, has its basis in a sympathy with nature rather than art, and, as interpreters of the beauty and sanctity of *what is to so many of us almost a lost province*, they may contribute new truths to poetry and refresh it as its source, provided they can criticise more carefully the organism of which they remain a part.[7]

I have emphasised '*What is to so many of us almost a lost province*' because it illustrates how 'woman', as a generic concept, was used paradigmatically for the personal life, spirituality and traditionalism which were threatened by post-war modernity.

The insistence on the difference of women's poetry and the attendant perception of the 'feminine' as intellectual weakness is palpably illustrated here in 'The Poetry of Women'. It is worth exploring the whole article at length because it is typical of discourses which did not distinguish literary women from the weakest popular verse-writers. Fay Inchfawn's *The Verse-Book of a Homely Woman*, published by *The Girl's Own* and *Woman's Magazine*, was easy fodder for the association of woman, the sentimental and the popular: 'But for ourselves we find something worth the knowing in a woman who can think of God amid her groceries and praise Him in her scullery.' The other two books prompted as much approval for women confining themselves to women's concerns, namely motherhood, but not writing about them:

---

6   'The Poetry of Women', review of *The House*, by Gladys Mary Hazel, *Poems of Motherhood*, by Dorothea Still, and *The Verse Book of a Homely Woman*, by Fay Inchfawn. *TLS* 9 December 1920: 810.

7   Ibid. (emphasis added).

Mrs Inchfawn can sing of her baby with as true and satisfying a restraint as Mrs Still can 'embed' hers (most uncomfortably) in the 'Silver of her kisses,' because she tries to impose a false decoration on an instinct which was too realistic to deserve expression. And while maternity should have its intimate poetry (though we are tempted to doubt whether a mother is best suited to express it), but a poetry, at any rate, distinct from that which is offered externally by man as an act of homage. Mrs Still would have been wise to avoid all those merely physical experiences of motherhood which are too absorbingly natural to be poetical. She is happiest when she escapes from both the fear and sentimentality which attach themselves to the mere fact of a child and universalises her experience in a moment of triumph.

The implication that women were intrinsically sentimental – occupied with religion, nature and the personal life – was relentless:

It is in a delicate echoing of nature's lyrical moments, to which man is possibly too philosophic to respond, that these writers obtain their happiest effects ... . Woman accepts the language of children and birds and trees, because she is of nature's household. Not even in her religion does she go abroad in quest of a fantastic grail.

The thrust of the review was to perpetuate the myths of the poetess through the rhetoric of binary opposition which conflates femaleness with femininity:

The inherent masculine faculty is to objectify, the feminine to express subjectivity: this is of course a broad distinction and infinitely transgressed (witness the number of poets who are parading their private sentiments to-day), but as a general principle we may say that woman sees and interprets life from within; she has neither to stoop nor to rise to nature – her response to it is only a wider expression of herself.[8]

Similarly, 'On the Threshold', a review of three women's books, demonstrates the effect of reviewing women in combination, whereby the womanliness and not the poetry is in focus. It fuelled the prejudices about women's poetry as domestic, derivative, traditional and consoling.[9]

The patronising platitudes about women's inherent interpretation of life 'from within' are not innocuous, since, as Cora Kaplan argues:

---

8   'The Poetry of Women', *TLS* 9 December 1920.
9   'On the Threshold', review of *The Gift*, by Margaret Cecilia Furse, *Three Days*, by Rose Macaulay, and *The Splendid Days*, by May Wedderburn Cannan. *TLS* 13 November 1919: 647.

> The emphasis on women's imagination relating to the private realm can be understood as the control of high language which is a crucial part of the power of dominant groups, and ... the refusal of access to public language is one of the major forms of the oppression of women.[10]

Critics confined women to the personal life but rubbished it as suitable for good poetry. Suzanne Clark points out that because sentimental discourse assumes sympathy through appeal to personal experience, it has become associated with personal experience; therefore, all expressive writing is perceived as sentimental.[11] Consequently, marginalised groups are deprived of a valid discourse for representing their histories.

It is noticeable how often 'sentimental' cropped up in discussions of women's verses. 'Sentimental' was a pejorative term, and, used conjunctively with 'poetess', it inflated the myths of universal womanhood. In *Practical Criticism* (1929), I.A. Richards included a chapter on 'Sentimentalism and Inhibition' in which he observed that 'sentimental' had become a term of abuse, often followed by the word 'rubbish'. He recognised that 'sentimental' was one of the most overworked words in the whole vocabulary of literary criticism but did not identify its particularly detrimental application to women.[12] Judging by the quoted extracts, however, there was some justification for the implications of sentimentality, but these three books of verse had been selected for review at length and the heading, 'The Poetry of Women', insidiously universalised them. This universality was magnified by encompassing women of the nineteenth century into 'women's poetry':

> Nature accepted at a bad moment may produce the formless fidelities of Mrs Browning, at a good the pure gallantry of Miss Coleridge. None of these poets discriminates altogether between wrong and right impulses.

During the interwar period, sentimental became further associated with women because it was linked to the growth of mass culture which became caricatured as women's magazines and Hollywood romances. The popular papers published women's verse and reinforced the association between women's poetry and sentimentality. In *Sentimental Modernism*, Suzanne Clark

---

10   Cora Kaplan, 'Language and Gender', in Deborah Cameron (ed.), *Feminist Critique of Language* (London: Routledge, 1990), 58.

11   Suzanne Clark, *Sentimental Modernism: Women Writers and The Revolution of The Word* (Bloomington and Indianapolis: Indiana University Press, 1991), 19.

12   I.A. Richards, *Practical Criticism*, 1929 (London: Routledge & Kegan Paul, 1982), 270.

describes the literary 'reversal against the sentimental' which 'located women's writing within the obscenity of the sentimental':

> Women, of course, have a privileged (or fatal) relationship with the sentimental. From the point of view of literary modernism, sentimentality was both a past to be outgrown and a present tendency to be despised. The gendered character of this condemnation seemed natural: women writers were entangled into sensibility, were romantic and sentimental by nature, and so even the best might not altogether escape this romantic indulgence in emotion and sublimity, or so it might seem to a criticism anxious to make distinctions.[13]

Since 'sentimental' became 'a shorthand for everything modernism would exclude',[14] the legacy of the conceptual link between women and mass culture is that literary women have been ignored by modernist histories.

Women were clearly conscious of the universal 'feminisation' of their work. In *The New Freewoman* in 1913, Dora Marsden recorded the battle between intellectual women and 'Woman':

> 'Woman' spelt with a capital, Woman-as-type, is an empty concept and should be banished from the language. If we take 'female reproductive organs' away from this concept Woman, what have we left? Absolutely nothing, save a mountain of sentimental mush … Woman? Is there such a thing even as a woman sensed from the inside?[15]

The expectation that women composed genteel nature lyrics is addressed by Anna Wickham in 'Explanation':

> It's so, good Sirs, a Woman-poet sings
> Sick self, and not exterior things,
> She'd joy enough in flowers, and lakes and light,
> Before she won soul's freedom in a fight.
> Thus half-creation is but half expressed,
> And the unspoken half is best.[16]

Significantly, in her poetry, Anna Wickham frequently substituted this limiting feminine stereotype with the emancipated New Woman.

---

13 Clark, 2.
14 Clark, 9.
15 Dora Marsden, 'Views and Comments', *New Freewoman* 2.1, 1 July 1913: 24.
16 'Explanation', *The Writings of Anna Wickham: Free Woman and Poet*, ed. R.D. Smith (London: Virago, 1984), 296.

It has to be recognised that the ideal of 'Woman' as the embodiment of high moral sensibility was as seductive to some women as it was to men. Women, too, unwittingly conspired with this preservation of idealised womanhood and represented the 'sentimentality' from which the progressive woman poet wanted to be dissociated. Conservative critics used their reviews to play upon women's sense of womanly duty. Eva Gore-Booth was described by Thomas Moult as 'mistress of victorious expression ... a superb example of noble vision combined with superb technique' although the brief review of *Broken Glory* in the *TLS* implied that she was right to place 'grace and distinction' above pacifism.[17] Alice Meynell was similarly constructed in terms of the feminine ideal in the literary press. *The Last Poems of Alice Meynell* (1923), got one and a half columns in the *TLS* and was approved for having the requisite combination of religious and poetic piety, albeit deficient in literary quality.[18] Consequently, they appear superficially to be more genteel than they really were.

Eva Gore-Booth (1870–1926), Alice Meynell (1847–1922) and Katherine Tynan (1861–1931) were respected literary women with successful publishing histories but are difficult to position. They seem caught between the competing pressures of feminist emancipation and prescribed femininity which were exaggerated by the First World War. The need for male approval may explain why, although involved in political and suffrage activities, they suppressed their politics in their poetry. Eva Gore-Booth published five books of prose, several newspaper articles and ten books of poems including a *Complete* and *Selected Poems*. She was born in Ireland and moved to Manchester where she supported movements for economic and political reform and for the enfranchisement of women; she was a member of the Manchester Education Committee and secretary to the women's trade union council.[19]

Although a vociferous suffragist, there is little feminist protest in her poems. Likewise, although Alice Meynell was an active member of the women's writing suffrage league and a respected voice for women's emancipation, her poetry seems curiously separate from her political life. She was a leading member of the Celtic literary revival and a friend to Yeats, Parnell, and Rossetti. In 1922, Meynell was considered to be one of the

---

17   Review of *Broken Glory*, by Eva Gore-Booth, *TLS* 3 October 1918: 471.
18   'The Poetry of Mrs Meynell', review of *The Last Poems of Alice Meynell* and *The Poems of Alice Meynell*, *TLS* 1 March 1923: 139.
19   Thomas Moult, review of *Shepherd of Eternity and Other Poems*, by Eva Gore-Booth, *Time and Tide* 10 July 1925: 673.

foremost women poets of the day, but she has suffered from having her earliest and weakest poems, such as 'The Shepherdess', chosen for anthologies.[20]

'Would-be manliness': Gender, Politics and Poetic Form

In the context of militant women's suffrage and an intense period of legislation concerning the rights of women, the feminisation of women's poetry can be seen as a symptom of male resistance to women's entry into the professions and public places. As Virginia Woolf observed, women had an unprecedented freedom to write and publish but the activities of the suffrage movement presented men with unprecedented challenges to their authority:

> And if it be true that it is one of the tokens of the fully developed mind that it does not think specially or separately of sex, how much harder it is to attain that condition now than ever before. Here I came to the books by living writers, and there paused and wondered if this fact were not at the root of something that had long puzzled me. No age can ever have been as stridently sex-conscious as our own; those innumerable books by men about women in the British Museum are a proof of it. The Suffragette campaign was no doubt to blame. It must have roused in men an extraordinary desire for self-assertion; it must have made them lay an emphasis upon their own sex and its characteristics which they would not have troubled to think about had they not been challenged. And when one is challenged, even by a few women in black bonnets, one retaliates, if one has never been challenged before, rather excessively.[21]

Virginia Woolf's *A Room of One's Own* (1929), was a key text for women writers and reflected a climate where the heightened consciousness of sex differences was counter-productive to their careers. Woolf's ideal of the androgynous imagination, the 'man-womanly' and the 'woman-manly' mind, was influential on intellectual women, but rarely entertained by men. As has been seen, part of asserting male values, was to assert the womanliness of women's poems. In a special edition of *Poetry Review* on 'Women-Poets', May 1912, the editor, probably Harold Monro, stated 'the truism that the great poet is neither man nor woman, but partially each'. In the rhetoric of binary opposition, however, he observed that 'Woman' had failed to represent herself in poetry 'through the belief that, in order to do so, she must become

---

20 For further discussion of Alice Meynell see Angela Leighton 1992.
21 Virginia Woolf, *A Room of One's Own*, 1929 (London: Granada, 1977), 107.

as Man'. He tellingly identified – and thus prescribed – a trend in the woman poet to develop her own kind of verse, following on from Rossetti: she must 'reveal that she is Woman indeed. In the poetess, perhaps, chiefly, this revelation is becoming apparent'.[22]

One of the difficulties in avoiding gendered associations was that traditional poetic form was identified with the best of male and the weakest of female writing. William Archer, apparently in praise of Alice Meynell, denounced women generically for failing with form:

> Few poetesses of the past have shown a very high developed faculty for strict poetical form. I am not sure that the works of any woman in any modern language are reckoned among the consummate models of metrical style ... ladies as a rule seem to have aimed at a certain careless grace rather than a strenuous complexity or accuracy of metrical structure ... Mrs Meynell is one of the rare exceptions to this rule. Within a carefully limited range, her form is unimpeachable.[23]

It is for her 'unimpeachable' form, however, that Alice Meynell is considered traditionalist by modernist and feminist critics. They have not recognised the pressure upon women to prove themselves as poets through adopting the metres of the English poetic tradition. For example, in 'The English Metres', Meynell paid tribute to the tradition of British poetry which was stabilised by metrical conformity:

> The rooted liberty of flowers in breeze
>   Is theirs, by national luck impulsive, terse,
> Tethered, uncaptured, rules obeyed 'at ease',
>   Time strengthened laws of verse.[24]

The militaristic language strengthened the association between masculinity and the poetic tradition. The gendering of poetic form cropped up again in 'The Laws of Verse':

> Dear laws, come to my breast!
> Take all my frame, and make your close arms meet

---

22   'Women Poets', leading article, *Poetry Review* May 1912: 199–200. Probably written by Harold Monro who was editor of *Poetry Review* from January–December 1912.

23   William Archer, cited in 'The Poetess of Poets: Alice Meynell Rediscovered', by Beverley Ann Schlack, *Women's Studies* 7, 1980: 111–26. See Schenck, 227.

24   'The English Metres', from *Last Poems*, 1923, *The Poems of Alice Meynell* (Oxford: Oxford University Press, 1940), 177.

Around me; and so ruled, so worked, so pressed,
I breathe, aware; I feel my wild heart beat.[25]

In the ambiguous image of the male embrace as imprisoning and companionate, there is an uncertainty about whether the laws of traditional prosody are limiting or liberating for the woman. Consequently, it is not clear whether the poem's energy derives from a battle against the straitjackets of metre and form or from the excitement of partnership with metre and form. Alice Meynell wanted to avoid being like all women poets 'self-conscious and melancholy'[26] but Edith Sitwell accused her of bringing women a bad name because she mismatched feminine sentiment with masculine technique: 'sheltering tenderly under the protection of those manly boomings and burstings ... we find Mrs Meynell's limp exhortations to virtue.'[27]

Celeste Schenck uses Alice Meynell's 'The Laws of Verse' as an example of 'the double bind of the woman poet ... [in her] simultaneous exile *from* and *to* poetic form':

> The whole idea of the 'genteel' against which modernism defined itself seems to be inextricably bound to these contradictory, even schizophrenic, notions of femininity ... If gentility in poetry carries the disparaging connotation of soft and female, or worse, not male enough, it can also bear the opposite meaning of conservative and rigid, rhymed and therefore masculine and hard. Given the impossibility of separating the two valences of the term, it is no wonder that women poets found themselves divided in the debate over genre.[28]

A poet like Edith Sitwell found herself, 'committed *both* to a separate tradition of women's poetry ... *and* to outdoing male poets in fashioning a poetics that is anything but wallowing and soft. Her recourse to form, then, was both prescribed and understandably defensive'.[29]

In an article on women's poetry in 1925, Edith Sitwell expressed this dilemma between identifying with feminine or masculine traditions in terms of formalism:

---

25 'The Laws of Verse', from *Last Poems*, 1923, *The Poems of Alice Meynell*, 173.
26 Leighton, 245.
27 Edith Sitwell, *Aspects of Modern Poetry* (London: Duckworth, 1934), 12.
28 Celeste M. Schenck, 'Exiled by Genre: Modernism, Canonicity, and the Politics of Exclusion', *Women's Writing in Exile*, ed. Mary Lynn Broe and Angela Ingram (Chapell Hill: University of Carolina Press, 1989), 228–9.
29 Schenck, 228.

Women poets will do best if they realise that male technique is not suitable to them. No woman writing in the English language has ever written a great sonnet, no woman has ever written great blank verse. Then again, speaking generally, as we cannot dispense with our rules, so we find free verse difficult.[30]

Notably, she endorses the connection between the sonnet or blank verse and masculine technique. In reviewing Charlotte Mew's poetry, Edith Sitwell similarly indicated her preoccupation with the difference which gender made to writing. She commended Mew for avoiding perceived feminine writing – 'It is usual for the poems written by women to be unendurably embarrassing when they deal with emotion ... there is a general lack of restraint, decency and dignity, to be observed'[31] – but in the above article on women's poetry she condemned Elizabeth Barrett Browning for 'trying to write as a man':

Most of the rules for women poets begin with a 'Don't' or an 'Avoid'. 'Avoid metaphysics.' 'Don't be pompous.' 'Avoid the sonnet form, and, when possible, long lines.' For poetry is largely an affair of muscle. When we ask ourselves why Christina Rossetti's 'Goblin Market' is one of the best poems ever written by a woman, and why Mrs Elizabeth Barrett Browning's 'Aurora Leigh' is not, the answer is this: It is not only a matter of inspiration: Christina Rossetti in her poem found only and made use of a technique and a manner suitable to feminine muscles, whereas Mrs Browning used a technique and a manner which is only suitable to a man. Failure was the inevitable result ... It is true that the lady writing under the initials H.D. writes admirable and suave free verse which is technically among the best free verse written today; but she is an exception. I like the contents of Amy Lowell's free verse, but I find it for the most part formless and tuneless. Though her poems please me faintly while I am reading them, they leave no impression on my mind, because they are not definite entireties, and for this reason: they have no organic form. Free verse is a form – for it should have organic form – more suitable to men ... how different is this ['Goblin Market'] from the clod-hopping, hearty tweed-clad manner of certain modern women verse writers, tumbling over everything they see, in their would-be mannishness![32]

---

30   Edith Sitwell, 'Some Observations on Women's Poetry', *Vogue* [London] 65, 5 March 1925: 117–8. *Edith Sitwell: Fire of the Mind*, ed. Elizabeth Salter and Allanah Harper (London: Michael Joseph, 1976), 187–192.

31   Edith Sitwell, review of *The Farmer's Bride* and *The Rambling Sailor*, by Charlotte Mew. *Criterion* IX. 34, October 1929: 130–4.

32   Sitwell, 'Some Observations on Women's Poetry'.

The lengthy extract indicates Sitwell's movement towards and retreat from the concept of a distinctive woman's aesthetic in preference to 'would-be mannishness'. Her association between metre and masculinity echoes men's critical discourses.

Like her male colleagues, Edith Sitwell found both feminine and seemingly pseudo-masculine treatment of form unsatisfactory. Laura Riding expressed similar ambivalence about women's competence with conventional poetic effects: 'Women poets are for the most part distinguished from one another by the literary mannerisms they assume in being as-it-were-men.'[33] Her phrase 'as-it-were-men' corresponds to Sitwell's 'would-be-mannishness' and Lowell's 'writing man-wise'. Like Harold Monro, they suggest that women tended to write as men but that their poetry failed according to the 'severe tests of a masculine standard'.[34] Worse, however, was to be judged as feminine in the face of mockery like Carlos Williams' jibe that bad poetry is made of 'sugar and spice and everything nice' and good poetry of 'rats and snails and puppy dogs' tails'.[35]

Reading through the literary periodicals of the period, it is striking that the values and prestige attached to conventional poetic form was an obsession with poetry critics and a particular issue when reviewing the work of women poets. Articles such as 'Originality and Poetry', which identified poetry with the male English tradition, added to women's, often unconscious, sense of exclusion:

> So long as England is the home of Englishmen, English Poetry will be what it has become through Chaucer, Shakespeare, Coleridge; its character is known … future poetry can only refine and diversify and superimpose.[36]

The psychological complexities surrounding poetic form have to be understood because women needed to show mastery of form to be associated with the literary traditions which they sought to enter. In the language of reviewing, formal prosody was associated with literary tradition and by association with nationalism:

---

33   Laura Riding, 'An Enquiry', *New Verse* 11, October 1934: 5.

34   'Women Poets', *Poetry Review* May 1912: 199.

35   William Carlos Williams in *No Man's Land: The Place of the Woman Writer in the Twentieth Century. Vol. 3. Letters to the Front*, by Sandra Gilbert and Susan Gubar (New Haven: Yale University Press, 1994), 74.

36   'Originality and Poetry', review of *Some Contemporary Poets*, by Harold Monro, *TLS* 30 December 1920: 889.

> Mr Bridges' experiments ... teach us, as nothing else can teach us, what prosody is, and what is meant by metre and rhythm and the opposition and reconcilement of the two.[37]

Robert Bridges, poet laureate until 1929, is ostensibly praised here for his 'technical experiment' but it was really for being 'English to the core' that he was prized. Before the War, Britain had held economic dominance and one quarter of the world flew the British flag, but the rejection of British imperialism, associated with the revolt against Victorian dogma, was both accentuated and mitigated by the First World War.

The War accelerated scepticism towards the rhetoric of nationalism but aroused caution regarding radical experiments because of their associations with violence. Consequently, the controversy over *vers libre* was tied up with post-war insecurities. Reviewers strengthened the association between 'form' and 'tradition' so that *vers libre* became synonymous with rebellion or was simply dismissed: 'we doubt indeed whether *vers libre* has any right to call itself verse, unless it is much less free than most *vers libre* actually is.'[38]

In Britain, reviewers in the *TLS* and J.C. Squire in the *New Statesman* and *London Mercury* played upon popular prejudice against new art forms. The perceived synonymy between revolutionary forms and revolutionary politics was repeatedly endorsed – 'Miss Sitwell and her little band of pilgrims – progressives, anarchists, or what you will, go on writing in their own way.'[39] 'Anarchist' is not accurate but demonstrates that radical poetics were taken to be synonymous with ideological extremism.

According to Philip Hobsbaum:

> The concern for form is a characteristic of a development in our poetry which has not, I think, been separately recognised. Perhaps it is best called English modernism – as opposed to the American brand of Eliot, Pound, Stevens and Lowell.[40]

This is misleading in suggesting that the American modernists were not concerned with form, but there is some accuracy in distinguishing different attitudes to formal verse. In a letter to Marianne Moore in 1915, H.D. expressed

---

37 'The Laureate's New Verse', review of *New Verse*, by Robert Bridges (Oxford: Clarendon Press) *TLS* 17 December 1925: 87–9.

38 Review of *Can Grande's Castle*, by Amy Lowell, *TLS* 16 December 1920: 853.

39 Thomas Moult, Review of *Poetry and Criticism*, by Edith Sitwell, *Time and Tide* 30 April 1926: 428.

40 Philip Hobsbaum, *Tradition and Experiment in English Poetry* (Basingstoke: Macmillan, 1979), 298.

the distinction between her reception in the United States and in England as indifference versus opposition:

> I know, more or less, what you are up against, though I escaped some five years ago! – There are terrible difficulties & discouragements, to be met on this side, too – But at least, it is a fight – there is something definite *To* fight! I felt so terribly when I was in USA, the putty that met my wheted [sic] lance![41]

In Britain, American women had to contend with prejudices against foreigners, free verse, mass culture – the influx of Hollywood films added to the association of America with popular culture – and 'women's poetry'.[42] The inescapable fact that most of the avant-garde women's poetry was written by Americans further endorses the importance of interpreting the tendency towards formalism by British poets in its cultural context.

Publishing and Literary Criticism: 'Our War is with Words'

Women needed to break into literary circles to contest the superiority of masculine intelligence and the feminising of their work. Although, as J.C. Squire observed in 1921, women were such a common sight in publishing houses, they frequently experienced only a nominal acceptance by their male contemporaries. In his introduction to *Some Contemporary Poets* (1920), Harold Monro's advice to young poets reinforced the sense of male exclusivity. He detected that poetry writing had become a professional and competitive occupation so that a poet needed 'a technical acquaintance with London Literary Circles'. He admitted that 'editors privilege publishers who advertise, friends and partisans of the paper, colleagues in the trade and great reputations'. The 'young poet' was implicitly male as he was advised to court fashionable women for sponsorship and young women for invitations to dinner.[43]

Male rivalry which excluded and inhibited women was aggravated during the 1920s by the growth industry of literary criticism. Muriel Bradbrook was conscious of the suppression of women when she went up to Girton in 1927. She recalled her weekly lectures by I.A. Richards, F.R. Leavis and Sir Arthur Quiller Couch who addressed the lecture hall as 'Gentlemen'. She realised,

---

41 H.D., letter to Marianne Moore, 21 August 1915, *The Gender of Modernism*, ed. Bonnie Kime Scott (Indianapolis: Indiana University Press, 1990), 137.

42 In 1920, 95 per cent of films shown in Britain were American.

43 Harold Monro, *Some Contemporary Poets* (London: Simpkins & Marshall, 1920), 14, 10, 212.

however, that despite their appearance of absolute authority there was no 'consensus of opinion' among these critical 'giants'.[44] Women did not feature in the influential critical texts of the period such as *The Sacred Wood* (T.S. Eliot, 1920), *Principles in Literary Criticism* (I.A. Richards, 1929), *Seven Types of Ambiguity* (William Empson, 1928) and F.R. Leavis' *New Bearings in English Poetry* (1932). Critical debate was also stimulated and sustained by the surge of literary periodicals, mainly based in London. Intellectual women needed to be recognised in the highbrow papers, namely T.S. Eliot's *The Criterion,* F.R. Leavis' *Scrutiny,* the *Times Literary Supplement* (*TLS*) and *The New Statesman,* but these tended to ignore or undermine them. Vera Brittain recorded how she and Winifred Holtby 'were the first victims of that "discrimination" on which, with some justice, the *New Statesman* has prided itself ever since' when their names were omitted from a list of contributors which included practically everyone else who had written for it. She found the discrimination significant because during the 1920s and 1930s the *New Statesman and Nation* became known for its 'intellectual brilliance' under its chairman J.M. Keynes.[45] Brittain's parenthetical phrase, 'with some justice', illustrates how even successful writers like her internalised a sense of inferiority. These cumulative exclusions entrenched 'femininity' and 'intellect' as binary opposites.

The number of new papers fuelled the prevailing spirit of competition but the publications shared a concern to preserve literary value and taste from contamination by mass culture.[46] Between 1900 and 1930, the newly literate public provided an extended market for books but inflamed concern about the erosion of literary standards. The division between high-, middle- and low-brow became a preoccupation of the literary papers. For example, the production of pocketbook *Everyman* poetry editions provoked debate about the cheapening of literature via widespread circulation. As David Perkins states, in the opening years of this century 'the partisans of poetic beauty were entrenched in the leading journals; if a poet offended their sense of values, their reviews could be gruesome'.[47] In the preservation of tradition from the masses, the *Times Literary Supplement* was clearly regarded as the major voice of literary value:

---

44 Muriel Bradbrook, *Women and Literature 1979–1982: Collected Papers of Muriel Bradbrook* (Sussex: Harvester, 1982), 115.

45 Vera Brittain, *Testament of Experience: An Autobiographical Story of the Years 1925–1950* (London: Virago, 1979), 64.

46 See, for example, review of *The New Criterion, TLS* 10 February 1927: 94.

47 David Perkins, *A History of Modern Poetry. Vol. 1. From The 1890s To The High Modernist Mode* (Cambridge, Massachusetts: Harvard University Press, 1976), 140.

An austere format; the maintenance of anonymity; a heavy emphasis (not least in the correspondence columns) on traditional scholarship; a general flavour of club, common room and parsonage; the link with the *Times* itself – in avant-garde eyes, these were the unmistakable stigmata of the Establishment.[48]

T.S. Eliot considered that to be invited to write for the *Times Literary Supplement* 'was to have reached the top of the ladder of literary journalism'.[49] He described a male enclave where drinks and lunches were part of the job.

Although it could condemn both men and women, its language of competition and almost exclusively male staff made the *TLS* seem impenetrable to women and its nationalistic sentiments were inhospitable to foreigners. Although it was usually inimical to them, the response of the *Times Literary Supplement* mattered to women because they needed approval from the literary establishment in order to be constructed as a writer rather than merely a woman. Virginia Woolf recorded in her diary that the review of *To The Lighthouse* hung over her like a 'damp cloud'.[50] (She did, however, work for the *TLS* from 1905 although she did not review poetry.)[51] Vita Sackville-West also articulated the desire for approval when *The Land* was published in 1926. She told Virginia Woolf of two good reviews, 'a very handsome tribute from Mr Drinkwater in *The Observer*. One is easily comforted',[52] and, 'I am so glad Julian [Bell] likes "The Land" – so glad he thinks me a poet,' but added, 'Now there remain [sic] the *Times Literary Supt.* for which I have an unreasoning respect.'[53]

Women were clearly aware on the one hand of the power of the literary journals which rarely treated their poetry as serious literature, and on the other, of the damagingly conservative leading popular papers, the *Daily Mirror* and the *Daily Express,* which sensationalised their personal lives. In an article, 'A Few Remarks on Sitwellism', in *Time and Tide* (1928), Edith Sitwell

---

48 John Gross (ed.), *The Modern Movement* (London: Harvill, 1992), xii. However, Gross believes that the conservatism of the paper became less solid when it recruited new blood like Richard Aldington.

49 'Bruce Lyttleton Richmond,' *TLS* 13 January 1961; Gross, 263.

50 Virginia Woolf, 'I write however, in the shadow of the damp cloud of the *TLS* review', 5 May 1927, *A Moment's Liberty: The Shorter Diary. Virginia Woolf,* ed. Anne Olivier Bell (London: Hogarth Press, 1990), 229.

51 Gross, xix–xx.

52 Letter from Vita Sackville-West to Virginia Woolf, 2 January 1927, *The Letters of Virginia Woolf and Vita Sackville-West,* ed. Louise De Salvo and Mitchell A. Leaska (London: Hutchinson, 1984), 175.

53 Letter from Vita Sackville-West to Virginia Woolf, 10 October 1926, De Salvo and Leaska, 160.

referred to the antagonism of both 'The crowd' which is taught to fear modern poets as 'alive and dangerous' (as opposed to the innocuous dead ones) and the reviewers who 'fly into a temper'. She satirised the tabloid obsession with her appearance – 'are poets liable to a beauty competition?' – and asserted that 'the people who attack artists to-day are not the real critics, but the gossip writers of certain of the cheaper papers'.[54] In 1928, The Six Point Group, which was dedicated to social equalities in law, advertised a debate on 'Women in the Press', the motion being 'That the influence of the Daily Press is detrimental to the position of Women'.[55] It alluded to the growth of 'trash' weeklies aimed at women as consumers. Women's weeklies helped to give them identity as a sub-culture but they also perpetuated the equation between the 'popular' and the 'feminine'.

Women's Initiatives

Critical writing provided intellectual women like Edith Sitwell, Laura Riding and Amy Lowell, with a means of overcoming the poetess stigma. Edith Sitwell's controversial claims in *Aspects of Modern Poetry* (1934) register her attempts to free critical practice from its stifling tones and limited responses. Laura Riding, with Robert Graves, published *A Survey of Modernist Poetry* (1927) which was a widely read attempt to identify current practice and which integrated men and women. This and her *Contemporaries and Snobs* (1928) stimulated substantial reviews in the *TLS*[56] but have been largely ignored in subsequent surveys of the period. Amy Lowell's *Tendencies in Modern American Poetry* (1917) was one of the first analyses of modern American verse and included H.D.

Although barred from the major literary papers, many women were involved in the more inclusive new magazines which became channels of poetry and criticism between the United States and Europe. In his foreword to *A History of American Magazines 1910–1930*, Frank Mott connects the little magazines with the literary revolution of the years 1910 to 1920. Malcolm Bradbury similarly attributes the small periodicals with democratisating literature without abasing it:

---

54 Edith Sitwell, 'A Few Remarks on Sitwellism', *Time and Tide* 6 April 1928: 332–3.

55 'Women in the Press', advert in *Time and Tide* 16 March 1928.

56 'Modernist Poetry', review of *A Survey of Modernist Poetry*, by Laura Riding and Robert Graves, *TLS* 19 January 1928: 40; review of *Contemporaries and Snobs*, by Laura Riding, *TLS* 5 April 1928: 254.

The tone of the important journals was *avant garde*: their circulation was small; they were addressed largely to a bohemian intellectual reading public. Such criticism as appeared in these magazines tended to be written by literary practitioners, like Pound and Eliot, Ford Maddox Hueffer and F.S. Flint, and was very much devoted to what Pound called, "making it New'. It was reformatory rather than considered; but it offered many critical insights that subsequent critics sought to pursue with greater precision. The twenties were a period of *critical* revolution.[57]

The promotion of the so-called 'avant-garde', was, however, one trend in a period of stylistic cross-currents and it was not exclusive to men. The papers adopted various political positions. The Poetry Society's *Poetry Review*, which started in 1912, was proudly reactionary and had a wide international readership. In 1913, Harold Monro left *Poetry Review* and set up *Poetry and Drama* as an alternative independent paper.[58] *New Age*, edited by A.R. Orage, was 'a socialist weekly of considerable influence though small circulation'.[59] *The Athenaeum*, *The Coterie* and the *New Coterie* were in sympathy with avant-garde poetry.[60] Other journals like *The Adelphi* (the *New Adelphi* from 1927), *Criticism*, *The London Magazine* and *Review of English Studies*, which sprang up during the 1920s, set out their varying editorial principles which tended to be liberal in their aims of being 'representative'.

Women were reviewed in and contributed to these papers. They also set up journals which were arguably more progressive, but in keeping with their dominant goal of equality rather than segregation, they published both men and women.[61] In the United States, Harriet Monroe's *Poetry: A Magazine Of Verse*, based in Chicago, ran from 1912. She remained its editor until her death in 1936. *The Little Review* was edited by Margaret Anderson and Jane Heap between 1914 and 1929. Its 'importance to the service of literature' is acclaimed in *The History of American Magazines*: '*The Little Review*'s record for publication of important contemporary writers is not surpassed – if indeed

57 Malcolm Bradbury in *A Modernist Reader: Modernism in England 1910–1930*, ed. Peter Faulkner (London: Batsford, 1986), 14.

58 See Joy Grant, *Harold Monro and the Poetry Bookshop* (London: Routledge & Kegan Paul, 1967) for an account of Monro's initial dealings with The Poetry Society and the inauguration of *Poetry and Drama*. He had been invited to edit *Poetry Review* but gave up after a year because he did not have enough autonomy and was prohibited from encouraging new writing.

59 Arthur Russell, *Ruth Pitter: Homage to a Poet*, ed. Russell (London: n.p. 1969), 23.

60 Lucas 1997, 178.

61 Frank Mott, *A History of American Magazines. Vol. V: sketches of twenty one magazines 1905–1930* (Cambridge, Massachusetts: Harvard University Press, 1968), x.

it is equalled – by that of any other magazine of the period'.[62] Ezra Pound became foreign editor for the *Little Review* and *Poetry*, although their editors, akin with Harriet Shaw Weaver at the *Egoist*, found him difficult to work with.[63] *The Dial*, formerly 'Chicago's conservative literary weekly', became an important outlet for poetry and criticism under the editorship of Marianne Moore. In the running controversy over the relative progressiveness of *The Dial* and *Poetry*, Frank Mott describes *The Dial* as 'the chief organ of the aesthetic experimentalist',[64] but *Poetry* is usually perceived as more consistently adventurous. In Britain, women forged *The Egoist*, formerly *The New Freewoman*, from 1914, and *Time and Tide* from 1920.[65] *The Egoist*, subtitled 'an individual review', was outspoken on women's issues such as women's sexual needs or how to be unmarried and happy.[66] Its stated aim, 'Our war is with words in every aspect: grammar, accidence, syntax', indicates the editors' conceptual association between literary and social revolution.[67] T.S. Eliot's opinion, '[Harriet Shaw] Weaver is the only woman connected with publishing whom it is really easy to get on with', is a tribute but also reflects the sex war involved even in the progressive journals.[68]

These publishing initiatives illustrate the significant presence of women within the international network of intellectuals. Not only did they promote modern poetry through journals and critical works, but also through bookshops and printing presses. Sylvia Beach's famous Shakespeare and Company bookshop and lending library in Paris was an important meeting place for writers interested in modernism. In London, Alida Monro became responsible for the Poetry Bookshop in Devonshire Street.[69] The bookshop was an international meeting place and eclectic in outlook. It provided a platform for new poets, including Frances Cornford, Charlotte Mew, May Sinclair and Anna Wickham, by publishing their work and organising readings. Nancy

---

62 John T. Frederick in Mott, 173–8.

63 Mott, 174.

64 Mott, 167.

65 For more discussion of *Time and Tide* see *This was My World*, by Lady Margaret Rhondda (Basingstoke: Macmillan, 1933) and *Women's Poetry of the 1930s*, ed. Jane Dowson (London: Routledge, 1996), 181–2.

66 See, for example, 'Women Who Did and Who do Yet', by 'G.W.', *Egoist* I, 1 January 1914: 16 and a response, 'Women, Education, Marriage', letter from R.S. Kerr, *Egoist* I, 15 January 1914: 39.

67 Editorial, *Egoist* II, 1 January 1915.

68 T.S. Eliot, letter to John Rodker, 1919, *The Letters of T.S. Eliot: Vol. 1. 1898–1922*, ed. Valerie Eliot (London: Faber, 1988), 348.

69 Alida Monro took over the Poetry Bookshop when Harold Monro was called for war service. He then became too unwell to run it and died in 1932. See Grant 1967.

Cunard's The Hours Press, in Réanville and then Paris, printed twenty-four books between 1928 and 1931, including the poetry of Richard Aldington, Louis Aragon, Robert Graves, Laura Riding, Ezra Pound, William Carlos Williams, Kay Boyle and Gertrude Stein, and most notably James Joyce's *Ulysses*. Laura Riding with Robert Graves ran the Seizin Press (1927–39) to encourage new, mostly male, poets and later edited *Epilogue* (1935–37), a critical review. These initiatives may partly have stemmed from her lack of acceptance by her male colleagues in America in the Twenties. According to Frank Mott, she was a prize-winner, her poems were often printed in *The Fugitive* (1922–25) and she energetically promoted the magazine and the group of 'Fugitive poets' but 'a woman could scarcely adapt herself to this unusual fellowship of gentlemen. Mrs Gottschalk quarrelled with Grand Master Hirsch, and though she was made a member of the board of editors, she was never a real Fugitive.'[70] The Fugitives also satirised Harriet Monroe as 'Aunt Harriet', playing upon her spinsterhood to imply that she, and therefore her magazine, were restrained and old-fashioned. The personal records surrounding these activities are important documentaries of the cultural climate.[71] Less well-documented are the dependence of many men and women on the patronage of Dorothy Wellesley and Winifred Bryher. Dorothy Wellesley put money into the Woolfs' Hogarth Press and Bryher provided funds for Robert MacAlmon's avant-garde Contact Publishing Company in Paris, Sylvia Beach's bookshop and the Egoist Press.[72]

The new female autonomy reflected in women's professional work and in the unorthodox aspects of their lives is also manifested in the developing stylistic independence of their writing. Their lifestyles contradict the myths of conventional femininity which were attached to the generic label of the woman poet. Upper-class writers such as Nancy Cunard and Edith Sitwell were distanced from the social snobbery and stifling traditionalism of their families, particularly because, as women, they could not hold power or inherit property. Vita Sackville-West, Dorothy Wellesley, Sylvia Townsend Warner,

70 Mott, 110.

71 Sylvia Beach, *Shakespeare and Company*, 1956 (London: Faber and Faber, 1960), Harriet Monroe, *A Poet's Life: seventy years in a changing world* (New York: The Macmillan Company, 1938) and Marianne Moore, '*The Dial*: A Retrospect', *Predilections*, 1931 (New York: Viking, 1955), 103–14.

72 For more discussion of Winifred Bryher, see Gillian Hanscombe and Virginia Smyers, *Writing for their Lives: The Modernist Women 1910–1940* (London: The Women's Press, 1987), 33–46. Contact Publishing Company published Bryher, H.D., Mina Loy, Mary Butts, Djuna Barnes, Gertrude Stein and an influential anthology, *A Contact Collection of Contemporary Writers* in 1925.

Valentine Ackland, Natalie Barney, Amy Lowell, H.D., Gertrude Stein and Djuna Barnes rejected heterosexual for lesbian relationships.[73] Leaving a marriage meant flouting the 'cult of femininity' propagated during and after the War. Dorothy Wellesley left her husband; H.D.'s marriage to Richard Aldington collapsed; Djuna Barnes divorced Courtney Lemon after two years and settled in Paris with Thelma Wood; Mina Loy divorced her first husband. (Her second husband died.) Laura Riding divorced her first husband and lived with Robert Graves and his wife in Mallorca before returning to America and a second marriage. Frances Cornford and Anna Wickham remained in conventional marriages with children but Frances Cornford suffered from severe depressions and Anna Wickham separated from her husband for a while and eventually committed suicide, alleging that she felt a failure as a mother. Elizabeth Daryush, who spent time in Persia with her husband, a Persian government official, decided not to have children. Edith Sitwell, Winifred Holtby, Charlotte Mew, May Sinclair, Stevie Smith and Ruth Pitter were single.

The un- and anti- conventional lives and their literary activities demonstrate that the ideals of femininity – marriage, motherhood and social conformity – in the rhetoric of criticism and in the popular magazines were alien to these poets. In reaction, they often chose rigorous prosodic principles in order to forge an image associated with the high literary forms of 'masculine' writing. Their poetry holds its own in the orthodox terms of stylistic categories, but at the same time requires a critical response which attends to their anti-feminine strategies. Where their poems seem ungendered, the woman-consciousness has to be perceived through its denial. The modernist concept of the 'persona', the masked identity of the poet on the page, was appropriated by some women to try out different masculine and feminine identities. Through these dramatisations, women developed a self-assertive colloquial voice. By their reworking of traditional forms, metres or symbols, and in their rejection of high poetic diction, all the poets participated in the literary revolt against Victorianism which was both precipitated and complicated by the First World War.

---

73   Edna St Vincent Millay is thought to indicate a suppressed lesbian sexuality in some of her poems See www.sappho.com/poetry/e–millay.htm.

Chapter Three

Rear-Guard Modernism

Introduction

Feminist revisionists who seek to free women writers from their alleged 'sentimentality', find themselves dually urged to defend and dismiss the stylistically cautious. Most commonly, they tend to dismiss women's war poetry and the so-called 'Georgians' due to their unadventurous versification and the apparent lack of gender politics. This poetry needs, however, to be reinstated for historical accuracy and for a more comprehensive cultural representation. It cannot be claimed that women's war poetry was influential at the time, but it is an important register of women's responses to war. As for the 'Georgians', Frances Cornford and Vita Sackville-West had successful publishing histories and Sackville-West was potentially the first woman poet laureate. They represent poets like Elizabeth Daryush (1887–1977), Ruth Pitter (1897–1992), Dorothy Wellesley (1889–1956) and Sylvia Lynd (1888–1952) who were popular between the wars. In particular, Pitter and Daryush attracted attention during the 1920s but their better work was published in the 1930s. All these women can be distinguished from the 'elder poets' such as Alice Meynell (1847–1922) by a more contemporary diction and technical versatility.[1] Like other interwar writers they indicate a 'conservative modernity' in that they rejected Victorian and Edwardian cultural conventions but psychologically deferred their entry into modernity.[2] They covered up their gendered perspective with the impersonality of universal voices and conventional forms, but there is often an unofficial discourse below the respectable, symbolised, textual surfaces.

One reason for the disappearance of these women's poems is that their formalism has appeared commendable but irrelevant to the movements of poetry in the hegemonic terms of modernist criticism. In *The Oxford*

---

1 Harold Monro, *Some Contemporary Poets* (London: Simpkins & Marshall, 1920). Alice Meynell is classified under 'A Glance Backwards' whereas Charlotte Mew, Edith Sitwell, Fredegonde Shove, Rose Macaulay, Anna Wickham, Helen Parry Eden and Frances Cornford are classified as 'Poets and Poetasters of our time'.

2 Alison Light, *Forever England: Femininity, Literature and Conservatism between the Wars* (London: Routledge, 1991), 10.

Companion to Twentieth-Century Poetry, Elizabeth Daryush is said to have 'established herself as a traditionalist poet writing in conventional prosody but (like her father) willing to experiment in non-traditional forms'; Pitter's poetry is described as 'usually but not always written in conventional prosody', and the entry on Sackville-West points out that her reputation rests on *The Land* which was 'deliberately anti-modernist and provincial, using regular iambic lines and archaic diction'.[3] Frances Cornford was posthumously classified as 'Georgian' in a commemorative *Poetry Review* which stated that she 'declined to follow the Eliot-Pound fashion in her poetry'.[4]

If the appearance of literary conservatism remains unchallenged, uninformed second- and third-hand commentaries evolve into a misleading consensus. Fleur Adcock was ambivalent about including the 'rear-guard' in *The Faber Book of 20th Century Women's Poetry*:

> It is not easy now to summon a great deal of enthusiasm for the more well-mannered, ladylike poets of the 1920s, 1930s and 1940s, such as Yeats's favourite Dorothy Wellesley (although my inclusion of Ursula Bethell, Frances Cornford and others is evidence that I think we should overcome this natural prejudice and not dismiss them all).[5]

Ruth Pitter is one of those 'others' and Vita Sackville-West is excluded for being 'outmoded'. Fleur Adcock considers Elizabeth Daryush as a 'borderline case' because 'Her experiments with syllabic verse were of interest, but unfortunately she disguised their novelty in a diction which was almost as archaic as that of her father, Robert Bridges.' Adcock is clearly more comfortable with 'technical innovators' like Marianne Moore.[6] As Donald Davie has pointed out, however, after her father died, Elizabeth Daryush's work on syllabic metres became more independent and corresponds to Moore's.[7]

The publication of *Scars Upon My Heart: women's poetry and verse of the First World War* (1981), one of the first anthologies of twentieth-century women's poetry, stirred up the female affiliation complex in feminist critics

---

3　*The Oxford Companion to Twentieth-Century Poetry,* ed. Ian Hamilton (Oxford: Oxford University Press, 1994), 429.

4　Editorial Board, *Poetry Review* 15. 4, October–December 1960: 197.

5　Fleur Adcock, Introduction, *The Faber Book of 20th Century Women's Poetry* (London: Faber, 1987), 7–8. Ursula Bethell (1874–1945) was a New Zealand poet who lived in Britain and Europe for a time and published *Collected Poems* (Oxford: Oxford University Press, 1985). See biographical note, Adcock, 306.

6　Adcock, 8.

7　Donald Davie, *Elizabeth Daryush: Collected Poems* (Manchester: Carcanet, 1976), 13.

because of the pronounced difference between women's and men's poems. In *Feminism and Poetry* (1987), the anthology is discussed under the heading 'The question of bad poetry' and described as 'conventional, sincere and amateurish'.[8] Jan Montefiore finds the poems valuable to the social historian, 'precisely because of their often uncritical handling of War, Sacrifice, Poetry and Religion: there is no professional finish to disguise thought and feeling', and to the literary critic for demonstrating 'the failed attempts to engage with masculine traditions and discourses'.[9] Such verdicts universalise the poetry from the weakest work and imply that realist modes, the intersection of historical and literary relevance or the wrong ideology were pertinent only to women's poems. Although largely realist, much women's poetry contributes to the ironic treatment of classical or nineteenth-century heroic verse which is associated with First World War poetry. The early imagist and Georgian departures, from high rhetoric in favour of conversational idioms and from the abstract to the ordinary, were taken up in war poems by both men and women.

War poetry complicated both pre- and post-War literary experiments. The three column review of *Georgian Poetry 1916–17* demonstrates how the association between form and cultural stability became embedded during the War:

> If these young poets write in metre and rhyme and shape, it is because they want to, because expression urges them to form. And it is mighty comforting –
> in these days when the spirit is hungry for any scrap of permanence and continuity
> – to see the old friendly boots shaping themselves thus kindly to the proud young feet.[10]

Although Georgian poetry was understood to represent some stability in a changing set of values, modernism was also characterised by nostalgia for a distant past and it did not cast off all formal effects; notably, T.S. Eliot maintained classical metres and traditional rhyming patterns. In 1932, F.R. Leavis wrote off the war poets on the grounds of technical caution in comparison with T.S. Eliot and Ezra Pound – 'the debilitated nineteenth-century tradition, then, continued without serious challenge, and there had been nothing to suggest a serious new start'[11] – but Quentin Bell linked the changes of mood and idiom to the spread of modernism:

---

8   Jan Montefiore, *Feminism and Poetry: Language, Experience, Identity in Women's Writing* (London: Pandora, 1987), 65.
9   Montefiore, 69–70.
10 'Georgian Poetry', review of *Georgian Poetry 1916–17*, *TLS* 27 December, 1917: 646.
11 F.R. Leavis, *New Bearings in English Poetry*, 1932 (London: Chatto & Windus, 1979), 58.

A certain scepticism, a certain uneasiness, replaced the glorious certainties of 1914. The war poets began to speak in a new tone of voice. In a word, the mood was one of disenchantment, and in that mood the British public was ready to listen to what Bloomsbury had to say.[12]

As Elizabeth Marsland indicates, although experimental writing was not common among war poets,

> there is little doubt that the conflict between pro-war and anti-war factors hastened the demise of nineteenth-century poetic conventions, when it disestablished amongst the young literati after the war the social attitudes that traditional verse expressed *pro-patria*.[13]

The post-War literary climate was marked by radical and reactionary cross-currents. Geoffrey Bullough detected at least five significant tendencies and observed the survival of traditional poetry.[14] A review of *The Best Poetry 1925* registers the co-existent tugs of the new and the old which were tied to poetic form:

> Here one sees represented the holding to old traditions, old forms and conventions, with the breaking into new forms, which beside the old seem almost of no form, but are none the less, indeed some will say, are the more, true poetry. Here is felt the restlessness, the desire for change, interwoven with the clear and steadfast faith which can be seen in the world this poetry mirrors.[15]

When *The Waste Land* was published in 1922 it was greeted with caution in the literary papers, partly because the First World War had put a brake on experimentation.[16] As David Peters Corbett states, Futurism and Vorticism lost their impact because radical art became associated with destruction: 'Modernism was irrecoverably associated with what the war was being fought to defeat and returns to figuration and realism were applauded.'[17] In 1925,

---

12   Quentin Bell, *Bloomsbury* (London: Weidenfeld and Nicolson, 1968), 82.

13   Elizabeth A. Marsland, *The Nation's Cause: French, English and German Poetry of the First World War* (London: Routledge, 1991), 5.

14   Geoffrey Bullough, *The Trend of Modern Poetry*, 1934 (London and Edinburgh: Oliver and Boyd, 1941), 44–5.

15   Review of *The Best Poetry of 1925*, ed. Thomas Moult, *Time and Tide* 12 February 1926: 154.

16   Review of *The Waste Land*, by T.S. Eliot, *TLS* 20 September 1923: 616.

17   David Peters Corbett, *The Modernity of English Art 1914–30* (Manchester: Manchester University Press, 1997), 50. See also 'The Death of Futurism', by John Cournos, *Egoist* IV, January 1917: 6–7.

Edith Sitwell recorded, 'Many of the poets labelled Georgian are still writing at the moment from the point of view as that which has prevailed since Wordsworth, and therefore seems less obscure and alarming to a certain portion of the press and of the public.'[18]

The importance of arguing that literary movements were less distinct than retrospective reductions commonly suggest is that the technical reserve of women has been falsely isolated or exaggerated to make them seem irrelevant to modern poetry. Although Harold Monro's Poetry Bookshop Press published the Georgian anthologies, edited by Eddie Marsh,[19] Monro believed that after the first two volumes they lost their cutting edge, and he published modernist poets like Ezra Pound through his chapbooks. He was in dialogue with Pound and other writers associated with *The Egoist* and with T.S. Eliot at *The Criterion*. However, the hostility of T.S. Eliot, Edith Sitwell and Virginia Woolf to the Georgians partly accounts for the exaggerated schism between Bloomsbury and 'Squirearchy'.[20] Eliot's condemnation of Georgian poetry in *The Egoist* in 1918 fatally separated Georgian from 'modernist': 'Georgian Poetry ...is inbred. It has developed a technique and a set of emotions all of its own ... [characterised by] "pleasantness".'[21] Eliot's disparagement of a mythologised comfortable Georgian coterie may have been intended to define himself as a modernist, but according to Quentin Bell, T.S. Eliot was not 'one of us' and 'no part of Bloomsbury ... A new Englander – Puritan. He wanted tradition'.[22] Bloomsbury was not the definable entity or close-knit group of literary mythology, nor were the 'Georgians' a settled gentleman's club. The number of poems by D.H. Lawrence in Marsh's anthologies illustrates that 'Georgians wrote modernist poems and modernists were anthologised in Georgian collections.'[23] War poems were included in both.

Nevertheless, modernist sanctions against the expressive have undermined the literary status of all war poetry. Similarly, since all Georgian poetry had regular form, there was and is a fallacious assumption that all poems with regular form were what Georgian came to stand for: out of touch, traditional and sentimental. The implications are particularly detrimental for the many

---

18 Edith Sitwell, *Poetry and Criticism* (London: Hogarth, 1925), 13.
19 Edward Marsh was private secretary to Winston Churchill and allegedly treated poetry as more of a leisure activity than a profession.
20 For information on J.C. Squire see Chapter Two, footnote 5.
21 T.S. Eliot, 'Verse Pleasant and Unpleasant', review of *Georgian Poetry* 1916–17 and *Wheels. A Second Cycle*, *Egoist* V, March 1918: 43–4.
22 Quentin Bell, *Bloomsbury* (London: Weidenfeld and Nicolson, 1968), 127.
23 Clive Bloom (ed.), *Literature and Culture in Modern Britain. Vol. 1. 1900–1929* (Essex: Longman, 1993), 18.

women who used conventional forms in order to identify themselves with the male tradition which they sought to enter.

In discussing the exiles from literary modernism, Celeste Schenck puts a case which is central to the re-evaluation of non-experimental writing:

> If ... the radical poetics of modernism often marks a deeply conservative politics, might it also possibly be true that the seemingly genteel, conservative poetics of women poets whose obscurity even feminists have overlooked might pitch a more radical politics than we had considered possible?[24]

It cannot be claimed that there is a 'radical' gender or class politics in the poetry considered here, as there is with the 'Female Modernists' or during the 1930s. However, women's war poems register the competing impulses regarding their national and gendered identities. The War came at a time when suffragism had awakened the concept of equal rights and equal access to male-dominated public places and professions but it separated the experiences of men and women and set demands for nationalism above social equality. The opportunities to take over men's work during the war were countered by the prescribed feminine dedication to keeping the home fires burning and by the requirement to return to domestic duties when it was over. Frances Cornford and Vita Sackville-West tended to conceal their gender but there is often a personal undertow to the superficially tame writing. Although they did not voice feminist protest, they investigated social conventions, notably concerning marriage and motherhood. Schenck's statement especially applies to Vita Sackville-West who qualifies stylistically as a Georgian yet whose covert lesbian agenda has rarely been recognised in her poetry.

One of the reasons why these poets have not been properly recognised is that where there is the possibility of different readings, women's poetry especially has been interpreted as simply traditionalist rather than as using the form of the tradition as a respectable cover for challenging traditional ideals. As Isobel Armstrong recognised in her revisionist history of Victorian poetry:

> The doubleness of women's poetry comes from the ostensible adoption of an affective mode, often simple, often pious, often conventional, but those conventions are subjected to investigations, questioned, or used for unexpected

---

24 Celeste M. Schenck, 'Exiled by Genre: Modernism, Canonicity, and the Politics of Exclusion', *Women's Writing in Exile*, ed. Mary Lynn Broe and Angela Ingram (Chapell Hill: University of Carolina Press, 1989), 232.

purposes. The simpler the surface of the poem, the more likely it is that a second and more difficult poem will exist beneath it.[25]

Women's Poetry and the First World War

Women's First World War writing records the cultural conflicts which centred on the ideologies of home and womanliness which had been inflamed before the War in reaction to suffrage activities and which were fanned during the War by equating motherhood with the 'Motherland'. This rhetorical synthesis had the dual purpose of quashing suffragism and of mustering support for the war effort. Recruiting propaganda required a reversion to traditional ideologies of gender yet women's war work meant that they crossed the conventional lines between male and female roles. A minority of poems seem to support the dominant rhetoric of patriotism, maternity and sacrificial love but the majority indicate women's psychological rejection of the idealised femininity on which the rhetoric depended. The separation of men's and women's experiences, through the opposition of 'Home' and 'Front', meant that women were confronted with the difficulty of writing about distinctly female experience when they wished to avoid the assumptions of gender-distinctive authorship. Additionally, neither the canons of traditional, that is classical or nineteenth-century, war poetry nor contemporary soldier poetry offered them relevant models for their experience.

Like much war poetry, women's is stylistically tame, but several poems operate as implicit or explicit critiques of both literary and popular war verse. The contemporary idiom and anti-heroic irony in many poems contribute to the rejection of high diction and imperialist rhetoric which began before the War and was given impetus by poets writing during it. In a tradition of women's poems, the First World War poetry indicates their negotiations between private lyric and public political discourse. Women projected themselves into male roles in order to engage imaginatively with the men at the Front, and dramatised various female roles for representing their new identities as workers, for protesting against pro-war propaganda or for faking the idealised femininity which the propaganda prescribed. The critical reception to women's poems registers the continuation of the pre-war reaction against women's suffrage in its endorsement of the values associated with traditional femininity.

It is important to include women in any conspectus of First World War poets because of the major impact which the War had on the British

---

25 Isobel Armstrong, *Victorian Poetry* (London: Routledge, 1996), 324.

consciousness, and because the cultural shifts have mostly been represented in male terms. Jacqueline Rose points to the intersection of the War's historical and literary significance: 'Neither *Jacob's Room*, nor *The Waste Land*, nor *Ulysses*, which also appeared in 1922, can be read without reference to the Great War.'[26] The interface between suffragism, pacifism and nationalism has, however, been more explored in women's fiction than in their poetry. Classifying and evaluating war poetry written by women is particularly problematic because of its quantity and because much of it is hard to position within the dominant category which foregrounds active service. Out of 2,225 British writers who published war poems, at least 532 were women – (pseudonyms and initials make exact figures impossible).[27] Their treatment of war was stylistically and politically diverse. The poetry which voices dedication to the homeland appeals little to contemporary readers and poems which appear to collude with government propaganda are a problem for contemporary, especially feminist, criticism.

Literary histories of war poetry have tended to build on the binary model of combatant versus civilian yet, as Robert Graves recognised, 'many soldiers wrote as though they had seen more of the war than they really had'.[28] Since women's experiences were more obviously 'at home', however, their writing has been prejudged as irrelevant in the terms of canonical trench poetry or the modernist opposition to domestic culture. War poetry, especially, confronted women with the impasse between masculine and feminine authorship. The Great War was the first time that a number of women were participants in, rather than spectators of, what had previously been understood as a male event, but their experiences were separated. Before the War,

> women were not then so concerned to express that area of their experience which was literally 'no-man's land', off-limits to men and so outside the dominant culture. Rather, their literature was concerned with women's entry into that exclusive part of the national culture which had previously been forbidden to women.[29]

---

26   Jacqueline Rose, Review of *Virginia Woolf*, by Hermione Lee, *London Review of Books* 23 January 1997: 3.

27   Catherine Reilly (ed.), *Scars upon my Heart: Women's Poetry and Verse of the First World War* (London: Virago, 1981), xxxiii.

28   Robert Graves, 1949, cited in Susan Schweik, 'Writing War Poetry Like a Woman', *Critical Inquiry* 13 (Spring 1987): 533.

29   Claire Tylee, *The Great War and Women's Consciousness: Images of Militarism and Womanhood in Women's Writings 1914–1964* (Basingstoke: Macmillan, 1990), 14.

Consequently, it was particularly hard for women to assume a universal voice when the universal voice was that of the male soldier poet. The borrowed robes of neither nineteenth-century war verse, nor classical heroics, nor the combat poems of their male contemporaries were suitable for their experiences and perceptions of the War. In several poems, women adopted the voice of the male soldier; in others, they voiced their experiences of war work, leave-taking, loss or alienation from male militarism.

If literary women were seeking an identity in the symbolic order which was distinct from the maternal function, writing war poetry involved particular conflicts. All women would reject the idealised image of motherhood but if they colluded with the dominant patriarchal sentiments towards the War, they were propelled towards patriarchal presumptions about femininity. Poetry like Jessie Pope's seem 'inauthentic', because it seems to follow the dominant order uncritically, although occasionally, a personal, non-symbolised, response to war peeps through. In the non-patriotic verse, women represented a resistance to the public language of war, but the most convincing poems report the specifically female areas of experience such as war work and nursing abroad. The best draw upon modernist disruptions of language and form, such as May Sinclair's and Charlotte Mew's depictions of a consciousness which is disengaged from or opposed to active fighting.

In all war writing, the pressure to report extreme experience meant that realist discourses took priority over modernist syntactical fragmentations. As Paul Fussell has pointed out, poets looked to the literature of war to represent their experiences and traditional epic, narrative and lyric forms were appropriated for maintaining or subverting the heroic ethos of war.[30] Helen Hamilton's 'The Romancing Poet' illustrates that women were aware that these literary uniforms were ill-fitting to the First World War and particularly to their perspectives:

> If you have words –
>   Fit words, I mean,
> Not your usual stock-in-trade,
>   Of tags and *clichés* –
> To hymn such greatness,
>   Use them.[31]

---

30 Paul Fussell, *The Great War and Modern Memory*, 1975 (London: Oxford University Press, 1977).

31 Helen Hamilton, 'The Romancing Poet', Reilly, 49–50.

As indicated here, women consciously negotiated with the male traditions of war poetry which they knew. The biographies at the end of Catherine Reilly's anthology indicate that most of her poets were well-educated and many were connected with literary groups. Some, like Charlotte Mew, May Wedderburn Cannan and Katherine Tynan, were published poets before the War.

The diversity and complexity of women's responses, which the poetry records, are an important antidote to the mythologies of the maternal sentimentalist depicted in the recruitment posters such as the best known, 'Women of England say "Go!"'.[32] As Claire Tylee puts it:

> The main thrust of the official propaganda was an essentially Victorian ideal of war, which has dominated the British imagination of the Great War ever since. It promoted a chivalrous myth of British soldiers as pure young men who sacrificed their lives, innocently and willingly, to save their Mother-country and their womenfolk from violation. All criticism of this myth which implied that the war was anything other than a holy crusade against the bestial hun, was ruthlessly suppressed.[33]

Since anti-war sentiment was suppressed, the poetry can be read as an instrument of women 'having their say' when they had no other means of public discourse. Margaret Sackville was a pacifist and in 'Nostra Culpa' she suggests that women were guilty of keeping quiet because of their need for male approval:

> We knew that Force the world has deified,
> How weak it is. We spoke not, so men died.
> Upon a world down-trampled, blood defiled,
> Fearing that men should praise us less, we smiled.[34]

The fact that several poets were active in feminist and socialist movements validates my investigation of the tension between superficial passivity and unarticulated rebellion. Along with statistics, memoirs and fiction, Margaret Sackville's depiction of the unspoken protest of women registers the suppressed resistance which often lay below the surface acquiescence to their prescribed response. In 1928, H.D. confessed,

---

32 Recruitment Poster, no. 75. See Gill Plain, 'Great Expectations: Rehabilitating the Recalcitrant War Poets', *Feminist Review* 51, Autumn 1995: 41–65, 53.
33 Tylee, 252.
34 Margaret Sackville, 'Nostra Culpa', Marsland, note 54, 125.

One of the most distinguished women of the political non-militant suffragettes said to me (in 1914) 'I have studied the problem from every angle, but I can dare not question [sic] our cause for going to war. If I questioned it for one moment, I should go mad.' I did not say to her then: 'well, go mad.' I would now.[35]

The disjunction between the ideologies of femininity, which were circulated by the powerful propaganda machines, and the individual experiences of women often provides the textual ambiguities which lifts the poetry above the merely documentary.

The frequent sense of liberation from domestic routine, which underlies the symbolic rhetoric of sacrifice and duty, is illustrated in Rose Macaulay's early war poem, 'Many Sisters to Many Brothers':

> Oh it's you that have the luck, out there in blood and muck:
>> You were born beneath a kindly star;
> All we dreamt, I and you, you can really go and do,
>> ...
>> But for me ... a war is poor fun.[36]

Rose Macaulay was apparently 'vilified for the seemingly naive sentiments' in this poem.[37] In the light of recruitment propaganda, the anti-feminine stance was subversive, but is cloaked by the childlike rhythm and rhyming. It is likely that the innocent persona was a conscious cover for her resentment since Rose Macaulay was well aware of the ways in which men and women were manipulated by propaganda machinery. She was educated in Oxford and became a well-known writer, connected to Bloomsbury.

Much poetry illustrates the ways in which women at home were caught between the patriotic discourses of the establishment, which surrounded them through the press, and the anti-war writing of the combatant poets. Ironically, the hostility to the idealised feminine figure famously expressed by Owen in his denouncement of 'a certain poetess,' understood to be Jessie Pope,[38] and by Sassoon in 'Glory to Women' was to a sentimental image largely constructed by men: 'You crown our distant ardours while we fight, / And mourn our laurelled memories when we're killed.'[39]

---

35 H.D., in Rose, 7.
36 Rose Macaulay, 'Many Sisters to Many Brothers', Reilly, xxxv.
37 Reilly xxxv.
38 Wilfred Owen made a mock dedication to 'a certain poetess' in an early draft of 'Dulce et Decorum Est'.
39 Siegfried Sassoon, 'Glory of Women', Craiglockhart, 1917, *Penguin Book of First World War Poetry*, ed. Jon Silkin (Harmondsworth: Penguin, 1981), 132.

In *Goodbye To All That*, Robert Graves reprinted the 'Letter from "A Little Mother"' which indicated the cult of motherhood propagated by the *Morning Post* and other conservative media.[40] It was published as a pamphlet and seventy five thousand copies were sold in less than a week. The 'Little Mother' asserted on behalf of the 'gentle-nurtured, timid sex' that the 'common soldier' would find the women of the British race at his heels, 'reliable, dependent, uncomplaining'. The fact that it was designed to oppose 'those who disgrace their sacred trust of motherhood' indicates the significant presence of the female rebels and makes one wonder whether the letter was an editorial fiction. Helen Hamilton's 'The Jingo-woman' represents vehement opposition to 'Little Mothers': '(How I dislike you!) / Dealer in white feathers, / Insulter, self-appointed.'[41] The white feather doled out to men who did not volunteer for war service was a ruse initiated by Admiral Penrose Fitzgerald. The rhetoric of poets like Hamilton indicates that women were still acutely 'sex-conscious'.

It is a myth that women lost the concept of equality during the War. In her leading article 'Women's Rights' in *The Egoist*, 1 October 1914, the former activist Dora Marsden assented to, but lamented, the halt of suffragism:

> The war – still the war – has brought the wordy contest about women's rights to an abrupt finish, and only a few sympathetic words remain to be spoken over the feminist corpse.[42]

May Sinclair's article, 'Women's Sacrifices for the War', published in *Collier's Magazine*, 1914, and *Woman at Home*, 1915, would have reached a wide audience. It detailed the ways in which women proved that they could do men's work equally well and argued that they would not collapse into preferring peace at any price. She insisted that it was not a question of 'sacrifice' but 'service' because women *wanted* to do men's work: 'If the war should last long and take a heavy toll of men, it would settle for all time the question of women's ability to fill all men's places.'[43] In June 1915, some seventy-eight thousand women had volunteered for clerical and shop work or war service in armament factories, agriculture and transport.

---

40 'Letter from "A Little Mother"', in *Goodbye to All That*, by Robert Graves, 1929 (Harmondsworth: Penguin, 1979), 187–8.

41 Helen Hamilton, 'The Jingo–woman', Reilly, 47.

42 Dora Marsden, 'Women's Rights', *Egoist* 1, 1 October 1914: 361–3.

43 May Sinclair, 'Women's Sacrifices for the War', *Collier's Magazine* 21 November 1914, reprinted in *Woman at Home* February 1915. See *Miss May Sinclair: Novelist. A Biographical and Critical Introduction*, by Theophilus E.M. Boll (New Jersey: Associated University Presses, 1973), 253.

Many women in Britain were pacifists, but were inhibited from articulating their hostility towards the War machinery. In America, there was less constraint. In an article on women and war in the *Little Review*, September 1914, 'A Spectator' explained that she had observed the pre-war military suffragism in England with a mixture of terror and admiration, but the War demonstrated its justification: 'for the first time I felt the real tragedy of the women of Europe whose business is to bring up sons for the man's game of war'.[44] The same issue printed 'Children of War', by Eunice Tietjens, a regular contributor to *Little Review*, which associated patriotism with patriarchy:

> And we shall pay – year after year, in our
> Frail bodies and our twisted souls shall we pay
> For your glorious patriotism.
> Out of the wounds of war we cry to you,
> We who have yet to be.[45]

The emotive device of unborn children's voices may have been deliberately appositional to the voice of the dead soldier which was a common strategy in men's war poems.

In her preface to *Tendencies in Modern American Poetry* (1917), Amy Lowell recorded, 'It is impossible for anyone writing today not to be affected by the war. It has overwhelmed us like a tidal wave.'[46] Harriet Monroe recalled that most of the poems submitted to *Poetry*'s competition in 1914 were protesting against the War, and in 1917 she expressed her 'suspicion of the propaganda which was gradually luring us into the conflict'.[47] In her editorial of September 1914, she argued for the role of poetry in constructing and changing man-made ideologies of war:

> Poets have made more wars than kings, and war will not cease until they remove its glamour from the imaginations of men.
>
> What is the fundamental, the essential and psychological cause of war? The feeling in men's hearts that it is beautiful. And who created this feeling? Partly, it is true, kings and their 'armies with banners'; but far more, poets with their

---

44 Sonya Levien, 'Women in War', *Little Review* September 1914: 5.

45 Eunice Tietjens, 'Children of War', *Little Review* September 1914: 6. Eunice Tietjens is one of Amy Lowell's regretted omissions, along with Rose Benét, from *Tendencies in Modern American Poetry*, 1917, Preface, viii.

46 Amy Lowell, Preface, *Tendencies in Modern American Poetry*, 1917 (Oxford: Blackwell, 1922), v.

47 Harriet Monroe, 'The New Era', *Poetry* January 1917; *A Poet's Life: Seventy years in a changing world*, by Monroe (New York: The Macmillan Company, 1938), 343–8.

war-songs and epics, sculptors with their statues – the assembled arts which have taken their orders from kings, their inspiration from battles. Kings and artists have united to give war its glamour, to transmute into sounds and colors and forms of beauty its ravages and horror, to give heroic appeal to its unreason, a heroic excuse to its rage and lust.

All this is of the past. The race is beginning to suspect those old ideals, to give valor a wider range than war affords, to seek danger not at the cannon's mouth but in less noisy labors and adventures. When Nicholas of Russia and William of Germany, in solemn state the other day, invoked the blessing of God upon their armies, the emotion that went round the world was not the old thrill, but a new sardonic laughter.

As Cervantes smiled Spain's chivalry away, so some poets of the new era may strip the glamour from war ... But the final word has not been said; the feeling that war is beautiful still lingers in men's hearts, a feeling founded on world-old savageries – love of power, of torture, of murder, lob of big stakes in a big game. This feeling must be destroyed, as it was created, through the imagination. It is work for a poet.[48]

Monroe believed that the reversal of the heroic ethos was not mere wishful-thinking because a new poetry of grim protest was emerging.

The alienation of women from male militarism is supremely represented by Virginia Woolf in *Three Guineas* (1938). In war, she says, a woman 'will find that she has no good reason to ask her brother to fight on her behalf to protect "our" country':

'Our country' she will say, 'throughout the greater part of its history has treated me as a slave; it has denied me education or any share in its possessions. "Our country" still ceases to be mine if I marry a foreigner. "Our" country denies me the means of protecting myself ... you are fighting to gratify a sex instinct which I cannot share; to procure benefits which I have not shared and probably will not share.'[49]

For Woolf, as Jacqueline Rose observes, 'the question of war is inseparable from that of gender or sex':

If at one level women find themselves bolstering up the system that maintains them ('our splendid empire') and then supporting war as one of the few opportunities to escape the tyranny of the home ('our splendid war') they none

---

48   Harriet Monroe, Editorial, *Poetry* iv. vi, September 1914: 232.
49   Virginia Woolf, *Three Guineas* (London: Hogarth Press, 1938), 197.

the less, because they are regularly excluded from the great civilisation – have a different take: 'what is this civilisation in which we find ourselves?'[50]

In Pauline Barrington's 'Education' the stock image of the woman knitting is undercut by the critique of women's collusion with militarism in allowing her sons to play with toy soldiers: 'Is the toy gun father of the Krupps?'[51] In poems like this, there are two competing discourses: the official and idealised depiction of the women at home and an underlying objection to the man-made concept of military glory which was alien to them and which devastated their personal lives.

Nationalism

Given the psychologically complex relationship of women with nationalism, the patriotic poems are difficult to digest. They are a testimony to the power of the propaganda machines which constructed the War in terms of duty, sacrifice and love. The poets who were most accommodating of the dominant pro-war ideologies, superficially, at least, were the ones who were most commercially successful and subsequently have been taken as more representative than they were. The most overtly patriotic poetry, such as Jessie Pope's *War Poems* (1915) and May Wedderburn Cannan's *In War Time* (1916), were used to promote nationalistic sentiments by the literary papers and the popular press. Reviewers of Katherine Tynan's *Flower of Youth: Poems in War Time* (1915) and *The Holy War* (1916) endorsed the conjunction of nationalistic and feminine qualities by applauding the perceived 'delicacy and tenderness' and 'appealing gentleness'.[52] Similarly, the *TLS* embraced an anthology, *Lest we forget* (1915), which was published to aid the Queen Mary Needlework Guild. According to the review, it was 'inscribed', as Baroness Orczy says in her foreword, 'to every individual woman and girl of Great Britain who today is bearing so heroically – so uncomplainingly – her own share of Britain's burden in this great war'.[53] In reviewing Irene Hammond's *War Verse and Others*, the alleged lack of 'poetic quality' was useful for

---

50 Jacqueline Rose, *Why War? – Psychoanalysis, Politics, and the return to Melanie Klein* (Oxford: Blackwell, 1993), 32.
51 Pauline Barrington, 'Education', Reilly, 6.
52 Review of *Flower of Youth*, by Katherine Tynan, *TLS* 10 June 1915: 199; review of *The Holy War*, by Katherine Tynan, *TLS* 8 June 1916: 275.
53 Review of *Lest we Forget: A War Anthology*, ed. H.B. Elliott, Foreword by Baroness Orczy (London: Jarrold, 1915), *TLS* 1 March: 96.

keeping women poets in their place.[54] Books like Rose Macaulay's *Three Days* (1919) and Margaret Cole's *Poems* (1918) which interrogate the ethics of war were less well advertised.

Lucy Whitmell's devotional verse 'Christ in Flanders', first printed in *The Spectator*, 11 September 1915, was one of the most reprinted poems of the War.[55] The Victorians had justified imperial militarism by Christian mythologies of chivalry and the prevalence of Christian imagery in early war poems was part of the construction of the War as a Christian crusade by the careful propaganda campaign of the British government.[56] Katherine Tynan's 'Mid Piteous Heaps of Dead' accordingly pointed to the comfort offered by the Catholic faith; the poem relates a young soldier's dying words which conformed to the promoted synthesis between the soldier and the crucified Christ and therefore between his mother and the Holy Mother.[57] The publishers of Tynan's *Flower of Youth* inflamed the popularity of the title poem by a note appended to the page: '*In response to numerous applications, the publishers can supply copies of this poem printed separately at twopence each. The profits will be given to the Dublin Castle Red Cross Hospital.*'[58] Like 'Mid Piteous Heaps of Dead', the poem offered consolations of Heavenly reward:

> They run and leap by a clear river
>   And of their youth they have great joy.
> God who made boys so clean and good
>   Smiles with the eyes of fatherhood.

The lines echo Rupert Brooke's renowned representation of war's purification, 'as swimmers into cleanness leaping'.[59] These poems of Katherine Tynan and Lucy Whitmell's 'Christ in Flanders' indicate the aspect of the female imagination which sought to enter into the events of war by imitating the well-circulated patriotic poems by Brooke and Rudyard Kipling.

Women allied themselves with men through depicting men's war service and using men's frames of reference. In *Flower of Youth* there are meditations

---

54 Review of *War Verse and Others*, ed. Irene Hammond (London: St Catherine's Press), *TLS* 22 April 1915: 139.

55 Lucy Whitmell, 'Christ in Flanders', Reilly, 127–8; Biographical note, Reilly, 140.

56 Tylee, 57.

57 Katherine Tynan, 'Mid Piteous Heaps of Dead', *Flower of Youth*, 39–40.

58 Katherine Tynan, 'Flower of Youth', *Flower of Youth*, 54–5.

59 Rupert Brooke, 'Peace', *Collected Poems*, 1932 (London: Sidgwick and Jackson, 1974), 146.

on soldiers and airmen in England and Tynan's native Ireland. The public school imagery in 'The Golden Boy' exemplifies how women projected themselves into the male arena:

> He plays the game, winning or losing,
>> As in the playing-fields at home;
>
> ...
>
> Gay at Eton or at Harrow,
>> Counts battles as by goals and runs:
> God keep him from Death's flying arrow
>> To give his England fighting sons.[60]

Although Tynan hints at the over-glorification of war, the protest is overshadowed by the endorsement of nationalism which made her poems successful. As Paul Fussell has detailed, the competitive public school ethos provided a common vocabulary and imagery for the British soldier poets; it also emphasised the male-only site of experience.[61]

Other poems depicted women's roles as men wanted to see them. In 'Play the Game' Jessie Pope's reinforcement of recruiting propaganda is in terms of male pursuits, football and shooting:

> A truce to the League, a truce to the Cup,
>> Get to work with a gun.
> When our country's at war we must all back up –
>> It's the only thing to be done![62]

She colludes with the 'Women of Britain say "Go!"' campaign, but the clichés demonstrate that the rhetoric is wholly adopted from the dominant discourses. Jessie Pope was educated at Craven House, Leicester and North London Collegiate School. Her poems, humorous fiction and articles were printed in *Punch* and other leading popular magazines and newspapers. Her books of poems were always promoted in the *Times Literary Supplement* with approving noises like, 'We are glad of another volume of those poems as full of point and sling as the previous volume.'[63] Her *Simple Rhymes for Stirring Times* (1916) had been individually printed in the *Daily Mail* and the *Daily Express*.

---

60   Katherine Tynan, 'The Golden Boy', *Flower of Youth*, 14–15.
61   Fussell 1977.
62   'Play the Game', *Jessie Pope's War Poems* (London: Grant Richards Ltd, 1915), 11.
63   Review of *More War Poems*, by Jessie Pope (London: Grant Richards Ltd, 1915), *TLS* 22 July 1915: 248.

Jessie Pope's apparent lack of critical response to the official propaganda is discordant with contemporary, particularly feminist, critics. However, the superficiality of these jog-trot verses may register the borrowed nature of the writing when women assume the identity created for them by men. It is possible to read into 'No' both a compliance with and a denial of the chivalric platitudes which required women to view themselves in need of protection:[64]

> And what of the girl who is left behind,
>> And the wife who misses her mate?
> Oh, well, we've got our business to mind
>
>> …
>> 'Are we downhearted?' – 'NO!'[65]

The almost parodic cheeriness could stem from a genuine sense of independence which women were forbidden to profess. The exaggerated regularity also foregrounds the fictionality of the stock responses which the poem purports to support.

In 'War Girls' Jessie Pope leaks a more palpable hint that women's injunctions on men to 'Go!' were fuelled by their enjoyment of the unprecedented opportunities provided by life without them:

> There's the girl who clips your ticket for the train,
>> And the girl who sweeps the loft from floor to floor,
> There's the girl who does a milk round in the rain,
>> And the girl who calls for orders at your door.
>>> Strong sensible, and fit,
>>> They're out to show their grit,
>> And tackle jobs with energy and knack.
>>> *No longer caged and penned up*,
>>> They're going to keep their end up
> Till the khaki soldier boys come marching back.[66]

Although the narrative capitulates to reinstating wife and mother as women's preferred roles, the energetic rhythm projects the pleasure of working 'like a man'. My emphasis on, 'No longer caged and penned up', is to underline the excitement which is also recorded in women's memoirs and fiction. After the War, many women admitted to having tasted an independence which was by no means unpalatable and which they wanted to retain.

---

64   Tylee, 57.
65   Jessie Pope, '"No"', *War Poems*, 10.
66   Jessie Pope, 'War Girls', Reilly, 90, emphasis added.

It cannot be denied that poetry like Jessie Pope's or Katherine Tynan's is stylistically claustrophobic, but as Elizabeth Marsland points out, all propaganda poetry, whether patriotic or protesting, was subject to cliché and conventional formalism. She divides war poetry into two categories: 'propaganda', which includes both patriotic and protest poems because they are similar in tone and language, and 'non-propaganda'. Both kinds of propaganda are prone to didacticism and both kinds are found in 'popular' verse. This stylistic link between protest and patriotic writing illustrates the double-speak which applauds anti-war but condemns pro-war polemic, ostensibly for aesthetic reasons. Most of the archaic patriotic verse was written in the early years of the War and, in accordance with a widespread move from idealism in 1914 to satire in 1918, the voice of protest was the more common after 1915.[67] In *Scars upon my Heart*, the majority of the poetry can be labelled as propagandist and the poems of protest outweigh those which support the War.

War Work

There is less disjunction between the dominant discourses of war and the writer's subjectivity in poems which represent women's actual, rather than imaginative or prescribed, identities as medical workers abroad and volunteers at home. They present complex responses to war in an easier idiom. Some poems like 'Women at Munition Making'[68] express resentment at producing weapons and indicate a conflict between pacifist, suffragist and nationalist impulses. Other poems depict a relish at the opportunities to be involved in the machinery of war. These depictions of women's differing psychological conditions are crucial to dispelling the myths that women universally supported the War or that they were by nature essentially pacifist. May Wedderburn Cannan's 'Rouen – 26 April–25 May 1915', was apparently very popular. The metrical similarity to John Masefield's 'Cargoes' and Rudyard Kipling's 'Mandalay' echo the sort of Edwardian narrative verse associated with imperial values but it expresses the excitement of independence, travel and access to male preserves which characterises much women's First World War writing:

> Can you recall those noontides and the reek of steam and coffee,
> Heavy-laden noontides with the evening's peace to win,
> And the little piles of Woodbines, and the sticky soda bottles,
> And the crushes in the 'Parlour', and the letters coming in?

---

67 See Jon Silkin on the four stages of consciousness; Introduction, Silkin 1981, 30–9.
68 Mary Gabrielle Collins, 'Women at Munition Making', Reilly, 24.

...
Can I forget the passage from the cool white-bedded Aid Post
Past the long sun-blistered coaches of the khaki Red Cross train
To the truck train full of wounded, and the weariness and laughter,
And 'Good-bye, and thank you, Sister', and the empty yards again?[69]

May Wedderburn Cannan was a VAD and in the Intelligence Service during the War; she also worked for the Clarendon Press in Oxford, which published government propaganda materials, and then became a librarian. Claire Tylee states that she was consciously conservative in her literary style, unashamed in her admiration for Rupert Brooke and an example of women who helped 'to make the War, and were intoxicated by it'.[70]

The subtext of welcome adventure in 'Rouen', along with records like May Sinclair's *Journal of Impressions in Belgium* (1915),[71] indicate that women were more intoxicated by their new opportunities than by patriotism. Like the men, however, they became disillusioned by the extreme conditions and the gulf between the suffering abroad and the idealism at home. May Sinclair went to Belgium for seventeen days with the Motor Ambulance Corps and was accepted by the Belgian Red Cross, but the advance of the Germans forced the Corps to retreat from Ghent to Bruges and then to Ostend.[72] She wrote three sets of verse about her experiences but only two were published, including 'Field Ambulance Retreat', subtitled 'Via Dolorosa, Via Sacra':

II

The road-makers made it well
Of fine stone, strong for the feet of the oxen and of the great Flemish hostess,
And for the high wagons piled with corn from the harvest.
And the labourers are few;
They and their quiet oxen stand aside and wait

---

69   May Wedderburn Cannan, 'Rouen', Reilly, 17–18. The poem was included in *The Oxford Book of Twentieth-century Verse*, ed. Philip Larkin (London: Oxford University Press, 1973). May Wedderburn Cannan published *In War Time* and *The Splendid Days* (Oxford: Blackwell, 1917, 1919). Her poems have recently been collected in *Tears of War*, ed. Charlotte Fyffe (London: Cavalier, 2000).

70   Tylee, 81, 83.

71   May Sinclair, *Journal of Impressions in Belgium* (London: Hutchinson and New York: Macmillan, 1915). A shortened version was printed as 'The War of Liberation: from a Journal' in *The English Review*, May, June and July 1915. See also her novels, *The Tree of Heaven* (London: Cassell and New York: Macmillan, 1917) and *Mary Olivier: A Life* (London: Cassell and New York: Macmillan, 1919).

72   Boll, 107.

By the long road loud with the passing of the guns, the rush of
armoured cars and the tramp of an army on the march forward to battle
And, where the piled corn-wagons went, our dripping
Ambulance carries home
Its red and white harvest from the fields.[73]

May Sinclair's approval of imagist objectivity, economy and clarity can be
discerned in the intensity of her description while the uneven line lengths are
characteristic of her experiments with stream-of-consciousness.

Like May Sinclair, Charlotte Mew can be described as modernist in her
representation of individual or collective consciousness.[74] In 'The Cenotaph:
September 1919', Mew explores the effect which the War memorial will have
on the passers-by through dramatic monologue:

Only, when all is done and said,
God is not mocked and neither are the dead.
For this will stand in our Market place –
    Who'll sell, who'll buy
    (Will you or I
Lie to each other with the better grace)?[75]

Mew was more preoccupied with psychological responses than with the events
or ethics of war. Rose Macaulay's experimental poems like 'The Shadow' are
also evasive in terms of their perspective on the War.[76] These oblique,
sometimes ambivalent, standpoints are implicit denials of jingoistic propaganda.

In the *Egoist*, J.G. Fletcher cited Amy Lowell's 'Bombardment' as one of
the best war poems, which, incidentally, appeared to be 'male-authored'.[77]
Her 'September 1918' describes 'the endeavour to balance myself/ Upon a
broken world' but accords with imagist principles of concrete observation:

    This afternoon was the colour of water falling through the sunlight;
The trees glittered with the tumbling of leaves;
The sidewalks shone like alleys of dropped maple leaves,
And the houses ran along them laughing out of square, open windows.
Under a tree in the park,
Two little boys, lying flat on their faces,

73   May Sinclair, 'Field Ambulance in Retreat', Reilly, 98–9.
74   I discuss May Sinclair's and Charlotte Mew's non-war poetry in 'Female Modernists'.
75   Charlotte Mew, 'The Cenotaph', 'May 1915', 'June 1915', Reilly, 71–2.
76   Rose Macaulay, 'The Shadow', Reilly, 68.
77   J.G. Fletcher, 'The Poetry of Miss Amy Lowell', *Egoist* II, 1 May 1915: 81–2.

Were carefully gathering red berries
To put in a pasteboard box.

Some day there will be no war.[78]

It is significant that the freer verse forms and more natural idioms are found
in these war-work poems and in anti-war poems which were detached from
the official discourses and propaganda. Even where the versification is regular,
it does not conform to Featherstone's types of popular doggerel or nineteenth-
century Romanticism. Iris Tree frequently manipulated the sonnet to challenge
the traditional celebration of honour and explore the male psychology of war
– 'will the fatted gods be gloried yet?' Nancy Cunard's sonnet 'Zeppelin'
investigates perception rather than events: 'I saw the people climbing up the
street/Maddened with war and strength and thought to kill'.[79]

Protest

Protest poetry can include bereavement poems because the articulation of
grief contradicted the makers of 'A Little Mother' who proclaimed that women
should resist 'the lonely anguish of a bereft heart' in order 'to carry on the
glorious work our men's memories have handed down for us now and all
eternity'.[80] Iris Tree's untitled poem interrogates the taboo on grief:

> No more! – And we the mourners dare not wear
> The black that folds our hearts in secrecy of pain,
> …
> We dare not weep who must be brave in battle – [81]

Gill Plain demonstrates how the public declaration of grief opposed the
'dominant patriarchal logic of war':

> Hence in the aftermath of war, these monuments, these calls to the dead, remain
> as semiotic irruptions within the symbolic order fundamentally unchanged by
> the ravages of war. In this context it is no surprise that these poems disappeared
> from the anthologies of war verse.[82]

---

78   Amy Lowell, 'September 1918', *Complete Poetical Works* (Boston: Houghton Mifflin,
     1955), 241.
79   Nancy Cunard, 'Zeppelins', from *Outlaws* 1921, Reilly, 26.
80   'A Little Mother', Graves, 190.
81   Iris Tree, untitled poem, Reilly, 115.
82   Plain, 61.

Plain's argument rehabilitates superficially sentimental and elegiac lyrics like Marian Allen West's 'The Wind on the Downs' which contradicts the palliative that women assumed a heroic stature through the deaths of their husbands.[83] Similarly, in the 'grief poems' by Katherine Tynan, Vera Brittain and May Wedderburn Cannan, the non-symbolised responses disrupt the symbolic by rejecting the dubious consolations of becoming heroines by the deaths of their men. In 'Lamplight', Cannan subtly critiques the logic of war by juxtaposing personal grief with the ideals of Empire.[84] Gill Plain also reads the bereavement poems in the terms of 'grief psychology', arguing that they demonstrate alternating moods of anger and passivity or the common phases of avoidance, postponement, keeping faith with the dead or reproaching them for leaving.

The grief poems further indicate that the loss of the men through whom women were given identity had the potential for allowing them to reconstruct themselves apart from the maternal function and therefore outside of the patriarchal order. Ruth Comfort Mitchell's rejection of the 'tinsel platitudes' paved the way for an identity which was independent of 'dominant patriarchal logic':

> *How much longer, O Lord, shall we bear it all?*
> *How many more red years?*
> *Story it and glory it all,*
> *In seas of blood and tears?*
> *They are braggart attitudes we've worn so long;*
> *They are tinsel platitudes we've sworn so long –* [85]

Although some grief poems indicate 'a retreat into conservative ideologies', voices like Mitchell's, above, register the ways in which many women's consciousness changed during the War.[86]

The anti-heroic poems will seem the most authentic to twenty-first century readers. Cicely Hamilton's 'Non-Combatant' dramatises her contempt for and fear of femininity projected through the monologue of a wounded soldier who finds the condition of passivity and dependence humiliating: 'With life and heart afire to give and give/I take and eat the bread of charity.'[87] Cicely Hamilton was a 'familiar figure on suffragette platforms' and a director of *Time and Tide*. She worked in a British women's hospital in France during the

---

83 Marian Allen West, 'The Wind on the Downs', Reilly, 1–2.
84 May Wedderburn Cannan, 'Lamplight', Reilly, 16.
85 Ruth Comfort Mitchell, 'He went for a soldier', Reilly, 76.
86 Plain, 60.
87 Reilly, 46.

War.[88] The poem could support the ideology that war service was the highest form of human activity, but it is an implicit indictment of the propaganda which made the soldier feel useless.

In order to censure recruiting talk, Vera Brittain dramatises the inglorious reception to the returning soldier in 'The Lament of the Demobilised': 'And no-one talked heroics now, and we/Must just go back and start again once more.'[89] S. Gertrude Ford similarly treats the euphemistic rhetoric of newspaper language with the satire of her male contemporaries like Siegfried Sassoon. In 'A Fight to Finish' she parodies the rhyming couplets associated with popular jingoism: '"Fight on!" the Armament-kings besought; / *Nobody asked what the women thought.*'[90] This almost parenthetical sentence depicts the silencing of women's anti-war complaints. Dramatisation enables her to shoot the invectives not expected of women. Ford was a socialist, feminist and writer. In addition to publishing poems in periodicals, she wrote *Lessons in Verse Craft* and edited the *Little Books of Georgian Verse*. Her concern for economic equality above warfare is expressed in 'The Tenth Armistice Day':

> Spend not on us your cares
> Your wreaths, for we have better flowers to gather.
> But lift the load our workless comrade bears:
> Flowers for the dead? Bread for the living rather![91]

She manipulates the device of the dead soldier's voice, which commonly called survivors to guilty or reverent remembrance, to challenge political priorities which arguably quickened war fever to distract from the social and economic crises in Britain.

In the protest poetry, the perceived enemy was rarely the German but the propagators of war. Elizabeth Chandler Forman's 'The Three Lads' consists of the parallel narratives of a German, Russian and English soldier fighting for the same allegedly just cause:

> 'Then hey! for our righteous king!' (he cries)
> 'And the good old God in his good old skies!
> And ho! for love and a pair of blue eyes, –
> For I'm off to the war and away!'[92]

---

88   Biographical note on Cicely Hamilton, Reilly, 133.
89   Vera Brittain, 'The Lament of the Demobilised', Reilly, 14.
90   S. Gertrude Ford, 'A Fight to Finish', Reilly, 38, emphasis added.
91   S. Gertrude Ford, 'The Tenth Armistice Day', Reilly, 38–9.
92   Elizabeth Chandler Forman, 'The Three Lads', Reilly, 40.

The ballad defies the nationalistic rhetoric and Christian-chivalric mythologies of war which were doled out to the recruits. The ironic register in a poem such as this is the dominant feature of British First World War poetry and consequently of subsequent twentieth-century poets.[93] Irony, which represents the discontinuity between language and experience,[94] figures in several poems, such as 'What Reward?' by Winifred Letts:

> You gave your life, boy,
>   And you gave a limb:
> But he who gave his precious wits,
>   Say, what reward for him?[95]

It has the satirical edge and the economy of Siegfried Sassoon. Other poems by Winifred Letts (1882–1971) are less acerbic but nonetheless anti-heroic. 'The Deserter' challenges recruiting pressure in its sympathy for the war refuser.[96] Winifred Letts was a VAD and in 'Screens' she describes the common experience of nurses who witnessed the deaths of young men. In 'The Veteran' Margaret Cole's tragically ironic depiction of a nineteen year old war victim is similar to Wilfred Owen's 'Disabled'.[97] Nosheen Khan is happy to point out that 'women were writing protest poetry before Sassoon and Owen' as an implicit measure of literary value, but is cautious about 'The Veteran' because of its 'moralising tone which stems from the writer's pacifist sympathies'.[98] The dramatic dialogue, however, has a dialectic which avoids didacticism. Margaret Postgate Cole was the daughter of a Cambridge professor, educated at Roedean and Girton, a classics teacher at St Paul's Girls School in London and the wife of G.D.H. Cole, 'socialist writer, economist, labour historian and author'. She became a prolific political and literary writer and took up political work in the Fabian Research Department from 1917.[99]

Women's activities and autobiographical records which testify to their deep-seated objections to war help dissolve any idea that they were simply

---

93 See Paul Fussell, 'A Satire of Circumstance', ch. 1, Fussell, 3–35.

94 Mutlin Konuk Blasing, *American Poetry: The Rhetoric of its Forms* (New Haven and London: Yale University Press, 1987), 12.

95 Winifred Letts, 'What Reward?', Reilly, 61–3.

96 Winifred Letts, 'The Deserter', Reilly, 61–2.

97 Margaret Cole, 'The Veteran', Reilly, 22–3. See also *Growing up into Revolution*, by Cole (London: Longmans, 1949).

98 Nosheen Khan, *Women's Poetry of the First World War* (London: Harvester Wheatsheaf, 1988), 15, 26.

99 Biographical note, Reilly, 131.

latching on to the trend for satire. They also reduce the simple polarisation between the suffering men at the Front and the pro-war civilians at Home. After the War, the insistence on women returning to their pre-war roles was channelled through the continual publishing of nationalistic early poetry, like Rupert Brooke's sonnets and Jessie Pope's *War Rhymes*, and through the terms of approval and disapproval of literary criticism. Conservative critics entrenched the association of women with the personal life and perpetuated the rhetoric of patriotism, maternity and love to brainwash away the goals of women's suffrage.

After the War

In the 'Afterword' to *Forever England: Literature, Femininity and Conservatism Between the Wars*, Alison Light concludes that there is 'still much work to be done exploring the full cultural meanings of that "war to end all wars" for British social life'.[100] The War had complicated the suffragist project because its leaders agreed to support the war effort and all women over thirty were granted the vote in 1918. At the same time, their taste of men's work and men's pay meant that they resented the requirement to return to prescribed domesticity when the men came back. It was difficult to overtly express any resentment when they were expected to honour the men who had fought for national freedom and to respect the memories of those who had died, many of whom were members of their own families. If women were attached to their homes as wives or daughters, however, it was often through duty or financial dependence, rather than affection or gratitude. Many were single at the end of the War and were aware of the surplus of women, but as Ruth Pitter stated, 'We knew very well that we couldn't all marry and we liked the idea of independence.'[101] Only sentimental histories maintain that women only thought of fulfilment through marriage. In 1914, in a letter to *The Egoist* headed 'Marriage is Dead', R.S. Kerr observed that 'the vast majority of educated women have left marriage behind them for ever'.[102] The War's 'brides who never were' became the emancipated career women of the 1920s and 1930s.[103]

---

100 Light, 210.
101 Ruth Pitter, in *Ruth Pitter: Homage to a Poet*, ed. Arthur Russell (London: n.p. 1969), 25.
102 R.S. Kerr, 'Women, Education, Marriage', *Egoist* 1, 15 January 1914: 39.
103 Judith Kazantzis, Preface, Reilly. xvi.

Between the Georgians and Bloomsbury: Frances Cornford (1886–1960) and Vita Sackville-West (1892–1962)

Introduction

The classification 'Between the Georgians and Bloomsbury' dismantles the misleading binary divide between the associated oppositions of tradition and experiment. It is precisely because their poems cut across stereotyped Georgian and modernist categories that it has lain in a no-man's land. Frances Cornford and Vita Sackville-West can be given modernist credentials through their personal connections or the psychological interest of their poems. At the same time, Vita Sackville-West was considered 'Georgian' in her day but does not feature in Georgian histories; Frances Cornford was well-known as a modern poet in the 1920s but labelled 'Georgian' in retrospect. Their publications and reputations should be recognised within the Georgian period but separated from the negative mythologies which have turned 'Georgian' into a critical term of abuse. Furthermore, since 'Georgian' can be a metonym for 'expressive', its rehabilitation has implications for harnessing poetry to politics because, as in First World War poetry, the language of extreme experience or protest tends towards realist modes. Although stylistically cautious, Frances Cornford and Vita Sackville-West eschewed the high rhetoric and abstractions associated with Victorian sentimentalism and the didacticism of Edwardian jingoism in favour of the clarity and directness of the Georgian. The formal restraint was also a symptom of feminine denial. Both espoused the theory of the androgynous mind, and Sackville-West used poetic conventions to mask her bisexuality. In the development of twentieth-century women's poetry, their male impersonations appear to liberate them from the self-denying aesthetic of the nineteenth century but to limit their stylistic freedom. They represent writers like Ruth Pitter and Elizabeth Daryush who had successful publishing histories but have been subsequently considered archaic because of their stylistic reserve.

In reassessing non-experimental women's poetry, it is particularly important to reject the binary polarities of modernists and Georgians because of the associated distance between the intellectual and weak-minded. As David Perkins argues,

> The conventional statement among critical sheep thus came to be: the modernists had displaced a school of Georgian poets; these poets had been unoriginal and

slack in technique, shallow in feeling, slight in intellect; their poetry specialised in insipid appreciativeness, false simplicity and week-end escapism.[104]

The homogenising of Georgian by its weakest aspects has exaggerated the predominance of high modernism. It is also misleading to homogenise 'Georgian' when it has always been a movable definition, sliding between periodisation – all poetry written during the reign of George V (1910–36), Edward Marsh's five *Georgian Poetry* anthologies published between 1912 and 1922, a list of variable names such as Rupert Brooke, John Masefield and Walter De La Mare, or as a certain kind of poetry characterised by rural setting, colloquial diction and regular verse form. It was not always a pejorative term with connotations of archaism. The first volume of *Georgian Poetry 1911–12* (1912) was introduced with 'the belief that English poetry is now once again putting on a new strength and beauty' and on being selected by Edward Marsh, Wilfred Owen famously celebrated, 'I am held peer by the Georgians; I am a poet's poet'.[105] In *The Trend of Modern Poetry* (1934), Geoffrey Bullough connected Georgian directness with the psychological realism associated with modernism: 'the value of [the Georgians'] experiments in the familiar poetry of commonplace incident lit by fancy, and their tentative probing of conscious thought-processes is insufficiently recognised today'.[106] Georgian poetry achieved some degree of cultural democracy because the contemporary idiom made it more widely accessible than the high diction of the Edwardians or Victorians and Marsh's Georgian anthologies reached a wide audience. The recorded sales of the first four volumes were between fifteen and nineteen thousand. They were followed by many other anthologies such as Thomas Moult's annual *Best Poetry* collections which brought poetry by American and British men and women to both literary and general readers. Additionally, several anthologies emerged from the 'provinces' such as Merseyside and Birmingham. Edith Sitwell's counter series *Wheels,* however, arguably exacerbated the conceptual polarity between tradition and experiment.

Vita Sackville-West was accommodated by Bloomsbury through her associations with Virginia Woolf. She was described by Quentin Bell as 'a friend and in some respects a Bloomsbury figure' yet several of her poems were published in the *Georgian Poetry* anthologies. Frances Cornford has

---

104 David Perkins, *A History of Modern Poetry. Vol. 1. From The 1890s To The High Modernist Mode* (Harvard University Press, 1976), 203–4.
105 Wilfred Owen, in Anthony Thwaite (*Twentieth-Century English Poetry* (London: Heinemann, 1978), 5.
106 Geoffrey Bullough, *The Trend of Modern Poetry*, 1934 (London and Edinburgh: Oliver and Boyd, 1941), 62–3.

been counted with the Georgians through her friendship with Rupert Brooke and Edward Marsh but she was never in his anthologies. Her poems were published by the Woolfs' Hogarth Press as well as by The Poetry Bookshop. If, as Quentin Bell believes, distaste for the besetting sins of nineteenth-century art, 'vulgarity, sentimentality and rhetoric', were the hallmarks of Bloomsbury, Vita Sackville-West and Frances Cornford were in tune with Bloomsbury.[107] At the same time, they aimed to write in the colloquial style associated with the Georgians.

There is a perceived 'outmodedness' about them which is this technical reserve. Their traditional formalism is a symptom of their quest for critical approval which meant disguising their gender. Given a chance, male reviewers reinforced the association between the conventional, feminine and sentimental in women's poems. The inclusion of a woman in *Georgian Poetry 1918–1919* was registered in the *TLS*: 'Mrs Fredegonde Shove' was 'the first poetess to appear in these anthologies. One wonders why. Hers is a happy talent with a novel quaintness. Quaintness seems to be rising in poetical estimation.'[108]

Both women's poetry and Georgianism were implicitly belittled by the pointed adjective 'quaintness'. It was galling for intellectual literary women not to be distinguished from the generic mythologies of 'women's poetry'. Frances Cornford recorded her lack of sympathy with anthologies of women's poetry, 'due to the horror in which all right-thinking people must hold the word "poetess". She, we all feel, is somebody with far too much fervent, personal emotion per square yard, so to speak. A woman poetess was "never gay"'.[109]

These poets grew up alongside suffragism but were not allied to the suffrage movement. Although there is no protest in their poems, there is a gender awareness in their avoidance of femininity. As Alison Light observed, following the First World War 'Even those who would not call themselves feminists were linked by a resistance to "the feminine" as it had been thought of in later Victorian or Edwardian times'.[110]

---

107 Quentin Bell, 114.
108 'Georgian Poetry New Style', review of *Georgian Poetry 1918–1919*, *TLS* 11 December 1919: 738. Fredegonde Shove, née Maitland, (d. 1949) published *Dreams and Journeys* (Oxford: Blackwell, 1918), *Daybreak* (London: Hogarth Press, 1922), *Christina Rossetti* (Cambridge: Cambridge University Press, 1931) and *Poems*, which include many previously unpublished as well as uncollected poems (Cambridge: Cambridge University Press, 1956). Shove is discussed in *Some Contemporary Poets*, by Harold Monro, 1920.
109 Frances Cornford, 'Views and Recollections of A Sunday Poet', Mss 58387, Journals and Literary Papers of Frances Cornford (London: British Library, Department of Manuscripts).
110 Light, 10.

For a start, they would have been alienated from the idealisations of motherhood propagated during and after the War. Frances Cornford recorded her suicidal exhaustion from the tension of being a wife, mother and poet; Ruth Pitter was single and worked for a living; Elizabeth Daryush married a Persian official, had no children and spent several years abroad; Dorothy Wellesley left her husband and became part of a love triangle with Virginia Woolf and Vita Sackville-West; Vita Sackville-West constructed a male identity in her affairs with Violet Trefusis and other women.[111]

It is debatable whether their success at avoiding a feminine, and therefore a personal, poetic voice is the achievement or weakness of the poets. Ruth Pitter and Elizabeth Daryush were clearly respected for their 'craftsmanship', but the paternalistic approval has distanced them from their so-called 'modernist' contemporaries. In *Ruth Pitter: Homage to a Poet*, Pitter's verse forms are commended as 'those of the mainstream English poetic tradition' and consequently, 'It would be possible to argue that Ruth Pitter is a man's poet.'[112] All had healthy publishing histories and won prizes.[113] Even at the time, however, there was a suspicion that prize-winning was a mark of literary conformity. Virginia Woolf was notoriously disparaging about Vita Sackville-West's Hawthornden prize (1927) and recorded her scepticism in *A Room of One's Own* (1929): 'the persistent voice [of male pedagogy] admonish[es] them [women] if they would be good and win, as I suppose, some shiny prize, to keep within certain limits which the gentleman in question thinks suitable.'[114] The result is a technical restraint which Virginia Woolf called the 'something muted' in Vita's poetry.[115]

It is clear from their literary papers and correspondence that Cornford and Sackville-West were attracted by Woolf's theory of the androgynous imagination – 'It is fatal for anyone who writes to think of their sex. Some collaboration has to take place in the mind between the woman and the man before the art of creation can be accomplished.'[116] Frances Cornford's ambivalence about whether writing was gendered was almost identical to Virginia Woolf's:

111 Vita Sackville-West dramatised herself as 'Julian' in her novel *Challenge*, which she withdrew from publication. See footnote 199.

112 See Lord David Cecil, Introduction to *Ruth Pitter: Homage to a Poet*, ed. Arthur Russell (London: n.p. 1969).

113 For further details see *Women's Poetry of the 1930s*, ed. Jane Dowson (London: Routledge, 1996).

114 Virginia Woolf, *A Room of One's Own*, 1929 (London: Grafton, 1977), 82.

115 See discussion of Sackville-West later in the chapter and fn, p. 93.

116 Woolf, *A Room...*, 112.

People will think that poetry is just the words you write, but really it's a state of mind. And I believe that when writers enter into that state of mind they are neither male nor female, they are androgynous, though fortunately the voice in which they describe the regions from which they return will be either a man's or a woman's.[117]

For Frances Cornford, Woolf's theory of 'woman-manliness' partially offered an intellectual resolution to the bind between assuming man's clothing – the 'old friendly boots' of metre and rhyme – and being dressed as a woman. It allowed women the concept of gender difference without chaining them to a woman's, that is feminine, 'voice'. The influence of, or like-mindedness with, Virginia Woolf is also evident in Vita Sackville-West's unpublished autobiography where she advanced her theory of the dual personality 'in which the feminine and masculine elements alternately predominate'.[118] The notion of androgyny provided her with a means of containing her 'duality', her term for her bisexuality. Fleur Adcock disparages Sackville-West's 'Miltonic or Virgilian' imitations but does not recognise that her recourse to these writers was a means of both entering into the British literary tradition and of masking her same-sex orientation.[119]

Frances Cornford

Frances Cornford was well-known to both intellectual and 'middlebrow' readers.[120] A review of *Spring Morning* (1915) in *Poetry: A Magazine of Verse*, recorded that 'Frances Cornford's verse has been known in Cambridge (England) circles these few years.'[121] In *Some Contemporary Poets* (1920), Harold Monro included her in his conspectus of current British poetry and a reviewer of Thomas Moult's *Best Poems of 1924* cited Frances Cornford in 'a list of names which attract attention even before their contributions are

---

117 'View and Recollections of a Sunday Poet', Tuesday 27 March 1956, Mss 58387, Literary Papers of Frances Cornford.
118 Vita Sackville-West, *A Portrait of a Marriage*, ed. Nigel Nicolson, 1973 (Basingstoke: Macmillan, 1980), 102.
119 Adcock, 8.
120 Alison Light defines 'middlebrow' culture as 'one whose apparent artlessness and insistence on its own ordinariness has made it peculiarly resistant to analysis', Light, 11–12. Virginia Woolf was disparaging about 'Middlebrows', for vacillating between High- and Low-brow cultures, in 'Middlebrow', *Collected Essays Vol. 2*, by Virginia Woolf (London: Hogarth Press, 1966), 196–203.
121 Review of *Spring Morning*, by Frances Cornford, *Poetry* 6. 5, August 1915: 255.

savoured'.[122] *Different Days* (1928) was reviewed in *The Criterion* where it was noted that 'She already has a reputation, and her technique is known to the wide world of readers of *Poems of To-day*'.[123] *Spring Morning* (1915) and *Autumn Midnight* (1923) were published by Harold Monro's The Poetry Bookshop press while *Different Days* (1928) was the first of the *Hogarth Living Poets* series. As is suggested by her association with both the Monros' and Woolfs' publishing houses, Cornford's poetry has both Georgian and modernist associations, an eschewal of high rhetoric and an interest in representing the interplay of conscious and unconscious thought processes.

The notice of Frances Cornford's death in *Poetry Review* is typical of records which make her poetry sound old-fashioned:

> Winner of the Queen's Medal for Poetry in 1959, Mrs Cornford, grand-daughter of Charles Darwin, declined to follow the Eliot-Pound fashion in her poetry, which was written from first to last in 'this Cambridge calm' – she had married a Cambridge University Professor. The April-June number of *The Poetry Review* was dedicated to her as a 'Georgian' poet and author of four books of verse.[124]

The tribute is inaccurate in that she actually published eight poetry books (and two books of translated poetry). It is also typical of the tendency to give her credentials through her father, husband or son, and to tether her to the kind of poetry which she consciously rejected. Helen Fowler records Cornford's 'predilection for craftsmanship' but also that ever since 'Brooke had lumped her with the "heart-criers" ... she seems to have been blamed for the sort of poetry which, in the main, she did not write'.[125] In her poetry readings and lectures, Cornford rated Rupert Brooke as a minor poet and explained that they had both struggled to resist 'turgid' Georgian metres.[126] Her success can be gauged by the fact that 'neither the advocacy of Rupert Brooke nor that of J.C. Squire could persuade Edward Marsh to put her work into his Georgian anthologies'.[127]

Frances Cornford's reputation has further suffered from being solely associated with, 'To a Fat Lady seen from a Train', largely because it is in W.B. Yeats' *Oxford Book of English Verse* (1936). As Joy Grant points out, it

---

122 Review of *Best Poems of 1924*, ed. Thomas Moult, *Time and Tide* 20 March 1925: 272.
123 Review of *Different Days*, by Frances Cornford, *Criterion* vii. 4, June 1928: 447–8.
124 Editorial Board, *Poetry Review* 15. 4, October–December 1960: 197.
125 Helen Fowler, 'Frances Cornford', *Cambridge Women: Twelve Portraits*, ed. Edward Shils and Carmen Blacker (Cambridge: Cambridge University Press, 1996), 154, 149.
126 'Notes for a Talk', Mss 58385, Literary Papers of Frances Cornford.
127 Entry on Frances Cornford in Hamilton, 99–100.

is striking for the way in which adult psychology is expressed in a child's language, but Frances Cornford wanted to be freed from her association with the poem:

> I should like to disassociate myself entirely from the Fat White Woman who walked through the field in gloves. But she, chiefly surely, because the average anthologist has a mind almost indistinguishable from the mind of sheep, she goes on and on.[128]

Cornford's literary papers record her conscious breaking away from the disreputable features of the Edwardians:

> [The reason why] I look at my early verses with a good deal of distaste is because I grew up in such a poor state of poetry ambience ... surrounded with faded poeticisms and lolloping turgid metres ... all 'finger thumping poets' as Sassoon called them ... I long to write much more in the stresses of my natural speaking voice though I think I only occasionally succeed at doing this.[129]

Similarly, in her notes for a reading at the Cambridge Literary Circle she regretted the 'moribund poeticisms and clichés, and many jog-trot sentimental rhythms, well sunk into our unconscious'. She believed that W.H. Davies and Siegfried Sassoon were admirable 'Georgian poets', but T.S. Eliot was 'joyful liberation'. These notes are illuminating for the vehemence with which she renounced her early work and with which she rejected Victorian rhetoric along with the jingoistic consolations of Edwardian verse: 'I cannot bear in poetry all those abstracts – the ineffable and eternal etc. which for me it is largely the business of poetry to suggest to the imagination in concrete images.'[130] To this end, like the Georgians, she aimed for a naturalistic idiom, using rhyme and regular rhythm. Like the Georgians, she concentrated on the local and specific, as in 'Cambridgeshire':

> The stacks, like blunt impassive temples, rise
> Across flat fields against the autumnal skies.
> The hairy-footed horses plough the land,
> Or as in prayer and meditation stand
> Upholding square, primeval, dung-stained carts,
> With an unending patience in their hearts.

---

128 'Notes for a Talk'.
129 'Lunchtime Talk at Foyle's', Mss 58386, Literary Papers of Frances Cornford.
130 Letters from Frances Cornford to Gilbert Murray, Gilbert Murray Papers (Oxford: Bodleian Library).

> Nothing is changed. The farmer's gig goes by
> Against the horizon. Surely, the same sky,
> So vast and yet familiar, grey and mild,
> And streaked with light like music, I, a child,
> Lifted my face from leaf-edged lanes to see,
> Late-coming home, to bread-and-butter tea.[131]

Her depiction of rural stasis is characteristically accompanied by a sense of transition. Her popular snapshots of familiar places such as university gardens and quadrangles also explore the psychological significance of place.

It is questionable whether Frances Cornford would have received more enduring publicity and whether her style would have been more orthodoxly modernist had she been more part of the Bloomsbury social milieu. Although drawn to the literary circles in London, she remained in Cambridge out of family loyalty or duty. At the same time, if as Quentin Bell observed, Bloomsbury was defined by a certain 'manner of speech', she qualifies for Bloomsbury.[132] Siegfried Sassoon identified her gift as the ability to represent universal feeling and her limitation as 'Cambridge intellectualism':

> She succeeds through keeping on her own ground of feeling and experience. She did feel and suffer deeply. But it is all overlaid by Cambridge intellectualism and refinement (one might say the same of Virginia Woolf?). It is a cultured humanistic mind speaking, with perfectionist versecraft. The power and the glory of spiritual aspiration are absent. Thoughts and emotions beautifully, sometimes poignantly, articulated. But never 'the roll, the rise, the carol, the creation'. Much as I admired her, I did feel that she was too intense, analytic and cultured for me. That vibrant voice of hers had a quality of academic aloofness in it. One couldn't imagine her outside of Cambridge.[133]

It is true that the culture of the economically comfortable is represented in some of the idioms and diction, like 'tucked-up children' and 'bread-and-butter tea', or the allusions to dressing-up and dinner parties. Although the framework of reference may be a cushioned world, Frances Cornford frequently demythologises the alleged securities of wealth and other idylls. In 'On August the Thirteenth', for example, what to the outsider would appear

---

131 Cornford, 'Cambridgeshire', from *Different Days*, 1928, *Selected Poems of Frances Cornford*, ed. Jane Dowson (London: Enitharmon, 1996), 12.

132 Quentin Bell, *Bloomsbury* (London: Weidenfeld and Nicolson, 1968), 9–10.

133 Siegfried Sassoon (1961), in *Siegfried Sassoon: A Poet's Pilgrimage*, by Dame Felicitas Corrigan (London: Victor Gollancz, 1973), 68–9.

a 'solid order' at 'The Mount, Marsden, Bucks' can be easily disturbed. The reason for the unspecified addressee's departure is presumably death:

> Out of this seemliness, this solid order,
> At half-past four to-day,
> When down below
> Geraniums were bright
> In the contented glow,
> Whilst Williams planted seedlings all about,
> Supremely geometrically right
> In your herbaceous border,
> You had to go
> Who always liked to stay.
> Before Louisa sliced the currant roll,
> And re-arranged the zinnias in the bowl,
> All in a rhythm reachless by modernity,
> Correct and slow.[134]

The narrative investigates but maintains the 'seemly' surface of cultural conventions while clockwork routine is represented as both secure and stifling. Such mixed feelings towards change are characteristic of a 'conservative modernity'.

Gwen Raverat's biographical *Period Piece: a Cambridge Childhood* indicates that she and her cousin Frances were not at ease with the social conventions of their childhood. For them, it was 'torture' to dress up properly, and they dreaded dancing classes, 'the worst of social events'.[135] However, in the large Darwin family they were more exposed to ethics than dogmas. Gwen and Frances were evidently independent spirits who worked through for themselves the questions of duty, religion and convention. It is interesting that a reviewer of Frances Cornford's early poems identified the tone of a 'rebellious protest against an unjust world'.[136] Although it cannot be claimed that she was political in any actively socialist sense, she speaks in the language of democracy. She combated the high modernist tendency to make poetry esoteric – 'Do not think of verse writing as some kind of sacred mystery' –

---

134 Cornford, 'On August the Thirteenth', from *Mountains and Molehills*, 1934, *SP*, 16. The poems in *Mountains and Molehills* were probably written between 1927 and 1933.
135 See chapters xiii and xiv on 'Clothes' and 'Society' in Gwen Raverat, *Period Piece: A Cambridge Childhood*, 1952 (London: Faber, 1960).
136 Review of *Poems*, by Frances Cornford, 1910, *The Times*, June/July 1910. Undated cutting in Mss 58421, Literary Papers of Frances Cornford.

and used popular forms such as ballad, epitaph and epigram.[137] She believed that the poet's role was to represent universal experience – 'I thought the poet's vision always incorporated the general in the particular, and this above all means the images, often concrete images.'[138] Her concept of universal experience usually assumed a human nature which was common to men and women. It connected to the liberal humanism of the early nineteenth-century Romantics but the difference in Cornford's poetry is that it is informed by early twentieth-century psychology. (She read Jung more than Freud.)

Of the many voices in the poems, it was the voice of the under-represented that Frances Cornford often aimed to present. In 'Notes for a Talk' she records that she wanted to show what it feels like to be old, a child or an animal.[139] She also assumed these personae of innocence in order to explore a psychological condition, most commonly regret, grief, alienation and divided duty. The ballad 'The Princess and the Gypsies', is not merely a fantasy, but an interrogation of fantasy. The rich, comfortable but confined princess is attracted by the liberties of the gypsies:

> 'O gentle, gentle gypsies
>> That roam the wide world through,
> Because I hate my crown and state,
>> O let me come with you!'

The gypsies educate the princess about the hardships of their nomadic life and the princess's decision to stick with her safe but stultifying situation leaves her broken-hearted:

> I hung about their fingers brown
>> My ruby rings and chain,
> And with my head as heavy as lead
>> turned me back again.

> As I went up the palace steps
>> I heard the gypsies laugh;
> The birds of spring so sweet did sing,
>> It broke my heart in half.[140]

---

137 Frances Cornford, undated lecture on poetry, Mss 58385, Literary Papers of Frances Cornford.

138 'Notes for a Talk'.

139 Ibid.

140 Cornford, 'The Princess and the Gypsies', from *Autumn Midnight*, 1923, *SP*, 7.

As in several poems, the impulse for freedom is in tension with the conservative impulse to keep things as they are.

Fairy tales were important to Frances Cornford, perhaps because they embody the distinction between hope and quotidian reality, especially as experienced by the developing child. Freud would interpret the sense of loss in terms of nostalgia for the pre-Symbolic mother/child unity. The ballad 'Fairy Tale Idyll for Two Voices' constructs the yearning for mythical fulfilment or pre-lapsarian perfection when 'All things were new'.[141] Again, albeit under a cloak of mere amusement, nostalgia for the 'fairy story place' is contrasted to the social world of convention and non-communication in 'Journeys End in Lovers' Meeting':

> I used to wish when I was 17
> …
> That I could find that fairy-story place
> Where there is everything that might have been[142]

In this, as in other poems, Hell is conceived of as the place of missed opportunities.

'Contemporaries' (original title, 'No Immortality'), a response to the number of young men killed in the First World War, particularly commemorates the death of Rupert Brooke:

> Most loved, on you
> Can such oblivion fall? Then, if it can,
> How futile, how absurd the life of man.[143]

Here, as in other poems, Cornford's treatment of death is stark. Her heightened awareness of death was part of belonging to a large family – her father was one of six children. She inevitably encountered deaths as a regular occurrence, but after her mother's death when she was 17, she suffered the first of three long depressions. In the First World War she lost several friends and her father died in 1925; her son John was killed in the Spanish Civil War (1936) and other friends and relatives in the Second World War. Her husband died in 1943. Nijinsky is mentioned in three poems and is a significant symbol of mental breakdown. The poem 'Grand Ballet' recounts an occasion when

---

141 Frances Cornford, 'Fairy Tale Idyll for Two Voices,' from *Mountains and Molehills*, 1934, *SP*, 25.
142 Cornford, 'Journeys End in Lovers' Meeting', *SP*, 45.
143 Cornford, 'Contemporaries' ('No Immortality'), from *Different Days*, 1928, *SP*, 15.

Frances and her husband saw the famous ballet dancer – an occasion upon which she often dwelt:

> That thunderous night
> We saw Nijinsky dance.
> Thereafter fell
> On the awaiting world the powers of Hell,
> Chaos, and irremediable pain;
> And utter darkness on your empty brain[144]

The Nijinsky image represents the fine line between sanity and insanity or life and death which is a preoccupation in many poems.

Frances Cornford's depressions, her sense of failure as a mother and her frustrations as a woman writer point to a level of non-symbolised experience in poems which have often been mistaken as simplistic or 'genteel'. In her account of The Poetry Bookshop, Joy Grant records that Frances Cornford was 'a sweet-hearted, domesticated woman bred among men of culture from whom she had learned discrimination. It was a creditable, but quite uncontroversial addition to the Poetry Bookshop's list'.[145] In fact, modernity for Frances Cornford involved repeated bereavement and the frustrating bonds of domestic duty. Although avoiding femininity, Cornford's poetry connects with other interwar writers who represent the unquiet depths 'beneath the apparently unruffled surface of sensible and quiescent womanhood'.[146] She studiously avoided the 'embarrassingly personal'. In fact, Sylvia Townsend Warner used her as an example of women writers who were adept at 'vanishing' out of their writing to effect immediacy: 'the writing is no longer propelled by the author's anxious hand, the reader is no longer conscious of the author's chaperoning presence.'[147] Placed in their cultural and biographical contexts, however, superficially agreeable poems like 'A Glimpse', carry a personal undertow. Read in conjunction with her later poem 'The Scholar', which depicts her husband's temperamental distance from his family, it suggests alienation from the male-dominated university territory where, as Woolf recorded in *A Room of One's Own*, women were trespassers:[148]

144 Cornford, 'Grand Ballet', from *Mountains and Molehills*, 1934, *SP*, 18.
145 Joy Grant, *Harold Monro and the Poetry Bookshop* (London: Routledge & Kegan Paul, 1967), 116.
146 Light, 13.
147 Sylvia Townsend Warner, 'Women as Writers', in *Collected Poems*, by Sylvia Townsend Warner, ed. Claire Harman (Manchester: Carcanet, 1982), 269.
148 Woolf, *A Room ...*, 10.

The figure of a scholar carrying back
Books to the library, absorbed, content,
Seeming as everlasting as the elms
Bark-wrinkled, puddled round their roots, the bells,
And the far shouting in the football fields.[149]

The scholar's occupation is represented as enviably peaceful and its male-only property endorsed by the reference to the sounds of a football match. Unusually, it avoids rhyme while the compound adjective 'Bark-wrinkled', here as in other poems, suggests the influence of Gerard Manley Hopkins.

Frances Cornford's correspondence constructs a cheerful compliance with the competing demands of family life and forays into the world of publishing, but her journal entries illuminate the 'not-waving-but-drowning' undercurrent:

> Mostly the sense of my being is a strain, hushed anxiety, and depression, guilt, not keeping going as if in a beleaguered city and, and of constant ill health and exhaustion to be skilfully dodged … I seem to myself to be only keeping my head just above water and complete neuroticism – a period comes and I dip under again.[150]

In 'She Warns Him', a series of metaphors signify the emotional deadness recorded in her diaries: 'a lamp that is out', 'a star that is dead', a 'shallow stream' and 'an empty book'.[151] It is debatable whether the childlike idiom and imagery are successful reconstructions of a disintegrating psyche or failed attempts to find a language which expresses women's experience without appearing feminine.

'The Sick Queen', from *Different Days* (1928), appears to vacillate between the self-negation of the nineteenth-century feminine ideal and the self-assertion of twentieth-century female modernists. Emotional and intellectual drowning are encoded in the extended symbolism but the more adventurous versification and bolder self-dramatisation exhibit greater stylistic freedom than many of Cornford's poems:

> I hear my children come. They trample with their feet,
> Fetched from their play to kiss my thin-boned hands lying on the sheet,
> Fresh as young colts with every field before them,
> With gazing apple-faces. Can it be this body bore them?

---

149 Frances Cornford, 'A Glimpse', from *Different Days*, 1928, *SP*, 13.
150 Frances Cornford, Journal, Mss 58390, Literary Papers of Frances Cornford.
151 Frances Cornford, 'She Warns Him', from *Different Days*, 1928, *SP*, 15.

(This poor body like an outworn glove,
That yet subdues a spirit which no more knows that it can love.)
All day is theirs. I belong to night,
The brown surrounding caverns made of dream. The long failing fight,
On and on with pain. Theirs is sweet sleep
And morning breakfast with bright yellow butter. They can laugh and weep
Over a tiny thing – a toy, a crumb, a letter.
Tomorrow they will come again and say: "Now are you better?"
'Better, my lords, today', the Chamberlain replies;
And I shall be too tired and too afraid to cry out that he lies.[152]

The effort to appear well for the sake of her family is projected through the ragged line lengths – the longest lines give the impression of trying to sit up in bed. The disjunction between the mother's role and her struggling subjectivity is indicated in the contrasting images: young colts, apple-faces and bright butter juxtaposed with bony hands, a worn out glove of a body and a mind consisting of dark caverns. The metaphors simultaneously represent and signify the unrepresentability of her pain.

The distortion of the fairyland persona in 'The Sick Queen' is a strategy of which Virginia Woolf would have approved because it kills the myth of woman as the angel of the house:

> I discovered that if I were going to review books I should need to do battle with a certain phantom … The Angel in the House. It was she who used to come between me and my paper when I was writing reviews … She was utterly sympathetic. She was immensely charming. She was utterly unselfish. She excelled in the difficult arts of family life. She sacrificed herself daily.[153]

The concealed weariness of the sick queen was a condition familiar to both writers and may largely account for their affinity. The following extract is from a letter to Frances Cornford on 29 December 1929, in which Virginia Woolf said that her poems had struck a chord with herself. Woolf was writing from Lewes, Sussex, where she sought respite from 'the chaos of London'. 'My book', is presumably *A Room of One's Own*:

> I was all a heap when I read your letter with pleasure that you should like my book. Everything had to be boiled to a jelly in the hope that young women would swallow it. I'm very happy that a wise and distinguished woman, with

---

152 Cornford, 'The Sick Queen', from *Different Days*, 1928, *SP*, 15.
153 Woolf, 'Professions for Women', *Collected Essays Vol. 11*, 285.

growing daughters, should find some sense in it. Yours is so much more important a contribution to life than mine. I am, or was till Christmas Eve, a harassed middle class middle aged (47 to your 43) woman, stepping into Hamley's toyshop and buying presents for nephews and nieces.[154]

Earlier exchanges of letters testify to the mutual appreciation between poet and novelist – 'I like your poems … I wish you did write more of them.'[155] On 12th November, 1923, Frances Cornford answered Virginia Woolf's 'delightful' letter – 'I've never had things said about my poems that I appreciated so much' – and on 1 February 1926, wrote enthusiastically about Virginia Woolf's essays in *The Common Reader* and *Mrs Dalloway*.[156] It is difficult to be certain about the degree of acquaintance between the two women. They were both associated with the Neopagans and the Cornfords had evidently met the Woolfs. There is correspondence between the husbands, Francis and Leonard, dating from 1913 and between the wives during the 1920s. Frances Cornford's letters express the regret at being unable to offer the Woolfs hospitality because of her busyness. In reciprocation, when Virginia Woolf made a plea for more poems, it was so that they could hold 'disembodied communion' since meeting up, although preferable, was impractical. The dual demands of professional and personal responsibilities dogged both wives and both feared mental breakdown. (Frances Cornford's third bout of depression lasted from 1934 to 1940; Virginia Woolf committed suicide in 1941.) With five children, Frances Cornford understood the *Room-of-One's-Own* struggle between family commitments and writing: 'none requires the expense of spirit as domestic life does on a woman.'[157]

The journal entries, notebooks, literary papers and correspondence indicate Frances Cornford's acute sense of the difficulties of the woman writer, yet she did not dramatise the concept of the New Woman in her poetry. She and her husband supported meetings for women's suffrage before the War but she demonstrates 'conservative modernity' rather than feminist protest in her depiction of women. Many of her poems, like 'Constant', allude to the altruism and silent grief of women suffering from 'the pain unknown' of loss. 'Mother and Child Asleep' reflects on the requirement for women to give all to their

---

154 Letter from Virginia Woolf to Frances Cornford, Mss 58422, Literary Papers of Frances Cornford.
155 Ibid.
156 Letters from Frances Cornford to Virginia Woolf 1923–6, Sx. Ms 18, MHL (VW) (Brighton: University of Sussex Library).
157 Frances Cornford, 'View and Recollections of a Sunday Poet', Tuesday 27 March 1956, Mss 58387, Literary Papers of Frances Cornford.

families and then to let them go. 'A Peasant Woman', included in *Twentieth Century Poetry* (1929), edited by Harold Monro,[158] objectifies the isolation and waiting which such women endure, without regret, at every stage of their lives:

> I saw you sit waiting with your sewing on your knees,
> Till a man should claim the comfort of your body
> And your industry and presence for his own.
>
> I saw you sit waiting with your sewing on your knees,
> Till the child growing hidden in your body
> Should become a living creature in the light.
>
> I saw you sit waiting with your sewing on your knees,
> Till your child who had ventured to the city
> Should return to the shelter of his home.
>
> I saw you sit waiting with your sewing on your knees
> – Your unreturning son was in the city
> Till Death should come along the cobbled street.
>
> I saw you sit waiting with your sewing on your knees.[159]

Characteristically, the poem is also about the effect of the subject on her observer. A question raised here, as in most of her poetry, is whether Frances Cornford's articulation of unfulfilled identity is liberated or stifled by its stylistic regularity. Significantly, she wrote to Virginia Woolf that she was conscious of writing back 'through one's fathers'.[160] This 'pseudo-male' lyricism both enervates and restrains her creativity. The tension between the two creates the energy of the writing.

Vita Sackville-West

The initial tendency to position Vita Sackville-West within the 'genteel' Georgian tradition partly explains why she was considered too 'archaic' for

---

158 *Twentieth Century Poetry*, ed. Harold Monro, 1929, revised and enlarged by Alida Monro (London: Chatto & Windus, 1933).

159 Cornford, 'A Peasant Woman', from *Mountains and Molehills*, 1934, *SP*, 23.

160 Letter from Frances Cornford to Virginia Woolf, 1 February 1926; letters from Frances Cornford to Virginia Woolf 1923–6, Sx. Ms 18.

The Faber Book of 20th Century Women's Poetry. In the review of *Collected Poems* (1933) in the *Spectator*, the features associated with Georgian poems were applied to her entire oeuvre:

> Speaking familiar language and of familiar things, Miss Sackville-West has written, not one or two lines or lyrics, but a body of verse, which will, I think, never be forgotten ... Her poetry does not merely describe nature; it does not merely express her feeling: she describes, and in what she writes Nature and her feeling are one.[161]

The view of Vita Sackville-West as 'archaic' can also be attributed to the narrow representation of her poems in anthologies and the unavailability of her work. The surprising lack of new readings of the poems, when feminist critics have take an interest in her other writing, can be accounted for by the fact that they have been out of print for over half a century. Victoria Glendinning has written up Vita's life in conjunction with the novels, travel writing and historical fictions and she has alluded to the significance of some poems, but recognises that there is more work to be done on them.[162]

Vita Sackville-West was connected by her social and amorous connections with the leading figures of both the conservative literary establishment and the Bloomsbury intellectuals. J.C. Squire and John Drinkwater dined at the Nicolsons' home at Long Barn in Kent and Vita was invited to publish with the Hogarth Press when Virginia Woolf was wanting to develop their acquaintance. As a poet, she qualifies as Georgian in all uses of the term: she was in Edward Marsh's anthologies; she wrote within the historical timespan (1910–36) – most of her poetry was written and published between 1918 and 1938, the best during the years 1926 to 1932 – and if Georgian means English pastoralism and a stylistic regularity, some of her poems conform to these characteristics. They also enlarge any canon of Georgian poetry in number and type because many of the ostensibly descriptive poems are coded love poems. They are difficult to categorise as simply 'Georgian' since the conventional versification operates as a cover under which she explores the duality of her sexual orientation. They qualify for the aspect of female modernism which investigates or rejects heterosexuality, conventional marriage and the literature which endorses the traditional family plot.

---

161 Review of *Collected Poems* by Vita Sackville-West (London: Hogarth, 1933). Printed at the back of *Solitude*, by Vita Sackville-West (London: Hogarth, 1938).
162 Victoria Glendinning, Preface, *Vita: The Life of Vita Sackville-West* (London: Weidenfeld & Nicolson, 1983).

It cannot be claimed that the poems are technically experimental, but the psychologically complex relationship with modernity and investigation of sexual politics have not yet been examined. Within the framework of conventional versification her impersonations of the male lover are symptoms of a 'masculinity complex', which is when women entertain fantasies of being men. According to Freud, the 'masculinity complex' is the condition of female homosexuals. As the controversy over the censorship of Radclyffe Hall's *The Well of Loneliness* (1928) registers, it was not acceptable to openly articulate lesbian love. Vita Sackville-West was on the side of the intellectuals who defended the book against the charge of obscenity. In a letter to Virginia Woolf, 31 August 1928, she stated 'I feel very violently about *The Well of Loneliness*. Not on account of what you call my proclivities; not because I think it is a good book, but really on principle ... I really have no words to say how indignant I am.'[163] Earlier, in 1920, two of the reasons she gave for writing her autobiography, which gives the impression that it was written for delayed publication, were that it would provide a record of same-sex connections because she had had to operate without any models, and because same-sex connections would be considered more natural in future times.[164] At the time, critics either ignored or did not recognise the lesbian coding. *King's Daughter* (1929), a sequence of love poems, was interpreted as a pastoral: 'Miss Sackville-West is known as the poet of good husbandry in these times.'[165] Jane Dunn places her 'romantic and backward-looking pastoralism' as typical of a homosexual subculture of the 1920s and 1930s: 'a prepubescent utopian dream, free of heterosexual conflict and oppression.'[166]

The Land (1926), dedicated to Dorothy Wellesley, won Vita Sackville-West fame as a poet, the Hawthornden prize (1927), and the serious proposal as Poet Laureate in 1929 when Robert Bridges died. Although mocked by experimentalists like Edith Sitwell, it reached a wide audience through the radio, public readings and newspapers – it was initially published in extracts – and anthologies. *The Land* is an important poem in the annals of Georgian practice. In its easy metre and country settings it was ultimately 'agreeable'

---

163 Vita Sackville-West, letter to Virginia Woolf, 31 August 1928, *The Letters of Virginia Woolf and Vita Sackville-West*, ed. Louise De Salvo and Mitchell A. Leaska (London: Hutchinson, 1984), 296.

164 Vita Sackville-West in Nicolson, *A Portrait*, 101.

165 Review of *King's Daughter*, by Vita Sackville-West. *TLS* 7 November 1929: 892. For further discussion of the lesbian aesthetic in *King's Daughter* see Glendinning, 219.

166 Jane Dunn, review of *Vita and Virginia: the work and friendship of Vita Sackville-West and Virginia Woolf*, by Suzanne Raitt, *Literary Review* March 1993.

poetry but it was also useful to Vita's persona as the contented home and country lover. As she recorded in her autobiography, 'secrecy was my passion', and her affair with Violet was 'that little undercurrent'.[167]

The Land is classically pastoral in addressing both the beauty and the rougher side of country life – the work and the war with the elements. It follows Virgil's *Georgics* in advising the reader about farming methods. It was carefully researched and an important record of rural customs which were disappearing. According to Victoria Glendinning, Vita Sackville-West set out to document the skills, processes and landscapes which were being modified by mechanisation. Her sources were her own observations, encyclopaedias of agriculture, old poems and farming treatises:

> She incorporated into her deliberately archaic verse-vocabulary country words still in use, and old place names and field names of the Weald, as well as words that were already falling into disuse: droil, yavy, reasty, undern, winsel, kexen, dwale, scrannel, fisking, eild, tedd, spline, yelm, stelch, sneath, yerk, weazen. (Of these, 'undern', meaning 'in the afternoon', became part of her private language with Virginia.)
>
> In this poetry of dung and marl and tilth and toil – classical Georgian verse, poetry in gumboots – she charted the Wealden farmer's yearly round: beekeeping, woodcraft, sheepshearing, sowing, haysel and harvest, craftsmanship, threshing, ploughing, cidermaking and hop-picking.[168]

Some pages of *The Land* seem hyperbolic and there is no evidence of the political engagement of Virgil nor the scope of his reference and use of myth, but the best passages detail and explore the psychology of rural rituals.

David Perkins defends Georgian poetry of the countryside by arguing that for the poet, it was not simply a case of either escapism from the grim reality of modern life or of clinging to poetic tradition, but an exploration of the craft of poetry: taking the Romantic poets as their standard, 'they were nature poets by inheritance'.[169] *The Land* invokes the Romantic tradition in the context of the modern environment. In the conventional juxtaposition of city and country, Vita Sackville-West may well have had her new Bloomsbury acquaintances in mind:

> Book-learning they have known.
> They meet together, talk, and grow most wise,

---

167 Vita Sackville-West, Nicolson, *A Portrait*, 17, 42.
168 Glendinning, 166.
169 Perkins, 215.

But they have lost, in losing Solitude,
Something, – an inward grace, the seeing eyes,
The power of being alone with earth and skies,
Of going about a task with quietude.[170]

These passages connect back to Wordsworth's imaginative 'bliss of solitude' but, albeit defensively, Vita professed animosity towards Wordsworth after reading *The Prelude*: 'I HATE Wordsworth, the old prig, bore, preachifying old solemnity.'[171]

Vita Sackville-West's writing exemplifies how women took their models from the male traditions on which they had been brought up, although it is not clear how far she modelled her poem on Virgil's *Georgics*. She is alleged to have denied knowledge of them, but Harold noted that she conceived a kind of 'English Georgics' in 1921 when she first started on *The Land*.[172] The poem ends with a direct allusion which seems somewhat nominal, as if to encourage readers to associate *The Land* with the *Georgics*:

Then thought I, Virgil! how from Mantua reft,
Shy as a peasant in the courts of Rome,
You took the waxen tablets in your hand,
And out of anger cut calm tales of home.
(Isfahan April, 1926).[173]

More significant here, however, is the reference to the anger behind Virgil's calm tales; this should be taken as a clue to the characteristic passions underlying Vita's apparently pleasant account of rural life. Whereas Virgil's Part Three was largely about war and implicitly the civil unrest which threatened the Roman world, section three of *The Land*, 'Summer', makes allusions to Persia where Vita revised the poem, having left a nearly completed manuscript with Virginia Woolf. The lyrical passage 'Summer Song' is a celebration of romantic love and some lines suggest personal lovesickness: 'This know, and know then how the heart can ache/With pining for the woods and clouds of home.'[174] Although accompanied by Dorothy Wellesley on her visit to Harold in Persia, at the time of finishing *The Land* Vita wrote several love letters to Virginia Woolf which include the famous profession, 'I am

---

170 Vita Sackville-West, *The Land* (London: Heinemann, 1926), 38.
171 Glendinning, 168.
172 Glendinning, 119.
173 *The Land*, 108.
174 *The Land*, 68.

reduced to a thing that wants Virginia ... I just miss you, in a quite simple desperate human way ... It is incredible how essential to me you have become.'[175] The reviewer in the *TLS* did not construe the professed heartache as sexual passion but as patriotism. Drawing attention to the 'postmark', Isfahan, he constructed *The Land* as a hymn to England, 'It is a learned love, the love of one who delights to attach herself to the countryside by a knowledge of its crafts and husbandry, its flora and its traditional lore.' It was a good and long review which approved the lack of sentimentality, 'she is careful not to indulge her emotion apart from the objects which inspire it'.[176]

Superficially, *The Land* can be read as an archetypal Georgian pastoral in its sketches of English country life. It deserves attention because it was important and well-known in its day. Vita Sackville-West was allegedly inspired by Edward Marsh's complaint against the 'short lyric cries' of modern poets, 'which exactly expresses the irritation that is driving me into trying the experiment of a volume of connected verse',[177] and she found favour with Marsh who called her the 'best living poet under 80'.[178] Although she appeared to Marsh to be taking arms against the sea of innovation, Vita also wanted to be well-received. In a letter to her mother, in 1922, she wrote that 'the people who make or destroy reputations are the professional critics ... and they start out naturally with a prejudice against the dilettante'.[179] Although *The Land* established Vita Sackville-West as a poet (it was on its third reprint by the end of January 1927), it also estranged her from the avant-garde. Edith Sitwell, who was exceptionally disparaging about Georgian poetry, caricatured Vita as the Georgian 'gentleman': 'Nobody is more able to tell you what country life in this English climate is like than she!'[180] Similarly, Peter Quennell played upon the easy mockery of *The Land* in *The Criterion*. He then moved on to *King's Daughter* which he found 'disappointingly flimsy'.[181] Far from 'flimsy', *King's Daughter* (1929), number eleven of the *Hogarth Living Poets* published by the Woolfs, is a pastiche of sixteenth-century courtly sonnet sequences. The persona of the male courtier allowed Vita to dramatise her fantasies with her female lovers.

---

175 Letter from Vita Sackville-West to Virginia Woolf, 21 January 1926, Glendinning, 153.
176 Review of *The Land*. *TLS*, 21 October 1926: 716.
177 Vita Sackville-West, letter to Eddie Marsh, 1924, Glendinning, 134.
178 Vita Sackville-West, letter to Virginia Woolf, 15 June 1927, De Salvo and Leaska, 178.
179 Glendinning, 125.
180 Edith Sitwell, 'Who Wants Poets Now?', *Evening News* 25 April, 1930; *Edith Sitwell: Fire of the Mind* ed. Elizabeth Salter and Allanah Harper (London: Michael Joseph, 1976), 186–8.
181 Peter Quennell, 'Books of the Quarter', *Criterion* ix. 35, January 1930: 358–62. *King's Daughter* was also reviewed in *New Adelphi* III. 3, March–May, 1930: 235.

Vita Sackville-West was not embraced by either the Georgian gentlemen or by the avant-garde, although the Woolfs encouraged her in what she wanted to be most of all, a 'good poet', by publishing her work. Virginia advised her to free up her technique, once she had shown that she could master formalism: 'the danger with you is your sense of tradition and all those words'.[182] Vita was aware of the possibilities of contemporary experiment; she invited Djuna Barnes to stay at Long Barn and she contemplated dedicating her *Collected Poems* to Edith Sitwell. However, she seemed unable to break away from the security of regular metre, rhyme and a slightly formal idiom, perhaps on account of the 'something muted' in her nature – which Woolf believed restrained her writing:

> And isn't there something obscure in you? There's something that doesn't vibrate in you; it may be purposely – you don't let it: ... something reserved, muted ... It's in your writing, too, by the by.[183]

In April 1926, Vita wrote, 'all I can say is, that rhythm and I are out of gear', and in December 1928, she considered 'going into mourning for my dead muse'. She wanted her poetry to be well received – 'I mind about that poem [*The Land*], never having minded about other books.'[184] She was, however, disillusioned with *The Land* for being 'damned bad. Not a spark in it anywhere. Respectable but stodgy'.[185] In later letters, she was similarly self-deprecating about her *Collected Poems* although it is likely that she was seeking Virginia's reassurance – 'all that tripe ... I can't rid myself of the idea that it is all a little pretentious' ... 'It [*Collected Poems*] is the only book of mine I shall ever have minded about – (i.e. I don't give a damn for my novels, but I do give 1/ 2 a damn for my poems, which is not saying much).'[186]

The *Collected Poems* (1933) is divided into thematic sections which make it difficult to link personal events and the poems or to look for stylistic development. There is greater psychological realism, freer versification and less forced rhyme schemes after her connection with Virginia Woolf and Bloomsbury in 1922, although *The Land* was already in draft and little influenced by Virginia's advice to free up her technique. Two sections in

---

182 Virginia Woolf, letter to Vita Sackville-West, 31 June 1927, De Salvo and Leaska, 187.
183 Virginia Woolf, letter to Vita Sackville-West, Glendinning, 169.
184 Vita Sackville-West, letter to Virginia Woolf, 15 March 1926, De Salvo and Leaska, 129.
185 Vita Sackville-West, letter to Virginia Woolf, 3 December 1928, De Salvo and Leaska, 315.
186 Vita Sackville-West, letters to Virginia Woolf, 24 June 1931 and 21 July 1933, De Salvo and Leaska, 403–4.

Collected Poems hive off 'People' and 'Love' whereas most of her poems can be read with reference to her relationships. The dedications alone indicate that Vita had people in mind when writing them. Read in conjunction with biography, the poems correspond to the investigation of sexuality and marriage in her letters, fiction, unpublished autobiography and diaries. Like her correspondence with her husband, they appear to construct a sense of order and control which mask her complicated relationship with social and sexual conventions.

A more complex poetic landscape, which can be detected after 1918, was the result of personal, rather than national, upheavals. Nineteen-eighteen was a year of psychological confusion for Vita due to Harold's need to tell her of his venereal infection. This disclosure also meant the revelation of his bisexuality which was accompanied by the acknowledgement of her own. Nineteen-eighteen was the year in which her relationship with Violet Trefusis, although formed in 1910, became openly passionate. As Victoria Glendinning puts it:

> She had to rethink her whole marriage and her picture of her husband, of his sexual nature – and her own. She had to recognise a parallel duality in her own nature that was sexual and not just temperamental. The unthinkable, after the first shock, becomes the thing most thought about. It was a turning point.[187]

'Dissonance', dated 1918, can be read in the context of this turning point. Like Frances Cornford, Vita Sackville-West seems to be struggling for a language which articulates her pain and alienation without appearing to be personal, that is feminine or sentimental:

> Clamour has riven us, clamour and din.
> My hand reaches blindly out for your hand, but within
> My mind cannot reach to your mind, because of the clamour and din.
>
> Clang as of brass, an uproar that will not cease.
> I would take from the strangest god or devil the gift of peace.
> If the strife that divides us were suddenly stilled and would cease,
>
> I could come to you, come under washed void skies,
> My thought in your thought embraced, my eyes and your eyes
> Levelly meeting without quick faltering of disguise.

---

187 Glendinning, 88.

> But all is harshness and rack in vain
> We strive through the grossness of flesh to discover our souls again,
> And the closer we clasp one another, the further apart remain.[188]

The rhymes offer aesthetic consolation but are dissonant with the harsh diction and declarations of separateness. The uneven line lengths and vocabulary of discord – 'din', 'clang', 'strife', 'rack' – overwhelm the images of unity. The depiction of mental and physical distance makes sense if it is read as if addressed to Harold after his confessions. However, given Vita's insistence on being able to love two people at once, it could also be addressed to Violet who was allegedly not as keen on sex as Vita.

The poem corroborates Virginia Woolf's depiction of Vita in *Orlando* (1928) where she has difficulty in composing a poem because the 'spirit of the age' inhibited her from writing about women:

> When she had written 'Egyptian girls', the power told her to stop. Grass, the power seemed to say, going back with a ruler such as governesses use at the beginning, is all right; the hanging crops of fritillaries – admirable; the snaky flower – a thought strong from a lady's pen, perhaps, but Wordsworth, no doubt, sanctions it; but – girls? Are girls necessary? You have a husband at the Cape, you say? Ah, well, that'll do.[189]

The episode ends with Orlando able to write freely because she has publicly conformed to the spirit of her age by marrying. Similarly, for Vita, traditional forms, harmonious rhyming and regular metres were respectable covers under which to explore her dual identity.

In a letter to Virginia Woolf dated 1928, Vita Sackville-West's phrase, 'I hate safety. I would rather fail gloriously than dingily succeed',[190] indicates her addiction to adventure. 'Night', dedicated to Harold Nicolson, seems to be recording a joyful return to her husband but it is likely that this was one of Vita's homecomings from her travels with Violet Trefusis which always made Harold anxious. It should, therefore, be read as an aesthetic representation of happy reunion:

---

188 'Dissonance', *Collected Poems* by Vita Sackville-West (London: Hogarth, 1933), 289.
189 Virginia Woolf, *Orlando*, 1928, ed. Rachel Bowlby (Oxford: Oxford University Press, 1998), 252–4.
190 Letter from Vita Sackville-West to Virginia Woolf, 21 August 1928, De Salvo and Leaska, 294.

My Saxon weald! my cool and candid weald!
Dear God! the heart, the very heart of me
That plays and strays, a truant in strange lands,
Always returns and finds its inward peace,
Its swing of truth, its measure of restraint,
Here among meadows, orchards, lanes, and shaws.[191]

The regular iambic metres provide a measure of stability but words like 'truant' and 'restraint' signify a psychological restlessness while the exaggerated enthusiasm approaches the parodic. Just as the letters fictionalise the closeness missing in their actual marriage, the self-dramatising dresses up her rejection of marriage as a social institution:

> The marriage of their correspondence was its platonic ideal, in which they both believed. If this was an instinctual psychological device to contain the looseness of their union, it was a successful one – so successful that it took on a life of its own. The more effectively they could meet on the page, the more separate they could be in the everyday. What began as a unifying process legitimised their separateness.[192]

Although the personal agenda of the poems is illustrated through biography, the poems are not 'confessional'. Vita frequently alluded to masks, and both male and female impersonations allowed her to try out different identities. As early as 1910, her novel *Behind the Mask* showed her to be deeply disillusioned about marriage, no doubt considering her parents' difficulties at this point: 'Is there anyone without the mask? ... Not the husband, not the wife, not the son whose every secret the mother thinks she knows.'[193] She and Harold talked publicly about marriage but most of the time she was involved in some 'emotional troilism' – with Violet Trefusis and Pat Dansey, a confidante of Violet Trefusis, among others.[194] Pat Dansey was initially an alibi for Violet and Vita but she became attracted to Vita and insanely jealous of Vita's lovers.[195] 'Black Tarn' records Vita's excursion to Wales with Dorothy Wellesley and Pat Dansey who competed for her attention. With reference to the 'mask' and her 'discontent with ... the safety, and the ease' she dramatises her inability to settle with one person:

---

191 Vita Sackville-West, 'Night', *CP*, 144–6.
192 Glendinning, 146.
193 Glendinning, 37.
194 Glendinning, 197.
195 Glendinning, 133–7.

> I have seen Black Tarn,
> Shivered it for an instant, been afraid.
> Looked into the waters, seen there my own image
> As an upturned mask that floated
> Just under the surface, within reach, beyond reach.[196]

Typically, the alternating long and short lines mirror the paradoxical reaching out and retreat of her temperament. The dedication to Pat Dansey and the elusive persona may have been strategies to provoke the possessiveness and dependence which Vita required of her friends.[197] These poems encode the dominant features of Vita's character as Glendinning describes it:

> … a distaste for the idea of marriage; an apparent candour with her intimates that was no candour at all; a capacity for sustaining multiple relationships; the division in her mind between passionate and companionate love; her fantasy – to be realised – of 'living alone in a tower with her books'; also, her disinclination to let anyone who loved her go – keeping them on a string, rebuffing them if they asked too much of her, but drawing in the line sharply if they showed signs of straying.[198]

The poems addressed to 'Eve', alias Violet Trefusis, such as the sonnet – 'This little space which scented box encloses' – have the potential for the most romantic reading.[199] Two other poems, 'Eve' and 'Eve in Tears',[200] dated 1919, are love lyrics to the *'grande passion'* of her life.[201] After the 'Eve' poems, the next most covertly passionate poems are the ones associated with Dorothy Wellesley who lasted through many of Vita's other lovers and with whom she went to Persia when Harold was first posted there. Dorothy Wellesley was described by Vita in the *Dictionary of National Biography*: 'Slight of build, almost fragile, with blazing blue eyes, fair hair, transparently white skin, she was a natural rebel, rejecting all conventions and accepted ideas, living to proclaim herself an agnostic, a fiery spirit with a passionate

---

196 Vita Sackville-West, 'Black Tarn', *CP*, 137–9.
197 Glendinning, 125.
198 Glendinning, 50.
199 Vita Sackville-West, 'Sonnet', *CP*, 153. In her novel *Challenge*, Vita Sackville-West fictionalises her affair with Violet, named 'Eve', and conceals her own identity by depicting herself as a male, 'Julian', It represents the conflict between love and duty. It was never published in England because it was thought that Vita and Violet were too easily identifiable and too well known.
200 Vita Sackville-West, 'Eve' and 'Eve in Tears', *CP*, 262–3.
201 Glendinning, 94.

love for beauty in all its forms.'[202] 'Full Moon', which was written for her, along with an extract from *The Land,* was printed in *Georgian Poetry 1920– 1922* and in the *Observer* in 1922; it was also in James Reeves' Georgian anthology (1962). The editors were no doubt unaware that the subject of the love sonnet was the wife of Lord Gerald Wellesley. She was referred to as 'Dottie' by Vita and Virginia and 'A', for 'Aprile', was Vita's pet name for her. 'Insurrection' from *Orchard and Vineyard*, dedicated 'To A', is a six page exploration of the sweet torments of sexual passion.[203] As Victoria Glendinning also points out, *Orchard and Vineyard* (1921) gave the impression of a collection of poems about Kent, but knowing the background, a reader can 'trace the emotional confusion of her preceding year, but the common reader in 1921 did not have the key'.[204]

King's Daughter (1929) included three of a group of eleven sonnets written during her affair with Mary Campbell (1927), wife of the poet Roy Campbell. Vita feared that the lesbian eroticism was too transparent in the other sonnets and made them unprintable. Mary Campbell was followed by Hilda Matheson, with whom Vita went to Val D'Isère in July 1929. (Hilda Matheson was director of talks at the BBC and promoted Vita's poems on the radio.) The love poems dated 1931 in *Collected Poems* are addressed to Evelyn Irons, a Scot who was the editor of the woman's page of the *Daily Mail*. She and Vita became lovers in 1931.

Given that Vita Sackville-West depicts fantasy personae in her poems and that the solitary writer was one of her fantasy images, *Solitude*, published in 1938, but begun in 1927 when she had little time to herself, has to be read as a self-dramatisation of that image. *Solitude* gives the impression of a 'worldly-sick' recluse exploring the liberties of her youth, but the line, 'Those cheap and easy loves! but what were they?' upset Vita's female lovers.[205] Although it appeared to be autobiographical, Hilda Matheson wrote to say that she 'found no clue, in this self-communing poem, to the things in you which I have failed to understand in the last few years. I am puzzled by your attitude to love – cheap and easy'.[206] Hilda Matheson echoed Virginia Woolf's earlier reference to the 'something muted' in Vita which limited her writing. Vita acknowledged it in a letter to Harold:

---

202 Glendinning, 113.
203 Vita Sackville-West, 'Insurrection', *CP*, 275–80.
204 Glendinning, 122–3.
205 Vita Sackville-West, *Solitude* (London: Hogarth, 1938), 27–8.
206 Glendinning, 197.

There *is* something muted ... Something that doesn't vibrate, something that doesn't come alive ... It makes everything I do (i.e. write) a little unreal; gives the effect of having been done from the outside. It is the thing which spoils me as a writer; destroys me as poet. But how did V. discover it? I have never owned it to anybody, scarcely even to myself. It is what spoils my human relationships too, but I mind less.[207]

Vita Sackville-West's adherence to rhyme, metrical rigidity and formal diction corresponded to the public persona of a traditional home and country lover which she constructed through her correspondence with Harold, her gardening columns and talks. Behind these impersonations of respectability lurked the non-conformist adventurer which is glimpsed in the ambiguities and coded passions of the poetry. Like Frances Cornford, her male impersonations appear to muffle a stylistic freedom but liberated her from the self-negating aesthetic of the conventional poetess. Although keen not to be identified as 'feminine', through dramatisation they addressed or resisted socially prescribed female roles. In retrospect, they alter the association of traditional versification with the worst of popular female or the best of male writing.

---

207 Vita Sackville-West, letter to Harold, 20 November 1926, *Vita and Harold: The letters of Vita Sackville-West and Harold Nicolson 1910–1962*, ed. Nigel Nicolson (London: Weidenfeld & Nicolson, 1992), 173–4.

Chapter Four

The British Avant-Garde: Edith Sitwell (1887–1964) and the Women of *Wheels* – Nancy Cunard (1896–1965), Iris Tree (1897–1968) and Helen Rootham (d. 1938)

Introduction

In the developments of twentieth-century women poets, the avant-garde demonstrate a new boldness in flouting or subverting literary conventions. They investigate the operations of consciousness, eschew or displace traditional literary effects and transgress the boundaries of genre. They qualify for the language-centred model of modernism and are distinguished from the 'Female Modernists' or 'Thirties' poets in the following sections whose poetry is specifically woman-centred, or explicitly engaged with social and gender politics, but is stylistically less adventurous. In separating 'avant-garde' and 'female' modernisms, however, it would be as wrong to suggest that the former group did not evoke a female consciousness as it would be to imply that the political commitment of the female modernists overwhelmed stylistic concerns. Although the avant-garde writers espoused the 'impersonality' of high modernist poetics, their motivation for overriding literary conventions was often associated with breaking into or away from male-dominated traditions. Their obvious, sometimes ostentatious, intellectuality was fuelled by opposition to the 'feminine' rather than by cultural elitism. Suzanne Clark identifies women as both losers and drivers in a literary climate which valued objectivity, impersonality and 'intellection':[1]

> The modernist revolution turned away from ordinary language and everyday life. This disconnection from social consequence, from history, has every-thing to do with the gendering of intellectuality ... Modernism developed its

---

1   'Intellection' was a favourite term of approval in T.S. Eliot's *Criterion*.

anti-sentimentality into a contemptuous treatment of women, who had to struggle both internally and externally with that contempt ... [and] these women seized the moment to escape from categories of gender.[2]

It is particularly important to situate women within the avant-garde because of its association with intellectuality and because their importance has been understated. These British women and the 'Anglo-American' poets in the next section were perceived as groundbreaking at the time but their cutting edge has subsequently been blunted.

During the 1920s, Edith Sitwell was synonymous with progressive poetics and her *Wheels* anthologies (1916–21), intended as an antidote to Edward Marsh's *Georgian Poetry* books, were a launch pad for a new generation of poets in which men and women were on equal terms. Socially, and through *Wheels*, she was associated with Nancy Cunard and Iris Tree, also daughters of aristocrats, and with Helen Rootham, her former governess who became a lifelong companion. Apart from John Pearson's *Facades*, their poetry and involvement in *Wheels* have barely been registered:

> To start with, there was Helen Rootham: she was a poet, a translator of French poetry and almost a member of the [Sitwell] family. Then there was the Eiffel Tower group, particularly that extraordinarily liberated pair, Nancy Cunard and Iris Tree. Both were poets, both had violently rejected their rich parents' world and what they had stood for, and both were emphatically against the war.[3]

Although they did not produce a large body of poetry, Iris Tree and Nancy Cunard provide strong models of women holding their own among the intellectual élite in London and Paris. Together with Edith Sitwell, they occupy the otherwise vacant space of the British avant-garde and indicate a new aesthetic freedom and confidence in women poets. Sitwell especially presented herself as a public poet through her poetry performances, lectures and criticism.

Edith Sitwell's significance to modern, and specifically modernist, poetry has been unevenly acknowledged. She has been ignored by feminist critics, probably because she did not articulate any sympathy for women's rights. She denounced 'women's poetry' and tended to adopt young male poets as protégés, but her radical experiments fractured the authority of British literary traditions and were activated by antagonism towards her social background.

---

2   Suzanne Clark, *Sentimental Modernism: Women Writers and The Revolution Of The Word* (Bloomington and Indianapolis: Indiana University Press, 1991), 13, 3, 4–5, 8.
3   John Pearson, *Facades: Edith, Osbert and Sacheverell Sitwell* (Basingstoke: Macmillan, 1978), 106.

She constructed a persona which was self-consciously antithetical to the poetess but she became mythologised as 'eccentric' in dress and behaviour.[4] Although vehemently opposed to affiliation with the 'feminine', she did not resort to perceived masculine writing. Her statements about the nature of poetry by women indicate her preoccupation with the relationship between women's poetry and tradition but her formal and syntactical subversions avoided connotations of either male or female practices.

There was frequent correspondence in the papers about 'the Sitwells', particularly Edith, in connection with the new poetry.[5] In the *TLS* review of Osbert Sitwell's *England Reclaimed: A Book of Eclogues* in 1927, one claim stands out in a climate where criticism rarely gave away accolades for innovation: 'Mr Osbert Sitwell and his brother and sister must have the credit of the discovery of a new poetic territory.'[6] They are usually perceived as an alternative Bloomsbury although they overlapped socially with the Bloomsbury artists and novelists and other literary groups. They were particularly popular with the Oxford-educated socially-ambitious post-war generation because in 'their rejection of Cambridge-orientated Bloomsbury intellectualism, their contempt for the plodding homespun virtues of squirearchy, and their attacks upon the conventional paternal wisdom of the old',[7] they represented free thought and glamorous lifestyles. John Pearson firmly positions the Sitwell group as luminaries of avant-garde poetry and his description of the moderns' fight against 'Victorian tradition' and 'tired convention' is imaginatively appealing:

> There was an extended line up for the battle. On one side, under the banner of tradition, stood a host of disparate but more or less united allies – the popular press, the middle classes, provincial little Englanders, admirers of academic art and Georgian poetry, puritans in general and the old in heart. Against them stood the forces of what Herbert Read still optimistically termed 'the future'. They were less numerous but more vocal than their enemy. They included left-wing politicians, 'intellectuals', 'dandy-aesthetes' with Wilde's green carnation still in the button-hole, admirers of experimental poetry and the latest painting from the school of Paris and the whole of Bloomsbury.

---

4 Current criticism perpetuates the personal mythologies. See, for example, headlines to reviews of the recent *Selected Letters of Edith Sitwell*, ed. Richard Greene (1997): 'Epistles of a great English Eccentric', by Philip Zeiger, *Daily Telegraph* 1 March 1997 and 'Withering Heights', by Miranda Seymour, *Sunday Times* 9 March 1997.

5 See, for example, letter from Lawrence Housman, *Time and Tide* 22 June 1928: 612.

6 Review of *England Reclaimed: A Book of Eclogues*, by Osbert Sitwell, *TLS* 27 October 1927: 760.

7 Pearson, 190.

The groupings were, of course, amorphous, and could change: so could the line of battle, with groups and individuals switching sides or even fighting on both sides at once. But the Sitwells never wavered.[8]

Contemporary histories testify to the Sitwells' success in sustaining interest in literary innovation. During the 1920s they rescucitated the revolutionary zeal which had inspired the imagist and other poets before the War. David Peters Corbett (1997) argues that the rejection of the authority of Victorian rhetoric and the loosening of social etiquette, achieved through the most progressive pre-war artistic practices, were replaced by a 'culture of tranquillity' – 'In the midst of a world changing utterly, the English pretend things are as they wish they had always been.'[9] This post-war yearning for stability is one explanation for the view that modernist poetry was largely an American affair. Corbett believes that the Sitwellian avant-garde represents the evasions and concealments of post-war modernity but it also opposed the reactionary 'culture of tranquillity':

> The Sitwells exploited simultaneously a nostalgia for the social thrill of pre-war modernist radicalism, and the refusal of the meanings of that stance which was current in the twenties. The bulk of their achievement after the immediate post-war years lies in the evocation of a pre-modern dream world, an imaginary alternative to modernity.[10]

Edith particularly maintained the momentum for stylistic innovation when the literary press was wary of revolutionary forms because they were conceptually associated with violence. Looking back on 'modern poetry' in 1938 Gwendolen Murphy believed that Edith's poetry was the most significant of the three Sitwells' for its 'free association', and 'skill in texture, new images and symbols, in synthaesthesia (strange to her readers yet itself old), in liveliness of metre, which suggested that a certain richness might again be possible in English poetry ... a world of bright surfaces'.[11]

---

8   Pearson, 145.
9   David Peters Corbett, *The Modernity of English Art 1914–30* (Manchester: Manchester University Press, 1997), 66. See also 'The Death of Futurism', by John Cournos, *Egoist* IV, January 1917: 6–7.
10   Corbett, 160.
11   Gwendolen Murphy, ed., *The Modern Poet: An Anthology* (London: Sidgwick & Jackson, 1938), 170–71.

Wheels (1916–1921)

The caution or animosity towards Edith Sitwell and the *Wheels* anthologies register how post-war sensibilities watered down the zeal of pre-war experiment. A reviewer in the *Morning Post* had 'no doubt whatever that fifty years hence, the publication of *Wheels* will be remembered as a notable event in the inner history of English literature'.[12] Eighty years on, some of the poetry in *Wheels* seems undeveloped and its radical edge seems less keen out of its original context. According to David Perkins in *The History of Modern Poetry*:

> *Wheels* makes rather tame reading, but sixty years ago some reviewers found it radically modern or avant-garde. The reasons they mentioned were chiefly that the *Wheels* poets did not write about country things and were often despairing. The major reason was probably the reputation for rebellious modernity that Edith and her two brothers, Osbert and Sacheverell, were already beginning to acquire.[13]

At the time, *Wheels* did not appear tame. The volumes had startling and provocative covers and the poetry stimulated controversy about the nature and directions of modern poetry. The perceived despair in some poems was their departure from pre-war jingoistic optimism and from the consolations of the weakest Georgian verses. The *Wheels* anthologies provided a collective opposition to the stereotyped complacency of the country gentleman associated with the Georgians:

> *Wheels* was intended to be an act of defiance, a deliberate rebellion against the stuffy canons of respectable, conservative society. It mocked explicitly or implicitly the standards of poetic decorum and middle-class romanticism associated with Marsh and his Georgians; it undermined the dignified postures of academic men of letters; its tone was anti-militaristic, sophisticated and cynical. Not surprisingly, it evoked abusive hostility and delighted applause.[14]

The hostile reviews, such as the sensational article titled 'Asylum School of Poetry' in the *Daily Express*, were still useful publicity.[15] Osbert wrote a carefully reasoned response, which was printed as 'Poet's Defence of "Asylum

---

12 *Morning Post*, 'Press cuttings', *Wheels* 1918: 102.
13 David Perkins, *A History of Modern Poetry. Vol. 1. From The 1890s To The High Modernist Mode* (Harvard University Press, 1976), 427.
14 John Press, *A Map of English Verse* (Oxford: Oxford University Press, 1969), 156.
15 Louis J. McQuilland, 'Asylum School of Poetry', *Daily Express* 20 July 1920.

School". Are they or their critics mad?' He explained that the principles behind the poetry were aesthetic – to create beauty out of life which is not intrinsically beautiful and that *vers libre* could have aesthetic qualities – and that they were not ignoring 'tradition' but were drawing upon Elizabethan concepts of wit in their poems.[16] Several reports in both the popular and literary papers were more seriously engaged with what *Wheels* was about.[17] Even T.S. Eliot, under the pseudonym 'Apteryx' in *The Egoist,* acknowledged the initiatives of *Wheels*:

> *Wheels* is a more serious book [than *Georgian Poetry 1916–17*] ... These are not the good boys of the Sixth Form. The book as a whole has a dilettante effect, refreshing after the schoolroom. The authors are certainly conscious of the fact that literature exists in other languages than their own ... they have extracted the juice from Verlaine and Laforgue.[18]

They were 'not the good boys of the sixth form' in their freedom from British literary conventions and in not being exclusively male.

In *Wheels*, men and women appeared to be equally responsible for pioneering a new kind of poetry. If it is mentioned at all, *Wheels* is usually attributed to Edith Sitwell, although her biographers suggest that it was as much the initiative of Nancy Cunard, whose eponymous poem was the first in the first volume. Certainly, Sitwell was not the named editor until the third volume, but it was she who secured its publication with Basil Blackwell. Interestingly, there was nothing woman-centred about the poems and, unusually, reviewers rarely mentioned gender. The review of *Wheels. A Third Cycle* in *The Athenaeum*, headed 'The Post-Georgians', made no distinction between the men and women contributors and identified the ways in which *Wheels* marked a change in fashion: '*Vers libre* and Cubism already existed, but *Wheels* at least acknowledged the fact; it showed a willingness to experiment, a tolerance of various emotions, and a complete indifference to simplicity.'[19] These writers would agree, however, that in terms of their individual development, the poems published in *Wheels* are not their best work; few are included in Edith Sitwell's *Collected Poems*, Iris Tree's *Poems*

---

16   Osbert Sitwell, 'Poet's Defence of "Asylum School". Are they or their critics mad?', *Daily Express* 22 July 1920.

17   See 'Press notices', cited at the end of *Wheels* 1917, 1918, 1919, 1920.

18   T.S. Eliot, 'Verse Pleasant and Unpleasant', review of *Georgian Poetry* 1916–17 and *Wheels. A Second Cycle, Egoist* V, March 1918: 43–4.

19   'The Post-Georgians', anonymous review of *Wheels. A Third Cycle, Athenaeum* 4641, 11 April 1919: 171–2.

(1920) or Nancy Cunard's books of poetry. In a letter to Robert Nichols, Edith confessed that the edition of *Wheels* was 'very bad this year [1919], for the reason that most of us have had books, all our better work was exhausted'.[20]

The six annual cycles of *Wheels* were an important outlet for experiments in conventional forms, free verse, verse drama and prose poems, not only by the Sitwells but also Aldous Huxley, Sherard Vines, Iris Tree, Nancy Cunard and Helen Rootham. These core contributors were more or less consistent throughout the cycles. *Wheels* published Wilfred Owen's war poetry and *Wheels. A Fourth Cycle* (1919) was dedicated to his memory. Edith Sitwell's correspondence with his mother, Susan Owen, records her enthusiasm for publishing a volume of Owen's poetry and her disappointment when Sassoon took over the project. She declared that to have arranged 'the greatest poetry of the generation for publication' would have been the greatest pride of her life.[21]

Wheels succeeded as a foil to the Georgian anthologies and it reinforced the conceptual opposition between traditional forms and radical free verse. A reviewer in *The Observer* stated, 'The second cycle of *Wheels* is a challenge like the first. Every page shouts defiance of poetic conventions.'[22] Although the poems in *Wheels* experiment with a range of forms as much as with free verse, the association of the avant-garde with anarchism is significant because it meant that there was less appetite for radical poetics after the War. Sitwell, however, was bold in her continuing promotion of innovation. In drawing upon surrealist and abstract art, she pressed upon the boundaries of poetry. Additionally, the anti-representational aspects of many poems transcended the problem of gendered identification with its negative connotations of femininity.

Edith Sitwell

Edith Sitwell's avant-gardism was renowned but not recognised as contiguous with her eschewal of 'the feminine'. Anthony Thwaite observes that, '[Edith Sitwell] was, in the popular mind, the leader of the 1920s avant-garde (far more so than Eliot), and her verbal and rhythmical fancies, such as *Facade*, took no notice of social matters.'[23] While rightly indicating her reputation,

---

20 Edith Sitwell, letter to Robert Nichols, March 1919. *Edith Sitwell: Selected Letters*, ed. John Lehmann and Derek Parker (Basingstoke: Macmillan, 1970), 14–15.

21 Edith Sitwell, letter to Susan Owen, February 1921, Lehmann and Parker, 25–6.

22 *The Observer*, 'Press Notices', *Wheels* 1918: 100.

23 Anthony Thwaite, *Twentieth-Century English Poetry* (London: Heinemann, 1978), 63.

the opposition between her 'verbal and rhythmical fancies' and 'social matters' is misleading. Her anti-realist strategies were an aspect of the psychological retreat associated with post-war modernity and were also evasions of a gendered identity. Sitwell's poetry negotiates between the anti-representational – her famous 'surfaces' – and psychological or social realism. In common with Nancy Cunard and Iris Tree, she combined the modernist ideals of impersonality with a sensitivity towards social inequality and a changing civilisation. Although preoccupied with rhythm and rhyme, and their equivalence to abstract art or music, Sitwell also talks of her poems as being 'about' something: 'In many poems the subject is the growth of consciousness … whilst some poems are about the materialism and the world crumbling to dust.'[24] She was influential in representing and investigating the unconscious through associated images using devices borrowed from contemporary art.

Edith Sitwell was remarkably successful in publishing poetry, prose and criticism. Her publishing history spans the years 1913, when 'Drowned Suns' was printed in the *Daily Mirror,* to 1982 when her *Collected Poems* was reprinted. Her most successful period was 1922 to 1929. Between the wars she published *Clowns' Houses* (1918), *The Wooden Pegasus* (1920), *Bucolic Comedies* (1923), *The Sleeping Beauty* (1924), *Troy Park* (1925), *Rustic Elegies* (1927), *Gold Coast Customs* (1929), *Collected Poems* (1930), *Five Variations on a Theme* (1933) and *Selected Poems* (1936). She was also a prolific literary reviewer and critic; she wrote a novel, historical and satirical biographies, edited several poetry anthologies and gave poetry readings and lectures on poetry in Europe and the United States. She was awarded the Royal Society of Literature's medal for poetry in 1934. She is usually grouped with her brothers but they tended to tread separate paths after 1924 when Sacheverell married. She visited Paris in the 1920s and moved there in 1932. In France she was influenced by European art and her meeting with Gertrude Stein in 1924 began an important alliance between the two champions of avant-garde poetics, although it became tinged with rivalry.

The impersonality of modernist principles provided a legitimate *sortie* from identifying herself as a woman. Edith Sitwell could not identify with male literary traditions because male critics insisted on women's difference and she was embarrassed by the alleged sentimentality of women's poetry. Her inability to identify with male or female traditions was also symptomatic of the rejection by both her father and mother. Her mother rejected her because she was the first child in a marriage into which she had been forced and later

---

24   Edith Sitwell, *Collected Poems,* 1957 (London: Macmillan, 1961), xvii. (All subsequent page numbers are from this edition.)

passed her over in favour of Sacheverell, the youngest. Her father had married for an heir and found his daughter 'unsatisfactory' for neither being male nor conforming to traditional models of femininity. Both parents persistently drew attention to her ugliness and she reacted against her privileged heritage at the family estate of Renishaw Hall, Derbyshire, because of her parents' cruelty. She refused the conventional 'coming out' for high society daughters and left home for London in 1914. This meant becoming financially self-supporting and holding her own among literary acquaintances who were mostly men. In a letter to Stephen Spender, Sitwell confessed that there had not been an adequate female model 'to point the way … I had to learn everything – learn, among other things, not to be timid, and that was one of the most difficult things of all'.[25] She also had to deal with the persistent taunting by her male colleagues and by critics who were challenged by the figure of a woman who did not fit the innocuous poetess stereotype. Nevertheless, she held weekly soirées and according to Geoffrey Gorer, the leader of the Cambridge University Poetry Society,

> These tea parties of hers really *were* one of the most extraordinary literary affairs of the twenties when you think of them. For there she was, all but penniless, in a dingy little flat in an unfashionable part of London. All she could offer was strong tea and buns. Yet because of who she was she attracted to that flat almost every major literary figure of the twenties.[26]

No Man's Land: 'Women will try to write like a man and can't'

Like other literary women who became public figures, such as Edna St Vincent Millay and Marianne Moore, Edith Sitwell cultivated a protective public image. She also channelled her sense of exclusion into the revolutionary forms of her poetry and retreated psychologically from the ill-treatment of critics and her parents through fantasy and dreamstate. Drawing upon her own 'hell of a childhood', Sitwell challenged the false appearances of happy families in an early poem, 'En Famille': 'for Hell is just as properly proper / As Greenwich, or as Bath, or Joppa.'[27] In a letter to John Lehmann, she connected the suppressed pain of her childhood with her writing:

> I can't tell the truth about my sainted mother. If I had been a slum child, I would have been taken away from her. But I wasn't a slum child, and motherhood is a

25 Edith Sitwell, letter to Stephen Spender, 16 March 1946, Lehmann and Parker, 136–7.
26 Geoffrey Gorer, Pearson, 155.
27 Edith Sitwell, *CP*: 129.

very beautiful thing! I often wonder what my poetry would be like if I had had a normal childhood.[28]

The long poem 'Mother', printed in the first volume of *Wheels* but not in her *Collected Poems,* is a disturbing monologue of a mother who is killed by her child, figured as a boy, presumably to detract from autobiographical associations. It ends with the mother speaking from beyond the grave:

> He did no sin. But cold blind earth
> The body was that gave him birth.
> All mine, all mine the sin; the love
> I bore him was not deep enough.[29]

This poem maintains and fractures the maternal ideal. Similarly, 'The Drunkard', also printed in *Wheels*, relates to her mother's drink problem. The monologue dramatises the murderous thoughts of the discarded child as she observes her mother's unconscious body:

> And if, to spite her, I dared steal
> Behind her bed and feel
>
> With fumbling fingers for her heart ...
> Ere I could touch the smart,
>
> One more wild shriek on shriek would tear
> The dumb and shuddering air ...
>
> Yet still she never speaks to me.[30]

These poems indicate the psychological conflicts surrounding the feminine ideal linked to women's maternal function. Edith Sitwell's inability to dismiss an ideal with which she could not identify and a function which she could not have illustrates the literal mother-daughter alienation which also operates at the metaphorical level of creativity. As Luce Irigaray poses:

> But there is no possibility whatsoever, within the current logic of sociocultural operations, for a daughter to situate herself with respect to her mother: because,

---

28   Edith Sitwell, letter to John Lehmann, 1951, *Edith Sitwell: A Unicorn Among Lions*, by Victoria Glendinning (London: Weidenfeld and Nicolson, 1981), 24.

29   Edith Sitwell, 'Mother', *Wheels* 1916: 45–8.

30   Edith Sitwell, 'The Drunkard', *CP*, 172–3.

strictly speaking, they make neither one nor two, neither has name, meaning, sex of her own, neither can be 'identified' with respect to the other. A problem that Freud dismisses 'serenely' by saying that the daughter has to turn away from her mother, has to 'hate' her, in order to enter into the Oedipus complex. Doesn't that mean that it is impossible – within our current value system – for a girl to achieve a satisfactory relation to the woman who has given her birth? … How can the relationship between these two women be articulated? Here 'for example' is one place where the need for another 'syntax', another 'grammar' of culture is crucial.[31]

Bucolic Comedies (1923), which consists of twenty one parts, operates on the level of verbal experiment, particularly rhythm and rhyme, and also explores the psychological effects of Sitwell's childhood. The images, drawn from the house and gardens at Renishaw Hall, and the rhythmic shifts interchange dream–or nightmare–and realism in the memories of her hellish past. In Osbert's words, Edith was driven from home by the 'atmosphere of violent hysteria' surrounding their mother, the 'Countess of [Hel]L':

> But Anne was five years old and must know
> Reality; in the goose-soft snow
>
> She was made to walk with her three tall aunts
> Drooping beneath the snow's cold plants.
>
> They dread the hour when with book and bell
> Their mother, the old fell Countess of L –
>
> Is disrobed of her wig and embalmed for the night's
> Sweet mummified dark;[32]

John Press suggests that 'her preoccupation with images of cold indifference, isolation, betrayal, corruption and suffering probably stemmed from her own terror and loneliness as a young child'.[33] In 'Colonel Fantock', dedicated to Osbert and Sacheverell, images of loneliness, like 'I think that only winged ones know the eyrie is so lonely', are woven into the tapestry of memory's associative details. 'Dagobert' and 'Peregrine' were Edith's pseudonyms for her brothers:

---

31 Luce Irigaray, *This Sex Which Is Not One*, trans. Catherine Porter with Carolyn Burke (New York: Cornell University Press, 1985), 143.

32 Edith Sitwell, 'Winter', *CP*: 33–5.

33 Press, 159.

> But Dagobert and Peregrine and I
> Were children then; we walked like shy gazelles
> Among the music of the thin flower-bells.
> And life, still held some promise, – never ask
> Of what, – but life seemed less a stranger, then,
> Than ever after in this cold existence.
> I always was a little outside life –
> And so the things we touch could comfort me;
> I loved the shy dreams we could hear and see –
> For I was like one dead, like a small ghost,
> A little cold air wandering and lost.[34]

The profession of alienation – 'I always was a little outside life' – reads simultaneously as a tormented memory and a means of psychic rehabilitation by aestheticising the memory. The 'old military ghost' represents their distinguished ancestry which haunted the children:

> All day within the sweet and ancient gardens
> He had my childish self for audience –
> Whose body flat and strange, whose pale straight hair
> Made me appear as though I had been drowned –
> (We all have the remote air of a legend) – .[35]

The psychological effects of her childhood appear to have dogged Sitwell throughout her life. She continually quipped about her parents' rejection and cruelty, particularly putting her in an iron brace, her 'bastille', allegedly to strengthen her long spine.

In *The Sleeping Beauty* (1924), set in her maternal grandmother's home at Londsborough,[36] Sitwell's violent opposition to her conventional upbringing is depicted in the image of her stuffed parrot in a cage:

> Imprisoned now in a gilded cage
> In her powder closet, far from the rage
> Of winter, it can only sing
> Roulades, and preen its bright clipped wing.[37]

---

34   Edith Sitwell, 'Colonel Fantock', *CP*: 174–7.
35   Ibid., 176.
36   Edith Sitwell, *Taken Care of: an autobiography* (London: Hutchinson, 1965), 61.
37   Edith Sitwell, 'The Sleeping Beauty', *CP*: 64–5.

Typically, Sitwell negotiates between psychological realism and a substitute world of dreams and enchantments. The poem also illustrates her experiments with the discordant effect of adjacent rhymes:

> The country bumpkins come, with faces round
> And pink as summer fruits, with hair as gold,
> Sharp-pointed, as the summer sun (that old
> Bucolic mime, whose laughing pantomime
> Is rearing pink fruits from the sharp white rime).[38]

As in Christina Rossetti's *Goblin Market*, which she admired, the fruit is both enticing and sinister. The difficulty of translating Sitwell's imagery signify the unpresentability of her memories. They disrupt recognisable systems of representation, including conventional constructions of female identity. In *The Sleeping Beauty*, she deftly subverts fairytale romance by foregrounding the fiction and temporality of its narratives: 'The fruits are cold as that sweet music's time – / Yet all those fruit like the bright snow will fade.'[39]

Edith Sitwell's difficult relationship with her mother – 'It was my mother, and not my father, who made my childhood and youth a living hell, – and I am not exaggerating'[40] – contributed to the vehemence of her female affiliation complex in relation to women poets. In a letter to Robert Nichols in 1919, she complained of 'a depressing evening where all the guests were female poets'.[41] Her antipathy to other literary women was no doubt also sparked by the dismissiveness towards women in reviews. Significantly, in a letter to Nichols the previous year she had complained about her poems being called 'trivial' in the *New Statesman*:

> Damn them, – oh damn them! If they only knew the amount of concentration I put into these things, the amount of hard work and the frayed nerves it entails. They grumble because they say women will try to write like men and can't – then if a woman tries to invent a female poetry, and uses every feminine characteristic for the making of it, she is called trivial. It has made me furious, not because it is myself, but because it is unjust.[42]

---

38   Ibid., 87.
39   Ibid., 87–8.
40   Edith Sitwell, letter to Geoffrey Singleton, 11 July 1955, Lehmann and Parker, 198–200.
41   Edith Sitwell, letter to Robert Nichols, March 1919, Lehmann and Parker, 14–15. Robert Nichols was a poet, a protégé of Edith Sitwell's and devotee of Nancy Cunard.
42   Edith Sitwell, letter to Robert Nichols, 26 December 1918, Pearson, 132.

Sitwell's reviews of women's books, her article 'Some Observations on Women's Poetry' (*Vogue*, 1925) and her frequent references to the nature of women's poetry illustrate her preoccupation with the gendering of poetic techniques which she confronted in the rhetoric of male criticism. Initially, she believed that women were different – 'Women poets will do best if they realise that male technique is not suitable for them'[43] – but later was more anxious to eliminate the ghettoising of 'women poets' – 'If one can't write like a man, one has no business to write at all.'[44] It is likely that she was attracted to Virginia Woolf's concept of the androgynous mind in *A Room of One's Own* (1929). Sitwell wrote an enthusiastic letter to Woolf in 1930: 'You know that you are one of the only living writers whom I can read with joy and perpetual astonishment and satisfaction, and the fact that you like my poems makes me proud and happy.'[45] Sitwell's famous renunciation of her literary foremothers explains one of her central aesthetic concerns, to negate the feminine, largely through avoiding the expressive or personal:

> Women's poetry, with the exception of Sappho (I have no Greek and speak with great humility on that subject), and with the exception of 'Goblin Market' and a few deep and concentrated, but fearfully incompetent poems of Emily Dickinson, is *simply awful* – incompetent, floppy, whining, arch, trivial, self-pitying, – and any woman learning to write, if she is going to be any good at all, would, until she had made a technique for herself (and one has to forge it for oneself, there is no help to be got) write in as hard and glittering a manner as possible, and with as strange images as possible – strange, but believed in. Anything to avoid that ghastly wallowing.[46]

Her admiration for Christina Rossetti, as already indicated, emerged in an early poem, 'Singerie', which is strikingly similar to passages in *Goblin Market*:

> Papagei, O Papagei,
> Buy our greenest fruits, oh buy,
> Melons misty from the bloom
> Of mellow moons on some hot night,
> Melting in the August light;[47]

43   Edith Sitwell, 'Some Observations on Women's Poetry', *Vogue* 1925; *Edith Sitwell: Fire of the Mind*, ed. Elizabeth Salter and Allanah Harper, 1956 (London: Michael Joseph, 1976), 189.
44   Edith Sitwell, letter to Lincoln Kirstein, May 1950, Glendinning, 164.
45   Edith Sitwell, letter to Virginia Woolf, 11 July 1930, Lehmann and Parker, 40.
46   Edith Sitwell, letter to Maurice Bowra, 24 January 1944, Lehmann and Parker, 116.
47   Edith Sitwell, *CP*, 8.

The collage of imagery in 'Singerie' illustrates that early on Edith Sitwell reformulated the French symbolists whom she admired into her ideal of self-contained aestheticism. In her notes, critical books and articles, Edith Sitwell consistently drew attention to what she called the 'texture' – the sounds and shapes – of language, in ways which can taunt and frustrate the reader because they test conventional systems of meaning. By displacing conventional symbols, she defamiliarised the reader for the purposes of invigorating their consciousness. The refusal to provide recognisable signifiers also unsettled conventional representations of gender.

Defamiliarisation

As early as 1934, Geoffrey Bullough detected the Sitwells' influence on exploring the contingency of language and consciousness which characterises avant-garde modernism:

> Their contribution to poetic technique was considerable for they enlarged the associational thought of their contemporaries by new similitudes, fostered rhythmical flexibility, by their experiments in metre and texture, invented a new instrument of satire, and vindicated a decorative art where 'All is surface and so must die'.[48]

The creation of 'decorative art' was certainly an aesthetic principle, but the anti-realist evasions also correspond to the facades which the Sitwell children constructed in their public life. The striking aural effects and imagery which draw attention to the constitution of the text mirror Edith Sitwell's outlandish clothing which created a dramatic persona for public appearances.

Rhythm and rhyme provide the unifying principles in Sitwell's work. She believed that rhythmical variety was the major instrument for enlarging consciousness. For her, the growth of consciousness meant a person achieving enlightenment about 'something beyond the conscious that is yet buried in sleep' and rhythm was 'one of the principle translators between dream and reality'.[49] Rhyme was integral to rhythmic effect:

> Most modernist poets are keenly interested in developing technique along the lines laid down for us by our predecessors. For myself, I spend much of my

---

48 Geoffrey Bullough, 'The Sitwell Group', *The Trend of Modern Poetry*, by Bullough, 1934 (London and Edinburgh: Oliver and Boyd, 1941), 120.
49 Edith Sitwell, *Taken Care of*, 44, 123.

time in experimenting in the effects that rhyme and texture have on rhythm. Many of the violent rhythms which I obtained in *Bucolic Comedies* were got largely by the use of rhymes, internal and external.[50]

Significantly, here, Sitwell situated her experiments away from the continuities of 'our predecessors'. Her juxtaposition of allusions from several traditions such as classical and Christian, literary and nursery rhyme, are part of this defamiliarising process and have an irreverence unencumbered by nostalgia for the traditions which she recast.

The Sleeping Beauty was the first of Edith Sitwell's works to appear simultaneously in an edition in the United States. In Britain, the *TLS* review says something about the respect she had gained during the 1920s:

> The greater part of the poem, its scenery and symbolism, has the individuality of form and colour which we have come to associate with this poet's work. The principal theme of the poem may be said to represent the subjection of youthful vision, personified by the princess, to the necessities of age and its accompanying malice in the figure of the evil fairy Laidronete. There are, of course, many undertones which can only be heard in the verse itself, and it is not the mortality of beauty which is mourned, but the impossibility of retaining the perception in our early purity. It is a profound theme, and one to which Miss Sitwell has brought her accustomed thoughtfulness and uncommon intellectual awareness.[51]

The reviewer appeared not to identify any autobiographical allusions but he did recognise that her fairies were 'drawn in Beardsley fashion' and therefore represented the aristocracy. He was alert to the way in which the shades of the prison-house closed around the growing princess and that there was no Prince Charming in her fairy tales.

Underneath the textual antics was the motive to shake off traditionalism. Julian Symons complained that there was 'no reference through symbols to reality as there is in Yeats'.[52] As she explained in her lengthy article, 'Modern Poetry', Sitwell was aiming to rescue literary language from stagnation:

> One of the principal aims of the new poets is to increase consciousness, and, to do this, we must use all the powers that nature and intelligence and insight and

---

50   Edith Sitwell, 'Modern Poetry', *Time and Tide* 30 March 1928: 308–9.

51   'Defeat of Youth', review of *The Sleeping Beauty*, by Edith Sitwell, *TLS* 3 April 1924: 204.

52   Julian Symons, 'Miss Edith Sitwell have and had and heard', *The London Magazine* IV. 8, November 1964: 63.

dream and fact have given us ... The modernist artist wishes us to see things for ourselves – not merely to believe the trees are green because we have been told so.[53]

Significantly, she identified herself as 'modernist' and also maintained that form and rhyme were not oppositional to modernist principles: 'We leave the weak, the formless, unformulated verse which is neither free verse nor anything else, to the café-haunters of Paris, both [sic] English, French and American'. The early eight part sequence *Marine* is a study of a semi-conscious crowd and section Six, 'Portrait of a Barmaid', seems Prufrockesque in its depiction of shifting perceptions and alienation:

> Metallic waves of people jar
> Through crackling green toward the bar,
>
> Where on the tables, chattering white,
> The sharp drinks quarrel with the light.
>
> Those coloured muslin blinds, the smiles,
> Shroud wooden faces; and at whiles
>
> They splash like a thin water (you
> Yourself reflected in their hue)![54]

Sitwell characteristically confuses the reader's senses by connecting the concrete with the abstract: conversations are figured as 'spinal bars of shunting light'. In mingling perspectives she resembles Cubist experiments with angles and dimensions.

Façade and Beyond

Façade marks the stage between the greater realism of Edith Sitwell's earlier and later work when she was experimenting with the equivalent to abstract art and with the rhythms of music, particularly dances like waltzes and fox-trots. According to Sitwell, *Façade* was a series of experiments with pacing, rhythm and syntax and the deceptive gaiety of the lyrics concealed her seriousness about aesthetics.[55] Her seriousness aesthetic principles incorporated

---

53   Edith Sitwell, 'Modern Poetry'.
54   Edith Sitwell, 'Marine', *CP*: 166.
55   Edith Sitwell, *Taken Care Of*, 124.

the self-contained status of art, her commitment to enlarging consciousness and her reaction against British conventionality. The title of *Façade* introduces the theme of socially constructed appearances which the poem explores. Disguise and facades became a way of life for the Sitwell children and is central to much of their work. Edith's anger towards her parents incited her satirical portraits of national traditionalism in *The English Eccentrics* (1933) and in her poems.

In 'Sir Beelzebub', the last section of *Façade*, the exaggerated versification is a swipe at the rigidity of Victorian values:

> Alfred Lord Tennyson crossing the bar laid
> With cold vegetation from pale deputations
> Of temperance workers (all signed In Memoriam)
> Hoping with glory to trip up the laureate's feet,
>   (Moving in classical metres) ...[56]

Here, the exaggerated metre parodies Victorian traditionalism but Sitwell denied reference to social realities: 'The poems in *Façade* are *abstract* poems – that is, they are, too, in many cases, virtuoso exercises in technique of an extreme difficulty.'[57] More specifically:

> My experiments in *Façade* consist of inquiries into the effect on rhythm and on speed of the use of rhymes, assonances, and dissonances, placed at the beginning and in the middle of lines, as well as at the end, and in most elaborate patterns. I experimented, too, with the effect upon speed of the use of equivalent syllables – a system that produces great variation.[58]

In 'Fox Trot' and 'Hornpipe', although attending to rhythmic effect, the customs of the aristocracy, such as foxhunting and dancing, are mocked through the caricatures of Queen Victoria and Lord Tennyson, emblems of British imperialism and literary heritage:

> Where Lord Tennyson in laurels wrote a gloria free,
> In a borelaic iceberg came Victoria; she
> Knew Prince Albert's tall memorial took the colour of the floreal
> And the borealic iceberg.[59]

---

56   Edith Sitwell, 'Sir Beelzebub', *CP*: 158.
57   Edith Sitwell, *CP*: xvi.
58   Ibid.
59   Edith Sitwell, 'Hornpipe', *CP*: 155.

The nonsense-verse imitation undermines the authority of high cultural tropes. 'Hornpipe' and 'Sir Beelzebub' exemplify her play with popular and literary forms – nineteenth-century nonsense and Tennysonian narrative verse – which anticipates postmodernism's conflations of cultural differences.

Many anecdotal references to the Sitwells relate to the first public performance of *Façade,* in the Aeolian Hall on 12 June 1923, which became 'part of the artistic history of the twenties, and central to the whole mythology of the Sitwells'.[60] Some mythologies were created by Noel Coward's parodic show, *London Calling*, but the event mostly became scandalised as a shambolic riot in the popular press, although according to the *Daily Express* the audience was 'in ecstasy'.[61] First-hand witnesses, however, found it respectable, if not subdued: 'Everyone was perfectly good-mannered and no one objected violently at all. There were certainly no boos or catcalls. On the other hand there wasn't much enthusiasm either.'[62] Three years later, the revised score by William Walton helped the performance of *Façade* at Chelsea to be a notable success:

> It became a demonstration of the support and interest which their name could now attract among the socially artistic cream of London. Diaghilev was in the audience, and Cecil Beaton found the hall so crowded that he could not get a seat and had to stand 'along with the mass of other thrilled and expectant people. Half the audience seemed nicely arty and the other half merely revolting arty.' The nicely arty and the revolting arty were for once united in their enthusiasm. There were repeated encores, and afterwards the Sitwells and their allies dined in triumph at the Eiffel Tower [restaurant].[63]

The reference to the Russian impresario Sergei Diaghilev is significant because the staging of Diaghilev's *Parade* in 1917 was considered to be one of the historic moments in the modern movement and inspired Sitwell's writing.[64] The sets and costumes of *Parade*, designed by Pablo Picasso, were described as 'surreal' by Guillaume Apollinaire, the first recorded use of the term.[65] John Pearson believes that Edith Sitwell's poems written around 1919 and 1920 were woven from nursery rhyme figures which were reworked into

---

60   Pearson. 183.
61   'Poetry through a Megaphone'. *Daily Express* 13 June 1923.
62   Angus Morrison, Pearson. 183–4.
63   Pearson. 205–6.
64   Sergei Diaghilev presented a season of Russian opera and ballet in Paris in 1909.
65   Philip Waller and John Rowett, *Chronology of the 20th Century* (Oxford: Helicon, 1995), 73, 75.

characters in a Diaghilev ballet. They were also set against brightly coloured backcloths like Picasso's paintings which she and her brothers admired.[66] The fact that when *Façade* was again performed in the Aeolian Hall twenty years later it was rapturously received, suggests that any initial resistance to the Sitwells was reactionary because they were too progressive for their time.[67]

Sitwell's poetry operates according to Bakhtin's theory of carnivalesque where high cultural signifiers are treated with irreverence. A reviewer of *The Bucolic Comedies* in the *TLS* appreciated the interpolation of pauses and still small voices among the 'audacious pell-mell carnival'.[68] Geoffrey Bullough also noticed the carnival realism, especially in *Façade*:

> Her clowns are the clowns of the *commedia dell arte*. They exist in her imagination side by side with Ethiops and Victorian ladies, Greek Nymphs and centaurs, wigs and patches, costumes of all ages, statues, fountains, waterfalls, fruits and flowers, unicorns, caves, modern servants and ancient queens, a phantasmagoria without limitation of place or time.[69]

Although Sitwell's fantastic imagery challenges what Bakhtin describes as the 'official seriousness' of traditional rituals and ceremony, she did not substitute the lower cultural order for the ruling class.[70] She depicted the *commedia dell arte* rather than street carnival. However, the absence of linearity and the transgression of social conventions allowed in the carnivalesque were strategies for rejecting literary traditions and avoiding stereotyped femininity. Through the carnivalesque suspension of identity, she trod the line between representing and aestheticising a mind troubled by the decaying culture of post-war modernity. The evocation of an outworn culture in *Façade* connects with *The Waste Land* (1922) which Sitwell admired. She first met T.S. Eliot in 1917 and their acquaintance continued, if somewhat intermittently, for many years.

The restorative potential of fantasy in Edith Sitwell's figurations of the unconscious was discussed in a good full-length column review of *Three Rustic Elegies* in the *TLS*: 'Miss Sitwell's poems have then the qualities but not the function of dreams. The function of dreams, in poetry at any rate, is mainly to

---

66 Pearson, 151.
67 Pearson, 354.
68 Review of *The Bucolic Comedies*, by Edith Sitwell, *TLS* 31 May 1923: 369.
69 Bullough, 112.
70 M.M. Bakhtin, 'Rabelais and His World', 1965, *The Bakhtin Reader: Selected Writings of Bakhtin, Medvedev, Voloshinov*, ed. Pam Morris (London: Edward Arnold, 1994), 195–244.

provide compensation'.[71] The poems were also well-received in *Time and Tide*,[72] but neither reviewer caught the ways in which the elegies subverted the Georgian pastorals through the surreal landscapes of the poems. The first Rustic Elegy, 'The Little Ghost Who Died for Love', commemorates a young woman who was hanged in 1708 for shielding her lover in a duel. Part 2, 'The Hambone and the Heart', dedicated to Pavel Tchelitchew, the homosexual painter with whom she was allegedly in love, consists of a dialogue between a girl and her heart. The cumulation of morbid imagery evokes a nightmare condition which is both personal and cosmic:

> For underneath the lime-tree's golden town
> Of Heaven, where he stood, the tattered Clown
> Holding the screaming Heart and the Hambone,
> You saw the Clown's thick hambone, life-pink carrion.[73]

In his introduction to *The Oxford Book of Modern Verse* (1936) Yeats described 'The Hambone and the Heart' as one of the most tragic poems of the time. The third part, 'The Ghost Whose Lips were Warm' is a tragi-comedy, based on a seventeenth-century tale of a man who is visited by the ghost of his first wife. The tone of the elegy is both sincere and irreverently parodic. It was included in the Parisian review *Échanges*, founded by Allanah Harper in 1929.[74] *Three Rustic Elegies, The Madness of Saul* and *Elegy on Dead Fashion* anticipate the move towards realism in *Gold Coast Customs* (1929) in dwelling upon a 'crumbling civilisation'.

   Gold Coast Customs (1929), dedicated to Helen Rootham, is based on the Ashantee ritual, 'Customs', of killing the poor and slaves to provide blood to put upon the dead body of an important person. In the poem, the crucified Christ is the emblem of suffering *in extremis* caused by human hands.[75] Sitwell explained *Gold Coast Customs* as a poem in which 'I have tried to produce, not so much the record of a world as the wounded and suffering soul of that world, its living evocation, not its history, seen through the eyes of a protagonist whose personal tragedy is echoed in that vaster tragedy'.[76] Inspired by the hunger marches, *Gold Coast Customs* was also an attack on fashionable society,

---

71   Review of *Rustic Elegies*, by Edith Sitwell, *TLS* 7 April 1927: 246.
72   Review of *Rustic Elegies*, by Edith Sitwell, *Time and Tide* 14 October 1927: 914.
73   Edith Sitwell, 'The Hambone and the Heart', *CP*: 181–6.
74   *Échanges*, ed. Allanah Harper, ran for five quarterly numbers. It included poems and an article 'Modernist Poets', by Edith Sitwell. See note 1, Lehmann and Parker, 38–9.
75   Edith Sitwell, *CP*: 249–50.
76   Edith Sitwell, *CP*: xli.

personified in Lady Bamburgher who hosts champagne parties while men starve; the inequalities of her 'Mayfair Jungle' mirrored the cannibal rites of King Munza of Ashanti.[77] In the poem, Edith Sitwell's opposition to economic injustice is characteristically communicated through insistent rhythm, adjacent and internal rhyming and assonance:

> Yet the time will come
> To the heart's dark slum
> When the rich man's gold and the rich man's wheat
> Will grow in the street, that the starved may eat, –
> And the sea of the rich will give up its dead –
> And the last blood and fire from my side will be shed.
> For the fires of God go marching on.[78]

As Michael Roberts indicated, this is performance poetry: 'The poetry of Edith Sitwell, like the poetry of Vachel Lindsay and E.E. Cummings, needs to be read aloud, with careful change of rhythm, volume, pitch, and tempo.'[79] He analysed Sitwell's manipulation of sound at some length in his Introduction to *The Faber Book of Modern Verse* (1936):

> Often an effect of logic in a poem, which when examined, proves illogical, is due to auditory rhetoric rather than to fantasy. The poetry of Edith and Sacheverell Sitwell shows, for example, not only an unusually vivid use of sensuous impression, of image patterns based, like nursery rhymes, on the compelling force of dreams, but also an effective use of sound-patterns having this convincing facility of speech.[80]

As in her earlier, more autobiographical work, the experimental 'auditory rhetoric' in *Gold Coast Customs* negotiates between expressing and aestheticising oppression. It got a lengthy and good review in the *TLS* although the social realities were denied: 'Respect for the moral indignation of the poetess, enjoyment of her curious versification and novel senses of vocabulary, cannot prevent us from feeling that the case against Lady Bamburgher is not sufficiently evidenced.'[81] In a later article, 'What is Slavery?' (1935), Sitwell was more direct:

77	Salter and Harper, 151.
78	Edith Sitwell, *Gold Coast Customs*, *CP*: 252–3.
79	Michael Roberts, *The Faber Book of Modern Verse*, 1936 (London: Faber, 1965), 29–30.
80	Ibid.
81	Review of *Gold Coast Customs*, by Edith Sitwell, *TLS* 21 February 1929: 137.

Have we not got the extreme swing back of the pendulum in the ugly curve of the slave system, when it swings from the 'hunger marcher', with his banner-inscription: 'Feed us, or shoot us', to the charity-dancer, with his card of admittance, and its 'champagne included'?[82]

Although *Gold Coast Customs* reflects her hatred for the abuse of social privilege, Edith Sitwell did not situate herself with the younger generation of thirties poets. Typically, if not able to join them, she belittled them as a clique of minor talent, remarking, 'if they hadn't all been at Oxford together, they would never have been heard of'.[83] The longer lines and the despair at human barbarity in *Gold Coast Customs* anticipate the style of 'Still Falls the Rain' (1940). This and other later poems like 'Street Song' and 'The Song of the Cold' demonstrate the pressure of responding to extreme national upheavals which was taking precedence over avant-garde aesthetics between the wars and particularly during and after the Second World War.

Nancy Cunard, Iris Tree and Helen Rootham

Introduction

The women in *Wheels,* a group of independent daughters of the upper classes, mark a developing boldness in twentieth-century poets which can be aligned with an aesthetic of self-dramatisation. Collectively, they presented a compelling and formidable front which contradicted the stereotypes of the feminine writer. Their poems record their attempts to deal with their guilt-ridden privileges through aestheticising their memories and exposing social differences. Their experiments with verbal textures register the influence of Edith Sitwell and also of the European artists and writers whom they encountered in Paris. Iris Tree had more poems than anyone else in *Wheels.* Her poems were also printed in other anthologies and magazines like *Vanity Fair* although *Poems* (1920) was her only published collection. Helen Rootham's contributions were fewer but included some unusual war poems and translations of prose poems by Rimbaud. Nancy Cunard's six poems in *Wheels* 1916 were her first to be published and there were others in most of the *Wheels* anthologies. Her poems were also printed in journals like *The English Review* and *New Age* and she published four collections: *Outlaws*

---

82 Edith Sitwell, 'What is Slavery?' *Sunday Referee* 3011, 19 May 1935: 12; Salter and Harper, 151–2.

83 Edith Sitwell, letter to David Horner, 18 May 1939, Pearson, 332.

(1921), *Sublunary* (1923), *Parallax* (1925) and *Poems (Two) 1925* (1930). She could work in several languages, writing poetry in English, French and Spanish, and was meticulous as a translator.

The collection of tributes and writings to Nancy Cunard in Hugh Ford's *Nancy Cunard: Brave Poet, Indomitable Rebel 1896–1965,* (1968) is the main source of information concerning Cunard and her cultural milieu. Iris Tree's entry, "'We shall never forget": for Nancy Cunard', reminisces about their rebellion against the aspirations of their parents. Born in Leicestershire, England, Nancy Cunard was the daughter of Maude Alice Burke, a Californian socialite, and Sir Bach Cunard, son of Samuel Cunard, the founder of the shipping company. She was often alone in her childhood and looked after by a governess. Her mother expected her to make a high society marriage, but she rejected the extravagance and élitism of the British upper class which she had experienced at home and in exclusive schools in London and abroad. She had a short unhappy marriage and moved to Paris in 1920 where she became a familiar figure in Montparnasse. Iris Tree was the daughter of Sir Herbert Beerbohm Tree. (The writer Sir Max Beerbohm was her uncle's half-brother.) She was educated by a governess and then at Miss Woolff's school where she became close friends with Nancy Cunard. Iris Tree's mother wanted her to be conventionally feminine but her father treated her as the son he would have liked. In Freudian terms, she thus experienced the alienation which would obstruct the development of 'normal femininity'. However, both parents enjoyed poetry and acting, and Iris's childhood was spent around artistic people and theatres. Against her parents' better judgement, she married an American, Curtis Moffatt, was separated from him by 1924 and divorced in 1933. During the 1920s she took an apartment in Paris where she met up again with Nancy Cunard and other intellectuals of the Left Bank. She later married Friedrich Ledebur and lived with him nomadically between the United States and London.

Although rarely mentioned in literary histories, they feature in literary reviews and the memoirs and correspondence of their contemporaries. According to William Carlos Williams, Nancy Cunard and Iris Tree stood out in a group of 'young and arresting young women' in Paris:

> I couldn't make them out. I'm sure I didn't look at them as women ... they were ... young, detached from reality, without passion. They, young as they were, had had bitter early experiences without emotional response. There was nothing left in either of them. They were completely empty, and yet they were young, appealing and unassailable.[84]

---

84   William Carlos Williams, *Nancy Cunard: Brave Poet, Indomitable Rebel 1896–1965*, ed. Hugh Ford (Philadelphia: Chilton Book Company, 1968), 56–7.

Here, Williams detected the damaging effects of their privileged but stifling backgrounds which had caused them to move away from their family homes. They investigated alternative subjectivities through self-dramatising in their appearances and writing. Retrospectively, Iris Tree perceived their 'forbidden artifice', such as white face powder, lip rouge and cigarette smoking, as costuming devices for assuming a different identity from their parents. Nancy Cunard also adopted fictional roles through mimicry and singing. At the beginning of the First World War, before the young men were taken away, they congregated secretly in studio attics, hotels, pubs, river barges and cab shelters. Iris Tree recorded the excited atmosphere of independence in a changing cultural climate:

> It was an epoch of romantic discovery which had outgrown the strictures and sentimentalities of Victorian-Edwardian England, yet kept its manners and classical scholarship articulate, satirical, poetical. Transition and danger were in the air. We responded like chameleons to every changing colour, turning from Meredith to Proust, to Dostoievsky, slightly tinged by the *Yellow Book*, and occasional Absinthe left by Baudelaire and Wilde, flushed by Liberalism, sombered by nihilistic pessimism, challenged by Shaw, inspired by young Rupert Brooke, T.S. Eliot, Yeats, D.H. Lawrence; jolted by Wyndham Lewis's *Blast* into cubism and the Modern French Masters, 'Significant Form,' Epstein's sculptures, Stravinsky's music (booed and cheered); the first Russian ballets and American jazz; nightlong dancing, dawnlong walks; exultant, longing, laughing, loves unspotted by respectable sin.[85]

As seen with Edith Sitwell's experiments, Iris Tree's references to the new art and music forms and to the Russian ballet are particularly significant because these provided sources for their poetry. The correspondences between avant-garde poetry and contemporary art was recognised in a particularly considered review of *Wheels* in *The Lancet*:

> The idea of these young poets is that the role of poetry is rather to crystallise fleeting views and aspects, to catch and fix vague and half-formed ideas, than to do any of the brave things associated in popular literature with the title of poet – to lead, to uplift, to amaze. The inspiration of these nine different writers – different in style, technique and standard of accomplishment – has been a common one. They strive to show that any impression received by one person should be communicable to others by the medium of symbolic word-pictures. We recommend the book to lovers of verse.[86]

---

85 Iris Tree, Ford, 18.
86 'Press Notices', *Wheels* 1917: 108–9; *Wheels* 1972: 19.

Like Edith Sitwell's, their canvases of fantastical figures are psychological evasions typical of the more radical post-war writing, but it resists romantic or pastoral nostalgia. In 'Iris of Memories', a tribute to Iris Tree and published in *Sublunary* (1923), Nancy Cunard's idealised version of the past is a self-conscious fabrication:

> Do you remember in those summer days
> When we were young how often we'd devise
> Together of the future?
> ...
> And there were wandering journeys to the sea
> In dusty trains; there thrilling on the sands
> Your scarlet dress grew vivid, and your hands
> Evoked with witty gesture, palms of glee,
> Things we had laughed at lovingly – for then,
> Ah even then we loved our memories – [87]

The poem also refers to their early efforts with writing poetry. At times in this poem, the attention to iambic pentameters and rhyming seems to drive the sense but also achieved a natural idiom in an easy and confident first person voice.

Like 'Iris of Memories', many of Cunard's poems in *Sublunary* address the intersection of the past and present in the operations of consciousness, but they do not retreat into nostalgia. The evocation of the pre-war long summer in 'Iris of Memories' is an interesting contrast to Cunard's assertion that she 'never grieves for things gone by' in 'To the Eiffel Tower Restaurant'. The poem considers, rather than participates in, the post-war 'culture of tranquillity':

> Espéranto ...
> The seal on your letter sets me thinking
> Of other days and places,
> And now I have the past to kneel before my present;
> Those old nights of drinking,
> Furtive adventures, solitary thinking
> At the corner table, sheltered from the faces,
> Inopportune invasion of the street.
> I feel
> Sharp tugs at my memory's sleeve:
> The sound of the clock going wrong,

---

87   Nancy Cunard, 'Iris of Memories', *Sublunary*, by Cunard (London: Hodder and Stoughton, 1923), 14–15; reprinted in Ford, 24–5.

The fleet
Procession of your waiters with their platters –
Drinks held long
In one hand, while the other unwinds a discussion.
I do not grieve,
I never grieve
For things gone by [88]

In addition to its treatment of memory, the poem is interesting for its experiments with a colloquial voice and free verse. It is also a record of the so-called 'Eiffel Tower group' who were located in 'Fitzrovia', between Bloomsbury and Soho, during the nineteen twenties and thirties. The Eiffel Tower restaurant in Percy Street became the centre of this 'Higher Bohemia':

I think the Tower shall go up to heaven
One night in a flame of fire, about eleven.
I always saw our carnal-spiritual home.
Blazing upon the sky symbolically ...
If ever we go to heaven in a troop
The Tower must be our ladder,
Vertically
Climbing the ether with its swaying group.
God will delight to greet this embassy
Wherein is found no lack
Of wits and glamour, strong wines, new foods, fine looks, strange-sounding
     languages of diverse men – [89]

As John Pearson records, 'in 1915 the Eiffel Tower had just been discovered by a number of the more intelligent and adventurous "artistic" children of the rich ... These included Beerbohm Tree's rebellious daughter Iris – already a distinctly *outrée* student at the Slade – Lady Diana Manners and Lady Cunard's nineteen year-old daughter Nancy, for whom the Eiffel Tower became "our carnal-spiritual home"'.[90]

Nancy Cunard, Lady Diana Manners and Iris Tree aroused fascination because they were allegedly 'an inseparable trio of beauties'[91] but defied conventional femininity. The fascination they aroused is projected in the various portraits of them. Iris Tree had attended the Slade School of Art and

---

88   Nancy Cunard, 'To the Eiffel Tower Restaurant', *Sublunary*, 93–5; reprinted in Ford, 67–8.
89   Ibid.
90   Pearson, 99–100.
91   Janet Flanner, 'Nancy Cunard', Ford, 97.

became a close friend of Dora Carrington who did her portrait. Her portrait was also painted by Vanessa Bell, Duncan Grant, Roger Fry and Augustus John. Nancy Cunard was frequently painted, sculptured and photographed by artists like Alvaro Guevara, Constantin Brancusi and Cecil Beaton. Together, these independent upper class women were strong public figures who constructed a new image of the woman artist as both beautiful and intellectual.

Nancy Cunard

According to William Carlos Williams, Nancy Cunard was 'one of the major phenomena of that world'[92] and, apparently, she 'knew everybody, was known by everybody' in the post-war London literary generation.[93] In addition to William Carlos Williams she met Edith Sitwell, Anna Wickham, Virginia and Leonard Woolf, Wyndham Lewis, Aldous Huxley, T.S. Eliot, and Ezra Pound – who helped her to become a poet. Some of her poems written in the nineteen twenties, such as 'By the Dordogne', 'Toulonnaise' and 'A Vis a Vis', record places which she visited in France.[94] In her own memoir, 'Glimpses of the Twenties', Cunard remembers moving around several apartments in Paris, where she attended and held parties.

Although Raymond Mortimer, perhaps with the romanticism of nostalgia, remembers, 'in those blissful days, her ruling passion was for poetry, not politics',[95] Nancy Cunard did not seem to polarise them. In a letter to Ezra Pound, dated 1946, her challenge to his ideological shift indicates her own standpoint: 'It is inconceivable to me that an "intellectual" should collaborate with fascism.' She recalled his influence on her in 1915 when he was 'an intellectual revolutionary' who taught her to aim for artistic toughness – 'as hard as the side of an engine'.[96] All through her writing, she connects ideological with aesthetic principles. Whether she underwent a sudden change from hedonism to socialism is debatable although Nancy Cunard clearly became more politically active towards the end of the 1920s and during the 1930 when she produced her compilation of black writing *Negro* (1934) and worked for the Spanish Republicans during the Civil War.[97] Her anti-racist

---

92   William Carlos Williams, Ford, 56.
93   Janet Flanner, Ford, 87.
94   Nancy Cunard, Ford, 64–6.
95   Raymond Mortimer, Ford, 48.
96   Nancy Cunard, letter to Ezra Pound, 11 June 1946; reprinted in *The Gender of Modernism*, ed. Bonnie Kime Scott (Indianapolis: Indiana University Press, 1990), 80–83.
97   For more discussion of Cunard's poetry in the 1930s, see *Women's Poetry of the 1930s: a critical anthology*, ed. Jane Dowson (London: Routledge, 1996).

activities were no doubt stimulated by her friendship with Paul Robeson in Paris during the 1920s.

In 1928, Nancy Cunard founded The Hours Press in order to help young poets and to promote contemporary poetry. The press was started at Réanville in Normandy, six miles from Paris, and moved to Paris at the end of the 1920s. According to Wyn Henderson, the former editor of Aquila Press who had worked there when his own press collapsed, The Hours Press in Rue Guengaud, was an important daily meeting place for writers at around five o'clock.[98] Her aim was to publish 'mainly poetry of an experimental kind', especially if it was not published anywhere else.[99] The Hours Press was an important instrument of the international network of modernist writing and in England she found promotional reports of The Hours Press in journals like the *Observer* and the *Nation*. It published, among others, George Moore, Norman Douglas, Richard Aldington, Robert Graves and Laura Riding, Samuel Beckett's 'Whoroscope' and a draft of Ezra Pound's *Cantos XXX*. It also printed six numbers of *Les Poètes du Mondes Défendent le Peuple Éspagnol*, which included poems by Neruda, Albertis and Tzara. Nancy Cunard aimed to distribute the new writing in London, New York, Paris and Florence.[100]

Nancy Cunard's poems are difficult to get hold of and many remain uncollected. Ford's anthology prints selections from all her published books and also from *Wheels* which are not her best. John Press picked out her 'Wheels' as an example of the dominance of 'the world of the opulent nursery' in the *Wheels* anthologies. Press's comment misrepresents the diversity of the anthologies, but it is true that 'Wheels' and some other poems by Cunard resemble the kaleidoscopic impressions of toyland or the circus:

> I sometimes think that all our thoughts are wheels
> Rolling forever through the painted world,
> Moved by the cunning of a thousand clowns
> Dressed paper-wise, with blatant rounded masks.[101]

Typically, she bridges personal and public discourses by moving between first person singular and plural. These carnival and nursery images, like the pierrots in Edith Sitwell's poems, can be read as imaginative retreats into the world of artistic fancy. Like Sitwell's, they are also symbols of a sensed chaos

---

98   Wyn Henderson, Ford, 158.
99   Nancy Cunard, *These Were the Hours: memories of my Hours Press Réanville and Paris 1928–1931* (London and Amsterdam: Walter Lowenfels, 1969), 7.
100 Nancy Cunard, *These Were the Hours*, 15.
101 Nancy Cunard, 'Wheels', *Wheels* 1916, vii.

underlying the respectable surface of modern life. 'The Carnivals of Peace' investigates the artist's dilemma between recording and aestheticising tragedy: 'I'd write a song to conquer all our tears,/lasting for ever through all the folding years.'[102] 'Uneasiness', on the same theme of a troubling modernity, was picked out for praise in the review of *Wheels* in Harriet Monroe's Chicago-based *Poetry: A Magazine of Verse*.[103]

Cunard was preoccupied with the possibilities of both metrical form and free verse and developed an aesthetic freedom away from the conventions of the British literary tradition. She drew upon newly available art forms to explore post-war nostalgia and social injustice. Her dominant form is the sonnet, but her work after 1920 was more adventurous with free verse and more allusive, although she was still attentive to rhythm and often worked in iambics. 'Ballad of 5, Rue de L'Etoile', set in Paris, uses dramatic monologue to explore the interaction between the environment and consciousness: 'I'll tell you how the women come and go/Seemly and neat – for love will have it so.'[104] Several of the poems in *Outlaws* (1921), like 'Voyages North' which is set in the streets of London, similarly, echo T.S. Eliot's 'The Love Song of J. Alfred Prufrock' in representing psychical detachment from Society:

> The strange effects of afternoons!
> Hours interminable, melting like honey drops
> In an assemblage of friends ...
> Or jagged, stretching hard unpleasant fingers
> As we go by, hurrying through the crowds – [105]

In France, Cunard was influenced by the dadaists and surrealists whose distortions of images which signify the unconscious emerge in some of her poetry. The two poems 'Simultaneous' and 'In Provins', which made up *Poems (Two) 1925,* originally published in 1930, mirror these new art forms in their free play of associated images:

> At one time
> The bottle hyacinths under Orvieto –
> At one time
> A letter a letter and a letter –

102 Nancy Cunard, 'The Carnivals of Peace', *Wheels* 1916: 29.
103 Ezra Pound, review of *Wheels* 1916. *Poetry: A Magazine of Verse*, reprinted in *Wheels* 1917: 110–11.
104 Nancy Cunard, 'Rue de L'Etoile', *Sublunary*, 17–19.
105 Nancy Cunard, 'Voyages North', *Outlaws* (London: Elkin Mathews, 1921), 47–8.

At one time, sleepless,
Through rain the nightingale sang from the river island –

At one time, Montparnasse,
Ánd all night's gloss
Splendour of shadow on shadow
With the exact flower
Of the liqueur in its glass.
      Time runs,
           but thought (or what?) comes
Seated between these damaged table-tops,
Sense of what zones, what simultaneous-time sense?[106]

The repetitions, particularly 'A letter a letter and a letter', the syntactical defamiliarisation and the displacement of common images parallel Gertrude Stein's anti-poetical devices. The frontispiece to *Parallax* (Hogarth Press, 1925) indicates Cunard's interest in perspective: '"Many things are known as some are seen, that is by parallaxis, or at some distance from their true and proper being" (Sir Thomas Browne).' She also explained that 'Parallax', 'Simultaneous' and 'In Provins' were influenced by Louis Aragon's technique of allusiveness, 'a kind of consequence'. (Aragon was one of the poets she promoted through the Hours Press.) Other poems like 'The Night',[107] set in Avignon, and 'From the Train', where the canvas is the Midlands and the North of England, further experiment with the verbal equivalent of French impressionist painting:

Smoke-stacks, coal-stacks, hay-stacks, slack,
Colourless, scentless, pointless, dull;
Railways, highways, roadways, black,
Grantham, Birmingham, Leeds and Hull.

Steamers, passengers, convoys, trains,
Merchandise travelling over the sea;
Smut-filled streets and factory lanes,
What can these ever mean to me?[108]

Although structuring a pictorial canvas, there is also an investigation of the

---

106 Nancy Cunard, 'Simultaneous', Putnam, 83–4.
107 Nancy Cunard, 'The Night', *Sublunary*, 56–7.
108 Nancy Cunard, 'From the Train', *Wheels* 1916: 34.

distance of the intellectuals and artists from the urban half of Britain associated with the 'mass' population.

Iris Tree

Apart from a reference in *The Trend of Modern Poetry* (Bullough 1941), Iris Tree's poems have been ignored by literary historians.[109] At the time, Raymond Mortimer considered her a 'gifted poet'[110] and she came out well in some reviews. 'The days come up as beggars in the street', impressed Edward Marsh who had it read at the Georgian Poetry Society.[111] In contrast, Geoffrey Bullough referred to the 'macabre' poems of Iris Tree as 'symptoms of an intellectual disease which was to afflict poetry for the next ten years'.[112] Although urgent about moving poetry away from its traditions, she often used regular forms, particularly in her war poems.

Most of Iris Tree's published poems were written between 1913 and 1918 and register her anti-war scepticism. The vehemence of her opposition to the First World War is likely to have been partly caused by its interruption to their liberated world and the loss of several friends put a stop to her carefree artistic pleasures. She also rebelled against the imperial principles which were propagated to justify the War:

> While we still cry to God for strength to kill,
> Reminding Him that Britain rules the waves,
> And grind young bones for the commercial mill,
> And build munition works among the graves.
>
> Still crying 'Honour', 'Country' and 'The Flag',
> 'The last heroic fight in Freedom's name!'
> Though Kings make mouths at Kings, and Prelates brag –
> They boast of murder and they reek of shame! ... [113]

Other poems similarly interrogate national pride and the ingloriousness of war.

---

109 Iris Tree's long narrative poem *The Marsh Picnic* (Cambridge: Rampant Lions Press, 1966) caused a small stir and she was congratulated by many readers.
110 Raymond Mortimer, Putnam, 49.
111 Daphne Fielding, *The Rainbow Picnic – a portrait of Iris Tree* (London: Methuen, 1974), 64–5. See 'Rear-Guard Modernism' for other reference to Tree's war poems.
112 Bullough, 198.
113 Iris Tree, 'Holy Russia', *Poems* (London and New York: John Lane, 1920), 65.

The rebellious tone provoked the judgement that Iris Tree was one of 'a school of revoltés at the present time who agree with her in making the world's perversity the first article in their creed, but from whom she differs in her communicativeness of candour'.[114] Tree's revolt was against the 'crumbling roads of worn-out creeds'.[115] The speakers in her poems represented a new generation who challenged an exhausted art, warmongering statesman, hypocritical church leaders and the self-satisfied rich of the older generation. The first poem in *Poems*, dated 1914, confronts the rhetoricians of Victorian morality by irreverently appropriating the regular form of nineteenth-century hymns: 'You preach to me of laws, you tie my limbs/With rights and wrongs and arguments of good.'[116] She connected the disabling anchor of the past with attachment to the excessive lamentation of traditional poetry. In 'My poems cannot laugh' she is 'Most tired of tunes that only learn to weep',[117] and the sonnet 'Shall we be christened poets' ends, 'How shall the world learn how to laugh again / When all its songs have only learnt to weep?'[118]

One aspect of modernity was a disillusion with the idealised pastoral combined with alienation from the urban environment. Several of Tree's poems, like 'Myself in the City', explore this psychological dislocation. 'Streets' is a lengthy free verse monologue which depicts the contradictory thrills and disorientations of city life:

> I know her well,
> The moaning highways,
> And whispering alleys,
> The chimney-dishevelled roofs
> Where the moon walks delicately
> As a stray spectral cat;
> The little forlorn squares
> Where one tree stands
> Drooping bedraggled fingers
> Over the benches where the people sit
> And stir not from their sullen postures.[119]

Here she seems versatile with the differing line lengths and cadences of free verse. She also experimented with polyphonic prose. Tree's voice of protest,

---

114 Review of *Poems* by Iris Tree, *TLS* 8 July 1920: 435.
115 Iris Tree, 'Holy Russia', ibid.
116 Iris Tree, untitled poem, *Poems*, 11.
117 Iris Tree, untitled poem, *Poems*, 79.
118 Iris Tree, untitled poem, *Poems*, 46.
119 Iris Tree, 'Streets', *Poems*, 109–11.

however, often inhabited familiar verse forms, including sonnets, quatrains and ballads. In these regular forms, the rhythmic changes accorded with Edith Sitwell's principles whereby rhyme and metre arbitrate between strangeness and reality. In an untitled poem, dated 1917, the insistent rhythm and rhyme associated with popular ballads mitigate the polemical tone. She took up the cause of the socially excluded who were caught in a cycle of poverty and crime:

> What will happen to the beggar, and the sinner, and the sad,
> And the drunk that drinks for sorrow, and the maimed, and mad;
> What will happen to the starving, and the rebel run from drilling,
> Cowardly afraid of fighting, and the child who stole a shilling?
> They shall go to prison black
> With a striped shirt on the back,
> Feast on bread and water there
> In a cell, without care.[120]

The combination of colloquial and formal diction is characteristic. Another poem, 'Pity the slain that laid away their lives', dated 1918, is on the same theme of the sinned-against disadvantaged. Like the previous poem it experiments with the effects of rhythm and rhyme in calling attention to social differences and war. The final verses are reminiscent of Edith Sitwell's *Gold Coast Customs* in their satire of London High Society which ignores the poor:

> Drowning our flutes, till the cries of the city
> Flurry us, flutter us, force us to pity,
> Force us to sigh and arrange a committee,
> Tea-party charity danced to a ditty ... [121]

The ending of the poem is weak and there are some unsatisfactory phrases, but Tree was shaking off archaic idioms and aiming for an effective speaking voice. Her passionate response to oppression links her to Nancy Cunard and to Winifred Holtby with whom she also developed a friendship.[122] Iris Tree's dominant themes were a sense of futility, war and city life. She also wrote some love lyrics, although the pronouns were gender neutral. In exploring identity, she drew on the terminology of psychoanalysis such as 'egoism' and 'introspection'. This move towards a more natural idiom and the difficulties

---

120 Iris Tree, untitled poem, *Poems*, 63.
121 Iris Tree, untitled poem, *Poems*, 70–1.
122 For a discussion and examples of Winifred Holtby's poetry, see Dowson, 62–8.

with articulating a response to social injustice without forgoing imaginative pleasure anticipate the artistic dilemmas of the thirties poets.

Helen Rootham

Helen Rootham did not have as many poems in *Wheels* as Edith Sitwell, Nancy Cunard or Iris Tree. She was, however, considered by the *Morning Post* to be the 'most profound and accomplished' of the contributors. She was gifted musically and is distinguished by her translations of Rimbaud which were commended as 'excellent' by Ezra Pound in *Poetry: A Magazine of Verse*.[123] Her poems also indicate the influence of the French symbolists, Baudelaire and Verlaine, whom she translated and whom she had introduced to Edith Sitwell, along with some contemporary poets, when she became her governess. She wrote a fine war poem, 'The Great Adventure', dedicated to the memory of E. Wyndham Tennant who was killed in action in 1917. As a monologue in which a young soldier's anticipation of personal glory turns into tragedy, it is similar to other contemporary mock-heroic poems. 'Envious Youth' investigates the generation war which much of the *Wheels* cycle seemed to be about:

> I am not old enough to claim the privilege of years,
> To sit apart and say to youth –
> 'Now watch my nodding wisdom.'[124]

Summary

Edith Sitwell, Nancy Cunard, Iris Tree and Helen Rootham were influential models of women poets who succeeded in avoiding the 'feminine' in their public image and poetry. Their difficulties in identifying themselves with their mothers and the symbolised maternal function for women arguably transferred to psychological conflicts with both the male literary tradition and the concept of a female line. As they dramatised their public images, so they experimented with new poetic effects, but their writing was rarely overtly woman-centred. Their appropriations of abstract art indicate a drive away from realist representations towards explorations of the contingency of language and consciousness. They manipulated the traditions of mainstream British poetry

---

123 Review of *Wheels* in *Poetry: A Magazine of Verse*. 'Press Cuttings', *Wheels* 1917, reprinted in *Wheels* 1972: 110–111.
124 Helen Rootham, 'The Great Adventure' and 'Envious Youth', *Wheels* 1916: 76–7.

and their resources were contemporary art, music and psychology. Their poetry represents an aesthetic freedom and confident individual voice in women and demonstrates that the avant-garde was not the exclusive property of men, nor of American poets. They proved that women could win respect in the intellectual atmosphere surrounding London and Paris and like their American counterparts, they took part in the battles for the progress of modern poetry against the reactionary popular and literary papers.

Chapter Five

The Anglo-American Avant-Garde: H.D. (1886–1961), Amy Lowell (1874–1925), Marianne Moore (1887–1972), Laura (Riding) Jackson (1901–1991), Gertrude Stein (1874–1946) and Mina Loy (1882–1966)

Introduction

Since high modernism has been gendered as male in British history, experimental poetics have become associated with men, yet contemporaneously women were significant participants in the avant-garde. The social and psychological independence, the critical writing and literary activities of these women indicate their involvement in new systems of representation and signification. I am adopting the classification 'Anglo-American' in recognition of the cultural interchanges effected by the magazines, which were often started or steered by women, and by the movement of writers between Europe and the United States. 'Anglo-American' also accommodates the ex-patriation of H.D. and Laura Riding, from America to England, and Mina Loy from England to New York.

To some extent these writers have been incorporated into the canons of twentieth-century American poetry but their status in Britain is still uncertain, largely because they do not fit orthodox classifications of 'British Poetry'. H.D. and Marianne Moore occasionally feature but Laura Riding and Amy Lowell are rarely included in critical works on literary modernism, although Lowell was one of the most active practitioners and promoters of imagism and free verse. H.D. and Gertrude Stein have had attention within American lesbian and feminist criticism but this has tended to dehistoricise their significance. One excuse for exclusion might be the difficulty of getting hold of their books, but there is no common formula. Much of Stein's work was not published in her lifetime and Mina Loy's poems were almost unobtainable until 1982, but Laura Riding and Marianne Moore have had healthy publishing histories, with several reprints and new editions. New biographies, the recent publication of Marianne Moore's letters (1998) and *Rational Meaning* by Laura Riding and Schuyler Jackson (1997) keep their reputations alive, but do not necessarily integrate them into modernist canons.[1] In this section, it is not possible or appropriate to fully assess each poet's work, but to register their significance to the avant-garde in Britain.

Through their travels, correspondence and the little magazines, these avant-garde women were instrumental in the international character of modernism, particularly during the nineteen twenties. The label 'Anglo-American' was used contemporaneously; it also proposes a co-operative and inclusive model of criticism in place of the more common rhetoric of competition. For example, Laura Riding was dismissed by Valentine Cunningham for being 'anyway, an American'[2] although she did not think it appropriate to be involved in an American number of *Twentieth-Century Verse*.[3] H.D. is often included in histories of modern American poetry although she settled in England for most of her writing career, yet Mina Loy is also identified as American when she crossed the Atlantic the other way. It is important to recognise the origins of these writers in order to read the sense of displacement in their work, often encoded through symbols drawn from their childhoods and their native locations. Their nationality does not, however, provide the prime reading position but they had to negotiate the complex intersection of their national and gendered identities in their public image as poets and in their creativity. H.D. and Amy Lowell, for example, were more united by Ezra Pound's betrayal of the imagists than by their American births.

The notable predominance of American poets in avant-garde modernism has been attributed to the caution of British post-war sensibilities which associated radical writing with violence or anarchism.[4] Morton Dauwen, assistant editor of *Poetry: A Magazine of Verse* from 1929 to 1936, however,

---

1   Bonnie Costello, Celeste Goodridge and Christanne Miller (eds), *The Selected Letters of Marianne Moore* (London: Faber, 1998); Laura Riding and Schuyler B. Jackson, *Rational Meaning: A New Foundation for the Definition of Words and Supplementary Essays*, ed. William Harmon, Introduction by Charles Bernstein (University Press of Virginia, 1997).

2   Valentine Cunningham, *British Writers of the Thirties* (Oxford: Oxford University Press, 1988), 26.

3   Julian Symons, 'How wide is the Atlantic? or Do you believe in America?', *Twentieth–Century Verse* 12–13, September–October 1938: 80–84.

4   See 'The Death of Futurism', by John Cournos. *Egoist* IV, January 1917: 6–7.

perceived that the First World War also hampered the optimistic mood and openness to experiment in the United States: 'The new poets were writing out of the havoc and agony of a troubled and disrupted world; they were no longer engrossed by the high excitements and novelties of the earlier decade.'[5] In the Editorial of *Poetry*, June 1914, Harriet Monroe claimed that 'In the United States we have naturally that direct break with the past which is artificial in European artists and poets',[6] but in the same year, W.B. Yeats observed that all Anglo-American poetry was traditionalist and that innovation came from France. In a speech in Chicago, cited in *Poetry*, April 1914, he commented, 'When I open the ordinary American magazine, I find that all we rebelled against in those early days – the sentimentality, the rhetoric, the "moral uplift" – still exists here. Not because you are too far from England, but because you are too far from Paris.'[7] The mutual influence of developments in America and England is difficult to measure but there is some evidence to support David Perkins' observation in 1976 that, 'the main single influence on both sides of the Atlantic over the last fifty years has, in each case, been the writing of the other country'.[8]

Although the British literary papers fuelled prejudice against America, and its association with 'mass' culture, *writers* were open to transatlantic exchanges. The American edition of the *Bookman* saw its role as mediating literary news between America and England, for 'Today as never before England and America are alive to a deepening intellectual sympathy and it is fitting that each knows the thought of the other as expressed in the best books on both sides of the Atlantic.'[9] In 1920, a Poetry Bookshop *Chapbook* 'gave English readers who regarded transatlantic poetry with patronising complacency, a much needed interpretation of ten writers', including Amy Lowell.[10] Publications like J.C. Squire's anthology, *American Poems and Others* (1923), Thomas Moult's *Best Poems* anthology in 1923, which set British and American writers side by side, *Our Best Poets: English and American* (1923), the *Anthology of Magazine Verse* and the *Yearbook of*

---

5 Morton Dauwen, 'The Last Fifteen Years: 1922–1936', ch. 34 in *A Poet's Life: seventy years in a changing world*, by Harriet Monroe (New York: The Macmillan Company, 1938).
6 Harriet Monroe, Editorial, *Poetry* 4. 3, June 1914: 107.
7 W.B. Yeats, cited in *Poetry* 4. 1, April 1914: 25.
8 David Perkins, *A History of Modern Poetry. Vol. 1. From The 1890s To The High Modernist Mode* (Cambridge, Massachusetts: Harvard University Press, 1976), vii.
9 Advertisement for the American edition of the *Bookman* in the London edition.
10 Poetry Bookshop *Chapbook*, no. 11. May 1920. Joy Grant, *Harold Monro and the Poetry Bookshop* (London: Routledge & Kegan Paul, 1967), 156.

American Poetry sustained the cross-cultural debates.[11] In 1938, a special edition of *Twentieth-Century Verse* admitted that American poets, including Marianne Moore and Laura Riding, had been underrated in Britain:

> In England we owe a great deal to these Americans, and especially to the American-Europeans; they have given us a lesson in austerity, and without them the poetry being written in England now could hardly be so various or so unsentimental as it is.[12]

As Sylvia Beach recorded, 'The best way of following the literary movement in the twenties is through the little reviews.'[13] Although the significance of the international network and the little magazines has been well written up in revisionary histories of modernism, I want to briefly centralise *women's* roles in them. In America, Harriet Monroe's *Poetry: A Magazine of Verse* was fundamental to the perceived literary renaissance before the First World War. Some commentaries have invented a meeting between Harriet Monroe and Ezra Pound in 1910 to exaggerate Pound's place in this renaissance.[14] As soon as 1938, Harriet Monroe recorded that her part was in danger of being forgotten:

> The battle which *Poetry*, from its first issue, fought for was a 'new movement' in the art – for freer technique, for stripped modern diction, for a more vital relation with the poet's own time and place, and especially for recognition of new talent – is in danger of being obscured by the mists of time and by propaganda for later literary interests. Babette Deutsch, for example, manages, with singular skill, to write a whole volume on Modern Poetry without a single mention of *Poetry* and its editor.[15]

---

11 Review of *Modern American Poets,* by Conrad Aiken (London: Martin Secker), *TLS* 2 November 1922: 703; review of *American Poems and Others*, ed. J.C. Squire (London: Hodder and Stoughton, 1923), *TLS* 28 June 1923: 436; review of *The Best Poems of 1923*, ed. Thomas Moult (London: Cape, 1923), *TLS*, 13 March 1924: 157; review of *Our Best Poets, English and american*, ed. Theodore Maynard, *TLS* 3 April, 1924: 210; review of *Anthology of Magazine Verse for 1926* and *Yearbook of American poetry*, ed. William Stanley Braithwaite (Boston: B.J. Brimmer), *TLS* 3 February 1927: 179.

12 Julian Symons, 'How wide is the Atlantic?': 83–4.

13 Sylvia Beach, *Shakespeare and Company* (London: Faber and Faber, 1960), 144.

14 Ellen Williams, *Harriet Monroe & the Poetry Renaissance: The first 10 years of Poetry 1912–1922* (Urbana: University of Illinois Press, 1977), 3.

15 Monroe, 362.

She was aware of the discrimination against women by The National Institute of Arts and Letters when she set up *Poetry* in 1912 and which continued when she was writing her memoir in the 1930s.[16] *Poetry* stimulated international correspondence and carried the *vers libre* debate during its first six years. Harriet Monroe gave prominence to Amy Lowell, T.S. Eliot and Ezra Pound – Pound was hardly known when the magazine started.[17] In the *Egoist*, J.G. Fletcher described Harriet Monroe as 'the editor who discovered imagism'.[18] She printed Pound's defence of imagism in Issue 1, October 1912, and the 'creed' in March 1913.[19] *Poetry* was advertised in the *Egoist* and made poets like Amy Lowell and William Carlos Williams more well known in Britain. Harriet Monroe travelled to Europe and made the acquaintance of many poets, including Edith Sitwell and Anna Wickham. In Paris she met other artists and writers on the Left Bank, and visited Sylvia Beach's bookshop *Shakespeare and Company* which had distributed *Poetry* in Paris. *Poetry* was initially run wholly by women – Alice Corbin Anderson became Harriet Monroe's editorial assistant – and it published more women than other journals did, notably Sarah Teasdale and Agnes Lee.[20] Articles on the Monros' The Poetry Bookshop in London were printed in *Poetry* and *The Little Review*.[21] *The Little Review* was established in New York in 1917 and Margaret Anderson and Jane Heap took it to Paris (1922–23) where they met writers like Gertrude Stein and Djuna Barnes who became important contributors. It was inclusive of women and European artists and writers. Its landmark was the serialisation of James Joyce's *Ulysses* which had been censored in Britain and for which the editors went on trial for obscenity. *The Dial* became more progressive when Marianne Moore took over as editor in 1925.

---

16 Monroe, 326–8. She is referring to *This Modern Poetry* by Babette Deutsch (London: Faber, 1936).

17 Harriet Monroe, letter to Ezra Pound, 13 October 1913; Ellen Williams, 78.

18 J.G. Fletcher, *Egoist* I, 30 December 1914: 174.

19 See Gillian Hanscombe and Virginia Smyers, *Writing for their Lives: The Modernist Women 1910–1940* (London: The Women's Press, 1987), 151–5.

20 Some women published in the magazines do seem to belong to the earlier tradition, but others like Sara Teasdale, Frances Gregg, Helen Hoyt, Agnes Lee – who was not well-known before Harriet Monroe promoted her work in *Poetry* – and Margaret Widner, whose work was frequently published in *Poetry,* are worthy of attention. For discussion of Teasdale, Hoyt and Lee, see Monroe 322–4. For discussion of Teasdale, see Ellen Williams, 77–280.

21 Amy Lowell, 'The Poetry Bookshop'. *Little Review* II, May 1915: 19–22 and Harriet Monroe, 'The Editor in England', *Poetry* XIII, October 1923: 35.

In Britain, *The Egoist* was initially edited by Harriet Shaw Weaver, Dora Marsden and Richard Aldington; H.D. became assistant editor in 1916.[22] Significantly, its subtitle, 'Our War is with Words' indicates that women like Dora Marsden associated modernism's revolution of the word with feminist politics. It stimulated debate about new poetry in Europe and America and published poems by women including Charlotte Mew, Anna Wickham, Frances Gregg, H.D., Amy Lowell, Marianne Moore and May Sinclair. It printed articles and correspondence with Harriet Monroe, 'the distinguished editress of *Poetry*',[23] and reported on the obscenity trial of *The Little Review*.[24] It also promoted *Poetry* and *The Little Review* through advertisements. The liberal feminist British journal *Time and Tide*, which started in 1920, was a women's initiative and published poetry and criticism by women, along with articles on the arts, politics and news. The reviewers of American and European literature were disposed to be favourable and it reported at length on America's progress towards equalities in law.[25]

In Paris, Nancy Cunard's The Hours Press and Sylvia Beach's *Shakespeare and Company* bookshop and lending library were also vehicles for promoting poets internationally. British and American poets came into contact with European ideas and art when they connected with writers and artists on the Left Bank. Gertrude Stein's revolutionary principles and writing most clearly influenced Mina Loy and to some extent Laura Riding and Edith Sitwell. However, I can only mention her briefly since, apart from *Tender Buttons* (1914), her poetry was barely published in the period.

Mutual support clearly happened in pockets of the modernist network of intellectuals, but their independence makes the poets difficult to manipulate into a literary movement. There are stylistic connections between the imagist principles of H.D. and Amy Lowell or the subversions and transgressions of genre by Marianne Moore, Laura Riding, Gertrude Stein and Amy Lowell. Sitwell's and Stein's experiments with 'texture', the verbal equivalent to

---

22 T.S. Eliot took over as editor of *The Egoist* in 1917. For Eliot's complaints about women's involvement in magazines, see letter from T.S. Eliot to Ezra Pound, 15 April 1915/ *The Letters of T.S. Eliot: Vol. 1. 1898–1922*, ed. Valerie Eliot (London: Faber, 1988), 418, and Sandra Gilbert and Susan Gubar, *No Man's Land: The Place Of The Woman Writer In The Twentieth Century. Vol. 3. Letters to the Front* (New Haven: Yale University Press, 1994), 67.

23 T.S. Eliot, *Egoist* V, November–December 1918: 133–4.

24 See T.S. Eliot, *Egoist* V, March 1918: 39.

25 For example, 'Aspects of British and American Feminism', by Anne Martin, *Time and Tide* 21 and 28 March 1924: 268 and 292. For more discussion of *Time and Tide*, see *Women's Poetry of the 1930s*, ed. Jane Dowson (London: Routledge, 1996), 181–7.

modern art and music, influenced Nancy Cunard and Mina Loy – Stein's principles were especially influential on Mina Loy's *logopoeia*. All poets aimed to awaken their readers to new levels of consciousness.

Within feminist criticism there are competing views over whether modernist subversions of orthodox language structures suppressed or liberated women: one view is that writers like H.D. or Marianne Moore were impelled by Ezra Pound's dictum to 'make it new' and 'broke form *for* the boys'.[26] The opposing perspective is that since the common aesthetic of modernist texts, understood as anti-narrative structures, mythmaking and elliptical syntax, are features associated with feminine writing, modernist experimentation was driven by women. The conjunction of modernist and feminist aesthetics, however, is in danger of producing the converse equation between non-experimental and patriarchal writing, without considering its subject matter or context. As with the 'British avant-garde', the poets in this section are stylistically experimental but also unsettle binary oppositions between 'personality' and 'impersonality' or 'expressive' and 'self-reflexive'. They avoid associations of femininity through various impersonations and transformations, including animals. Their challenges to linguistic conventions which dismantle traditional systems of representation also contest conventional prescriptions of gender. Although the gender politics is rarely overt, even the most abstract verse of Marianne Moore and Laura Riding shows an interest in changing gender relations. The lesbian love poetry by Stein, Lowell and H.D. can be situated as one of several modernisms. The single status of Marianne Moore, Laura Riding and Edith Sitwell was also radical in a social context which only recognised heterosexual marriage as a valid arrangement.[27]

As Alicia Ostriker observes,

> In an age when it was widely believed that 'women are the cause of modernism, whatever that is' – as one journalist put it – these writers were at the provocative edge of the avant-garde … with the advent of modernism, they strove to escape the ghetto of feminine poetry by the leaps and bounds of undisguised intelligence.[28]

---

26 Celeste M. Schenck, 'Exiled by genre: Modernism, Canonicity, and the Politics of Exclusion', in Mary Lynn Broe and Angela Ingram (eds), *Women's Writing in Exile* (Chapell Hill: University of Carolina Press, 1989), 246, n. 6.

27 Laura Riding had divorced her first husband and lived in Europe as a single woman, albeit in a *ménage a trois* with the Graves in Mallorca.

28 Alicia Ostriker, *Stealing the Language: The Emergence of Women's Poetry in America* (London: The Women's Press, 1987), 48.

The common aesthetic is their avoidance of femininity by strategies of masking and dramatisation 'Masking' was a motif of male modernism – T.S. Eliot's 'objective correlative', Yeats' masks and Pound's *Personae*[29] – and although much women's poetry seems genderless in its conscious substitution of objectified emotion for the personal subject of traditional, that is early nineteenth-century Romantic lyric poetry, there is often a gendered awareness in their work – what Ostriker calls, 'evasive self-representation':

> the avant-garde women modernists veil their critique of culture behind a dazzle of stylistics, a film of distance – Lowell's jocularity, Stein's wordplay, Loy's jagged form, H.D.'s Greece, Moore's enamelled objects and embroidered quotations.[30]

H.D., Amy Lowell and Imagism

Labelled as imagists, H.D. and Amy Lowell have been tied to a movement of debatable significance, yet even their roles as imagists have been unevenly registered in British literary histories. The instability of their status also results from the difficulty in classifying them because they blur distinctions between personal and impersonal or male and female poetics. As Susan Friedman observes: '[H.D.] forged an impersonal lyric discourse that deeply encoded gender issues but did not directly address them. Her hard crisp lines with no excess word or sentiment defied the stereotype of the feminine "poetess"'.[31] As an American who spent most of her life in London, H.D. also crosses national delineations. She rarely features in records of modernism in Britain, although she has been canonised by the lesbian academic communities in Europe and the United States. Revisionary criticism has attempted to rescue her from the imagist label by looking at her early work in the context of her literary development rather than of the imagist movement. Viewing imagism as a precursor to modernism both elevates and diminishes its status but there is no consensus about its validity. Writing imagist poems was important to the stylistic development of writers like H.D., Amy Lowell and Richard Aldington, and the imagist credo and anthologies provoked controversy which

---

29   Ezra Pound, *Personae: The Collected Shorter Poems of Ezra Pound*, 1909 (USA: Boni and Liveright, 1926).

30   Ostriker, 53.

31   Susan Friedman, *The Gender of Modernism*, ed. Bonnie Kime Scott (Bloomington and Indianapolis: Indiana University Press, 1990), 86.

influenced contemporary practice. A case can be made that H.D. and Amy Lowell were mobilisers of imagism, without confining them to it, and that imagist principles of concrete observation, clarity and specificity were a 'kick-start' to the eschewal of personal lyrics and high rhetoric which has come to characterise modernist principles.

Peter Faulkner (1986), like John Press (1969) and John Williams (1987), places imagism in the centre of modernism: 'imagism fell apart as a group, but it had administered a sharp critique of prevailing poetic practices which, in complex association with the grim effects of the great war on the English sensibility, was to help to change English poetry in undeniable ways'.[32] The imagists also contributed significantly to establishing connections between poets in Britain and the United States. *The Egoist* produced a special number 'devoted to the works of the young Anglo-American group of poets known as "The Imagists"', whose names included Amy Lowell, H.D., Marianne Moore and May Sinclair.[33] Frank Mott endorses imagism as a significant Anglo-American movement: 'The group of English-American imagists broke up after publishing a few anthologies, and a reaction set in during the late twenties; but a certain liberating effect continued.'[34]

According to Andrew Thacker, imagism is widely acknowledged as 'the first significant Anglo-American movement in modernist poetry' but the tendency to view imagism through Poundian eyes overlooks the centrality of H.D. and Amy Lowell:

> It would be more appropriate to view H.D. as the stylistic innovator of the group, rather than as the poet whose work was labelled and cultivated by Pound as 'H.D. imagiste'. Lowell, attacked by Pound for hijacking the very term 'imagisme' and for blurring its aesthetic of 'hard, light, clear edges', arranged for three imagist anthologies to be published with far more commercial success than Pound's first anthology. Lowell conceded that Pound invented the name 'imagism' but argued that 'changing the whole public attitude from derision to consideration came from my work'. Lowell also produced the first critical book on American and modern verse – *Tendencies in Modern American Poetry* (1917) – which introduced Bryher to the poetry of her future partner H.D., and exhaustively promoted the new poetry across America by public readings

32 Peter Faulkner (ed.), *A Modernist reader: Modernism in England 1910–1930* (London: Batsford, 1986), 18.

33 Advert in *Egoist* III, 1 April 1915: 63.

34 Frank Luther Mott, *A History of American Magazines. Vol. V: sketches of twenty one magazines 1905–1930* (Cambridge, Massachusetts: Harvard University Press, 1968), 230.

(including perhaps the first reading of modernist poetry on American radio) and journal articles.[35]

Although Ezra Pound's naming of H.D. as 'imagiste' in the British Museum tea-room is a literary legend, the damaging effect of his desertion of imagism is less publicised. In her letters to Amy Lowell, H.D. expressed her gratitude at being rescued from Pound's manipulation:

> R[Richard Aldington] asks me to say that *in no event can we now appear under the direct title of 'imagiste'* – It is obviously E[Ezra]'s plan to prevent our publication and he believes that Macmillan is printing the book. Our dropping the title gives him the satisfaction of feeling that he has secured a victory and gives us the exquisite relief of being free of him.[36]

Given that she dropped the 'imagiste' title in 1914 and was later critical of the prescriptiveness of the imagist movement, it is an historical irony that H.D. was persistently connected with imagism and consequently underestimated during her life. Additionally, the desertion by Pound has been perceived as a deliberate feminisation of the 'movement' when it is likely that H.D. and Amy Lowell espoused the anti-sentimental principles of imagism partly to avoid feminine identification.

H.D.

H.D. was involved in the making of avant-garde poetics through her promotion of Marianne Moore and Amy Lowell and through the influence of her poems on them, particularly Lowell. She also helped to free women from the poetess stigma by the respect which she won from her male contemporaries, famously Ezra Pound, Richard Aldington and D.H. Lawrence. It is difficult to measure her explicit influence on women in Britain, but she enjoyed the mutual regard of May Sinclair, Dorothy Richardson and Edith Sitwell. H.D. initially became known in Britain and America through the imagist and other anthologies and through the progressive journals. In 1912, Harriet Monroe professed that she did not know H.D. but admired her poems and published them periodically in *Poetry* to represent the 'essence' of imagism.[37] H.D. was widely reviewed

35   Andrew Thacker, 'Amy Lowell and H.D.: The Other Imagists', *Women: a cultural review* 4. 1 (Spring 1993): 49–59.
36   H.D., letter to Amy Lowell, 17 December 1914; Scott, *Gender of Modernism*, 134.
37   Harriet Monroe, *Poetry* 1. 1 and 1. 6, October–March 1912/3: 118, 150–3.

and anthologised as the perfect imagist after *Sea Garden* (1916).[38] In 1915, she was awarded *Poetry*'s Guarantor's Prize and in 1917 won the *Vers Libre* contest in *The Little Review*. In 1917, D.H. Lawrence sent Edward Marsh a copy of the *Imagist* anthology, adding, 'I think H.D. is good: none of the others are worth anything', and a week later reiterated, 'Don't you think H.D. – Mrs Aldington – writes some good poetry? I do – really very good.'[39] He singled out 'The God' and 'Adonis' for Marsh and sent them to *The Egoist* which printed her poems in about half its editions. In *The Egoist,* although T.S. Eliot denounced Amy Lowell for being 'remorselessly intimate', he proposed that some works of H.D. and Fletcher 'entitled them to international standing'.[40]

The simultaneous recognition of H.D.'s work in Britain and the United States indicates how the international network constructed the reputations of new writers. Richard Aldington published a promotional article, 'A Young American Poet', in *The Little Review*, in which he argued that H.D. had been neglected because her output was small, the originality made her poems seem obscure, the use of her initials was off-putting and she had no friends among the professional critics. He appealed to the Americans to have a more open attitude than the British traditionalists: 'You must remember that there are very, very few people in England who have the faintest idea what is meant by *vers libre.*'[41]

When he sent H.D.'s poems to Harriet Monroe for *Poetry* magazine, Ezra Pound decreed them to be 'modern' in the terms of imagist principles:

I say modern, for it is the laconic speech of the imagistes even if the subject is classic. At least H.D. had lived with these things since childhood, and knew them before she had any book-knowledge of them.

This is the sort of American stuff that I can show here and in Paris without it being ridiculed. Objective – no slither; direct – no excessive use of adjectives, no metaphors that won't permit examination. It's straight talk, straight as the Greek! And it was only by persistence that I got to see it at all.[42]

---

38   H.D.'s 'The Last Gift' ('The Gift' in *CP*), 'The God', 'Adonis', 'Pygmalion' and 'Eurydice' were printed in *The Egoist* 1916–7 and these last four were included in *Some Imagist Poets*, ed. Amy Lowell, 1917.

39   D.H. Lawrence, letter to Edward Mash, 21 and 29 January 1917, *The Letters of D.H. Lawrence*, Vol. 2, June 1913–October 1916, ed. George J. Zytaruk and James Boulton (Cambridge: Cambridge University Press, 1981), 61, 84.

40   T.S. Eliot, 'Disjecta Membra', review of *Some Tendencies in American Poetry*, by Amy Lowell. *Egoist* V, April 1918: 55.

41   Richard Aldington, 'A Young American Poet', *Little Review* March 1915: 22.

42   Letter from Ezra Pound to Harriet Monroe, n.d. (October 1912). *The Selected Letters of Ezra Pound 1907–1941*, ed. D.D. Paige (New York: New Directions, 1950), 11.

As Pound suggested, H.D.'s poetry exemplifies the objectivity which was a central tenet of literary modernism, but it is not, as he suggested, 'straight talk'. She was not rejecting poetic conventions of form and symbolism for a universal language but for a new system of signification. She defamiliarised the reader by displacing traditional symbols like the red rose:

> Rose, harsh rose,
> marred and with stint of petals,
> meagre flower, thin,
> sparse of leaf,
>
> more precious
> than a wet rose,
> single on a stem –
> you are caught in the drift.[43]

H.D. typically interrogates literary representations of women through distorting conventional symbols of femininity and romance – 'nouns are delicately beautiful things which the verbs violate; cultural clichés and the treatment of women as delicate flowers are under attack'.[44] 'Sea Rose' was anthologised in influential anthologies like Harold Monro's *Twentieth-century Poetry* (1929) and *The Faber Book of Modern Verse* (1936). It illustrates that for women imagists, at least, the principles were not an end in themselves but techniques for bypassing literary conventions and awakening new perceptions.

'Hermes of the Waves', another of her most frequently printed and analysed poems, was used by Richard Aldington to exemplify imagism in 'Modern Poetry and the imagists', published in *The Egoist*, 1914.[45] He applauded the paradigmatic mixture of personality and objectivity: 'hard, direct treatment, absolutely personal rhythm, few and expressive adjectives, no inversions, and a keen emotion presented objectively.' The untranslatable metaphors drew attention to the unpresentable aspects of personal, as well as national, consciousness:

> Wind rushes
> Over the dunes,

---

43   H.D. 'Sea Rose', *Collected Poems 1912–1944*, ed. Louis L. Martz (New York: New Directions, 1983), 5.

44   A.D. Moody, 'H.D. Imagiste: An Elemental Mind', *Agenda* 25, 3–4 (Autumn/Winter 1987): 82.

45   Richard Aldington, 'Modern Poetry and the Imagists', *Egoist* I, I June 1914: 201–2.

And the coarse, salt-crushed grass
Answers.

Heu,
It whips round my ankles![46]

Identity, like the creative act, is foregrounded as a *process* here. In responding to Harold Monro's non-committal assessment of imagism in *The Egoist*, May Sinclair called 'Hermes of the Ways' the perfect poem: 'The poetry of H.D. *proves* the power of the clean, naked, sensuous image to carry the emotion without rhyme – *not*, I think, without rhythm; the best imagist poems have a very subtle and beautiful rhythm – and always without decoration.'[47] In a lengthy and discerning review of *The Poems of H.D.*, also in *The Egoist*, F.S. Flint praised her excellent combination of precision and evocation in 'Hermes of the Ways', 'Sitalkas', and 'Pines': 'Is it not evident that we have a woman who is creating a body of poetry that is original in its form, spirit and imagery?' He identified H.D.'s simultaneous dissolution and reconstruction of personality through symbol.[48] In *The Little Review*, Richard Aldington cited 'Hermes of the Ways' to illustrate H.D.'s paradoxical 'accurate mystery', achieved by her combination of the local and the remote, the sea coast of New England and ancient Hellenic myths.[49] One of the most convincing recent discussions of 'Hermes of the Ways' as a modernist text is by Hanscombe and Smyers. Like Flint and Aldington, they identify how the immediacies of experience intersect with 'timeless moments':

> The development of the image in H.D.'s poem follows the lyric of association rather than the logic of discourse: it is not necessary to know – but it is wonderful to know – that the wind and the grass rush and whip.[50]

H.D. specifically investigated the interplay between various states of consciousness. Her 'Notes on Thought and Vision' never had the chance to be an influential articulation of modernist poetics in its time, but it explains her theory of 'over-mind' – or 'super-mind' – and 'sub-conscious mind'. She believed that the job of an artist was to represent the condition of

---

46 H.D., 'Hermes of the Waves', *CP* 1983, 37–9.
47 May Sinclair, 'Two Notes', *Egoist* II, 1 June 1915: 88–9.
48 F.S. Flint, review of *The Poems of H.D. Egoist* II, 1 May 1915: 72–3.
49 Richard Aldington, *Little Review* March 1915: 22.
50 Hanscombe and Smyers, 173–4.

'over-conscious mind' which is 'the world of waking dreams and the world great lovers enter, spiritual lovers, but only the greatest'.[51]

I have indicated how H.D. was considered by men and women to exemplify imagist principles and that she was also implicitly a modernist in her representations of the changing conditions of consciousness. To this end, she defamiliarised readers' expectations through her textual mystifications. Her refiguring of literary forms and symbols were also deliberate appropriations of male cultural authority. It is well-documented that she studied the representation of women in the major genres of classical literature. Between 1918 and 1920 she wrote many notes on Greek authors and reviewed classical works for *Adelphi*.[52] Imagist principles of economy and observation contradicted the epic's attention to the heroics of war which excluded or idealised women. Her refabrications of ancient myths subverted traditional inscriptions of gender and her reworking of Sappho and classical poetics was particularly important to the transference of cultural power, because they were the starting points of western literary tradition.

In 'Eurydice', printed in *The Egoist*, May 1917, H.D. literally reverses the male gaze; through dramatic monologue, Eurydice complains against Orpheus whose looking back condemned her to the underworld for ever:

> So you have swept me back,
> I who could have walked with the live souls
> above the earth,
> I who could have slept among the live flowers
> at last;
>
> so for your arrogance
> and your ruthlessness
> I am swept back [53]

Eurydice's fate represents the relegation of women to an eternal subculture. The poem does not finally contradict this fate because it reinvents her capitulation to male mastery.

Gilbert and Gubar consider that H.D.'s early explorations of female immobilisation, as in 'Eurydice', both accepted and rebelled against the literary tropes of feminism, but that she progressed from this initial dependence on the male tradition to autonomous creativity:

51   H.D. 'Notes on Thought and Vision', Scott, *Gender of Modernism*, 93–109.
52   DuPlessis, 4 and 133, n. 9.
53   H.D., 'Eurydice', *CP* 1983, 51–5.

Thus H.D. evolved beyond submission to a paternal literary lineage, which Freud defined as the normative father-daughter paradigm; she suffered the renunciation of (aesthetic) desire that Freud saw as the source of female 'frigidity'; and she eventually recuperated what Freud called 'the original mother-attachment' through the recovery of a female muse of her own. H.D.'s efforts to achieve literary potency therefore can serve to summarize the various stages of development that we have used to define the twentieth-century woman writer's affiliation complex. At the same time, her poetic progress implies a critique of Freud's theory of female maturation.[54]

As they suggest, H.D.'s career can be traced in Freudian terms of development from male love objects – Ezra Pound and Richard Aldington – to a female love object, Winifred Bryher. However, even in these early poems, she was not just seeking approval in male terms of avant-garde innovation. As Celeste Schenck argues, 'For Woolf and H.D. the notion of breaking sentence and sequence was a way of rupturing political assumptions of great pertinacity and of making a radical criticism of power and status.'[55] H.D.'s eschewal of high literary form and her concern with the textual politics of gender and race blur the binary divide between 'high' and 'female' modernisms.

Amy Lowell

Amy Lowell was an important mediator of poetry and criticism between the United States and Britain. She promoted new poets and her critical writing and poetry drew attention to the possibilities of imagism, free verse and polyphonic prose. She published twelve poetry books, starting with a *Dome of Many Coloured Glass* (1912), and her poetry was printed in American and British magazines such as *The Bookman* and the *North American Review*, not just *Poetry* and *The Egoist* with which she had personal connections. She reviewed British poetry for American readers[56] and *Tendencies in Modern American Poetry*, which discussed paired poets including H.D. and J.G. Fletcher, was a groundbreaking survey of contemporary practice which was debated in both Britain and the United States. In his preface to the *Complete*

---

54 Sandra Gilbert and Susan Gubar, *No Man's Land: The Place of the Woman Writer In the Twentieth Century. Vol. 1. The War Of The Words* (New Haven: Yale University Press, 1988), 169–71.

55 Schenck, 246, n. 6.

56 For example, her lengthy review of *Georgian Poetry 1911–1912* in *The Dial* drew attention to the new writers, including Anna Wickham. See also, Amy Lowell, 'Weary Verse', review of *Georgian Poetry 1911–12*, *The Dial* 1920, reprinted in *Georgian Poetry: The Critical Heritage*, ed. Timothy Rogers (London: Routledge & Kegan Paul, 1977), 253–4.

Poetical Works of Amy Lowell (1955), Louis Untermeyer anticipated that her place in the history of American literature would be secured by future generations:

> In any case, the importance of her influence remains unquestioned. Underneath her preoccupation with the need for novelty, the disruption of traditional patterns and other theoretical departures, she was a dynamic force. She was not only a disturber but an awakener. Her exhilarating differences invigorated the old forms while affecting the new techniques. Her pioneering energy cleared the field of flabby accumulation and helped establish the fresh and free searching poetry of her day.[57]

I am not certain whether her contribution to opening up readers' minds to new poetry is recognised any more in America than it is in Britain.

Amy Lowell's promotion of imagism through the imagist anthologies and her lectures meant that she became the paradigmatic imagist. On reading H.D.'s poems, she famously declared, 'I too am an imagist' and went to England in 1914 to meet the imagists, research her book on Keats and publish her poems.[58] When she financed and took over the annual anthologies (1915–17), Ezra Pound shook the dust of the imagists off his feet, but she was clearly respected by other contemporaries who were sympathetic to imagist principles. *The Egoist* published several of her poems and two long articles about them. In 'The Poetry of Amy Lowell', J.G. Fletcher explained her work to British readers and predicted for her a 'permanent place in English Literature', picking out her irony, clear and concrete visualisations, her sense of narrative and her exceptional range. He believed 'Bombardment' to be one of the best war poems, appearing to be 'male-authored'. Tellingly, he described others like 'See! I give myself to you, Beloved!' as feminine poems, implying that expressiveness was the give-away trait of feminine authorship.[59]

In connection with her promotion of imagism, Amy Lowell was an influential champion and writer of free verse. In her Preface to *Sword Blades and Poppy Seed* (1914) she addressed the prevailing myths about *vers libre,* particularly the false opposition between 'traditional' and 'free' verse forms. She preferred the label 'unrhymed cadence' since free verse had 'not entirely abandoned the more classic metres' but was built upon 'the rhythm of the speaking voice with its necessity for breathing, rather than upon a strict metrical

---

57   Louis Untermeyer, Preface, *The Complete Poetical Works of Amy Lowell* (Boston: Houghton Mifflin, 1955).

58   Amy Lowell, *John Keats* (Boston: Houghton Mifflin; London: Jonathan Cape, 1925).

59   J.G. Fletcher, 'The Poetry of Amy Lowell', *Egoist* II, 1 May 1915: 81–2.

system'.[60] 'August: Late Afternoon', printed in *The Egoist*, 1916, is faithful to imagist principles of brevity and precision:

> Smoke-colour, rose, saffron,
> With a hard edge chipping the blue sky,
> A great cloud hung over the village,
> And the white-painted meeting-house,
> And the steeple with the gilded weather-cock
> Heading and flashing to the wind.[61]

Richard Aldington's review of *Sword Blades and Poppy Seed* in *The Egoist* judged some of the short *vers libre* poems 'extremely good' and promoted her precision in the manner of the Greek tradition and her experiments with rhythm and images. He recommended 'Miscast 1' and 'Miscast II', 'Music in a Garden', 'The Taxi', 'The Tree of Scarlet' and 'The Epitaph of a Young Poet'.[62] The literary papers tended to give her lengthy consideration but were sceptical about free verse. A long review of *What's O'Clock,* headed 'The Poetry of Miss Amy Lowell', is an interesting register of her reputation and the free verse controversy which her poems fanned. The reviewer debated the state of modern poetry, acknowledged that she had 'a famous name' but called her enthusiasm 'schoolgirlish'.[63] *Can Grande's Castle* (1920) had long reviews in the *TLS* which referred to her fame in the United States where she cultivated 'polyphonic prose'.[64] Richard Aldington cited 'In a Castle', 'The Forsaken' and 'The Basket' as models of polyphonic prose for all young poets, declaring 'for I am not a bit ashamed to confess that I have myself imitated Miss Lowell, in this, and produced a couple of works in the same style'.[65] She defined polyphonic prose as 'prose only in its typographical arrangement', and explained that it employed poetic strategies such as metre, rhyme and alliteration but the aim was to produce an orchestral effect. It broke down binary oppositions and allowed for the articulation of plurality. Louis Untermeyer reckoned that Amy Lowell was the first to experiment with

---

60 Amy Lowell, Preface to *Sword Blades and Poppy Seed* (London: Macmillan, 1914), x–xii.

61 Amy Lowell, 'August: Late Afternoon', *Egoist* III, 1 March 1916: 37; *Complete Poetical Works*, 223–4.

62 Richard Aldington, review of *Sword Blades and Poppy Seed*, by Amy Lowell, *Egoist* I, 16 November 1914: 423.

63 For example, 'The Poetry of Miss Amy Lowell', a long review of *What's O'Clock*, by Amy Lowell, *TLS* 14 February 1926: 114.

64 Reviews of *Can Grande's Castle*, by Amy Lowell, *TLS* 21 October and 16 December, 1920: 687 and 853.

65 Richard Aldington, review of *Sword Blades and Poppy Seeds*, *Egoist* 1914.

polyphonic prose, although it derived from the French poet Paul Fort, whom she included in *Six French Poets* (1915), a study of contemporary literature.

Although best known for her crusade for *vers libre*, Amy Lowell was also part of the vogue for a return to more orthodox forms, such as ballads, and for Japanese and Chinese poetry. Her first volume, *A Dome of Many Coloured Glass* (1912), consisted mainly of lyrical forms but she was more adventurous in the next volume, *Sword Blades and Poppy Seed* (1914), and *Pictures of a Floating World* (1919) which was in its fourth edition by 1921 and which best demonstrates her stylistic range. 'Ely Cathedral' is a humorous satire on British culture, which is unusual in its rhyming but typical in its associational progression of images: 'Anaemic women, stupidly dressed and shod / In squeaky shoes, thump down the nave to laud an expurgated God.'[66] The confidently ironic voice strategically eschews idealised feminine passivity or piety. Lowell's satirical register is acerbic in the free verse narrative 'Astigmatism: to Ezra Pound with much friendship and Admiration and some Difference of Opinion'. She depicts 'The Poet' stalking through the countryside, scything daisies with his walking stick which he considers to be an *objet d'art*:

> The Poet came to a meadow.
> Sifted through the grass were daisies,
> Open-mouthed, wondering, they gazed at the sun.
> The Poet struck them with his cane.
> The little heads flew off, and they lay
> Dying, open-mouthed and wondering,
> On the hard ground.
> 'They are useless. They are not roses', said the Poet.

> Peace be with you, Brother. Go your ways.[67]

Her jibe at Pound was obviously tied up with his splintering of the imagist group and his self-appointed artistic superiority. As Andrew Thacker comments, Lowell's representation of Pound's walking stick as a phallic emblem 'poke[d] fun at Pound's notion of poetry as a pen-craft fit only for men'.[68]

'The Sisters', to which I have referred in the Introduction, and 'A Critical Fable' investigate the creative bind for women in their negotiations with the

---

66 Amy Lowell, *Complete Poetical Works*, 230.
67 Amy Lowell, *Complete Poetical Works*, 34.
68 Thacker, 54.

male literary tradition. Lowell could not find inspiration in women poets of the past and found herself undermined by men. Furthermore, her lesbian orientation exacerbated the difficulty of self-definition. In 'Middle Age', one of her many haikus, the painful processes of subjectivity are represented through impersonal concrete images:

> Like black ice
> Scrolled over with the unintelligible patterns
>   by an ignorant skater
> Is the dulled surface of my heart.[69]

Harriet Monroe believed that Amy Lowell was a 'good workman, even though at times the mere workmanship is a bit too apparent'.[70] D.H. Lawrence, who thought her a 'very good friend', was also reticent about her achievement[71] and similarly identified an imaginative 'posturing': 'Why do you deny the bitterness in your nature, when you write poetry? Why do you take a pose? It causes you always to shirk your issues and find a banal resolution at the end.'[72] He was writing about her early work in *Sword Blades and Poppy Seed*, and did not seem to recognise her application of the imagist credo which promoted objectivity. Nevertheless, he was touching on the alienation in language of the non-symbolised lesbian identity. The self-masking both restrains and liberates her creativity.

Lowell particularly needed to mask her lesbian desires. As Hanscombe and Smyers point out, 'the intimacy of lesbian life could hardly have been openly depicted in the poetry of the time, not only for the obvious reasons that social opprobrium would result, but more seriously because the masculine tradition of lyric writing had not been questioned'.[73] In the love lyrics to Ada Russell, such as 'In Excelsis' or 'Opal', conventional images, particularly the juxtapositions of heat and cold, encode female sexuality:[74]

> You are ice and fire,
> The touch of you burns my hands like snow.

---

69 Amy Lowell, *Complete Poetical Works*, 226.
70 Harriet Monroe, *Poetry* 5. 3, December 1914: 137.
71 D.H. Lawrence, letter to Amy Lowell, 21 January 1917, *The Letters of D.H. Lawrence*. Vol. 3, ed. James T. Boulton and James Robertson (Cambridge: Cambridge University Press, 1984), 61. Amy Lowell sent D.H. Lawrence money, a typewriter in 1914 and promoted his poems in the imagist anthologies and in her talks on modern poetry in America.
72 D.H. Lawrence, letter to Amy Lowell, 18 November 1914, Zytaruk and Boulton, 234–5.
73 Hanscombe and Smyers, 69.
74 Thacker, 56.

You are cold and flame.
You are the crimson of amaryllis.
The silver of moon-touched magnolias.
When I am with you,
My heart is a frozen pond
Gleaming with agitated torches.[75]

Through her famous flower metaphors, Lowell often harnessed traditional symbols of femininity to lesbian desire. In 'A Decade' the food imagery is eroticised:

When you came, you were like red wine and honey,
And the taste of you burnt my mouth with its sweetness.
Now you are like morning bread,
Smooth and pleasant.
I hardly taste you at all for I know your savour,
But I am completely nourished.[76]

Andrew Thacker illustrates that Lowell and H.D. use the condensed discourse of orthodox imagist precepts but their images are more sensual and relational. The imagist principle of directness was problematic for the representations of lesbian or bisexuality which had to be coded or voiced indirectly. In other words, versions of modernism have to take into account 'the articulation of very different desires and vocabularies than those expressed in Pound's version of imagism'.[77]

Marianne Moore, Laura Riding, Gertrude Stein and Mina Loy

Like Edith Sitwell, H.D. and Amy Lowell, Marianne Moore, Laura Riding, Gertrude Stein, and Mina Loy disturbed or rejected conventional systems of signification. They were pioneers of defamiliarising experiments, such as displacing traditional symbols or distorting conventional syntax. They avoided realist representations in favour of constructing the operations of consciousness. They endorsed the tenets of 'high' modernism – intellectuality, objectivity and impersonality – which avoided gender identification and it is significant that the 'poetess' label was rarely applied to them. They are difficult to pin down in

---

75　Amy Lowell, *Complete Poetical Works*, 214.
76　Amy Lowell, 'A Decade', *Complete Poetical Works*, 217.
77　Thacker, 56.

terms of party or gender politics, but their avoidance of gendered affiliation is usually the place to look for a gendered awareness. They also challenged the idealisations of femininity maintained by literary tradition, myth and fairytale.

Marianne Moore

Marianne Moore influenced poetry in the United States and Europe through *The Dial* and through the publication of her poetry, articles and reviews in other papers, notably *The Egoist* and *The Criterion* in Britain, and through her energetic correspondence.[78] In the American academy, she is often numbered with male modernists although the final panel of a two-day centenary symposium in Chicago (1987) were hesitant about her place in literary history.[79] Like H.D. and Amy Lowell, her status as a poet is uncertain in Britain, partly due to the lack of consensus about her identity as a poet. Reputed for her knowledge and intellectuality, she earned respect within the literary establishment which showered her with prizes. She also became a popular figure whom putatively 'threw the first pitch of the baseball season, went to prize fights with George Plumpton, dined with Cassius Clay, as he then was, and was hired, unavailingly, to give a name to a new Ford car'.[80] The continuing debate about whether her verbal tactics were aimed at unsettling the reader, at concealing her gender or at contradicting cultural banalities, is a testimony to her skilful textual mystifications. Although the poems rarely seem gendered, there is an implicit feminist politics in her transgressions of genre.

The studied inscrutability of Marianne Moore's texts sends readers to biography. Her lifelong closeness with her mother and her determined celibacy support mythologies of a writer who was sanitised by her spinsterhood. Although she and her mother were members of the Women's Suffrage Party of Pennsylvania in 1915, her poetry does not specifically explore a feminist consciousness, but her disguising of the feminine voice and the respect which she earned for her 'craftsmanship' helped the credibility of the woman poet. In identifying the two-pronged critical reception to women like Moore, Alicia Ostriker presents the case for the radical poet:

---

78 See Costello, Goodridge and Miller 1998.

79 Robin Gail Schulze, '"The Frigate Pelican"'s Progress: Marianne Moore's multiple versions and Modernist Practice', *Gendered Modernisms: American Women Poets and Their Readers*, ed. Margaret Dickie and Thomas Travisano (Philadelphia: University of Pennsylvania Press, 1996), 117–142.

80 Frank Kermode, 'First Pitch', review of *The Selected Letters of Marianne Moore*, ed. Costello, Goodridge and Miller, *London Review of Books* 16 April 1998: 16.

As to Moore, the connection between the personal and sexual self-effacement which was one source of the respect she received in élite poetic and critical circles, and the limitations which readers have complained of in her work, can scarcely be doubted. To advocates and critics alike she had been the pre-eminent poet of the filigreed and polished surface, who is 'unassuming' and 'unpretentious' and whose 'humility is vast.' That her anger and her ambition were equally as vast has not been noticed. She has been all too thoroughly accepted, represented in anthologies by her most maidenly and least threatening work, and her subversiveness has been virtually invisible.[81]

In both America and Britain, Marianne Moore was renowned for her professionalism and prosody, particularly in the syllabic cause, which influenced W.H. Auden, although she moved on to free verse. As she explained in 'The Accented Syllable', published in *The Egoist*, 1916, her interest in developing syllabic verse was for the purpose of creating definite but naturalistic intonation.[82] During the 1920s, her poetry was published and reviewed in most of the literary and progressive papers in America and Britain. Her poems were included in the imagist anthologies and she published *Poems* in Britain (Egoist Press, 1921) and *Observations* in America (Dial Press, 1924). Her *Selected* and *Collected Poems* (1935, 1951) were severely pruned and do not include several poems which appeared in the two collections or in journals. Of all the poems published in *The Egoist* only 'The Fish' and 'He Wrote the History Book' are in her *Collected Poems*. She corresponded with Harriet Shaw Weaver at *The Egoist* which is where she mainly found an outlet in Britain. She became a central figure in the New York literary scene from 1915 and won the approval of her male colleagues. John Crowe Ransom contrasted 'Miss Marianne Moore' favourably with Edna St Vincent Millay because she was not 'deficient in masculinity' which he equated with 'intellectual interest'.[83] Moore admired Wallace Stevens and knew William Carlos Williams and Alfred Kreyburg, among other modernist intellectuals.[84] In a letter to Ezra Pound, 1919, she pointed out the positive reception to her work in *The Egoist*, *Poetry* and *The Little Review*, but professed dissatisfaction with the way it 'jerks and rears'.[85]

---

81   Ostriker, 53–4.
82   Marianne Moore, 'The Accented Syllable', *Egoist* III, October 1916: 151–2.
83   John Crowe Ransom, 'The Poet as Woman', *The World's Body* by Ransom, 1938 (New York: Kennikat Press, 1964), 98. John Crowe Ransom (1888–1974) was a member of the Fugitive Group.
84   Moore's famous review of Wallace Stevens, 'Well–Moused, Lion', was published in *The Dial* 76, January 1924: 84–91.
85   Marianne Moore, letter to Ezra Pound, 1919, Hanscombe and Smyers, 209 and 265, n. 19.

This proclaimed dissatisfaction could have been faked modesty, since she was well-received by her contemporaries and her poetry was reviewed at length in the *TLS,* albeit with reservations.[86]

In Britain, Marianne Moore's debut in *The Egoist* was her review of *Prufrock and Other Observations* and she brought T.S. Eliot's criticism to the attention of America with her review of *The Sacred Wood* in *The Dial*.[87] In *The Dial* she also wrote discerning reviews of H.D.'s *Heliodora and Other Poems* and Edith Sitwell's *The Sleeping Beauty.* She carried on a long and formal correspondence with T.S. Eliot who encouraged her to produce her *Selected Poems* which he introduced and he had her work reviewed in *The Criterion.* In April 1921 he wrote, 'How much I admire your verse. It interests me, I think, more than that of anyone now writing in America. I wish that you would make a book of it, and I should like to try to get it published here.'[88] In his review of the *Others* anthology in *The Egoist,* May 1918, T.S. Eliot raised up Marianne Moore with the 'living writers', 'Mr Pound, Mr Joyce and Mr Lewis':

> Miss Moore is utterly intellectual, but not abstract; the word never parts from the feeling; her ideas, imageless, remain quite personal ... She has an admirable sense of form ... being an American has perhaps aided her to avoid the diet of nineteenth-century English poetry.[89]

He much admired 'The Steeple Jack' for her method of running a prose sentence across stanzas, and he placed it at the beginning of her *Selected Poems.* In his Preface to *Selected Poems,* T.S. Eliot, suggested that the minute detail of her observations, which could provoke either irritation or admiration, was best seen in non-referential terms, as investigations of language rather than records of experience. He explored her combinations of internal rhyme and rhymed and unrhymed endings: 'Miss Moore's use of rhyme is in itself a definite innovation in metric ... of the *light* rhyme Miss Moore is the greatest living master; and indeed she is the first, so far as I know, who has investigated its possibilities.'[90] As well as 'master', he called her 'modernist' and placed the poems in 'part of the small body of durable poetry written in our time'. It is not necessary to use T.S. Eliot's compliments to add to her credentials, but

---

86 For example, review of *Poems*, by Marianne Moore, *TLS* 21 July 1921: 471.
87 Marianne Moore, review of *The Sacred Wood*, by T.S. Eliot, *Dial* March 1921.
88 T.S. Eliot, letter to Marianne Moore, 3 April 1921, Valerie Eliot (ed.), 442.
89 T.S. Eliot, under the pseudonym of 'Apteryx', review of *Others*, ed. Alfred Kreymborg. *Egoist* V, May 1918: 69–70.
90 T.S. Eliot, Preface to *Selected Poems*, by Marianne Moore, 1934.

they do register how she was perceived as an innovator and honorary male modernist.

Although Marianne Moore was identified as a modernist early on in Britain, she was initially associated with the imagists through the imagist anthologies and the promotion of her reputation in *The Egoist*. 'Evocations', printed in *The Egoist*, 1 April 1915, suggests the influence of H.D. but Moore rejected the 'imagist' along with every other label. In *The Faber Book of Modern Verse*, Michael Roberts perceived that later imagist developments, such as Amy Lowell's, had influenced her.[91] Conversely, in *A Survey of Modernist Poetry* (1927) Laura Riding and Robert Graves singled her out as an exemplar of modernist, as opposed to showy imagist, poetry because she was 'wholly concerned' with the technical discipline of poetry rather than with novelty for novelty's sake.[92] Their analysis of her 'Steam-Roller' and 'Poetry' was one of the first critical responses which recognised her ironic parody of the 'plain reader's' expectations: 'Miss Moore, who turns her poetry into matter-of-fact prose demonstrations in order to avoid mystery, thus expresses the plain reader's antagonism to poetry that perplexes rather than entertains.'[93]

If she were aiming for highbrow status and male approval, Marianne Moore was clearly successful and would have been delighted by Richard Aldington's praise in *The Criterion* in 1925: 'Miss Moore is indeed the most highbrow poet in the world ... Miss Moore's poetry is entirely intellectual'. This review of *Observations* is a useful record of a reception to Moore's poems among the British intellectuals and for an attentive analysis. Aldington confessed to having read the book three times, to his difficulty in finding an appropriate language of appraisal, and to a sense of her 'most menacing superiority' – 'one is conscious of a clear piercing gaze and an unfavourable judgement of oneself somehow emanating from the pages. Instinctively one straightens one's tie.' He believed that the superiority stemmed from her 'whimsical and sophisticated irony' and array of references.[94] Moore's range of reference can be construed as a highbrow fortification against the masses, but her levelling of classical or sacred with mundane texts anticipates postmodernist conflations of high- and low-brow referents. The conflation of literary and ordinary discourses

---

91 Michael Roberts, *The Faber Book of Modern Verse*, ed. Michael Roberts (London: Faber, 1936), 15.
92 Riding and Graves 1927, 111.
93 Ibid., 113.
94 Richard Aldington, review of *Observations* by Marianne Moore, *Criterion* III, 12, 12 July 1925: 588–92.

represents her internal contradictions concerning the conventional structures of poetry.

While appearing to be highbrow, Marianne Moore exposed the pretensions and élitism of highbrow poets. Her similarities with T.S. Eliot – the literary references and explanatory notes – can thus be read as parodic. 'Why I buy Pictures'[95] is characteristically ironic about the misplaced reverence for authors – 'Yes the authors are wonderful people / Particularly those who write the most'. 'Picking and Choosing' mocks the esoteric rhetoric of literary criticism:

> Literature is a phase of life. If
> one is afraid of it, the situation is irremediable; if
> one approaches it familiarly
> what one says of it is worthless. Words are constructive
> when they are true; the opaque allusion – the simulated flight
>
> upward – accomplishes nothing. Why cloud the fact
> that Shaw is self-conscious in the field of sentiment but is otherwise
> re-warding; that James is all that has been
> said of him if feeling is profound? It is not Hardy
> the distinguished novelist and Hardy the poet, but one man
>
> 'interpreting life through the medium of the
> emotions'. If he must give an opinion, it is permissible that the
> critic should know what he likes.[96]

Typically, the poem sets up and distorts rhythmic norms. Marianne Moore avoided rhyme because it impeded a 'naturalistic' voice and she preferred the scope of free verse for varying intonation.[97] Her well anthologised 'Poetry' (1921) similarly deflates poetry's mystique; its mixture of formal and informal diction investigates the line between literary and non-literary discourses. This combination may also represent an internal contradiction in her relationship with 'high-' and 'middle-' brow cultures.[98] She seems to both reject and sustain the concept of cultural sanctification by high literature.

Moore's defamiliarisations involved a redefinition of genre since she was preoccupied with the nature and status of literary tradition, particularly the

---

95 Marianne Moore, *Collected Poems* (New York: Macmillan; London: Faber & Faber, 1951), 67.

96 Marianne Moore, *CP* 1951, 51–3.

97 Marianne Moore, 'The Accented Syllable', *Egoist* III, October 1916: 151–2.

98 See 'Rear-Guard Modernism' for more discussion of 'middlebrow'.

conflict between its hierarchical structures and democratic ideals. H.D.'s review of Marianne Moore in *The Egoist* recognised the despairing bafflement of her readers and addressed the big question, 'does it mean something?'[99] She chose 'Feed me, also, river God' and 'He made the screen and Talisman' as examples of Moore's 'perfect craft'. H.D. argued that the meaning was found in the disdain of the artist who playfully engages then eludes the reader: '[Miss Moore] is fighting in her country a battle against squalor and commercialism' in the cause of the 'beautiful English language'. As H.D. indicated, there is a vehemence in Moore's depictions of 'The vast indestructible necropolis'[100] but her disdain was for élitist culture. In 1936 Marianne Moore declared her support for the Spanish Republicans 'against Franco, against Fascism; against any suppression of freedom by tyranny masked as civilisation'.[101] Lisa Steinman argues that Moore's commitment to interrogating the unequal distribution of cultural capital was partly a response to T.S. Eliot's 'Tradition and The Individual Talent', published in 1920.[102] In common with Eliot, she was concerned with extending the scope of poetry which encouraged stock responses in order to expand consciousness. It has to be acknowledged, however, that, like Eliot's, her writing remains self-referentially literary rather than achieves a widely accessible idiom.

The detachment or distance of Moore's speakers can give the impression that she assumes the high moral ground. Her revising and cutting, however, support the view that her aesthetic was more self-contained and that she was primarily testing the limits of genre. She refused the labels 'poet' or 'poetry', explained her syllabic verse as 'an arrangement of stanzas, each stanza being an exact duplicate of every other stanza' and referred to her poetry as 'my observations, experiments in rhythm, or exercises in composition'.[103] She continually reworked her poems. 'Poetry', begun in 1912, and published in *Poems*, was originally thirty lines but was reduced to thirteen lines in *Observations* (1921); it was thirty-eight lines long in *Selected Poems*, and four lines in *Collected Poems*. The indeterminacy of the texts mitigates the impression of a fixed moral purpose. The poems are best approached as a

---

99   H.D., review of Marianne Moore, *Egoist* III, August 1916: 118–9, reprinted in Scott, *Gender of Modernism*, 125–7.

100 Marianne Moore, 'People's Surroundings', *CP* 1951, 61.

101 Marianne Moore, 'Writers Take Sides: Letters about the war in Spain from 418 American Authors' (New York: League of American Writers, 1938).

102 Lisa M. Steinman, 'Marianne Moore and Literary Tradition', Dickie and Travisano, 97–116.

103 Marianne Moore, letter to Ezra Pound, 1919, Hanscombe and Smyers, 209 and 265, n. 19.

series of impressions and investigations into the processes of representation. 'England', for example, seems to be primarily descriptive, but it is also about stereotyping and the hindrance of clichés to fresh awareness: 'To have misapprehended the matter is to have confessed / that one has not looked far enough.'[104] Her poems interrogate the binary opposition between poetry and prose, personal and impersonal discourses or expressive or self-reflexive modes. She explained, 'One writes because one has a burning desire to objectify what is indispensable to one's happiness to express.'[105] This impersonal expression of the personal is typical and by littering quotation and adopting different subject positions she eludes a fixed identity.

Moore's 'impersonality' avoids the voice of female experience but she sometimes investigates gender relations. The overkill of 'Poetry' and 'The Steeple Jack' in anthologies has eclipsed longer poems like 'Marriage', a nine page exploration of the psychological effects of legalised partnership. It begins:

> This institution
> perhaps one should say enterprise
> out of respect for which
> one says one need not change one's mind
> about a thing one has believed in,
> requiring public promises
> of one's intention
> to fulfil a private obligation.[106]

Through an unidentified persona Moore questioned the validity of marriage and of cultural prescriptions of gender or sexual relations. Alicia Ostriker cites 'Marriage' as an example of how Moore's elliptical surfaces can hide 'a rather absolute critique of patriarchy and its central institution'.[107] Marianne Moore's review of H.D.'s *Hymen* is a rare polemic against the mythologies of women as either feminine or frigid:

> Talk of weapons and the tendency to match one's intellectual and emotional vigor with the violence of nature, give a martial, an apparently masculine tone, to such writing as H.D.'s, the more so that women are regarded as belonging

---

104 Marianne Moore, 'England', *CP* 1951, 51–53.

105 Marianne Moore, 'Idiosyncrasy and Technique', *The Complete Prose of Marianne Moore*, ed. Patricia Willis (London: Faber and Faber, 1987), 507.

106 Marianne Moore, 'Marriage', *CP* 1951, 69–78.

107 Ostriker, 51.

necessarily to either of two classes – that of the intellectual freelance or that of the eternally sleeping beauty, effortless yet effective in that indestructible limestone keep of domesticity. Woman tends unconsciously to be the aesthetic norm of intellectual home life and pre-eminently in the case of H.D., we have the intellectual, social woman, non-public and 'feminine'.[108]

It is likely that Moore's ostentatious intellectuality was a strategic distancing from 'feminine' sentimentality. Similarly, her device of animal voices, as in 'The Fish', 'The Frigate Pelican' and 'The Buffalo', enabled her to transcend gendered identification by avoiding human figurations altogether. She did not, however, hide under cover of male-associated conventions but consciously distanced herself from all literary categories and transgressed the traditional boundaries of genre. Although avoiding gendered affiliation in her poetry, Marianne Moore did not display symptoms of the female affiliation complex in her relations with other literary women. She and H.D. were university colleagues at Bryn Mawr and although H.D. came to London before the First World War, she and Moore remained mutual supporters and reviewed each other's work. Like H.D., she received guidance, wanted and unwanted, from Ezra Pound, but she withstood his 'text-bashing' and interferences concerning funding, contributing to and working for *The Dial*.[109] In addition to her friendship with H.D. she knew Mina Loy, Amy Lowell, Djuna Barnes and Margaret Anderson, and met Sylvia Beach when she went to Europe in 1911.

Laura Riding

Laura Riding left the United States in 1926 but did not settle with the ex-patriates on The Left Bank in Paris and spent her time in Mallorca and London. She published ten books of poems during the 1920s and 1930s, including her *Collected Poems* in 1938. She influenced some younger poets whom she took as protégés and published through her Seizin Press in Mallorca and London (1927–39). In spite of her publishing success, her promotion of new poets and her involvement in developing awareness about modernist poetry, literary criticism in Britain has been sparse and evasive about her status as a writer, partly because of her antagonism to anthologies and towards critics who did not share her puritanical view of language, and partly because of the

---

108 Marianne Moore, review of *Hymen*, by H.D., *Broom* 4, January 1923: 133–5, reprinted in Willis (ed.), *Complete Prose*, 79–82.
109 For example, Ezra Pound, letter to Marianne Moore, 16 December 1918, reprinted in Scott, *Gender of Modernism*, 359–362.

mythologies concerning her relationship with Robert Graves and her notorious suicide attempt in 1929. The disdain with which she was treated by some male poets and critics has also overshadowed the respect of others. Michael Roberts consulted her extensively during the formation of *The Faber Book of Modern Verse* (1936) and nine of her poems were included in it.

In the debate about whether she has been over- or underestimated, John Lucas states, 'That Laura Riding's poetry should be so little discussed or known is pretty disgraceful ... No account of the poetry of the 1920s can afford to ignore this collection [*Poems: A Joking Word*, 1930].' As Jeanne Heuving observes, one reason for the neglect is that she is difficult to position: 'Within existing periodizing concepts, (Riding) Jackson's poetry can only be seen as a strange kind of amalgam of modernist, New Critical, and postmodernist poetics.'[110] She did not align herself with literary groups, although she associated with members of the Paris–Bloomsbury avant-garde including Virginia Woolf, T.S. Eliot, Ezra Pound, Edith Sitwell and Gertrude Stein. She has been largely ignored by feminist histories, probably because, like Edith Sitwell, and to some extent Marianne Moore, her poems are difficult to read in terms of gender. A female affiliation complex is projected in her hostility towards women-only anthologies, to avoid what she saw as the general 'declassing' of woman poets.[111] However, in *These were the Hours* (1969), Nancy Cunard records that during the 1920s, Riding was an esteemed poet but considered difficult. Cunard also described her as feminist and believed that Riding's rhythms and repetitive syntax were influenced by Gertrude Stein.

As a woman and an American in Britain, Riding was doubly displaced. She did not identify herself as American and was aware of 'The most foolish instance[s] of critical segregation' because of her sex.[112] In a letter to *The Criterion* in 1927, Robert Graves took issue with John Gould Fletcher's review of Laura Riding's *The Close Chaplet*, particularly its implication that she was derivative of himself, and also of Gertrude Stein, Marianne Moore and John Crowe Ransom.[113] Graves explained why, in each case, Laura Riding could not have copied them and made the general objection to the self-publicising of reviewers:

---

110 Jeanne Heuving, 'Laura Riding Jackson's "Really New" Poem', Dickie and Travisano, 192–213.

111 Laura Riding, Preface to *Collected Poems* 1938, reprinted in *The Poems of Laura Riding* (Manchester: Carcanet, 1980), 418.

112 Ibid.

113 J.G. Fletcher, 'Recent Books', review of *The Close Chaplet*, by Laura Riding Gottshalk, *Criterion* VI. 2, August 1927: 170–1. See also review of *The Close Chaplet*, *TLS* 20 January 1927: 47.

What happens is that this sort of reviewer makes a point of knowing the 'names' in fashion at the moment as the leaders of the advanced movements in poetry, and of discovering exactly at what price the stock of, say, Gertrude Stein (rising), Edith Sitwell (steady), Marianne Moore (not very steady), Ezra Pound (sinking), and John Masefield (sunk), is being quoted in Bloomsbury, Paris and Greenwich Village.[114]

Graves' complaints register that Laura Riding's poetry was likened to other avant-garde writers, that poets objected to the 'false writing that passes as criticism' and that the reputations of Moore, Stein and Sitwell were established in the international modernist network. Additionally, Graves referred to 'Mr Fletcher's well-known anti-feministic bias [which] is only relaxed in the case of "names"'. Although the extent of the mutual influence of Laura Riding and Robert Graves is debatable, he became more avant-garde when working with her.

As with Edith Sitwell, Gertrude Stein, Amy Lowell and Marianne Moore, Laura Riding's criticism was an important instrument and record of modernism. The term 'Modernist' was first used by Riding and Graves in *A Survey of Modernist Poetry* (1927). They exposed the paradox that modernism's insistence on innovation had become an orthodoxy.[115] *A Survey of Modernist Poetry* was allegedly a 'word by word collaboration' between Riding and Graves so it is difficult to ascertain its significance as a woman's text, although it was inclusive through integrating British and American men and women. It was taken for granted that Marianne Moore, H.D., Gertrude Stein, Edith Sitwell and Nancy Cunard were as well-known to the readers as T.S. Eliot, William Carlos Williams, Ezra Pound and W.B. Yeats.

Like Marianne Moore's, Laura Riding's poems appear to elude gender distinctness through their impersonality. Like Moore, she wished to free readers from stock responses by confronting them with unfamiliar linguistic arrangements and, like Moore's, her poems often read as philosophy in verse – she was proud of W.H. Auden's description of her as 'the only living philosophical poet'.[116] Poems like 'The Talking World' and 'Come, Words, Away' illustrate her interest in extending her readers' consciousness by moving them away from familiar verbalisation, 'on and on, as far as poems could take':[117]

114 Robert Graves, letter to the editor, *Criterion* VI. 4, October 1927: 357–9.
115 Riding and Graves 1927, 155–6.
116 Laura Riding, *Poems* 1980, 410.
117 Laura Riding, *Poems* 1980, 408.

Come, words, away from mouths,
Away from tongues in mouths
And reckless hearts in tongues
And mouths in cautious heads –

Come, words, away to where
The meaning is not thickened
With the voice's fretting substance ... [118]

Riding's poetry is illuminated by her Preface to *Collected Poems* (1938) where she explains that her experiments with shedding 'literary conventionalities of poetic idiom' – rhyme, image, symbol or form – were aimed at achieving the diction of uncontaminated thought.[119] She believed in absolute 'meaning' and that words should point the way to moral and spiritual development in the individual: 'where language is converted into the mere instrument of an art, it loses its virtue as the expressive instrument of humanity.'[120] Riding's ideal of cultural sanctification through linguistic purity is also illustrated in the publication of *A Pamphlet against Anthologies* in 1928. Since she believed that modern poetry must make demands on the reader in order to be 'new', she saw the growth of popular anthologies as impeding progress.

Laura Riding aimed for a new language which would enlighten human consciousness; she also realised that in the past, 'universality' had meant male experience and, as Jean Heuving puts it, 'crucial to (Riding) Jackson's utopian vision of a new human universality is her gender critique'.[121] 'Postponement of Self' is ostensibly autobiographical and investigates the relationship between language and identity:

At six little girls in love with fathers.
He lifts me up.
See. Is this Me?
Is this Me I think
In all the different ways till twenty.
At twenty I say She.[122]

---

118 Laura Riding, 'Come, words, away', *Poems* 1980, 134.

119 Laura Riding, *Poems* 1980, 1.

120 Laura Riding and Schuyler B. Jackson, *Rational Meaning: A New Foundation for the Definition of Words and Supplementary Essays*, ed. William Harmon (Charlottesville & London: University Press of Virginia, 1997), 23–4.

121 Heuving, 192.

122 Laura Riding, 'Postponement of Self', *Poems* 1980, 59.

The alternation of first and third person pronouns is common in modernist women's writing; it indicates that subjectivity consists in the interplay between semiotic, that is non- or pre-symbolised, language and symbolic articulations. This poem mimics Freud's theory of the development of femininity from identification with the father to identification with the mother.

In 'Memories of Mortalities', ostensibly an examination of childhood, Laura Riding contradicts Romantic notions of universal essentialised human nature in representing the socio-linguistic construction of gendered identity:

> But the world pressed a mirror on my shyness.
> 'Not shy', to the no one in that mirror
> I not self-recognized protested … [123]

Here, drawing more upon Lacanian theory of the infant's mirror phase, the process of self-definition corresponds to the initiation of the female child into the prison-house of the Symbolic, that is patriarchal, language systems:

> I had learnt to be silent
> And yet to be.
> I had learnt how the world speaks. [124]

The interpretation that the childhood repression represented here is specifically female is reinforced by earlier poems like 'I Am' where she states, 'I am an indicated other', and by her reference to the 'patriarchal leer' in 'Divestment of Beauty'. [125] The prose text, *The Word "Woman"*, written in 1933 but not published until 1993, registers more explicitly Riding's thinking about the terminology of tradition and gender. It was intended to 'strip literature of its mythologies of ludicrous pieties' and looks at the alienation of women in language. [126] She believed that 'Woman', like 'God', was a concept by which Man enlarged his nature and defined himself: '"Woman" is the more co-operative kind of "otherness", which assists him practically (he does not know or care why) in his attempts to create identity between his own meanings and all the "other" meanings which may be.' [127]

---

123 Laura Riding, 'Memories of Mortalities', *Poems* 1980, 261.
124 Ibid., 263.
125 Laura Riding, 'I am', 'Divestment of Beauty', *Poems* 1980, 96, 267.
126 Laura Riding and Schuyler B. Jackson, *The Word 'Woman' and Other Related Writings*, ed. Elizabeth Friedman and Alan J. Clark (New York: Persea, 1993), 13.
127 Laura Riding, ibid., 19.

Laura Riding explores the psychological conflict between men and women, particularly in her early poems where she often parodies literary representations of romantic love and the sexual stereotyping of women.[128] In 'Helen's Faces', a monologue by Helen of Troy, she states that 'the original woman is mythical' and refigures the feminine paragon as cold and hard in her mockery of men's fantasies:

> Bitterly have I been contested for,
> Though never have I counted numbers–
> They were too many, less than all.
> And kindly have I warded off
> Contest and bitterness,
> Given each a replica of love,
> Beguiled them with fine images.
>
> To their hearts they held them.
> Her dear face, its explicitness![129]

In 'The Tiger' she similarly subverts the contradictory idealisations of women as 'queens and shepherdesses' through traditional fairy tale:

> ...
> Long since, when like a tiger I was pursued
> And the first pursuer, at such and such a date,
> Found how the tiger takes the lady
> Far away where she is gentle.
> In the high forest she is gentle.
> She is patient in a high house.
> Ah me, ah me, says every lady in the end,
> Putting the tiger in its cage
> Inside her lofty head.
> And weeps reading her own story.
> And scarcely knows she weeps.[130]

Laura Riding was acutely conscious of gender distinctions and stereotypes; like other avant-garde women, she both follows and defies Freud's and Lacan's

---

128 Jeffrey Walsh, 'Alternative "Modernists": Robert Graves and Laura Riding', *British Poetry 1900–1950: Aspects of Tradition*, ed. Gary Day and Brian Docherty (Basingstoke: Macmillan, 1995), 131–50: 137.

129 Laura Riding, 'Helen's Faces', *Poems* 1980, 63.

130 'The Tiger' and 'Lucrece and Nara' were printed in *The Faber Book of Modern Verse*, ed. Michael Roberts, 1936. *Poems* 1980, 64–7, 36.

negative theories of female development. She believed that women had a distinctive spiritual sensitivity and envisaged a condition of pre-lapsarian sex equality: 'The Lady of the Apple, she will eat, / She will reclaim Eden of gloom and sun'.[131] Her poems confront the difficulties for women in symbolising their identities in alien poetic forms and effects. She exercises a psychological and aesthetic control over the mythologies which essentialise and fix gender identities whereby women are always the passive or absent counterpart to men.

Gertrude Stein

When Gertrude Stein came to Britain in 1902, she connected with Bloomsbury and frequented the British Library Reading Room. She was invited to lecture to the Oxford and Cambridge societies in 1926 and 1936 and the former lecture, 'Composition as Explanation' was printed in *The Dial* and published by the Hogarth Press.[132] Her poem 'A Description of the Fifteenth of November: A Portrait of T.S. Eliot', was printed in *The Criterion* in October, 1929.[133] Stein was stylistically close to Edith Sitwell who had written constructive reviews of her pioneering work in 1923 and 1924, before they met in 1926. She had promoted Stein in Great Britain and arranged the invitations from Oxford and Cambridge universities. After they met, Sitwell wrote an enthusiastic review of Stein's *The Making of Americans* in *The Criterion*.[134] She visited Gertrude Stein and Alice Toklas when she lived in Paris, until the famous soirée at Sylvia Beach's Bookshop in 1931 when she snubbed Stein by reading from Shakespeare, the Elizabethan poets and her own work, but not from Stein's.

Gertrude Stein's 'Sitwell Edith Sitwell' is a verbal portrait of Edith in relation to her brothers:

> In a minute when they sit around her.
>   Mixed it with two who. One two two one two two. Mixed it with two who.
>   Weeks and weeks able and weeks.
>   No one sees the connections between Lily and Louise, but I do.

---

131 Laura Riding, 'The Lady of the Apple', from *The Close Chaplet*, 1926, Preface to *The Word 'Woman'*, v–vii.

132 Gertrude Stein, 'Composition as Explanation', *Stanzas in Meditation and Other Poems 1929–33* (New Haven: Yale University Press, 1967), 21–30.

133 Gertrude Stein, 'A Description of the Fifteenth of November: A Portrait of T.S. Eliot', reprinted in Scott, *Gender of Modernism*, 525–8.

134 Edith Sitwell, review of *The Making of Americans*, by Gertrude Stein, *Criterion* 2 April 1926: 391.

After each has had after each has had, after each has had had had had it.
Change in time.
A change in times is this, if a change in time, If a change in time is this.If a
change in time.[135]

It was first read by Stein to the Oxford Poetry Society in a packed lecture hall.
It operates both as a parody of and a tribute to Sitwell's attempts at the verbal
equivalents of music, dance and visual art. Stein combines Sitwell's style
with her own and connects them through their common purpose of cultural
change. Equally, Stein's poetry brought rare praise from Edith who described
it in terms of her own experiments with 'texture': '[Gertrude Stein] is bringing
back life to our language by what appears, at first, to be an anarchic process.
First she breaks down predestined groups of words ... then she examines
their texture and rebuilds them into new and vital shapes.'[136] Sitwell reinforced
the equation between anti-realist or anti-representational writing and
anarchism. Gertrude Stein's reputation in Britain as an anarchist was endorsed
in the 'Conclusion' of *A Survey of Modernist Poetry* (1927) where Laura Riding
and Robert Graves briefly discussed her for representing the 'new barbarism'.
Although not politically anarchist, Stein is arguably the most extreme of all
modernists because her writing lacks the yearning for a mythical past or for
entry into received traditions which encumbers other texts.

Both Gertrude Stein and Edith Sitwell were brave in their textual
subversions, but whereas Sitwell used rhythm and rhyme for aural impact
and plundered a range of traditional verse forms, Stein rejected recognisable
literary effects as systems of signification. Like Sitwell, her sources were
contemporary art and music. Laura Riding and Robert Graves recognised
that Stein's 'rhythms have a peculiar hypnotic power not met with before. It
has kinship with the saxophone'.[137] In her useful essay on Stein, published in
Transatlantic Review, 1924, Mina Loy observed, 'It has become the custom
to say of her that she has done in words what Picasso has done with form.
There is certainly in her work an interpenetration of dimensions analogous to
Cubism.' The other significant aspect, according to Loy, was her success in
making the reader a participant: 'In reading Gertrude Stein one is assaulted
by a dual army of associated ideas, her associations and your own.'[138] Stein

---

135 Gertrude Stein, 'Sitwell Edith Sitwell', Scott, *Gender of Modernism*, 528–30.
136 Edith Sitwell, *Poetry and Criticism* (London: Hogarth, 1925), 23.
137 Riding and Graves 1927, 274–5.
138 Mina Loy, 'Gertrude Stein', *Transatlantic Review* 2.2. 1924: 305–9, 427–30, reprinted in
    Scott, *Gender of Modernism*, 238–45.

also broke new ground with an Anglo-American lexical duality and in 'The Work of Gertrude Stein', published in *The Little Review*, 1916, Sherwood Anderson praised her ability to recast life in the city from American and British words.[139]

Gertrude Stein's critical writings illuminate the principles behind her revolutionary syntax and form. In order to eliminate received systems of meaning she rejected the boundaries of genre and freed up concepts of syntactical correctness through the creation of the prolonged present and removal of punctuation. She famously explained to a student that the line 'Rose is a rose is a rose' parodied how literary symbols had become dead through overuse. 'A Valentine to Sherwood Anderson' (1922) extends the principles of 'Rose is a rose is a rose' and demonstrates her favoured strategies of repetition, parody and displacement:

> Very fine is my valentine.
> Very fine and very mine.
> Very mine is my valentine very mine and very fine.
> Very fine is my valentine and mine, very fine very mine and mine is my valentine.

She typically breaks down conventional literary structures by mixing poetry and prose but coherence is constructed through visual and rhythmic patterning. Typically too, as in 'Rose', the mimicry undermines the ideal of romantic love.

In discarding recognisable literary devices, Stein refused to use symbols to represent the abstract. *Stanzas in Meditation* was written parallel to *The Autobiography of Alice B. Toklas* (1933) where her articulated intention was to achieve the 'exactitude of abstract thought'; she also believed that it was 'her real achievement of the commonplace'.[140] *Stanzas in Meditation* was completed in 1938 but not published until 1956. It is orthodoxly modernist in exploring the contingency of thought and speech. The cohering principle, the voice, which represents socially constructed identity, is also the subject of the poem.

Stein's radically innovative aesthetics unstitch rather than make meaning and evoke a prelinguistic female identity. She was not active in socialist or feminist movements but was committed to fracturing the cultural authority of male-dominated literary traditions. 'Patriarchal Poetry' (1927), explicitly

---

139 Sherwood Anderson, 'The Work of Gertrude Stein', *Little Review*, January–February 1916.
140 Gertrude Stein, *The Autobiography of Alice B. Toklas*, 1933 (Harmondsworth: Penguin, 1986), 230.

indicates her association between traditional poetry and patriarchy and her formulation of a post-patriarchal aesthetic. In this polyphonic text, she constructs a kind of supra- or sub-standard English which appears like the effort of foreigners or babies to master English grammar. It approximates to the concept of women's semiotic speech, which functions in the pre-symbolised mother/daughter union, in its absence of linearity or syntactical organisation:

> Fairly letting it see that the change is as to be did Nelly and Lily love to be did Nelly and Lily want to see and to see which is if could it be that so little is known was known if so little was known shone stone come bestow bestown so little as was known could which that for them recognisably.
> Wishing for Patriarchal Poetry.[141]

These compositions which confront the indeterminacy of interpretation invite intense debates about their meanings. Feminist criticism variously considers how Stein's tactics free language from the repressions of patriarchal traditions and articulate lesbian desire, particularly in *Lifting Belly* and *Tender Buttons*.[142] *Tender Buttons*, written during the pre-war years, 1911–14, is a group of prose poems which Stein called 'verbal still lifes'. Like 'Patriarchal Poetry', they seem preoccupied with avoiding signification and at the same time invite the reader to participate in a re-construction of meaning. Her poems represent the ways in which the modernist challenges to representation were driven by women since they destroyed the assumptions that gender was natural rather than socially determined.

Mina Loy

I have placed Mina Loy (Mina Gertrude Lowy) at the end of this section because she most palpably bridges avant-garde and female modernisms. Contemporary records indicate that she was a significant modernist who has since been overlooked.[143] Her radical departure from syntactical orthodoxy

---

141 Gertrude Stein, 'Patriarchal Poetry', *The Yale Gertrude Stein*, ed. Richard Kostelanez (New Haven: Yale University Press, 1980), 107.
142 Margaret Dickie, 'Recovering the Repression in Stein's erotic poetry', Dickie and Travisano, 3–25.
143 Virginia M. Kouidis, *Mina Loy: American Modernist Poet* (Louisiana State University Press and London: Baton Rouge, 1980), 141. Virginia Kouidis provides a comprehensive bibliography of Loy's published work and notes that many poems, plays and prose remain unpublished in the Collection of American Literature at the Beinecke Rare Book and Manuscript Library, Yale University.

means that it is hard to edit her unpublished writing, and much of it was unattainable before 1985. Ellen Stauder likens Mina Loy to Costantin Brancusi in that her originality poses 'a dilemma of placement on the cultural map', although unlike Brancusi, Loy 'was associated with nearly all of the significant art or literary movements of the modernist period'. Whereas Brancusi has become surrounded by a body of scholarship, 'Loy's visibility on the cultural horizon has been eclipsed ... Loy's poetry has been out of print for a number of years, she is almost never anthologised and is rarely mentioned in histories of modernism.'[144]

Mina Loy can justly be claimed as 'a pioneer of international modernism'.[145] Her influence on her contemporaries can be gauged by the number of memoirs in which she features. In addition to critical essays, stories and plays, she published two books of poems in her lifetime, *Lunar Baedeker* (1923) and *Lunar Baedeker and Time-Tables* (1958), but individual poems were printed in *The Dial*, *The Little Review* and other experimental journals.[146] Her work initially appeared in *Camera Work* and *Trend* in 1914 and she was instrumental in the anthologies of *Others*, edited by Alfred Kreymborg and published in 1916, 1917 and 1920. *Others* promoted her 'Love Songs to Joannes' which 'were much talked about in New York avant-garde circles'.[147] The promotional reviews of *Others* by Ezra Pound and T.S. Eliot helped draw attention to her poetry in Britain. Her involvement in the development of experimental poetry will have indirectly influenced poets in Britain, particularly those who met her in Europe or New York. Her writing was available in Sylvia Beach's bookshop in Paris which was visited by Anna Wickham and Edith Sitwell. Her verse portrait 'Nancy Cunard' registers a degree of acquaintance and admiration, on Loy's part, at least.[148]

'Anglo-American' is a particularly fitting label for Mina Loy. She was born in London but was never published in England. She took American citizenship and was called a 'young American' in *Poetry*.[149] In her article 'Modern Poetry' (1925), Mina Loy identified herself as American because

---

144 Ellen Keck Stauder, 'On Mina Loy', *Modernism/modernity* 4. 3 (The Johns Hopkins University Press, 1997): 141.

145 Fleur Adcock (ed.), *The Faber Book of 20th Century Women's Poetry* (London: Faber, 1987), 7.

146 Mina Loy, 'Lion's Jaws', *Little Review* September–December 1920, 'Anglo-Mongrels and the Rose', *Little Review* Spring 1923, and Autumn/Winter 1923–4.

147 Hanscombe and Smyers, 114.

148 Mina Loy, 'Nancy Cunard', *Nancy Cunard: Brave Poet, Indomitable Rebel 1896–1965*, ed. Samuel Putnam (Philadelphia: Chilton Book Company, 1968), 103.

149 *Poetry* 1. 2, November 1912: 65.

she was self-consciously avant-garde in her manipulation of language and poetic conventions: 'The new poetry of the English language has proceeded out of America … For the true American appears to be ashamed to say anything in the way it has been said before.'[150] Nevertheless, the alienation suggested in Loy's long poem 'Anglo-Mongrels and the Rose' needs to be understood in the context of the cultural duality experienced by emigrants; it also stemmed from being the daughter of a Jewish immigrant father and a bourgeois English mother.

Loy's commitment to revolutionise the versification of the English tradition was fuelled by her antipathy towards her English background. In July 1915, she remarked,

> I don't believe the men in England have got any of the new consciousness about things that is beginning to formulate in some of us – they cannot evaluate a reaction to any stimulus except through juggling with standard poetical phrases – if only they would realise that art always begins with a man's being quite simply honest with himself.[151]

Loy would have been brought up on British literature and her first husband was the English painter Stephen Haweis whom she met in Paris in 1903. In Paris they knew writers like Guillaume Apollinaire and Gertrude Stein. Like her American and British contemporaries, her verbal experiments drew upon the techniques and structures of modern European visual art, especially Futurism and Cubism.

As she outlined in 'Modern Poetry', Loy also wanted the new poetry to take from the new music:

> This unexpectedly realized valuation of American jazz and American poetry is endorsed by two publics; the one universal the other infinitesimal in comparison. And why has the collective spirit of the modern world, of which both are the reflection, recognized itself unanimously in the new music of unprecedented instruments, and so rarely in the new poetry of unprecedented verse? It is because the sound of music capturing our involuntary attention is so easy to get in touch with, while the silent sound of poetry requires our voluntary attention to obliterate the cold barrier of print with the whole 'intelligence of our senses'.[152]

---

150 Mina Loy, 'Modern Poetry', *Mina Loy: The Lost Lunar Baedeker*, ed. Roger Conover, 1982 (Manchester: Carcanet, 1997), 157–61. First published in *Charm* 3.3, April 1925: 16–17. According to Conover, *Charm* was an 'eclectic magazine published in the 1920s, devoted to women's fashion and clothing': Conover, Loy 1997, 217.

151 Kouidis, *Mina Loy*, 108.

152 Loy 'Modern Poetry', 157.

In 'The Widow's Jazz', Loy can be seen to use the rhythms of jazz to overcome 'the cold barrier of print' – 'White man quit his actin' wise/colored folk hab de moon in dere eyes.'[153] 'The Widow's Jazz' is an elegy to the memory of her second husband, an American, Arthur Cravan. (Loy and Haweis divorced in 1917.) Loy first read the poem at Natalie Barney's salon on 6 May 1927, but it was not published until 1931, in the New York magazine *Pagany: a Native Quarterly.*[154]

Like other modernists, particularly T.S. Eliot and Edith Sitwell, Mina Loy was influenced by Baudelaire in her belief that artists had a prophetic role. In 'Apology of Genius' she represents their vocational isolation: 'Ostracised as we are with God / The watchers of the civilised wastes.'[155] In 'O Hell', she implies that the poet's function is to release the common mind into further enlightenment: 'Our person is a covered entrance to infinity / Choked with the tatters of tradition.'[156] The poem was first published in *Contact* 1, December 1920, which was edited by Robert McAlmon and William Carlos Williams. Conover notes that this marked the third time that 'Mina Loy's work had appeared in the inaugural issue of an American magazine dedicated to experimental writing'. The other two were *Rogue* and *Others*.[157]

By revising familiar systems of meaning, Mina Loy believed that the individual would gain a greater grasp of reality which consisted of full self-awareness. The influence of the French philosopher Henri Bergson can be seen most directly in her doctrinaire 'Aphorisms of Futurism', fifty-one prescriptions for self-liberation. The agenda of the doctrine is to achieve total consciousness by escaping from the psychic restraints of tradition and convention which forge 'the mechanical re-actions of the subconsciousness, that rubbish heap of race-tradition'.[158] The characters in Loy's poems are frequently able to envisage such self-fulfilment but rarely achieve it. The three poem sequence 'Italian Pictures' (1914) depicts Italians leading difficult lives but their vitality is a foil to the staidness of the British. In the first poem, 'July in Vallombrosa', an elderly invalid Englishwoman and her attentive daughter are perceived as wasting their lives, in contrast to the more carefree Italians:

153 'The Widow's Jazz', Loy 1997, 95–7.

154 *Pagany: a Native Quarterly*, which ran from 1930–1933, was supported by William Carlos Williams. For a lengthy discussion of the magazine and the poem, see Conover's editorial note in Loy 1997, 203–4.

155 'Apology of Genius', Loy 1997, 77–8.

156 'O Hell', Loy 1997, 71.

157 Conover, Loy 1997, 194.

158 'Aphorisms of Futurism', Loy 1997, 152.

I cannot imagine anything
less disputably respectable
Than prolonged invalidism in Italy
At the beck
Of a British practitioner
...
While round the hotel
Wanton Italian matrons
Discuss the better business of bed-linen
To regular puncture of needles [159]

According to Bergson, humans need a moment of self-comprehension to save them from wasting their lives. In Loy's 'Parturition', childbirth is this moment of self-awareness for the female subject. The lines 'For consciousness in crises races / through the subliminal deposits of evolutionary processes' correspond to the urgency of 'Aphorisms of Futurism' where she announced, 'TODAY is the crisis in consciousness'.

In imitating the linguistic construction of consciousness Mina Loy anticipates postmodernism. She exemplifies what Pound termed, '*logopoeia* or poetry that is akin to nothing but language, which is a dance of intelligence among words and ideas and modifications of ideas and characters'.[160] He applied the term to Loy and Moore and asserted that their poetry was a 'distinctly national product'. Pound's review was taken up by T.S. Eliot in his review of the same *Others* anthology in *The Egoist*, May 1918.[161] Loy's tribute 'Joyce's Ulysses' registers the major publishing event of modernism and exemplifies the 'dance of intelligence among words':

The loquent consciousness
of living things
pours in torrential languages

with Ireland's wings
flap pandemoniums
of Olympian prose
and satirize
the imperial Rose

159 'July in Vallombrosa', Loy 1997, 9–10.
160 Ezra Pound, review of *Others*, second anthology, ed. Alfred Kreymborg, *Little Review* 4. 11, March 1918: 55–8.
161 T.S. Eliot, under the pseudonym of 'Apteryx', review of *Others* second anthology, ed. Alfred Kreymborg, *Egoist* V, May 1918: 70.

of Gaelic perfumes
– England
the sadistic mother
embraces Erin –

Master
of meteoric idiom
present [162]

Typically, image and sound tend to replace metre and rhyme as the controlling devices of the poem. She closely followed the events surrounding the censorship of *Ulysses* in Britain and America and its publication by Sylvia Beach's Bookshop in Paris in 1922. Loy met Joyce in Paris and the poem appeared in *Vanity Fair*, April 1922.

Loy's critical essay on Gertrude Stein indicates her understanding of the *logopoeia* which she applied to her own poetry. Loy made the case that by involving readers in interpretation and by destabilising high cultural norms, modernism worked on democratic principles: 'through cubism the newspaper has assumed an aesthetic quality, through Cézanne a plate has become more than something to put an apple upon, Brancusi has given an evangelistic import to eggs, and Gertrude Stein has given us the Word, in and for itself.'[163] Her admiration for Stein is also evident in her pre-publication review of *The Making of Americans* for *Transatlantic Review*, 1924,[164] and in her verse portrait 'Gertrude Stein':

Curie
of the laboratory
of vocabulary
          she crushed
the tonnage

of consciousness
congealed to phrases
          to extract
a radium of the word [165]

---

162 'Joyce's Ulysses', Loy 1997, 88–90.
163 Mina Loy, 'Gertrude Stein', *Transatlantic Review* II. 2, 1924: 305–9, 427–30, reprinted in Scott, *Gender of Modernism*, 238–245.
164 Mina Loy, review of *The Making of Americans*, by Gertrude Stein, *Transatlantic Review* II, September and October 1924: 306, 429–30. See Hanscombe and Smyers, 227–8.
165 'Gertrude Stein', Loy 1997, 94.

Like Gertrude Stein, Loy dismantles familiar signifying processes and involves the reader in new ones. Like Stein, she experimented with the textual correspondences to modern art. In 1899, she studied art in Munich and then moved to Paris where she observed that everyone admired the Impressionists. In 1903 she went to Florence and then to New York. In Florence she met the Futurists, Carlo Carrà, Flippos Marinetti and Giovanni Papini, and it is believed that she had affairs with Marinetti and Papini. She was influenced by the Futurists' aesthetic principles and the freedom of abstract artistic practice,[166] but she was not in sympathy with their promotion of a machine age or the hygiene of war. Poems like the 'Italian Pictures' sequence explicitly drew upon painterly techniques and their kinetic dimension appropriates the Futurist goal of representing movement and energy rather than the fixed object of realist art. This enabled her to combine the main techniques of Futurism with the philosophy of Bergson who advocated that a poem should be an uninterrupted sequence of images. In this way, the interpretative distance between reader and text is reduced. The uninterrupted series of images is achieved in 'Mexican Desert', first published in *The Dial*, June 1921:

> The belching ghost-wail of the locomotive
> trailing her rattling wooden tail
> into the jazz-band sunset ...
>
> The mountains in a row
> set pinnacles of ferocious isolation
> under the alien hot heaven
>
> Vegetable cripples of drought
> thrust up the parching appeal
> cracking open the earth
> stump-fingered cacti
> and hunch-back palm trees
> belaboured the cinders of twilight.[167]

---

166 Futurism, which originated in Italy, repudiated the literary past and celebrated industrialisation, violence and war. It violated familiar syntax and at its extreme, words and symbols were used interchangeably. Flippos Marinetti came to England in 1913 and the *Book of Futurists* sold 35,000. Vorticism was associated with the magazine *Blast* edited by Wyndham Lewis. It was similarly anti-representational in order to destroy received dogmas through destroying their discourses. The First World War interrupted their activities. See Grant, 54–5.

167 'Mexican Desert', Loy 1997, 74.

The equivalent effect to visual portraits is achieved through juxtapositions, compounds and the sequence of images. According to Roger Conover, 'Mexican Desert', was a 'collaged recollection of Mina Loy's traverse of the parched Mexican desert in 1918 with her second husband, Arthur Cravan (né Fabian Avenerius Lloyd, 1887–?)'.[168] Cravan had disappeared to avoid military service and was later reported dead in a Mexican desert.

Marinetti's literary theories were influential on Loy's experiments with figuring motion. In the 'Technical Manifesto of Futurist Literature' (1913) he advocated radical departures from conventional literary form and image, such as 'One must destroy syntax and scatter one's nouns at random', 'abolish the adjective', 'abolish the adverb' and 'Every noun should have its double: that is, the noun should be followed, with no conjunction, by the noun to which it is related by analogy'.[169] These techniques can be detected early on, such as in 'At the Door of the House',[170] first published in the second *Others* anthology. It represents the prevalent imagery of eyes and houses in Loy's work. Houses are often signs of the female body and they symbolise the ambivalent containment and availability of women's sexuality.

Loy's alignment with Gertrude Stein and the woman-centredness of her poems demonstrate that she was clearly interested in the processes of identity. Oppression is represented in psycho-sexual rather than socioeconomic terms; for example, in 'Magasins du Louvre' (1915), the third of a three poem sequence, 'Moments in Paris', the glass-eyed dolls are symbols of female blindness.[171] Whether or not they are to blame for their blindness is ambiguous. In her polemical 'Feminist Manifesto', Mina Loy stated that women had the capacity to change themselves: 'Leave off looking to men to find out what you are **not** – seek within yourselves to find out what you **are**.' She advocated that women should free themselves from dependence by destroying in themselves the desire to be loved, by overcoming 'the feeling that it is a personal insult when a man transfers his attentions from her to another woman' and by defying the superstition that sex is impure.[172] The manifesto makes feminist readings of poems like 'The Effectual Marriage' problematic, although the poem endorses Loy's constant concern for mental freedom through self-

---

168 Conover, Loy 1997, 195–6. Loy and Cravan had married in January 1918; he disappeared in November 1918 and was last seen in Mexico.
169 Kouidis, 56.
170 'At the Door of the House', Loy 1997, 33–5.
171 'Magazines du Louvre', Loy 1997, 17–18.
172 'Feminist Manifesto', Loy 1997, 153–6.

awareness rather than through social change. To this end, the disruption of familiar language conventions was crucial.

Ezra Pound picked out 'The Effectual Marriage' (1915) as one of the most memorable poems of the period. In his enthusiastic interference, he reduced it to one fifth of its original length and reprinted it as 'Ineffectual Marriage' in two anthologies – thereby erasing the title's irony.[173] The characters Gina and Miovanni are thinly disguised inversions of Mina Loy and Giovanni Papini:

> In the evening they looked out of their two windows
> Miovanni out of his library window
> Gina from the kitchen window
> From among his pots and pans
> Where he so kindly kept her
> Where she so wisely busied herself
> Pots and Pans   she cooked in them
> All sorts of silalogues
> Some say   that happy women are immaterial
> ...
> What had Miovanni made of his ego
> In his library
> What had Gina wondered   among the pots and pans
> One never asked the other [174]

Like Marianne Moore's 'Marriage', the poem appears to be primarily about the oppression of women within a marriage, but it explores the effect of the social institution on both partners. Loy suffered a mental breakdown between 1914 and 1920, which is likely to have stemmed from the breakdown of her first marriage, aggravated by her father's opposition to divorce, and the death of her second husband.

Loy's thirty-four part sequence 'The Love Songs or Songs of Joannes' is the most difficult to interpret and to position. 'Joannes' represents Giovanni Papini. It can be read as a satire on gender roles, or as a more tragic exploration of the failure of love and the violence and anger of sexual conflict:

> We might have coupled
> In the bed-ridden monopoly of a moment
> Or broken flesh with one another

---

173 Conover, Loy 1997, 185.
174 'The Effectual Marriage', Loy 1997, 36–9.

At the profane communion table
Where wine is swill'd on promiscuous lips
…
Let us be very jealous
Very suspicious
Very conservative
Very cruel
Or we might make an end of the jostling of aspirations
Disorb inviolate egos

Where two or three are welded together
They shall become god

Oh that's right
Keep away from me   Please give me a push
Don't let me understand you   Don't realise me
Or we might tumble together
Depersonalised
Identical
Into the terrific Nirvana
Me you – you – me[175]

The injunctions concerning mutual sexual relations arguably pick up or contradict the principles of 'Feminist Manifesto' which urge women not to depend on a man, to desire or to be jealous of him.

Mina Loy was publicly identified as the emblematic 'Modern Woman' by the New York *Evening Sun*, 13 February 1917.[176] According to Roger Conover, she operated in public via various masks which allowed her to try out different identities and roles:

Rather than allowing herself to be fixed by an identity, she interloped, using her various identities to transform the cultures and social milieus she inhabited. Feminist and Futurist, wife and lover, militant and pacifist, actress and model, Christian Scientist and nurse, she was the binarian's nightmare ... She wore femininity as a mask, sometimes to disguise what she often called her 'Masculine side', sometimes to draw the masculine to her side and sometimes to make her feminism less threatening. Loy wore mask upon mask; she was a poet of sophistication, in the word's true sense. She knew something about constructing

---

175 'The Love Songs or Songs of Johannes', Parts III and XII, Loy 1997, 53–68.
176 Kouidis, 1.

myth and she knew something about violating the rules of heterosexual discourse.[177]

In exploring the construction and representation of female identity, Mina Loy connects to Marianne Moore and Djuna Barnes. She and Barnes were reputed beauties and were puzzling figures because they putatively looked like ladies but were frank about female sexuality in their writing and art. Djuna Barnes' fiction and poetry reached an international audience through *The Little Review* and other magazines, but received late attention as modernist texts. *The Book of Repulsive Women* (1915) and *Ladies Almanack* (1928) indicate her aversion to the social ideals of femininity.[178] Like the other avant-garde women, both Barnes and Loy prefigure the self-contained, closed linguistic discourses of postmodernism and draw attention to the violations and inadequacies of representation. They also portray women and social misfits on the margins of society. Loy was sympathetic to the Dada trend in twentieth-century art but not to its nihilism; in her words, she aimed 'to depict the strivings and disappointments of average or destitute humanity'.[179] 'Der Blind Junge'[180] indicates her attempts to redeem 'the bums', by finding beauty in the seedy and mundane, and she dealt more with low life in her later poems.[181] Although Mina Loy did not identify herself with one group, nor exclusively with women, her preoccupation with social inequality and female subjectivity, particularly in relation to sexuality and language, means that her poetry also contributes to the following category of female modernism.

---

177 Conover, Loy 1997, xliv–xlv.
178 For example, *Nightwood* (1936) has been hailed as a representative modernist text. For more discussion of Barnes as a neglected modernist, see Mary Lynn Broe, 'Djuna Barnes', in Scott, *Gender of Modernism*, 19–29.
179 Loy 1997, 116.
180 'Der Blind Junge', Loy 1997, 83–4. First published in '1921–2' section of *Lost Lunar Baedeker*. It means 'The Blind Youth' in German, and was considered to be one of her best poems by Yvor Winters.
181 See section 'Compensations of Poverty' (1942–49), Loy 1997.

Chapter Six

Female Modernism

Introduction

The category of 'Female Modernism' is constructed around poetry which is concerned with representation, particularly the representation of women's lives. Modernism's anti-realist aesthetic is ostensibly at odds with women's attempts to find a public voice for their experiences of cultural change, particularly concerning their new roles and rights. It is also at odds with their attempts to realise an identity which is distinct from the maternal function. The poets in this section variously reflect their preoccupation with psychological freedom and free expression as much through a feminist perspective or social conscience as through radical experiment. Female modernists did not dress themselves up as men but identified themselves as women by centralising women's experiences in their writing. They adopted and adapted male-associated poetic conventions; by appropriating the tradition to women's agendas, they changed its association with exclusive masculinity. In displacing literary symbols, reversing gender stereotypes or challenging depictions of idealised femininity, female modernists culminate the progress of the modern woman poet towards aesthetic freedom.

Charlotte Mew and May Sinclair tended to juxtapose voices of social conformity with the voice of independent will or sublimated desire while Edna St Vincent Millay, Anna Wickham and Sylvia Townsend Warner dramatised the psychological and sexual autonomy of the New Woman. Mainly through interior monologue or dialogue, all poets reflected contemporary debates about equality in marriage which accompanied the advances in legislation concerning women's rights. As with the other sections, my selection has been based upon any evidence of a poet's recognition in Britain. Consequently, I have included Edna St Vincent Millay but not other Americans, Dorothy Parker (1893–1967), Louise Bogan (1897–1970), Elinor Wylie (1885–1928) or Sara Teasdale (1884–1933).[1]

---

[1]   Elinor Wylie (neé Martyn) married in 1905 but eloped to England with Horace Wylie in 1910. They married in 1916 after her first husband committed suicide. In 1921 she left Wylie. Her poems were published in various magazines; she wrote historical novels and she became literary editor for *Vanity Fair*. She died from a stroke in 1928. The publication of Wylie's books was registered in some literary papers in Britain but rarely discussed. Her poetry was admired by Edna St Vincent Millay and Winifred Holtby.

One reason for the neglect of female modernists is that they defy classification as either 'experimental' or 'traditional' in the binary terms of modernist histories. Their dramatisations of women's identities, gender relations and class differences negotiate with the impersonality of modernist principles and blur a clear-cut division between so-called sentimental rhetoric – the register which is expressive – and avant-garde or anti-realist poetry. High modernism has been defined by stylistic innovation without recognising the complex relationship between women poets and poetic formalism. Additionally, feminist criticism has tended to equate feminist with avant-garde writing and therefore to concentrate on the formally experimental. By implication, it assumes that non-experimental texts support patriarchal structures. Although broadening the boundaries of modernism, Sandra Gilbert and Susan Gubar explore the restraints of patriarchal literary conventions on female creativity in the work of Edna St Vincent Millay, Marianne Moore, H.D. and prose writers. Gillian Hanscombe and Virginia Smyers also major on prose and confine modernism to experimentalism in their synthesis of a radical lifestyle and radical writing:

> Like the well-known Bloomsbury Group, our more hidden network shared that feature of early twentieth-century *Zeitgeist* in which the radical chasm between life and art is breached, so that experimentalism and autobiography became inevitably enmeshed and the static drives impelling the transformation of literature also power the need to live anti-conventionally. The manifestation of the *Zeitgeist* particular to literary creation has become known as 'modernism'.[2]

The emphasis on rupturing literary norms as the only means of breaking the sequence of male-dominated literary tradition is, nevertheless, only one strand of criticism. The other, headed by Bonnie Kime Scott, Celeste Schenck and Suzanne Clark, challenges language-centred interpretations of modernism, 'favoured in the canonisation process from Ezra Pound to Julia Kristeva', which ignores other breaks with tradition.[3] Suzanne Clark considers whether a poet like Millay betrays feminine discourse – 'since Millay practises no subversions against the linguistic forms of the fathers, she offers no challenge against the phallocentrism embodied in these forms except by the small incongruity of her girlish figure' – but suggests that in writing sonnets, Millay 'subverts male modernism by appropriating conventional male poetics from

---

2   Gillian Hanscombe and Virginia Smyers, *Writing for their Lives: The Modernist Women 1910–1940* (London: The Women's Press, 1987), 7.

3   Bonnie Kime Scott (ed.), *The Gender of Modernism* (Indianapolis: Indiana University Press, 1990), 86, 5.

a more classic past'.[4] In proposing to reclaim poems which cannot be described as technically avant-garde, it is not a case of claiming subversiveness where there is no conscious negotiation with received linguistic codes, but of proving that poetic form, *per se*, is not the mark of either traditionalism or modernism. The 'Female Modernists' particularly demonstrate that women could write within traditions of poetry without being enslaved by them. These poets experimented with metrical variation, free verse, irregular line lengths, half-rhyme, new symbolism and colloquial idioms.

Feminist criticism, then, needs to contest the binary opposition of 'conservatism' versus 'experimentalism'. Women negotiated between the anti-realist aesthetic, which was symptomatic of an intellectual loss of belief in an essential knowable self, their search for identity and their struggles for equal representation. Female modernists parodied or subverted conventional representations of femininity and gender roles, particularly in marriage. The characterisation in much of their poetry draws upon the vocabulary of psycho-analysis and connects with other modern literary practice and criticism which register the widespread reading of the newly translated psychology among intellectuals. Sigmund Freud's *The Interpretation of Dreams* (1900) was translated into English in 1913 and Carl Jung's *The Theory of Psychoanalysis* published in 1912, the *Psychology of the Unconscious* in 1916 and *Psychological Types* in 1923. In reviewing his fellow imagist, Amy Lowell, in *The Egoist*, Richard Aldington declared, 'we are now primarily interested in the poet's personality'.[5] The following poets create dreamstates, investigate female consciousness and dramatise the psychology of domestic or sexual conflict.

Unlike the avant-garde poets, female modernists acknowledge their gender and are more direct in exploring its social construction. Through the monologues and dialogues of various personae, usually women, they draw attention to the processes of representation. It is debatable whether they simply depict or subvert systems of oppression. For Gilbert and Gubar, such 'female female impersonation' intimates the necessary disjunction between everywoman's self and the self-presentation Western culture labels "feminine"'.[6] Referring to the line "what a fine shroud!" from Dorothy Parker's poem 'The Satin Dress'

---

4   Suzanne Clark, *Sentimental Modernism: Women Writers and The Revolution of the Word* (Bloomington and Indianapolis: Indiana University Press, 1991), 92, 71.

5   Richard Aldington, review of *Sword Blades and Poppy Seeds*, by Amy Lowell (London and New York: Macmillan, 1914). *Egoist* 1, 16 November 1914: 423.

6   Sandra Gilbert and Susan Gubar, *No Man's Land: The Place of the Woman Writer in the Twentieth Century. Vol. 3. Letters to the Front* (New Haven: Yale University Press, 1994), 58.

(1926), however, they question whether these self-dramatisations are limiting or liberating for writers:

> The dress of the female female impersonator may free her into an exhilarating fictionality, yet it may also finally shroud her. For a poet, in particular, the artifice of 'the feminine' threatened aesthetic reification even while it fostered creativity.[7]

It is instructive to register that Dorothy Parker suffered from depression and that Charlotte Mew and Anna Wickham committed suicide. There were different reasons for their internal conflicts but writing was a source of pleasure and liberation. In 'Return of Pleasure', Anna Wickham identifies freedom with linguistic adventurousness:

> I thought there was no pleasure in the world
> Because of my fears.
> Then I remembered life and all the words in my language.
> And I had courage even to despise form.
> I thought, 'I have skill to make words dance,
> To clap hands and to shake feet,
> But I will put myself and everything I see, upon the page.'[8]

For Anna Wickham, the guilt attached to the tension between writing and fulfilling the womanly duties which society prescribed is what shrouded her.

Luce Irigaray sees 'female female impersonation' as a consequence of women being 'exiled from themselves'.[9] It is possible, however, to conclude that by dramatising these disjunctions, women gained control of them and were thus able to develop a specifically female creativity. It is significant that these women did not display symptoms of the female affiliation complex, either in their perception of their nineteenth-century predecessors or in their relationships with contemporary female writers. There is sometimes a restraint in the versification or projection of female desire in Mew's and Sinclair's poems, but the metrical versatility and confident play with identities by Millay, Wickham and Warner indicate artistic freedom.

The 'female modernists' invalidate Freud's essentialised prescription for 'normal' femininity which involves envy for patriarchal traditions. They did

---

7   Gilbert and Gubar, *Letters to the Front*, 61.
8   Wickham, 'Return of Pleasure', *The Writings of Anna Wickham: Free Woman and Poet*, ed. R.D. Smith (London: Virago, 1984), 194.
9   Gilbert and Gubar, *Letters to the Front*, 39.

not disguise themselves as men nor dissociate themselves from each other. Charlotte Mew and May Sinclair appropriated and recast traditional poetic forms, metres and symbols. Their alienation from the conventional roles for women was implicit in their exploration of the psychological tensions between self-renunciation and self-realisation. Edna St Vincent Millay tended to structural ironies by writing sonnets in the voice of the autonomous woman. Anna Wickham equated stylistic with mental freedom and developed free verse lyrics. Sylvia Townsend Warner was the most rigorous in her prosody but the most unorthodox in her politics and sexuality. Collectively, the new consciousness of women, which was effected by suffragism and the First World War, is manifested in these diverse rejections of the social and literary representations of the feminine.

'Female Consciousness': Charlotte Mew (1869–1928) and May Sinclair (1863–1946)

Both Charlotte Mew and May [Mary Amelia] Sinclair were steeped in the Brontes but their probing of female repression and the shifting states of consciousness registers their twentieth-century context. They connect to their Victorian predecessors in their depictions of tragic women who are victims of social proprieties and male-domination, but they are distinctly modernist in their psychoanalytical evocations of repressed desire; May Sinclair was responsible for promoting the term 'stream-of-consciousness' in her review 'The Novels of Dorothy Richardson'.[10] It is reasonable to identify a mutual influence between her and Mew in their experiments with psychological narratives in verse. After Mew and Sinclair were introduced to one another by their mutual friend Catherine Amy Dawson Scott in 1913,[11] Sinclair championed Mew's poems. Suzanne Raitt's discussion of the relationship between Charlotte Mew and May Sinclair could place them within Hanscombe's and Smyers' version of modernism in which female friendships were vital to female creativity, but they are not included in *Writing for Their Lives 1910–1940*.

---

10   May Sinclair, 'The Novels of Dorothy Richardson', *Egoist* V, April 1918: 57–9.
11   A profile of May Sinclair by C.A. Dawson Scott was published in the *Bookman* October 1920: 7.

Charlotte Mew

Charlotte Mew presents a challenge to historians of literary modernism because she was a significant figure in her day but her work is hard to classify. Reviews of the recent fictional biography of Thomas Hardy's relationship with Mew, *His Arms are Full of Broken Things*, variously refer to her as 'a largely forgotten Victorian writer' and 'an early modernist writer'.[12] In considering Mew's significance in the context of modernism there seems to be an uncertainty about whether she wrote a handful of good poems or whether a new critical vocabulary is required so that her whole *oeuvre* can be reassessed. It is not stylistically 'avant-garde', but her experiments with free verse and the investigations of female psychology distinguish it from Victorian or Georgian writing. Charlotte Mew is a female modernist because she acknowledges female desire and the interworking of social conventions, particularly marriage laws, and women's identity. Her encoded lesbian orientation is also common to female, as well as avant-garde, modernists.

Records of the contemporaneous reception do not help to find a critical vocabulary for Mew's work but they do endorse the fact that she crosses literary groups. Thomas Hardy's good opinion – 'far and away the best living woman poet who will be read when they [the others] are forgotten' – has added to her credentials.[13] It is documented that he wrote a favourable review of *The Farmer's Bride* in 1916 and copied out 'Fin de Fête'.[14] Her literary centre was the Poetry Bookshop where she helped Alida Monro. However, the fact that Edward Marsh rejected Harold Monro's suggestion that Mew be the token woman for the third and fourth books of *Georgian Poetry*, 1917 and 1918, in favour of Fredegonde Shove, can be taken as a sign of Mew's stylistic adventurousness. It is rumoured that Walter de la Mare advised Marsh against Mew because of her uneven metres.[15] Her poems were printed in Harold Monro's *New Shilling Magazines* and various periodicals, including *The Egoist*, and anthologies of modern poetry. She appealed to avant-garde writers

---

12   Reviews of *His Arms are Full of Broken Things,* by P. B. Parris (New York: Viking, 1996). Maggie Gee, 'Inside the Prickly Poet'. *Daily Telegraph* 1 March 1997; Kate Flint, 'Public antics, private angst'. *Guardian* 6 March 1997; Julie Myerson, 'Getting to know all about Mew'. *Independent on Sunday* 2 March 1997.

13   Penelope Fitzgerald, *Charlotte Mew and Her Friends* (London: Collins, 1985), 170–4.

14   Sidney Cockerell, literary executor for Thomas Hardy, found 'Fin de Fete' copied out among Hardy's papers after his death in 1928.

15   De La Mare later revised his original opinion of her. See Fitzgerald, 194.

like Virginia Woolf, who famously called her 'the greatest living poetess',[16] and Edith Sitwell. In *The Criterion*, Sitwell disassociated both herself and Mew from the abhorrent 'wallowing' of the stereotyped poetess,[17] and in *Time and Tide*, she situated Mew in the higher echelons of literary practice since only the few 'who care anything for poets are reading her work ... cheap and vulgar women poets write about "love" affairs and give women a bad name'.[18]

Charlotte Mew's reputation was largely established by *The Farmer's Bride* in 1916. The Poetry Bookshop printed one thousand copies, in spite of the wartime paper shortage, and it was reviewed in *The Nation* when it was difficult to get properly reviewed unless you were writing from the trenches at that time.[19] In 1919, *The Farmer's Bride* was still selling steadily and in 1921, it was reprinted with new poems and simultaneously published with an American edition called *Saturday Market*. In America it caught the eye of Louis Untermeyer and at home it received favourable reviews by Edith Sitwell in *The Daily Herald*, *The Criterion* and *Time and Tide*.[20] Nineteen twenty-four and 1925 were successful years and the new edition of *The Farmer's Bride* continued to sell steadily; she met supporters like Robert Bridges, Siegfried Sassoon and Louis Untermeyer, and her reputation spread. After Mew's suicide in 1928, Sitwell paid tribute to her 'spiritual integrity', her hard work and suffering which drove her to her death, but noted, 'She died and her work is still unrecognised ... posthumous fame is a cold and grave thing.' By 'still unrecognised' Sitwell presumably meant that her poetry had not been properly appreciated by the major literary papers.

In aiming to 'pin down' the nature of Mew's poetry, the thematic arrangement of *Collected Poems* (1951) makes a largely unclassifiable range

---

16 Virginia Woolf, letter to Vita Sackville-West, 9 November 1924, *A Change of Perspective: The Letters of Virginia Woolf. Vol. 3 1924–1928*, ed. Nigel Nicolson (London: Hogarth, 1977), 140–41. An editor's note suggests that this was Hardy's opinion, not Woolf's. Earlier, however, Virginia Woolf had written, '[I] have got Charlotte Mew's book [*The Farmer's Bride*], and think her very good and interesting and unlike anyone else'; Virginia Woolf, letter to Robert Trevelyan, 25 January 1925, *The Question of Things Happening: The Letters of Virginia Woolf. Vol. 2. 1912–1922*, ed. Nigel Nicolson (London: Hogarth, 1976), 419.

17 Edith Sitwell, review of *The Farmer's Bride* and *The Rambling Sailor*, by Charlotte Mew (London: The Poetry Bookshop, 1921, 1929), *Criterion* IX, 34, October 1929: 130.

18 Edith Sitwell, review of *The Farmer's Bride* and *The Rambling Sailor*, by Charlotte Mew, *Time and Tide* 21 June 1929: 755.

19 May Sinclair in Fitzgerald, 160.

20 Edith Sitwell, review of *The Farmer's Bride*, by Charlotte Mew, *Daily Herald* 4 April 1922, Fitzgerald, 179.

seem manageable, but it does not allow for consideration of her stylistic evolution. Val Warner's recent collection (1997) is more usefully chronological and includes prose selections. There is a convincing case that she developed a stream-of-consciousness technique after meeting May Sinclair in 1913, although she constructed states of mind in her earlier poems. 'The Farmer' Bride', 'The Quiet House', 'In Nunhead Cemetery', 'Ken', 'Fame', 'Pécheresse', 'Beside the Bed' and 'The Sunlit House', were all written about 1912/13, before she met Sinclair. The disproportionate attention to 'Madeleine in Church' and 'The Farmer's Bride', obscures the range of her subjects and the novelty of her war poems such as 'The Cenotaph' and 'May 1915' (considered by Sitwell to show Mew 'at her best'). These, as Celeste Schenck points out, are 'pacifist hymns', suitably 'rhymed, metered, divided conventionally into stanzas'.[21] It has to be remembered that the ambivalent attitude to victory in these war poems was daring at the time because of its refusal to collude with official propaganda which required women to celebrate male militarism.

Mew's depiction of the conflicting drives towards and away from emancipation are typical of women's writing and connect to Victorian poets. Her bold female psychology and manoeuvres with verse forms are, however, markedly modernist. The tension between social conformity and personal liberty is structurally supported through the combined adherence to and departure from regular rhyme and metre. As Val Warner observes:

> Her innovative modernist technique of rhyming free verse, probably derived from Matthew Arnold and others, was closer to the iambic beat than her later work. Recent feminist or lesbian criticism, sometimes citing her use of repeated rhyme which chimed with her American champion Marianne Moore's concerns, often places Mew outside 'male-dominated' modernism, yet within this movement Mew innovated.[22]

Most striking is Mew's experimentation with line lengths. These and their attendant enjambments allow the representation of identity as a process, as in the opening lines of 'On the Road to the Sea':

> We passed each other, turned and stopped for half an hour, then went our way,
>   I who make other women smile did not make you –

---

21 Celeste M. Schenck, Introduction to Charlotte Mew, Scott, *The Gender of Modernism*, 320.

22 Val Warner, Introduction, *Charlotte Mew: Collected Poems ... Selected Prose*, ed. Val Warner (Manchester: Carcanet, 1997), 45. Hereafter, referred to as *Collected Poems*.

> But no man can move mountains in a day
>   So this hard thing is yet to do.
>
> But first I want your life: – before I die I want to see
>   The world that lies behind the strangeness of your eyes.[23]

May Sinclair was particularly bothered by Mew's uneven line lengths and wanted them tidied up although she conceded that they worked when read aloud by Mew.[24] Paradoxically, it is likely that Mew's experiments with representing associational thought were influenced by Sinclair's, although Val Warner suggests that Mew was more interested in moments of heightened response than the 'chance detritus of the everyday'.[25]

One reason for the heightened response is Charlotte Mew's concealment of her love for women which is suggested in the enigmatic phrase 'I who make other women smile did not make you –'. In 'On the Road to the Sea', the subject is tormented by what she cannot have: 'But I want your life before mine bleeds away – / Here – not in heavenly hereafters – soon'. The elusive identities of lover and loved one codify the same-sex passion. Her speakers are anonymous but implicitly women. A woman is the object of love in ostensibly male monologues, but these 'male impersonations' enabled Mew to express her repressed love for women. She was clearly successful because W.S. Blunt, missing the coded same-sex desire, questioned the 'sexual sincerity' in her poems and recommended that women should not write from the man's point of view.[26] Mew's dramatic monologues unsettle conventional representations and social expectations of gendered identities, most successfully in poems like 'The Rambling Sailor' and 'The Farmer's Bride'.

Mew's dramatisations of freedom and dominance in human relations engaged with contemporary debates surrounding changing legislation. The Royal Commission on Divorce and Matrimonial Causes was approaching the end of its deliberations when 'The Farmer's Bride' was first published in the *Nation* in 1912.[27] The poem attracted correspondence over the farmer's lack of condemnation for his runaway bride:

---

23   'On the Road to the Sea', *Charlotte Mew: Collected Poems*, 32–4.
24   Fitzgerald, 127.
25   Val Warner, *Charlotte Mew: Collected Poems*, xviii.
26   William Blunt, Fitzgerald, 170.
27   For further discussion of 'The Farmer's Bride' and other poems in relation to contemporary legislation, see Kathleen Bell, 'Mew, T.S. Eliot and modernism', *Kicking Daffodils – Twentieth-Century Women Poets*, ed. Vicki Bertram (Edinburgh: Edinburgh University Press, 1997), 13–24.

'When us was wed she turned afraid
Of love and me and all things human;
Like the shut of a winter's day
Her smile went out, and 'twadn't a woman –
– More like a little frightened fay
       One night, in the Fall, she runned away.'
...
'Not near, not near!' her eyes beseech
When one of us comes within reach.
The women say that beasts at stall
Look round like children at her call
I've hardly heard her speak at all.

Although not directly appealing for women's right to divorce, their case is implicitly represented. The farmer appeals for the reader's sympathy, but we are propelled towards the absent and silent bride. The silent woman is a recurring image in Mew's writing and, as here, creates the dramatic interest. The common interpretation of the wife's hurried exit from her new husband is marital rape but if the bride is drawn to other women, her terror would be the confrontation with her forbidden desire in the context of a binding heterosexual partnership. Characteristically, however, Mew exploits the monologue's ambiguities and dialogic to avoid and destabilise fixed perceptions and preconceptions. Reviewing *The Farmer's Bride* in *The Egoist*, H.D. identified Mew's success with characterisation in lyrical form, 'Miss Mew has chosen one of the most difficult forms in the language – the dramatic lyric ... [she has] succeeded like no others of the present generation, except Hueffer and Frost'.[28]

'The Farmer's Bride' illustrates Charlotte Mew's combination of a colloquial idiom with formal regularity. The trite rhyme scheme evokes a disturbing undertow of psychic dislocation of haunting intensity. Such powerful evocation was identified by Edith Sitwell as 'an elliptical way of leaving out events, or certain explanations'.[29] It is the urge to know what is unspoken by the *dramatis personae* which is haunting. In reassessing Mew, there is a more than usual shuffling between the human interest and the aesthetics of her poems. In 'The Quiet House' the first person voice and specific allusions to Mew's early experiences of early loss invite a biographical reading:

---

28 H.D., review of *The Farmer's Bride*, by Charlotte Mew, *Egoist* III, September 1916: 135.
29 Edith Sitwell, review of *The Farmer's Bride* and *The Rambling Sailor* by Charlotte Mew, *Time and Tide* 21 June 1929: 755.

> When we were children old Nurse used to say,
>   The house was like an auction or a fair
> Until the lot of us were safe in bed.
> It has been quiet as the countryside
> Since Ted and Janey and then Mother died
> And Tom crossed Father and was sent away.
> After the lawsuit he could not hold up his head.
>   Poor father, and he does not care
>   For people here, or to go anywhere.

Biography explains the references to the children, their father and their nurse, Elizabeth Goodman. Three out of the seven Mew children died in childhood and Mew's father suffered a debilitating sense of social inferiority to his wife, the daughter of his erstwhile employer. Nurse Goodman was a source of security and companionship, but also of guilt and alienation. Apparently, she instructed 'Lotti' to number her sins in confessional prayer based on severe doctrines of retribution. In the poem, unuttered grief and guilt are projected through distorting familiar images and conventional colour symbolism:

> Red is the strangest pain to bear;
>
> … A Rose can stab you across the street
>   Deeper than any knife:
> As the crimson haunts you everywhere –
> …
>   I think that my soul is red
> Like the soul of a sword or a scarlet flower!
> I am burned and stabbed half through,
>   And the pain is deadly sweet.

The depiction of pain as excruciating but enervating is a mark of Mew. At the end of 'The Quiet House', language peters out as the attempt to represent and reconstruct the self ends in failure:

>   Tonight I hear a bell again –
> Outside it was the same mist of fine rain,
> The lamps just lighted down the long dim street,
>   No-one for me –
> I think myself I go to meet:
> I do not care; some day I *shall* not think; I shall not *be*[30]

---

30   Charlotte Mew, 'The Quiet House', *Collected Poems*, 20–21.

The absence of a full stop at the end is an effective pointer to 'not being'; the repeated oxymoronic 'shall not' suggests that, like pain, oblivion is a state to be both wished and feared. 'The Quiet House' was written in 1913 and was, in Mew's words, 'perhaps the most subjective to me of the lot'.[31] On the other hand, Alison Light views 'The Quiet House' as a representative interwar text which centres on the private life. Typically, the strangling codes of propriety – 'family ties, respect for elders, the notion of womanly sacrifice, of home sweet home' – violate the individual.[32]

Like 'The Quiet House', 'Asylum Road' and other asylum poems such as 'Ken'[33] become more harrowing if read in the context of Mew's family fortunes but they also expose the treatment of the mentally ill. Her older brother Harry developed schizophrenia and her younger sister Freda had a mental breakdown and was sent to an asylum on the Isle of Wight. Charlotte and her sister Anne vowed not to have children for fear of passing on their mother's hereditary tendency to mental illness which eventually killed her brother and sister.[34] 'In Nunhead Cemetery', which commemorates Harry's burial, was picked out by Edith Sitwell for illustrating Mew's success in avoiding sentimentality while producing emotive power since she could 'hardly read [it] without tears'.[35] Although stating that '[Charlotte Mew] did not help the progression of poetry in any way', Sitwell found that she expressed the passions of love, of grief, of personal loss, 'with such a bare force that we are filled with respect'.[36] Interestingly here, Sitwell espouses modernism's 'impersonality' by setting expression of the passions in opposition to the progression of poetry. The 'asylum' poems also explore the psychological condition of the outsider which is a common preoccupation in Mew's poems, most notably the female prostitute and the female homosexual.

Mew's female subjects are frequently alienated by social conventions which prescribe them a role which is at odds with their search for a self. The parodied formal intercourse in 'Afternoon Tea' depicts the rigidity of Edwardian etiquette and morality which she found unendurably stifling but difficult to discard:

---

31 Charlotte Mew, Fitzgerald, 88.
32 Alison Light, *Forever England: Femininity, Literature and Conservatism between the Wars* (London: Routledge, 1991), 5.
33 Charlotte Mew, 'Ken', *Collected Poems*, 16–19.
34 Charlotte's brother Harry died in Peckham House lunatic asylum in 1901 and is buried in Nunhead Cemetery.
35 Edith Sitwell, review of *The Farmer's Bride* and *The Rambling Sailor*, *Time and Tide* 21 June 1929.
36 Edith Sitwell, review of *The Farmer's Bride* and *The Rambling Sailor*, *Criterion* IX, 34, October 1929.

> 'Please you, excuse me, good five o'clock people,
>   I've lost my last hatful of words,
> And my heart's in the wood up above the church steeple,
>   I'd rather have tea with the birds.'[37]

The deliberate ironies of the strained rhyme and exaggerated metrical regularity intimate the suppressed impulse to escape from the restriction of social conventions. Her simultaneous rejection and acceptance of the 'laws of morality' recur throughout her writing. In 'At the Convent Gate', the first of the 'Early Poems' in *Collected Poems* (1953), the dilemma between the free spirit and religious discipline is supported by the colloquial voice conjunctive with the sonnet form. The formal structure aptly depicts the discipline of Holy Orders which is foreign to the individual will. The opposition is indicated in the fragmentation of the young girl's monologue:

> Why do you shrink away, and start and stare?
>   Life frowns to see you leaning at death's gate –
>   Not back, but on. Ah! sweet, it is too late:
> You cannot cast these kisses from your hair.[38]

Although it is the first poem in the collection, Charlotte Mew did not depart radically from this type of dramatic monologue which combines formal structures with conversational idioms. Also, in mood and tone it is typical of her later poems which evoke a yearning for what is not there, whether God, a lover, or in the absence of these, death.

The yearning for an absent one is a nineteenth-century motif but Mew's treatment of denial connects with twentieth-century scepticism of social or religious taboos. Like 'The Farmer's Bride', 'Madeleine in Church' indirectly registers the debates surrounding the new legislation for marriage and divorce:

> Is that why I see Monty now? equal to any saint, poor boy, as good as gold,
> But still, with just the proper trace
> Of earthliness on his shining wedding face;
> And then gone suddenly blank and old
> The hateful day of the divorce:
> Stuart got his, hands down, of course
> Crowing like twenty cocks and grinning like a horse.[39]

---

37 Charlotte Mew, 'Afternoon Tea' was an early poem but first printed in *The Rambling Sailor*, 1929, *Collected Poems ... Prose*, 61–2.

38 Charlotte Mew, 'At the Convent Gate', *Collected Poems*, 58

39 Charlotte Mew, 'Madeleine in Church', *Collected Poems*, 25.

'Madeleine in Church' was written during the years 1913–16, the period of Mew's friendship with May Sinclair, when she was developing stream-of-consciousness in verse. This monologue also represents Mew's fascination with the Magdalene figure which allegedly started when the family's weekly sewing woman, Miss Bolt, lamented the fate of her niece who became a prostitute. It is likely that Charlotte Mew wrote about fallen women as a projection of her own struggle to marry a transgressive sexuality with an Anglo-Catholic church upbringing. Her inability to reconcile them accounts for what Val Warner calls 'a celebration of passion deeply felt, but always denied'.[40]

In 'Saturday Market', the woman's terrible secret is not named but is implicitly an abortion or miscarriage, the child which Mew would not have because of the congenital mental illness in her mother's family and because of her desire for women:

> See, you, the shawl is wet, take out from under
> The red dead thing –. In the white of the moon
> On the flags does it stir again? Well, and no wonder!
> Best make an end of it; bury it soon.[41]

The associational imagery in 'Saturday Market' makes it 'one of the most successful things Charlotte Mew ever wrote', according to Penelope Fitzgerald.[42] She suggests that Mew's childhood habit of tossing her head when she had adopted a short haircut was a symptom of her agonised preoccupation with what is absent. Similarly, Suzanne Raitt argues the significance of hair as the symbol for lack in several poems such as 'The Farmer's Bride' and 'The Forest Road',[43] which was written in 1914 when May Sinclair allegedly rejected Mew's advances:

> Oh! hidden eyes that plead in sleep
> Against the lonely dark, if I could touch the fear
> And leave it kissed away on quiet lids –
> If I could hush these hands that are half-awake,
> Groping for me in sleep I could go free
>
> ...
>
> See, dear, your hair –
> I must unloose this hair that sleeps and dreams

---

40 Val Warner, *Collected Poems*, xvii.
41 Charlotte Mew, 'Saturday Market', *Collected Poems*, 37–8.
42 Fitzgerald, 139.
43 Suzanne Raitt, 'Charlotte Mew and May Sinclair: A Love Song', *Critical Quarterly* 37. 3 (Autumn 1995): 3–17.

About my face, and clings like the brown weed
To drowned delivered things, tossed by the tired sea
Back to the beaches. Oh! your hair![44]

The allusions to concealed lesbian desire are always ambiguous. They can be connected with Mew's masculine clothing and her alleged fixation with women. At school, she adored her lesbian teacher Lucy Harrison, in whose home she boarded and read English Literature. Later, Mew became notoriously obsessed with her unrequited love for May Sinclair. In 'The Fête', female sexuality is typically both benign and threatening:

At first you scarcely saw her face,
You knew the maddening feet were there,
What called was that half-hidden, white unrest
To which now and then she pressed
Her finger-tips; but as she slackened pace
And turned and looked at you it grew quite bare:
    There was not anything you did not dare: –
Like trumpeters the hours passed until the last day of the Fair.[45]

The excruciating void of an unutterable and unpresentable love is registered by the elliptical dash.[46]

Mew's biographers agree that her love for women remained unresolved and is projected on to her representations of mental conflict. The latent lesbian eroticism in poetry like Mew's is one aspect of a distinctive female modernism. It is difficult to make a clear-cut opposition between radical content and conventional forms, since Mew's versification has a range and is often experimental with free verse rhythms and the displacement of conventional literary symbols. Charlotte Mew's essay 'The Poems of Emily Bronte' indicates what she admired and was hoping to achieve in her own work – the way that 'scenes and moods and thoughts are flashed upon our consciousness' and a sense of colour, passion and imagination. She recognised that Elizabeth Barrett Browning and Christina Rossetti were the 'most prominent women poets of

44   Charlotte Mew, 'The Forest Road', *Collected Poems ... Prose*, 23–5.

45   Charlotte Mew, 'The Fête', *Collected Poems*, 4–8; Celeste Schenck, in Bonnie Kime Scott, *The Gender of Modernism,* 317.

46   'Lesbian' was recorded as a medical term in German psychoanalysis in 1890. Its first use in literature was 1931. 'Sapphist' was used by Virginia Woolf in 1923, *OED*.

the nineteenth century', but their writing never surpassed Emily Bronte's, 'this lovesong of a woman who never loved'.[47]

May Sinclair

Although well-known as a writer during her life, like Charlotte Mew, May Sinclair is not easy to classify and her poetry has not been easily available. As Bonnie Kime Scott states, she 'deserves to be much better known as a maker and connector of modernism … [Sinclair] proved adept at practising and detecting in others' work the new formal and psychological aspects of modernism'.[48] She was involved in three intersecting arenas of cultural change: women's suffrage, the First World War and psychoanalysis. Her biographer, Theophilus Boll (1973), 'could not understand why she had been denied a place in the main procession of English novelists'. He connects May Sinclair with George Eliot in that they were similarly musical, respected by the intellectual leaders at the time and wrote literary criticism of the 'highest merit'.[49] Like George Eliot, her talent as a poet was 'minor' to her gift with innovative prose, although Sinclair's first ambition was to be a poet. Furthermore, like George Eliot, she did not have children and wrote about the woman's dilemma of being a dutiful daughter and a developing individual. However, Sinclair's novels, short stories and poems draw on twentieth-century psychology to explore the psychic distance between parents and children and between men and women. Her early poems were published in 1880 and 1886 under the pseudonym 'Julian Sinclair' but, unlike George Eliot, she dropped her male disguise and identified with other women writers. She was friends with Alice Meynell, Rose Macaulay and Katherine Tynan. According to Frances Gregg: '[May Sinclair] knew her stuff, and was no sentimentalist. No woman is, of course, though the false, fair, sidling creatures ape that quality.'[50] She belonged to the non militant Women Writers Suffrage League which published her pamphlet 'Feminism' in 1912, and supported the Women's Suffrage Bill.

Although associated with women's suffrage, May Sinclair was respected by her male literary colleagues whom she knew through the Society of Authors.

---

47   Charlotte Mew wrote an introductory essay to preface a new edition of Emily Bronte's poems, but she was beaten to it. See 'The Poems of Emily Bronte' in *Collected Poems … Prose*, 363–5.

48   Bonnie Kime Scott, *Refiguring Modernism. Vol. 1: The Women of 1928* (Bloomington and Indianapolis: Indiana University Press, 1995), 58.

49   Theophilus E.M. Boll, *Miss May Sinclair: Novelist. A Biographical and Critical Introduction* (New Jersey: Associated University Presses, 1973), 9.

50   Frances Gregg Wilkinson, unpublished memoirs, 1345–47, Hanscombe and Smyers, 21.

Her correspondents included T.S. Eliot, Thomas Hardy, Ezra Pound, H.G. Wells and Hugh Walpole. She was committed to syntactical innovation and wrote discerning reviews on progressive writing. She enjoyed the company of the imagist poets, Richard Aldington, H.D. and Ezra Pound, although she had some reservations about imagism. Nevertheless, she was interested in its novelties and wrote a studied defence of H.D. and imagism in *The Egoist*,[51] and an essay, 'The poems of H.D.' was published in *Fortnightly Review* and *The Dial*.[52] '*Prufrock* and other observations, a Criticism', which was published in *The Little Review*, December 1917, was a defence of Eliot's 'stark realism'. She introduced Ezra Pound to her literary acquaintances and helped to promote his writing. 'The Reputation of Ezra Pound', published in the *English Review*, April 1920, and *North American Review*, May 1920, was an important explanation of Pound's refusal to be 'a respecter of respectable persons' for the sake of progress.[53] *The Divine Fire* (1904), an imaginative fiction about the identity of a poet was widely read and reviewed. Her novel *The Tree of Heaven* (1917) is a family saga which examines the psychological impact of the First World War and women's suffrage on the different generations and sexes. As her fiction and criticism were published in the United States and England, she became known as an advocate of modernist developments, particularly in the move towards 'Reality' as perception, as explained in her books on philosophy, *Defence of Idealism* (1917) and *The New Idealism* (1922). She also contributed to the institutionalisation of psychoanalysis in Britain.

    May Sinclair concentrated on prose after 1900, but her poetry should be recognised on the maps of modernism. Some poems were printed in the journals and her free verse narrative *The Dark Night* was published in 1924. Her engagement with developments in modern poetry is reflected in her published articles, her Introduction to a book of *vers libre* by Jean de Bosschere (*The Closed Door*, 1917), and in reviews such as 'The Poems of F.S. Flint' and 'The Poems of Richard Aldington' in *The English Review*, 1921.[54] These critical writings, particularly 'Notes' on H.D. and 'On Imagism' indicate her intentions of avoiding abstractions, imagery and symbolism in order to put nothing between the writer and the object.[55] She is successful in 'After the Retreat', an uncollected poem printed in *The Egoist* in 1915. It records her experiences in Belgium during the First World War:

51   May Sinclair, 'Two Notes', on H.D. and imagism, *Egoist*, 1 June 1915: 88–9.
52   May Sinclair, 'The Poems of H.D.', *Fortnightly Review* 121, March 1927: 329–40.
53   May Sinclair, 'The Reputation of Ezra Pound', *English Review* 30, April 1920: 326–335.
54   May Sinclair, 'The Poems of F.S. Flint', *English Review* 32, January 1921: 6–18; 'The Poems of Richard Aldington', *English Review* 34, May 1921.
55   May Sinclair, 'Two Notes', *Egoist* 1915.

If I could only see again
The house we passed on the long Flemish road
That day
When the army went from Antwerp, through Bruges, to the sea;
The house with the slender door,
And the one thin row of shutters, grey as dust on the white wall.
It stood low and alone in the flat Flemish land.
And behind it the high slender trees were small under the sky.[56]

Among Sinclair's poetry and fiction published in *The Little Review* was 'The Child', a three part poem which depicts the search for identity in the developing child. It was also printed in *The Egoist* in 1917[57] and Part 1, 'Visionary' was in Thomas Moult's magazine *Voices* in 1920. Through the child's perspective it investigates the Romantic ideal of infant innocence:

I grin
With joy that isn't utterly pure from sin;
And at last I say:
'Don't you wish you were me,
To be able to see
God?'

The characteristic monologue indicates Sinclair's interest in psychology, and the process of perception is the centre of interest. Part II, 'Prison House', depicts the same girl at seven years old and 'Fright' explores her unspoken desolation at her mother's refusal to speak to her. This mother/daughter bond is explored throughout her autobiographical novel *Mary Olivier: A Life* (1919). It is difficult to formulate a critical response to 'The Child', because, like Mew's 'The Quiet House', it shifts between realism and dreamstate. Its reconstruction of consciousness, however, is clearly influenced by Freud and Jung, with whose work Sinclair was occupied at the time of the poem's composition. In August 1916, she started a book on sublimation and published 'Symbolism and Sublimation', a review of *Jung's Psychology of the Unconscious*, for the Medical Press.

The book-length poem *The Dark Night* (1924) is a thirty-three part woman's dramatic monologue and was published the year after May Sinclair gave a paper 'Primary and Secondary Consciousness' to her fellow members of the Aristotelian Society for the Systematic Study of Philosophy.[58] The

---

56 May Sinclair, 'After the Retreat', uncollected poem, *Egoist* II, 1 May 1915: 77.
57 May Sinclair, 'The Child', *Egoist* IV, February 1917: 24.
58 Boll, 256.

ability to 'get closer to reality', by which she meant to present the fragmentary consciousness 'that life imposes on us' and which she admired in Dorothy Richardson, is what she aimed for. *The Dark Night* drew admiration for its ambitious experiments with narrative free verse. It was written during her period of declining health but brilliant creativity. Nine hundred copies were printed and it was also published in America. It was admired by E.A. Robinson, Harriet Monroe sent a letter of approval and T.S. Eliot wrote, 'It seems to me a very remarkable thing to have accomplished, and, perhaps, too, an important step in the transition of the novel into some other form, which I feel is an inestimable development already foreshadowed in some of your own work as well as in that of Joyce and a few others'.[59] It also reflects contemporary debates about the changing nature of marriage which surrounded the 1923 Matrimonial Causes Bill and other legislation.

The Dark Night explores the fluctuations of desire and repression in a virtuous woman, Elizabeth, who falls in love with a poet, Victor Rendal, through reading his work:

> He is Victor Rendal,
> The poet,
> And I am only Elizabeth.
> It is wonderful
> That I should have a secret that he knows,
> And that I should read it there
> In his poems. (iii)

They eventually meet, and he requites her fantasy but breaks off their engagement because he fears that marriage will confine him:

> I saw myself caught and shut
> In the beautiful cage.
> And I know I could never get out.
> I am not what you think of me,
> A gentle thing, full of kindness and delicate thoughts,
> I am a beast untamed that must go alone. (xv)

Although this is Victor's voice, it is an aspect of Elizabeth's memory. After a spell abroad he returns to marry Elizabeth. Later, she finds herself left in charge of her cousin's fifteen year old daughter, Monica, who moves in with

---

59   T.S. Eliot, Boll, 144.

them. Upon her adolescent sexual awakening, Monica falls in love with Victor who succumbs to her flirtations. They leave, have a baby and become destitute. They are rescued by Elizabeth who gives them her house and pays a servant to look after the child, although she is tortured by the sight of Monica with the child that she could not have:

> We sat together,
> He with the child in his arms,
> And I with my arms empty,
> And my heart aching. (xxix)

The scene echoes Charlotte Bronte's recurring dream of holding a crying child whom she could not stop.[60] The tragic plot is likely to have been informed by Sinclair's reading of the three Bronte women. She published *The Life of Charlotte Bronte* in 1908 and *The Three Brontes* in 1912.[61] At the end of *The Dark Night*, Monica leaves Victor who returns to Elizabeth as a blind dependant, a reversal of power similar to that between Mr Rochester and Jane Eyre. Central to *The Dark Night* is the philosophical investigation of such nineteenth-century narratives of female self-abnegation which are critically reproduced in Elizabeth's unconditional love for Victor, for her difficult niece Monica and in her prayers to God.

May Sinclair's interest in the psychology of faith may have stemmed from the influence of Miss Dorothea Beale, the Principal at Cheltenham Ladies College who aimed to instil Christian doctrine and a strong sense of duty into her pupils. Passages like 'So / Out of my Hell / I have built up Heaven!' (xxix) are represented as narratives of psychic survival. They raise the questions of whether such altruism is freely willed and whether renunciation is liberating or repressive. It is possible that the hero was modelled on Richard Aldington who may have been the unnamed person whom she alleged to have 'loved once but could not marry'.[62] Whereas for Charlotte Mew unconsummated love was tormented, May Sinclair was apparently fulfilled by abstinence and intrigued by the psychological operation of sublimation.[63]

---

60 Elizabeth Gaskell's account of this dream of Charlotte Bronte's allegedly haunted Charlotte Mew; Fitzgerald, 48.
61 May Sinclair, *The Life of Charlotte Bronte*, 1908 (London and New York: Dent, 1966). May Sinclair, *The Three Brontes*, 1912 (London: Hutchinson, 1938).
62 Boll, 120.
63 Raitt, 1995.

The relationship between language, the unconscious, sublimation and the self is explored throughout *The Dark Night*. At the beginning, Elizabeth has no developed identity:

> All my life long
> I have hidden my real, secret self
> In silence;
> I was safe in silence,
> Nothing could harm me there. (iv)

When Victor returns her love, however, she models herself according to his version of her:

> I look at myself in the glass,
> I turn this way and that,
> To find out how I appear to him. (xiv)

The fictional ideal of love is a construction of Elizabeth's fantasy which is fed by reading Victor's poetry. Idealised romance is further deflated by the distortion of romantic symbolism, such as the red rose. A sinister dark rose represents Monica, the archetypal seductress:

> Her beauty burns darkly like the splendour of a dark rose,
> Half-folded, half-open;
> She is enchanted with the image in the glass. (xxii)

The recurring symbolism, such as mirrors and flowers, achieves narrative coherence. Sinclair also developed structural coherence through the single consciousness which engages the reader's sympathy. Where dialogue is reported, it is of course, through Elizabeth's perspective. When they discuss the relevance of marriage laws, sympathy is therefore, directed towards Elizabeth's position:

> 'and I can't ask you to love me outside the law?'

> 'No.
> For the law was made for weak women and their children.'

> 'That is not true.
> The law was made for the husband,
> To protect them from bastards got by other men.' (xv)

The lyrical passages, such as the hymn to love after the first reconciliation between Elizabeth and Victor,[64] are enhanced as fictions in juxtaposition with these more realist sections of the monologue. *The Dark Night* should be considered in the chronicles of modernist writing for its dramatisation of contemporary debates about marriage and the nature of women and for its sustained narrative in free verse. It represents May Sinclair's ability to construct a psychological state which corresponds to what she admired in T.S. Eliot: 'His reality ... may be an ordinary human mind suddenly and fatally aware of what is happening to it ... live thoughts, kicking, running about, jumping nervily, in a live brain.'[65]

New Woman Poets: Edna St Vincent Millay (1892–1950), Anna Wickham (1884–1947) and Sylvia Townsend Warner (1893–1978)

These female modernists voice the 'New Woman' preoccupations with social equality. Their 'female impersonations' subvert the idealisations of romantic love and feminine identity perpetuated in literary tradition, social conventions and women's popular culture.

Edna St Vincent Millay

Edna St Vincent Millay's relevance to British poetry between the wars has not yet been explored although her name was well-known in the literary press. In America, the Skidmore centenary conference (1992) registered the range of current approaches to her poetry which oscillate between the formalist and biographical. Cheryl Walker investigates whether the renewed interest in Millay [in America] implies that 'academic criticism, heavily influenced by T.S. Eliot, [which] came to dominate the literary scene in the late thirties has lost its grip'.[66] However, Jan Montefiore's dismissal, because 'modernism passed her by', reflects the disinterest of feminist criticism in Britain.[67] Millay

---

64 May Sinclair, *The Dark Night* (London: Jonathan Cape, 1924), xvii.

65 May Sinclair, '*Prufrock* and other observations, a Criticism', *Little Review* 4. 8, December 1917: 8–14. Reprinted in Scott, *Gender of Modernism*, 448–53.

66 Cheryl Walker, 'Anti-modern, Modern and Post–modern Edna St Vincent Millay: Contexts of Revaluation', in Margaret Dickie and Thomas Travisano (eds), *Gendered Modernisms: American Women Poets and Their Readers* (Philadelphia: University of Pennsylvania Press, 1996), 170–88.

67 Jan Montefiore, *Feminism and Poetry: Language, Experience, Identity in Women's Writing* (London: Pandora, 1987), 115.

does not easily fit literary modernism because she was conscientious about traditional literary form. Her appeal to a broad constituency of readers, who consumed her personal life from the women's magazines which published features on her appearance and home, can also discredit her in the currency of high modernist cultural sanctification. In her poems she turned the relentless feminisation of her image by popular and literary journals into parodic impersonations of different feminine stereotypes.[68]

Edna St Vincent Millay's adherence to form, particularly the sonnet, and her attention to syllabic metres meant that for a long time she was rarely identified within modernist practices. Colin Falck claims, 'The occulting of Millay's reputation has been one of the literary scandals of the twentieth century and it is time we found a proper place for this intense, thoughtful and magnificently literary poet.'[69] He believes that her skills in both old forms and the 'Whitmanian tradition of cadenced free verse', which have been perceived as her weakness, is her achievement. Millay was buried 'by the generation that needed to get modernism established', and which did not look beyond the appearance of tradition: 'her use of traditional forms is often deceptive; attention should be given to the interplay between the grand manner and the artless conversational'.[70] This interplay with traditional form and a conversational voice is the mark of her poems and of the kind of realist modernism which anticipates much 'thirties' writing.

The story of the rise and fall of Edna St Vincent Millay is familiar in histories of women poets. During the 1920s and 1930s she had a brilliant career in terms of publishing, international reputation, awards and prizes, reading tours and radio broadcasts. After the immediate success of *Renascence* (1917), she published poetry books in 1920, 1921, 1923, 1928, 1931, 1934 and 1939; her *Collected Poems* came out in 1949 and was reprinted several times. The reception to *The Harp Weaver and Other Poems* (1923) helped her to become the first woman to receive the Pulitzer Prize. In addition to writing poetry, she translated Baudelaire, wrote verse drama and satirical journalism, sometimes under the pseudonym of 'Nancy Boyd'. She directed a play and acted; she was a correspondent for *Vanity Fair* in Europe from 1921 until 1923 when she married Eugen Boissevain. They travelled further before moving to New York City in 1925 and by 1926 she was allegedly a 'National

68   Gilbert and Gubar, 'Female Female Impersonators: The Fictive Music of Edna St Vincent Millay and Marianne Moore', *Letters to the Front*, 57–120.

69   Colin Falck, 'Introduction: The Modern Lyricism of Edna Millay', in Colin Falck (ed.), *Edna St Vincent Millay: Selected Poems* (Manchester: Carcanet, 1992), xiii–xxx.

70   Falck, xxiv.

Figure' with a wide and enthusiastic following. In 1933 she gave a series of poetry readings on national radio and was awarded honorary DLitts by the University of Wisconsin and Russell Sage College. After the 1940s she became remade as a 'poetess' and was dropped from histories of American poetry.[71] In the second half of the twentieth century, her reputation has peaked and troughed, and although there are signs of revived interest with new editions of her *Collected Poems* in 1981, 1984 and 1988 and her *Selected Poems* in 1992, Edna St Vincent Millay is virtually unrecognised in British literary canons or academic courses.

Several of Millay's books were published simultaneously in New York and London and her poetry was clearly known to British writers and readers. Thomas Hardy said that 'one of the two great things in America was the poetry of Edna St Vincent Millay',[72] A.E. Housman, allegedly told an American reviewer, 'I get more enjoyment from Edna St Vincent Millay than from either Robinson or Frost', and wrote to Sidney Cockerill in 1932, 'some things of Edna St. Vincent Millay which I have seen make me think her the best living American poet'.[73] In the literary papers, however, she was misrepresented as a sentimentalist. In *Time and Tide*, Thomas Moult mocked her bohemian image by referring to a 'young American author who wrote a poem of most brilliant promise, "Renascence", but since then she has travelled the world and learned in the Latin quarters of all the capitals what it is to be "artistic"'.[74] In *The Criterion*, F.S. Flint said she 'takes refuge in a landscape of convention'[75] and the *TLS* review of *Poems*, was headed 'Emotion and Sentiment'. The article did, however, indicate her reputation by referring to *Renascence* as 'a volume which has passed through several editions, known itself to numerous English readers, and by report to many more'.[76]

The early inability of reviewers to hold together the two faces of Millay, the lyrical love poet and the political commentator, reduced her to mythologies of the sentimental which clouded subsequent critical readings. 'The author of

---

71   For examples of the omission of Millay from critical works, see Gilbert and Gubar, *Letters to the Front*, 63–9.

72   Thomas Hardy, quoted in an advert for *The Buck and the Snow*, by Edna St Vincent Millay, *TLS* 6 December 1928: 965. The book had a long review in the *TLS* 10 January 1929: 27.

73   Allan Ross Macdougall (ed.), *Letters of Edna St Vincent Millay* (New York: Grosset and Dunlap, 1952), 163–4, n. 21.

74   Thomas Moult, review of *Poems*, by Edna St Vincent Millay (London: Martin Secker, 1923), *Time and Tide* 20 June 1924: 593.

75   F.S. Flint, review of *The Buck in the Snow* by Edna St Vincent Millay (New York and London: Harper and Brothers, 1928), *Criterion* VIII, 32, April 1929: 532–4.

76   Review of *Poems*, *TLS* 1 November 1923: 724.

Renascence' was John Crowe Ransom's example of the emotionally excessive woman poet in his notorious article 'Poet as Woman' published in 1938. It represents the prejudice against women during the 1920s which continued into the 1930s. Ransom, apart from declaring that 'Miss Millay is rarely and barely very intellectual, and I think everybody knows it', accused her of 'the mechanical determinism of metrical necessity'.[77] He distinguished the sonnets in 'Fatal Interview', her 'mature work', from 'her little-girl things' and recognised that he used a conventional symbol, 'which I hope was not objectionable, when I phrased this lack of hers [intellectuality], deficiency in masculinity'. His main criticism was directed at her formalism:

> She is not a good conventional or formalist poet, and I think I have already suggested why: because she allows the forms to bother her and to push her into absurdities. I imagine there are few women poets of whom this is not so, and it would be because they are not strict enough and expert enough to manage forms – in their default of the disciplines under which men are trained.[78]

The article by Ransom and the reception to Millay's poetry exemplify the pressure upon women to prove their poetic muscles by manipulating metre and form.

Millay was not temperamentally conventional and positioned herself outside of the conservative literary establishment which she believed gave her prizes 'more for moral than aesthetic reasons'. In a long letter to Arthur Davison Ficke, she registered her view that Elinor Wylie had never received the Pulitzer Prize because 'she had left her husband and child and run off to Europe with a married man'. Similarly, she [Millay] had not been awarded it a second time because she had protested against the execution of Sacco and Vanzetti:

> Suggesting that President Lowell of Harvard was withholding evidence which might have freed these men ... with how much affection following this action of mine would an aged professor of Harvard look upon my subsequently published volumes? With how much affection would any aged and conservative governor of a New England state look thence forward upon the published works of a person who had agitated as I had done against the governor of a neighbouring New England state?[79]

---

77   John Crowe Ransom's essay, 'The Poet as Woman' (1938) was a review of *Edna St Vincent Millay and Her Times*, by Elizabeth Atkins (University of Chicago Press, 1936). The review was originally printed in *Southern Review* 2, Spring 1937: 784.

78   John Crowe Ransom, 'The Poet as Woman', *The World's Body*, Ransom 1938 (New York: Kennikat Press, 1964), 103.

79   Millay, letter to Ficke, 25 May 1938, Macdougall, 294–6.

She also recorded her opposition to the murder trial of Nicola Sacco and Bartolomeo Vanzetti in 1927 in poetry.[80] Millay was an active suffragist and her sonnet 'To Inez Milholland' – 'Upon this marble bust that is not I' – was read on 18 November 1923, in Washington at the unveiling of a statue of three leaders in the cause of Equal Rights for Women.[81] She was clearly aware of what Laura Riding called the 'declassing' of women poets; referring to Louise Bogan in a letter to Edmund Wilson, Millay observed, 'Isn't it wonderful how the lady poets are coming along?'[82] Significantly, Louise Bogan depicted unashamed female desire. In 1931, Millay wrote, 'I have noticed with considerable fun that many of the English women writers like 'Fatal Interview' and not so many of the men.'[83] She met Anna Wickham in Paris in 1922[84] and was acquainted with her poetry, which acknowledges female sexuality and investigates women's competing impulses for freedom and duty. Like Anna Wickham's, the ironic register of much of her poetry is that of the emancipated woman.

Millay's strong public image and the assertiveness of her poetic voice indicate the progression away from literary mythologies of self-denying femininity. Many of her speakers express the sexual assertiveness of the New Woman which her contemporary male critics found difficult to marry with the stereotypical poetess:

> What lips my lips have kissed, and where, and why,
> I have forgotten, and what arms have lain
> Under my head till morning.[85]

The love lyrics are distinctively twentieth-century in substituting desire for romance. In the famous epigrammatic, 'My candle burns at both ends' or the parodic, 'Oh, oh, you will be sorry for that word', the flippancy is deliberately

80   Nicola Sacco and Bartolomeo Vanzetti were anarchists convicted of murder on slim evidence. There was a public outcry and they were eventually given posthumous pardons in 1977.

81   Millay, 'To Inez Milholland', *Collected Poems* (New York and London: Harper and Brothers, 1956), 627. Inez Milholland was the first wife of Millay's husband.

82   Millay, letter to Edmund Wilson, Gilbert and Gubar, *Letters to the Front*, 57–120. For more discussion of Louise Bogan, see Suzanne Clark, 'Medusa and Melancholy: The Fatal Allure of Beauty in Louise Bogan's Poetry', Clark 1991, 99–126 and *Stealing the Language: The Emergence of Women's Poetry in America*, by Alicia Ostriker (London: The Women's Press, 1987).

83   Millay, letter to Eugene Saxton, 30 December 1931, Macdougall, 244.

84   Millay, letter to Edmund Wilson, 20 July 1922, Macdougall, 153–4.

85   Millay, *SP* 1992, 56.

dissonant with fictionalised idealisations of women in love. In 'I being born a woman', Millay's depiction of female psychology is typically teasing:

> I being born a woman and distressed
> By all the needs and notions of my kind,
> Am urged by your propinquity to find
> Your person fair, and feel a certain zest
> To bear your body's weight upon my breast.[86]

The absence of a specific context, speaker or addressee makes it difficult to identify her subject position. The *TLS* review of *The Buck in the Snow* (1928), headed 'Modernism and Romance', objected that the majority of poems 'display[ed] more emotion than she felt' although it conceded some element of 'impersonation'.[87] As here, reviewers did not have a critical terminology for Millay's mocking exaggeration or reversal of literary stereotypes, particularly combined with the deceiving innocence of familiar formalism.

In some of her most assertive sonnets in *The Harp Weaver and Other Poems* (1923), Edna St Vincent Millay appropriates the form to substitute women's sexual desires for courtly love:

> Pity me not the waning of the moon,
> Nor that the ebbing tide goes out to sea,
> Nor that a man's desire is hushed so soon,
> And you no longer look with love on me.[88]

Idealised romance is also deflated through mocking final twists or through the ironic treatment of fairytale. Gilbert and Gubar interpret Millay's preoccupation with the Bluebeard story as a symptom of the anti-romantic imperatives which drove her subversions of conventional roles: 'specifically from *A Few Figs from Thistles* onwards, Millay masquerades as a *femme fatale* in order to expose the artifice and absurdity of romance while recreating conventional love scenes as interviews fatal to male rather than female lovers.'[89] She set forward the image of a woman having every right to sexual pleasure with no obligation to fidelity.[90]

---

86 Millay, *SP* 1992, 55.
87 Review of *The Buck in the Snow* by Edna St Vincent Millay, *TLS* 10 January 1929: 27.
88 Millay, *SP* 1992, 53.
89 Gilbert and Gubar, *Letters to the Front*, 77–8.
90 www.sappho.com/poetry/e–millay.htm.

The dramatic monologue allows Millay to expose and reject feminine stereotypes while inviting sympathy:

> Oh, oh, you will be sorry for that word!
> Give back my book and take my kiss instead.
>
> …
>
> Some sane day, not too bright and not too stormy,
> I shall be gone, and you may whistle for me.[91]

In the context of debates about gender roles and equal rights in marriage, Millay's representations of women being proactive in leaving a man were radically opposed to post-war injunctions of womanly duty.

Through a series of characters, the poems explore the construction of identities, and frequently represent the psychological alienation of women in the contexts of domesticity and married love. In the sonnet 'Tenderly, in those times', a monologue by a woman nursing her sick husband, there is a disconcerting disjunction between her situation and her capacity to envisage freedom:

> And she could see in her mind's vision plain
> The magic World, where cities stood on end.
> Remote from where she lay – and yet – between,
> Save for something asleep beside her, only the window screen.[92]

The woman's internal conflict is projected through her differing perceptions of her husband, as a helpless child, a friend or 'something asleep'. Millay modernises the yearnings of Emily Dickinson's or Emily Bronte's women for an elusive liberty or lover through a contemporary idiom. The sympathy evoked for the trapped wife endorses women's goals of freedom. The recurring representation of aloneness is not sentimental but is often contextualised by the inability of the sexes to communicate or by death. The discipline of the sonnet form combined with the colloquial idiom reconstruct women's divided impulses between liberation and containment.

It is possible to read the formalism either as oppressing or as liberating Millay's imagination. Gilbert and Gubar believe that the sonnet operated as 'a kind of archaic costume in which the rebellious poet sometimes seriously, sometimes paradoxically attired herself to call attention to the antiquated garb

---

91 Millay, *SP* 1992, 54.
92 Millay, *SP* 1992, 67.

of femininity'.[93] Debra Fried identifies the suitability of the sonnet for women poets to explore the fictionalising of women through literature: 'For women writing poetry in the years between the wars, the ... shaky fiction of new sexual freedom for women made the sonnet an apt form in which to scrutinise the inherited stances of men toward women and poets towards their muses.'[94] The ease of the colloquial idiom and the range of dramatisations suggest that Edna St Vincent Millay was liberated in her parodies, reversals and contradictions of traditional stereotypes.

The ironic love lyrics in *A Few Figs from Thistles* (1920) are mainly sonnets but from *The Harp Weaver and Other Poems* (1923), Edna St Vincent Millay was more experimental with form and voices. 'City Trees' has the verbal economy of imagism and her manipulation of cadenced free verse developed during the 1930s. Others, like 'Above these cares'[95] or 'Time, that renews the tissues of this frame',[96] a sonnet which reverses the dismal portrayal of ageing, are difficult to link to a modernist canon but would be a loss if cut from literary records simply for that reason. Suzanne Clark concludes her illuminating chapter on Millay by reiterating her importance to the literary history of the 1920s and 1930s. She anticipates that Millay's status will depend on the extent to which she is credited for negotiating well with what is perceived as masculine literary language:

> Edna St. Vincent Millay does not seem a likely candidate to be called a feminist writer. Does she offer any of the elements Teresa de Lauretis lists as essential to feminism: 'a critical reading of culture, a political interpretation of the social text and of the social subject, and a rewriting of our culture's "master narratives"'? That may depend on how we read her, and whether or not we take seriously her real power during the 1920s and 1930s to represent women's writing as a part of literary history. Her struggle provokes our awareness of the contradictory status of the woman author, whose authority, as de Lauretis emphasises, comes from a masculine literary language. Her status, then, depends not on any absolute literary value but on a criticism which extends its interest to the difference that gender makes in literature.[97]

It is a paradox, as Clark points out, that Millay accrues an authority through her competence with the sonnet which has been associated with male poets.

---

93   Gilbert and Gubar, *Letters to the Front*, 113.

94   Debra Fried, 'Andromeda Unbound: Gender and Genre in Women's Sonnets', *Twentieth-Century Literature* 32.1, 1986: 11, 17; Gilbert and Gubar, *Letters to the Front*, 114.

95   Millay, *SP* 1992, 104.

96   Millay, *SP* 1992, 99.

97   Clark, 96.

However, in appropriating the form, by writing sonnets *as a woman*, the associations of literary conventions no longer remain exclusively male.

Anna Wickham

Celeste Schenck joins Charlotte Mew and Anna Wickham for writing the 'overtly feminist poetry that has escaped notice for its failure to adhere to the experimentalist demands of a masculinist modernism'.[98] They were exact contemporaries, yet in her subversions of masculinist ideals of femininity, Anna Wickham is more similar to Edna St Vincent Millay who saw 'a great deal' of her in Paris and thought many of her poems unpolished 'but some splendid, and all interesting'.[99] She exemplifies the female modernist in her investigation of the social construction of gender. Not only was her articulation of women's frustrations and desires, radical – why else would her husband want to lock her away on hearing that her poems were to be published?[100] – but her experiments with assonance and half-rhyme were pioneering. Her reputation was at its height, especially in the USA, after the First World War. She is more direct than Mew, Sinclair or Millay in addressing social inequality. Since there are frequent connections between the situations of the poems and her own difficulties with combining marriage, motherhood and writing, her female 'impersonations' operate as self-dramatisations which are not disjunctive to her sense of multiple identities. Although female identity is usually projected as unfulfilled, women in her poems are oppressed by social laws rather than suffering from the essentialised feminine deficiency prescribed by Freud. Like other modernist women, she expresses the internal conflicts involved in refuting self-renunciation as an ideal.

The publication of *The Writings of Anna Wickham* in 1984 brought out her poetry from obscurity. In spite of her overt gender politics, Anna Wickham's poetry has seldom figured in feminist studies of literary modernism yet she was well known in Britain, Paris and the United States. British born, she grew up in Australia, returned to Britain in 1904 and married Patrick Hepburn in 1906. She held soirées at their home in London, with music, entertainment

---

98 Schenck, in Scott, *The Gender of Modernism*, 613.
99 Millay, letter to Edmund Wilson, 20 July, 1921, Macdougall, 153–4.
100 David Garnett relates the gruesome incident in 1915 when Anna Wickham put her hand through a glass door during a quarrel with her husband when he discovered that her poems were to be published by The Poetry Bookshop: he 'thought anything she wrote worthless and in any case had no intention of allowing his wife to be a poet: she was not to do it again. Anna exploded with rage and found herself certified as insane'. David Garnett, Introduction, *Selected Poems*, by Anna Wickham (London: Chatto & Windus, 1971), 8.

and lectures on women's suffrage. Her literary acquaintances included Nancy Cunard, the Poetry Bookshop crowd, such as the Monros and David Garnett, and the bohemian writers in London associated with D.H. Lawrence.[101] She spent five months in Paris in 1922, during which she met Ezra Pound as well as Natalie Barney, Sylvia Beach, Robert MacAlmon, Edna St Vincent Millay, and Djuna Barnes. Temporarily, she became part of the circle of women who lived on the Left Bank and Natalie Barney became an emotional centre. Although there is no evidence of any sexual involvement, they maintained 'a correspondence of passionate love letters' which were also passionate discussions about the woman artist.[102] Domestically, she felt a failure: she had a still born child and a miscarriage before her first son James was born; he was followed by three more children but her third son died of scarlet fever in 1921. She had a stormy marriage and when her husband died from a climbing accident in 1929, she was freed from the bonds of marriage but not of motherhood.

Anna Wickham's poetry is not formally traditional, but seems distant from the impersonality of male modernist doctrines. Surprisingly, some poems were included in *Edwardian Poetry* (1937) and *Neo-Georgian Poetry* (1937) but they have nothing of the formal restraint or agreeableness associated with either of those groupings. Editors and literary critics did not know what to make of her. The reviewer of *The Little Old House* (1921) commented on her 'lively rhythm and vigorous expression' but undermined the poems as 'flung-off stanzas' and 'sudden unrevised inspirations, sometimes even despising punctuation in her haste'.[103] Yvor Winters' review in *Poetry* in 1922, titled 'A Woman with a Hammer', accused her of generalities about men and women 'which do not constitute poetry'.[104] He did not tune in to her ironies nor observe the metrical and metaphorical processes by which she *constructed* the mental hammering of marital conflict.

The poems from *The Man with a Hammer* (1916) are particularly preoccupied with transgressing literary conventions. 'Examination' is a rare

---

101 Anna Wickham was a good friend of Nancy Cunard and they were neighbours at Parliament Hill, London, for a while. She was also friends with Freda and D.H. Lawrence. Alida Monro was apparently jealous of her because Harold was in love with her, as was David Garnett. For these and other details I am grateful to George (her son) and Margaret (her daughter-in-law, wife of James) Hepburn whom I visited on 28 July 1997.
102 R.D. Smith, *The Writings of Anna Wickham*, 24. The letters are with George and Margaret Hepburn.
103 Review of *The Little Old House*, by Anna Wickham, *TLS* 18 August 1921: 535.
104 Yvor Winters, *Poetry* XX. 2, May 1922: 94–5, reprinted in Francis Murphy (ed.), *Uncollected Essays and Reviews of Yvor Winters*, 1973 (London: Allen and Lane, 1974), 3–5.

but loosely structured sonnet – 'I write my thought in a ragged way'.[105] In 'The Egoist', first published in *The Contemplative Quarry* (1915), the speaker flaunts an irreverence for metrical regularity while making it clear that she can 'master' it in order to shore up her credentials as a poet:

> Of the dead poets can I make a synthesis,
> And learn poetic form that in them is;
> ...
> It was as fit for one man's thoughts to trot in
>   iambs, as it is for me,
> Who live not in the horse-age, but in the day of
>   aeroplanes, to write my rhythms free.[106]

The association between free rhythm and the modern day 'of aeroplanes' is symptomatic of her intellectual connection between stylistic and psychological freedom. Her association of old techniques with tired thought recurs throughout her work – 'How can I put the liquor of new days / In the old pipes of rhyme?'[107] In 'The Egoist', above, she refers to her discovery of the 'near perfect rhyme' for holding together idealised happiness and humdrum quotidian experience. Matt Holland's discerning discussion in *Poetry Review* (1988) identifies her self-referential use of rhyme to convey predictability and flat routine, the stultifying effects of British conventionality.[108] At other times, exaggerated rhyme signals that the socially prescribed calm surface of middle class respectability belies disturbing undercurrents of repressed impulses for freedom.

Anna Wickham's poems deal with women's identities and particularly the nature of the woman artist. These 'female impersonations' also dramatise her internal conflicts, frequently through dramatic monologue. The desire to be freed from gender when she creates is the subject of 'A Woman in Bed': at times the poet seems to be overwhelmed by the hindrance of femaleness, but on good days, 'I can forget my skirt, / I hide my breast beneath a workman's shirt, / And hunt the perfect phrase.'[109] 'The Fresh Start' collects together her irresolvable tensions concerning the competing roles of wife, mother and artist:

---

105 Wickham, 'Examination', *Writings*, 193.
106 Wickham, 'The Egoist', *Writings*, 173.
107 Wickham, 'Formalist', *Writings*, 195.
108 Matt Holland, 'Anna Wickham: Fettered Woman, Free Spirit', *Poetry Review* 78. 2 (1988): 44.
109 Wickham, 'A Woman in Bed', *Writings*, 197.

O give me back my rigorous English Sunday
And my well-ordered house, with stockings washed on Monday.
…

Two years now I have sat beneath a curse
And in a fury poured out frenzied verse.

It is not clear whether the feminist sensibility here is mitigated by nostalgia for the old ideologies of clear-cut gender roles or merely impersonating this nostalgia. It follows the pattern of several poems where the female imagination envisages freedom but capitulates to socially prescribed duties:

When this hot blood is cooled by kindly Time
Controlled and schooled, I'll come again to Rhyme.
Sure of my methods, morals and my gloves,
I'll write chaste sonnets of imagined Loves.[110]

If there is a wish for clear gender roles, it is only for relief from the demands of her competing identities: 'if any ask why there's no great she-poet, / let him come live with me, and he will know it'. 'New Eve', a previously unpublished poem in *Writings*, articulates the impossibility of reconciling the 'two sides of me' – 'Why was I born beneath two curses, / To bear children and to write verses?'[111] Anna Wickham never did win her battle over the conflicting priorities of home and writing and took her life believing that she had failed her family. She also believed that she had failed as a poet.

It is clear from poems like 'Suppression'[112] – 'If you deny her right to think, / If you deny her pride of ink' – and 'Woman and Artist'[113] – 'There's no excuse for expression from a woman / Unless she be representative human' – (both undated) that writing was an act of freedom. Freedom of expression is her central preoccupation in *Fragment of an Autobiography*:

The relief of writing will give me nervous and physical energy to continue with my task. I write also because I am a woman artist and the story of my failure should be known. I have a European reputation: my poetry is mentioned with honour in the *Encyclopaedia Britannica*: that should give me the right to live. I have very little newspaper reputation. I have always avoided it as a part of my phobia.[114]

110 Wickham, 'The Fresh Start', *Writings*, 240.
111 Wickham, 'New Eve', *Writings*, 324.
112 Wickham, 'Suppression', *Writings*, 327.
113 Wickham, 'Woman and Artist', *Writings*, 331.
114 Wickham, *Fragment of an Autobiography, Writings*, 52.

Confronting her internal sense of failure, Anna Wickham noted the lack of positive role models, 'there have been few women poets of distinction', and, significantly, the high suicide rate among her predecessors, which she increased by hanging herself in 1947.

Like Edna St Vincent Millay's, several of Anna Wickham's poems have the anti-romantic purpose of New Woman novels and some are outspoken representations of a feminist consciousness. Nevertheless, freedom is a troubled concept in her work. 'The Scapegoat', 'The Dilemma' and 'Envoi' articulate the warring claims of liberty and restraint. The strict parental régime of her childhood and severe Roman Catholic education had instilled the habit of obedience but also provoked rebellion against discipline. She felt an outsider in Australia and particularly in the convent where it was known that her father was anti-religious. R.D. Smith reads the frequent images of beating and whipping in terms of Anna Wickham's violent treatment by her mother, who was envious that her father showed more sympathy with his daughter than with his difficult wife. In her one hundred and six page *Fragment of an Autobiography*, she recorded that her mother's jealous anger 'was to be the most destructive agent in my life'.[115]

The uneasy relationship with her mother no doubt inhibited a wholehearted acceptance of radical feminism and accounts for Wickham's ambiguous treatment of the sex war. Additionally, gender was a complicated concept because her mother wanted her to be feminine and her father wanted her to be like a boy. In 'The Angry Woman' the concept of the androgynous imagination parallels other women's search to avoid gender imperatives when writing: 'There is the sexless part of me that is my mind.'[116]

'The Angry Woman' is a lengthy disclosure on gender differences and equality: 'In many things are you and I apart / But there are regions where we coincide / Where law for one is a law for both.' The speaker also questions the value of marriage for women: 'If sex is a criterion for power, and never strength, / What do we gain by union?' Similarly, in 'Definition', she questions whether a wife's identity is anything more than a mother and bed partner.[117]

The complex psychology at work in domestic conflict is dramatised in 'Marriage', where civilised fighting, symptomatic of a couple's competing instincts for love and liberty, are depicted as inextricable and inevitable. *Fragment of an Autobiography*, however, relates the unrelenting oppression in Anna Wickham's own marriage:

---

115 Wickham, *Fragment, Writings*, 105.
116 Wickham, 'The Angry Woman', *Writings*, 202–4.
117 Wickham, 'Definition', *Writings*, 201–2.

For twenty-nine years I have been attempting to order the house. For twenty-five years of my misery, it has been my passionate preoccupation. I began in the first year of my marriage with a sort of amiable unction. Three years after my marriage, my domestic happiness was in ruins … It was during my pregnancy that the shades of the prison house began to close in on me. My husband, Patrick Hepburn, from being my devoted lover seemed to become my enemy and my judge.[118]

Although the poems operate in conjunction with the autobiography, they are not confessional. The coexistence of sympathy and antipathy, particularly towards men, seems rooted in Anna Wickham's own relationships. She broke off two engagements before marrying Patrick Hepburn. In the autobiography she vacillates between blaming him or blaming herself for their inability to get on. She states that her father ruined her life but also 'My father's love for me was a refuge from the passion of men of my own generation against which I always reacted.'[119] She was, however, consistent in her resentment at giving up her promising singing career when she got married. 'The Silent Singer'[120] represents the way in which her absorption in her husband's interests – photographing Romanesque churches and cathedrals – necessitated silencing her own identity: 'But from the wealth of living I have proved / I must be silent if I would be loved.'[121] 'The Slighted Lady' is a lengthy exploration of the psychological fossilisation which happens to women when they surrender their minds to men's authority. It has none of the buoyancy of other poems where a jaunty rhythm offsets the weight of the message: 'And the man possessed her and grew in ecstasy, / And he talked while the woman listened and smiled.' The husband could see no further than his needs – 'this woman is no goddess, but my wife; / And no perfection, but the keeper of my house' – so she succumbs to the relative ardour of a younger man:

'My husband has not looked at me for many days –
He has forgot that flesh is warm,
And that the spirit hungers.
I have waited long within the house,
I freeze with dumbness and I go.'

118 Wickham, *Fragment, Writings*, 51–2.
119 Wickham, *Fragment, Writings*, 124–5.
120 Wickham, 'The Silent Singer', *Writings*, 285. The poem first appeared in Harold Monro's *Chapbook*, March 1923. It was one of a trio of poems, 'Three Love songs', along with 'The Way of Sleep and Fear'. I am grateful to James Hepburn for this information in a letter to me 15 December 1993.
121 Wickham, 'The Affinity', *Writings*, 176.

Then she stept down from her high window
And walked with her young lover, singing to his lute.[122]

The poem demonstrates Anna Wickham's skill as a storyteller and her predilection for fracturing fairytale idealism.

In the context of the emphasis on women's duty as homemakers during and after the First World War, Wickham's dramatic monologues of female infidelity and free will were bold. 'Divorce' seems to have few if any precedents or contemporaries in its disrespect for marriage laws, although it resembles Charlotte Mew's 'The Farmer's Bride' and Edna St Vincent Millay's portraits of the independent woman lover.[123] Even more shocking would have been Wickham's 'The Revolt of Wives' which challenged the idealised maternal function of patriarchal discourses. It contradicts the idea that childbearing was woman's greatest gift, goal and pleasure:

Nor for my very pleasure will I vex
My whole long life away in things of sex,
As in those good Victorian days
When teeming women lived in stays.
...
Show us the contract plain, that we may prove
If we are loved for children, or are loved for love.[124]

The coupled rhymes in tension with the colloquial voice structurally support the subject, the conflicting demands of individual choice and social propriety. Internal tension between freedom and duty is similarly constructed in 'The Wife':

My brain dies
For want of exercise,
I dare not speak
For I am weak.
...
'Twere better for my man and me,
If I were free,
Not to be done by, but to be.
But I am tied.[125]

---

122 Wickham, 'The Slighted Lady', *Writings*, 187–9.
123 Wickham, 'Divorce', *Writings*, 166.
124 Wickham, 'The Revolt of Wives', *Writings*, 180–81.
125 Wickham, 'The Wife', 'Definition', 'The Angry Woman', *Writings*, 199, 201, 202.

Wickham's hatred of routine and conformity recurs in both her poetry and prose. A prose piece, 'The Deficit', begins with characteristic mimicry, 'I know some dull people. They live in a dull house, in a dull street in Bloomsbury, which has not always been dull.'[126] Irony is a favourite weapon against the mediocrity and social snobbery of the suburban middle classes, most memorably caricatured in 'Nervous Prostration':

> I married a man of the Croydon class
> When I was twenty two.
> And I vex him, and he bores me
> Till we don't know what to do!
> It isn't good form in the Croydon class
> To say you love your wife,
> So I spend my days with the tradesmen's books
> And pray for the end of life.[127]

The jog-trot rhythm mimics the pedestrian routine of marriage, but the woman's death-wish is a disconcerting undertow. Wickham encountered the 'Croydon class' in the Hepburns:

> While my husband's family, the Hepburns, were filling the great Croydon villa with their pride, their efficiency and their gold, my people were in Wimbledon, at war with all that villas stood for.[128]

In 'Meditation at Kew', it is likely that she had in mind her husband's sister Ellen who became engaged to someone the Hepburns believed was socially beneath her. She encouraged the match, partly because Ellen was living with her in Paris and trying her patience:

> Alas! for all the pretty women who marry dull men,
> Go into the suburbs and never come out again,
> Who lose their pretty faces and dim their pretty eyes,
> Because no one has skill or courage to organise.[129]

In his review of *The Contemplative Quarry* (1915) in *The Egoist*, Richard Aldington picked out this last line as an example of Anna Wickham's tendency to ruin a perfectly good poem with 'doggerel'. Apart from this weak phrase,

---

126 Wickham, 'The Deficit', *Writings*, 379.
127 Wickham, 'Nervous Prostration', *Writings*, 210.
128 Wickham, *Fragment, Writings*, 53.
129 Wickham, 'Meditation at Kew', *Writings*, 45.

however, he admired her manipulation of rhyme and conceded the logic of her argument:

> [It is] the humorous protest of a sane woman observing the insane things which are excited from her sex by bourgeois rules. She manages to say bitter and satiric and true things with a good deal of humour (she runs the eighteenth-century trick of antithetical rhyme). Her misfortune is to be clear-sighted among the blind, vital among the insipid, natural among the affected, sane among the stupid ... You get the impression of a woman (you seldom get the impression of femininity from a woman's book) who is very interested in life and especially in her own life. She wants to know what the devil women are to do with their lives.[130]

The parenthetical observation, '(you seldom get the impression of femininity from a woman's book)' exemplifies my argument throughout this book, that the majority of women were preoccupied with resisting femininity.

The satire of 'Meditation at Kew' and 'Nervous Prostration' typically has an acerbic edge in the depiction of marital routine and mediocrity as literally soul-destroying. *Fragment of an Autobiography* explains in detail why Anna Wickham's background ignited her hostility against the oppression of social snobbery and conventional gender roles. The lectures at the back of *Writings* indicate her interest in social welfare and class warfare.[131] Her portraits of poor women were motivated by sympathy for their doubly oppressed social position. 'The Town Dirge', which dramatises the plight of the poor works as a political tract. It centres on the death of a child who was born into poverty:

> O you who are strong in the town,
> Mighty to build, mighty to shield the weak,
> Join with us that we may say,
> Under God's grace, and of our good care,
> No child shall die.[132]

The seven stanza narrative corresponds to an incident mentioned in Anna Wickham's lecture 'School for Mothers' (probably written 1909–10). In this lecture she explained her welfare work and argued for greater respect for the families depicted in her poem:

---

130 Richard Aldington, 'New Poetry', review of *The Contemplative Quarry*, by Anna Wickham (London: The Poetry Bookshop, 1915) *Egoist* II, 1 June 1915: 89–90.

131 Wickham, 'Notes for a Lecture', *Writings*, 374–6.

132 Wickham, 'The Town Dirge', *Writings*, 167–8.

The educated classes, the comfortable classes, are not keeping their ranks filled up: we are getting our population from the cottage and the tenement. It seems to me that God's poor are doing God's work. We have to look through the veil of dirt and ugliness in their houses, the rags and sometimes the unloveliness of neglected children, and see human souls, and do the best with our material. And we really have to decide that the material is not so bad after all.[133]

Another verse portrait, 'Laura Grey: died June 1914, in Jermyn Street', published in the *Daily Herald*, 16 June 1914, commemorated the suicide of a pregnant woman and questioned why society blamed her instead of asking, 'where was the man?'[134] In the same lecture about the school for mothers she also crusaded for women like Laura Grey and her child who need not have died:

A man is thrown out of work through some change in trade, a fashion is altered, there is another strike, and his living is gone; there is no food for the mother and for the child. Now this is very unfair; and in a great rich town like London, and a town so full of clever people who can contrive, of women who are good housekeepers, it seems a very stupid, thriftless thing that pregnant women should be without food.[135]

According to Aldington, *The Contemplative Quarry* 'registers the revolt of the human sort of mind from the exasperating pretensions and limitations of English Middle Class life'.[136] Similarly, orderliness is linked with the stifling of love in 'Tidiness and Order': 'And duty fills all silence /And leaves no room for song.'[137]

Love is a common emblem in Anna Wickham's poetry, often as the signifier of God and never sentimental. Wickham's tricky relationship with religion is likely to stem from the over-sensitised conscience of an ex-convent girl. In refiguring God as female, she again seems to be ahead of her time: 'In nameless, shapeless God found I my rest, / Though for my solace I built God a breast.'[138]

In her various depictions of spiritual search, there is a mixture of Christian doctrine and the new psychoanalysis of personality and motivation. 'Two Egotists' depicts a self-satisfied pedant who accuses his silent companion of

---

133 Wickham, Lecture 'School for Mothers', *Writings*, 372–3.
134 Wickham, 'Laura Grey', *Writings*, 335.
135 Wickham, Lecture 'School for Mothers', *Writings*, 372–3.
136 Aldington, 'New Poetry'.
137 Wickham, 'Tidiness and Order', *Writings*, 261.
138 Wickham, 'Inspiration', *Writings*, 169.

not doing anything about the poor, the sick and the unemployed.[139] 'The Individualist' is a lengthy and intriguing interrogation of a man's self-sufficiency and possessiveness towards his child.[140] It is one of several discourses which recognise the social construction of male as well as female gender.

The dialectical treatment of gender relations and social conventions in Anna Wickham's poems sets up mixed responses; the voices may be assertive, but they are rarely polemical. Her knowledge of theatre, ballet and the music hall are reflected in her poetry's dramatic qualities and strong rhythms. 'The Cherry Blossom Wand' (1915), for example, was meant to be sung and was very popular. Wickham's mix of form and formlessness manipulates the association between metrical formalism and the restraints of social conventions. R.D. Smith makes the useful comparison between Wickham's epigrammatic dramatisations and Stevie Smith's 'quirky, cheeky way with truthfulness', particularly in a poem like 'The Tigress'.[141] Like Stevie Smith, Anna Wickham crosses conventional boundaries of genre and having to ask the question, 'is this poetry?' unsettles literary conventions and exposes the limitations of traditional literary criticism.[142] They both dramatise the subordination of women and the socially disadvantaged. Stevie Smith could be grouped with 'female modernists' but since she did not publish until the end of the nineteen-thirties I have placed her in my final section.

Sylvia Townsend Warner (1893–1978)

Sylvia Townsend Warner operated within the conventional poetic form and syntax with which she had been educated. Her poetry best unhinges the association between formal verse and political conservatism. She was the most formalist yet the most active in socialist and communist movements. Furthermore, she rejected heterosexuality for the lesbian partnership with Valentine Ackland and therefore the marriage and motherhood expected of women. Jane Marcus endorses Celeste Schenck's case for 'elasticising' stylistic considerations in order to include writers like Warner:

> Revising modernism to include this poem [*Opus 7* (1931)] unsettles definitions … If we privilege lyric fragmented voices from this period, what to do with this

---

139 Wickham, 'Two Egotists', *Writings*, 299–301.
140 Wickham, 'The Individualist', *Writings*, 216–7.
141 Wickham, 'The Tigress', *Writings*, 38.
142 See Martin Pumphrey, 'Play, fantasy and strange laughter: Stevie Smith's uncomfortable poetry', *Critical Quarterly* 28. 3 (Autumn 1986): 85–96.

other tradition, the daughters of *Aurora Leigh*? Townsend Warner wrote the verse novel as well as Tudor metrical conceits, the dark and dramatic Hardyesque as well as the committed communist ballad. Her multivoicedness and creation of character in dramatic soliloquy call out for a critical extension of Bakhtin's work on the novel to poetry. In the age of metropolitan modernism, Warner politicizes the pastoral ... she set all the forms at her disposal dancing to the tune of politics.[143]

Including Sylvia Townsend Warner's poetry in the chronicles of modernism is not over-stretching the boundaries. She published *The Espalier* in 1925 and *Time Importuned* in 1928. In October 1929, she recorded that she was writing a poem a day. Her poems were printed in literary journals and anthologies, and she contributed articles on contemporary literature to *Time and Tide*. She engaged with the issues of equality and the gendering of women's writing raised by Virginia Woolf in *A Room of One's Own* (1928). Joining the Communist Party in 1933 concluded her journey to Marxism during the 1920s.[144] Her politics was rarely acknowledged in contemporary reviews which centred on her formalism. *Time Importuned* (1928) was given a long review in the *TLS* which complimented her stylistic versatility.[145] In *The Criterion*, it received a favourable verdict from J.G. Fletcher, although he used the 'poetess' word: 'Now that Miss Charlotte Mew is dead, I think Miss Warner should be proclaimed the best poetess in England.'[146]

   'Wish in Spring', which is concerned with the right to write, echoes poems by her predecessors, such as Anne Bradstreet or Elizabeth Barrett Browning, and by her contemporaries like Anna Wickham. Unusually, for Warner, it is in free verse:

> But as I am only a woman
> And not a tree,
> With piteous human care I have made this poem,
> And set it now on the shelf with the rest to be.[147]

Warner self-consciously used homely images – 'cups and saucers on a shelf' – to register the competition between the woman's domestic role and her

---

143 Jane Marcus, 'Sylvia Townsend Warner', Scott, *Gender of Modernism*, 531–8.

144 John Lucas, *The Radical Twenties* (Nottingham: Five Leaves, 1997).

145 Review of *Time Importuned*, by Sylvia Townsend Warner, *TLS* 20 September 1928: 665.

146 J.G. Fletcher, review of *Time Importuned*, by Sylvia Townsend Warner (London: Chatto & Windus, 1928). *Criterion*, VIII, 30, September 1928: 128.

147 Sylvia Townsend Warner, 'Wish in Spring', *Collected Poems* (Manchester: Carcanet, 1982), 83–4.

identity as a poet. Her gentle meditation on the barriers to women poets becomes more taut when informed by her diary entry of November 1927, 'I want to read and write nothing but poetry'.[148] Probably on account of its confident voice or political subject matter, much of her poetry was unpublished or uncollected.

Warner's poems written in the 1920s tend to be about country people and places, often in the democratic forms of ballad or narrative quatrains. Through examining the plight of individuals, she 'politicises the pastoral' as she does in her highly imaginative, socialist feminist novel *Lolly Willowes* (1926) and later in the narrative poem *Opus 7* (1931). Warner's interest in the formulation of gender is represented through dramatisations, particularly of country women. An uncollected poem,'Ornaments of Gold', is a dialogue about conventional femininity between a mother and daughter:

> Mother, why do you hang in each hurt ear
> those bobbing rings of gold?
> To tweak men's glances thither from my face to behold.
> …
> And when I am woman grown, shall I dress like you?
> Yes, child, you may depend,
> Woman-kind shall go thus till our world's end.[149]

'The Rival' is ostensibly a light-hearted monologue by a farmer's wife about her husband's absorption in his work, but it depicts her sense of confinement and neglect which is typical of women's interwar writing:

> The farmer's wife looked out of the dairy:
> She saw her husband in the yard;
> She said: 'A woman's lot is hard,
> The chimney smokes, the churn's contrary.'
> She said:
> 'I of all women am the most ill-starred.
>
> Five sons I've borne and seven daughters,
> And the last of them is on my knee.
> Finer children you could not see.
> Twelve times I've put my neck into the halter:

---

148 Warner, *The Diaries of Sylvia Townsend Warner*, ed. Clare Harman (London: Chatto & Windus, 1994), 78.
149 Warner, 'Ornaments of Gold', *CP*: 5.

You'd think
So much might knit my husband's love to me.'[150]

As a reviewer observed in *Time and Tide*, Warner's poems bridge nineteenth-century Romanticism and twentieth-century modernist innovation in their combination of pastoral and stream-of-consciousness: 'There is no doubt that Miss Warner is a poet, but there are epitaphs and ironic tragedies on the roads of Wessex and psychoanalysis.'[151] It was similarly noted in the *TLS* that 'her verses present a collection of accidental images'. Like other female modernists, Warner's depiction of freedom refutes the self-renunciation to which nineteenth-century texts often capitulated. 'The Absence' complements poems about restraint by reversing the romantic myths and depicting carefree independence: 'How happy I can be with my love away!'[152] These poems fulfil her aim of evoking frames of mind with few images; instead, she uses conceits and intellectual stresses to construct poetry which was 'formally tight in thought and expression'.[153] The dialogic voices avoid political polemic but allow the poet to direct the reader's response to the dramatised conflicts and debates.

Sylvia Townsend Warner's lesbian love lyrics with Valentine Ackland are chronologically thirties poems. They can also be added to the body of 'Sapphic' modernist poetry which contributes to a canon of lesbian writing. Sylvia Townsend Warner and Valentine Ackland were unusually confident in expressing their mutual desire, albeit with gender indeterminate pronouns. These love lyrics link them to Vita Sackville-West, Amy Lowell, H.D., Gertrude Stein, Djuna Barnes and Charlotte Mew. I am looking at Warner's and Ackland's love and political poems in the next section since most of them were written during the 1930s.[154]

---

150 Warner, 'The Rival', *CP*: 162.
151 Naomi Boyd Smith, Review of *Time Importuned*, by Sylvia Townsend Warner, *Time and Tide* 3 August 1928: 29.
152 Warner, 'The Absence', *CP*: 12.
153 Claire Harman, *Sylvia Townsend Warner: A Biography* (London: Minerva, 1985), 79.
154 For more discussion of Warner as a modernist, see Jane Marcus in Scott, *Gender of Modernism*, 531–8.

Chapter Seven

The 1930s: Cultural Politics and the Poetry of Sylvia Townsend Warner, Valentine Ackland, Nancy Cunard, Winifred Holtby, Naomi Mitchison and Stevie Smith

Introduction

The two strands of modernist negotiations with the British literary tradition, the more stylistically conventional and the avant-garde, continued into the 1930s. The work and public image of experimentalists like Marianne Moore, H.D., Amy Lowell and Edith Sitwell had helped to diminish the 'poetess' stigma. Reviewers were less able to draw upon the myths of feminine simplicity, conservatism and piety but they still positioned women in a literary sidestream. However, as I have set out in *Women's Poetry of the 1930s*, they were rarely mentioned in histories of 'thirties' poetry.[1] Because 'thirties poets' have been associated with left-wing politics, the omission of women has perpetuated the prejudices that they are politically conservative and concerned with the private life. The fierce egalitarianism of Stevie Smith, and the political engagement of Sylvia Townsend Warner, Valentine Ackland, Naomi Mitchison, Winifred Holtby and Nancy Cunard challenge the lingering assumptions that women's concerns are with personal, not public, experience. These poets were active in communist, socialist and feminist movements and attempted to write poetry of commitment which avoided propaganda. Their woman-centred poetry deflates idealised femininity or domesticity and also documents literary women's complex relationship with women's emancipation.

By including the 1930s, I am endorsing a cultural, rather than a language-based, model of modernism and the pluralisation of modernisms, since the hegemony of high modernism is partly responsible for sidelining women. Additionally, to cut off modernism in 1929 would falsely suggest that thirties

---

1   *Women's Poetry of the 1930s*, ed. Jane Dowson (London: Routledge, 1996).

poetry suddenly ceased to be stylistically innovative or that twenties poetry was not political.[2]

The diversity of poetry by women demonstrates the diversity of the decade and the woman-centred poetry further challenges the orthodox versions of the 1930s. Even the alternative histories by John Lucas (1978) and Adrian Caesar (1991) do not record the number of women who wrote and published during the 1930s. Several had successful publishing histories during the period and Frances Cornford, E.J. Scovell, Nancy Cunard and Sylvia Townsend Warner also published translated poetry. Women were involved in making poetry broadcasts, running printing presses and bookshops, editing anthologies, and producing literary periodicals, notably Lady Rhondda's *Time and Tide*. The key journals and anthologies published women's poems. In *The Faber Book of Modern Verse* (1936), Michael Roberts included Edith Sitwell, Laura Riding, Marianne Moore, and H.D. while W.B. Yeats published Frances Cornford, Vita Sackville-West, Edith Sitwell, Dorothy Wellesley, Michael Field, Charlotte Mew and Sylvia Townsend Warner in *The Oxford Book of English Verse* (1936). These poets, along with Ruth Pitter, Kathleen Raine, Laura Riding, Lilian Bowes Lyons, Dorothy Wellesley, Margaret Stuart and Anna Wickham. were recurring names in other representative anthologies like *Recent Poetry* (1933) and *Poems of Today* (1938). Significantly, however, their political poems were not selected and the overtly political writers, Naomi Mitchison, Nancy Cunard, Winifred Holtby and Stevie Smith, were only included in liberal and left-wing publications and not always in these.

Women have had particular difficulty in being counted in the records of thirties poetry because, as Adrian Caesar argues, literary value has become equated with liberal humanism masquerading as left-wing ideology so that where women are concerned they have been perceived as either too reactionary to be relevant or too radical to have any literary value. In the context of the thirties, the association of conservative forms with conservatism has meant that the formalists, Vita Sackville-West, Elizabeth Daryush, Frances Cornford and Ruth Pitter, all of whom were particularly successful in term of publishing and critical reception, have appeared to be out of synch with their time. Instead of counting as achievements, awards like the Hawthornden Prize (Sackville-West and Pitter) and the Queen's Medal for Poetry (Cornford and Smith) have identified them with the conservative literary establishment. On the other hand, an unorthodox poet like Sylvia Townsend Warner, who combined polemical communist ideals and a couched lesbian sexuality with regular poetic form, has been difficult to position and remained largely underestimated:

---

2   See John Lucas, *The Radical Twenties* (Nottingham: Five Leaves, 1997).

An exile from the pages of literary history … her politics labelled radical in the social text of the twentieth century and her poetic and fictional forms conservative in the Modernist canonical text, she is known by the epithet – *lady* communist, as Stephen Spender sarcastically dismissed her, and a *communist* writer who contributed to the *Left Review* as those who purport to write the literary histories of the Spanish Civil War and the 1930s list her.[3]

Although here he mocks the unfamiliar image of a politically radical woman, Spender did include one of Warner's poems in his anthology *Poems for Spain* (1939).

Sylvia Townsend Warner's combination of traditional form and modern idiom is, in fact, a discernible aesthetic of the period. In 'Poetry and Revolution' (1933), Spender spoke of his difficulty in getting outside the tradition of poetry:

The artist today feels himself totally submerged by bourgeois tradition, he feels that nothing he can write could possibly appeal to a proletarian audience, and therefore he finds himself becoming simply the bourgeois artist in revolt, in short, the individualist.[4]

In *The 1930s and After* (1978), he recalls that they were writing Romantic poetry about revolutionary feeling:

The essence of the modern movement was that it created art which centred on itself and not on anything outside it; neither on some ideology projected nor on the expression of the poet's feelings and personality … [in the 1930s] we were putting the subject back into poetry. We were taking the medium of poetry which to them [modernists] was an end in itself and using it as an instrument for realising our felt ideas about the time in which we were living.[5]

For the intellectuals, however, the process of reporting ordinary life was not straightforward because they realised that they were remote from the experiences and states of mind which they should be recording. C. Day Lewis referred to their aim of creating 'a literature that expressed the lives of those whose voices had not been heard'[6] and W.H. Auden more or less admitted

---

3 Barbara Brothers, 'Writing Against the Grain: Sylvia Townsend Warner and the Spanish Civil War', in Mary Lynn Broe and Angela Ingram (eds), *Women Writers in Exile* (University of Carolina Press, 1989), 362.

4 Stephen Spender, 'Poetry and Revolution', *New Country*, March 1933. See Stephen Spender, *The Thirties and after: Poetry, Politics People 1933–1975* (London: Collins/Fontana, 1978, 48.

5 Spender 1978, 25.

6 C. Day Lewis, 'English Writers and a People's Front', *Left Review*, Vol. 2, October 1936: 671–4.

that he was primarily interested in social deprivation for its artistic possibilities: 'When an artist writes about the slums or disease or Hell, it is quite true that he wants them to be there because they are his material, just as a dentist wants people to have decaying teeth'.[7] To cite C. Day Lewis, Spender and Auden is not to reinforce their monopoly as 'Thirties Poets' but to support the argument that ideology and writing were not as clear cut as has been suggested. All poets negotiated between high modernist and socially realist discourses and between political and aesthetic concerns, uncertain whether direct polemic was the aesthetic or 'anaesthetic' of art.[8]

The simultaneous attempt to maintain modernist principles of impersonality, objective observation and linguistic economy but also to develop a more democratic aesthetic by drawing upon popular forms, engaging with mundane realities and reproducing conversational idioms marks most of the poets writing in this period. The development of photography and film was accompanied by a new documentary realism in art – associated with the Documentary Film Movement from which Mass Observation came. New translations of Freud and Jung meant that psychoanalysis continued to influence the idiom of artists and writers and the Surrealist Exhibition in 1936, which was attended by twenty thousand people, inspired them to find new forms for representing the unconscious and dream images. Stylistically, the rejection of the anti-democratic principles of high modernism allowed for a return to narrative forms and representational characterisation, along with Geoffrey Grigson's principle of clear direct observation: 'report well, begin with objects and events; a stone begets vision.'[9]

Looking back, Julian Symons said 'the technical problem that faced these poets was that of expressing revolutionary sentiments, which was something "new" in English poetry, in some appropriately "new" language' yet nothing in the 1930s was as stylistically radical as the twenties *avant garde*.[10] Thirties poets, then, were sensitive to social realities but collectively created a climate of mixed literary styles. The 'MacSpaunday'[11] poets were a talking point but

---

7   Auden, 'Poetry, Poets and Taste', *The English Auden: Poems, Essays and Dramatic Writings 1927–1939*, ed. Edward Mendelson (London: Faber and Faber, 1977), 358–60.
8   See, for example Edgell Rickword, 'Art and Propaganda', *Left Review*, No. 2, November 1934: 44 and Julian Symons, *The Thirties: A Dream Revolved* (London: Faber, 1975).
9   Geoffrey Grigson, *New Verse: an anthology* (London: Faber, 1939), 15.
10   Julian Symons, *The Thirties*, 25.
11   MacSpaunday was the name given by the poet Roy Campbell to Louis MacNeice, Stephen Spender, W.H. Auden and C. Day Lewis. See R. Carte (ed.), *Thirties Poets: 'The Auden Group'* (London: Macmillan, 1984), 12.

memoirs and records testify to the continuing influence of T.S. Eliot, Ezra Pound, D.H. Lawrence and W.B. Yeats. New names like Roy Fuller, Clifford Dyment, Dylan Thomas, David Gascoyne, Hugh MacDiarmid, Richard Church and John Betjeman were equally present in literary publications and broadcasts. In his anthology of the 1930s and after, Grigson concluded, 'one cannot talk too much of schools and generations and directions'.[12] The importance of pointing out that the 'pits and pylons' poets are not the only luminaries of the period and that there was ideological and stylistic diversity, is to contest the continuing application of a hypothetical 'Audenesque' style as the standard for all poets. Several poets contributed to an identifiable 'thirties poetry' which both continued and also broke from the principles of high modernism.

Women's poems represent the diversity of poetry in the 1930s and the impossibility of aligning political and stylistic radicalism. Sylvia Townsend Warner, Valentine Ackland, Naomi Mitchison, Winifred Holtby and Nancy Cunard were the most politically active, in terms of communism, socialism and feminism. They tended to adopt narrative and other verse forms whereas Laura Riding, who was the most adventurous stylistically – 'dispens[ing] with literary conventionalities and poetic idiom' – was the most politically conservative.[13] With Henry Kemp, Robert Graves and others she issued *The Left Heresy in Literature and Life,* which was advertised as 'a virile indictment, by distinguished poets, of left wing sectarianism and its intrusion in literature, psychology, politics etc. Criticism of many well-known literary experiments of left-wing ideology are included'.[14] Stevie Smith was not a political activist but her textual subversions went further than any other thirties poet and were an aspect of her temperamental egalitarianism which was sympathetic to socialism and feminism. Other poets who have been overlooked or sidelined because of what Caesar terms 'an inevitably ideological view of literary value'[15] include Ruth Pitter, E.J. Scovell, Elizabeth Daryush, Anne Ridler, Lilian Bowes Lyons, Laura Riding and Dorothy Wellesley. Frances Cornford and Vita Sackville-West also count but I have discussed their work in 'Rear-Guard Modernism'.

---

12 Geoffrey Grigson, *Poetry of the Present: an anthology of the Thirties and after* (London: Phoenix House, 1949, 24.

13 Laura Riding, *The Poems of Laura Riding,* new edition of *Collected Poems* 1938 (Manchester: Carcanet, 1980), 12.

14 Advert for *The Left Heresy in Literature and Life,* Laura Riding Henry Kemp, Robert Graves and others, *Twentieth-Century Verse,* June/July, 1939: 57.

15 Adrian Caesar, *Dividing Lines: Poetry, Class and Ideology in the 1930s* (Manchester: Manchester University Press, 1991), 37.

The Literary Context

In a literary climate of change, diversity and their new rights in law, it was possible for women with money to move in literary circles. In Britain, they ran publishing houses, bookshops and journals and they became editors, reviewers and journalists. Laura Riding (with Robert Graves) ran the Seizin Press and the critical periodical *Epilogue*. Nancy Cunard started the Hours Press; Dorothy Wellesley edited the Hogarth Living Poets series; Anne Ridler worked with T.S. Eliot at Faber and Faber. Winifred Holtby was a director of *Time and Tide* and E.J. Scovell was among its editors. Janet Adam Smith was instrumental in the poetry programmes on the radio and edited the anthology of broadcast poems, *Poems of Tomorrow*, in 1935. During the war, and later, when her husband's ill-health prevented him from doing so, Alida Monro ran The Poetry Bookshop, which was a meeting point for poets as well as a marketing and publishing industry.[16] Nevertheless, as Anne Ridler recalled, 'It was difficult for women poets to achieve publication in the 1930s' and still more difficult 'to be treated as a poet pure and simple, rather than as a woman poet'.[17] Several encountered resistance and found the atmosphere of competition to be inhibiting.[18] Although there was less use of the pejorative label 'poetess', there was still a conceptual segregation of women's poetry. Form was still an issue: although there was an openness to both free verse and a return to traditional form, particularly popular forms, women recorded that they had difficulty in freeing up their rhythms to imitate the speaking voice, probably because they could not construct themselves in terms of male or female authorship. Most would have read *A Room of One's Own* (1929) and been attracted by Virginia Woolf's theory of the androgynous imagination which traversed the binary oppositions of gender. In her lecture notes, Frances Cornford is tellingingly similar to Woolf:

> One more point about any woman who writes poetry ... I believe that when writers enter into that state of mind they are neither male nor female, they are androgynous; though fortunately the voice in which they describe the regions from which they return will be either a man's or woman's.[19]

16 See letters from Edith Sitwell and Alida Monro, *Time and Tide*, 2 and 9 April 1932: 371, 395.

17 Anne Ridler, letter to Jane Dowson, 1 September 1992.

18 For individual accounts of prejudice from male poets and critics see Introduction and sections on Kathleen Raine, Naomi Mitchison, Laura Riding, Anne Ridler and E.J. Scovell in Dowson 1996.

19 Cornford, 'Views and Recollections of A Sunday Poet', Tuesday 27 March 1956, *Literary Papers of Frances Cornford*, Mss 58387, London: British Library, Department of Manuscripts.

In *New Verse* in 1934, Laura Riding wrote that women were ineffectual when they 'assume the manner of men'[20] and Edith Sitwell advised women to 'forge their own technique'. In practice, however, they still tended to avoid gender identification through the use of initials, adopting male pronouns and drawing upon traditional forms. Their other preoccupation was with avoiding the personal and propaganda while representing their experiences, ideals and political commitment.

Women recorded successes and frustrations about combining the impersonal poetics of modernism with clear reporting and a more natural idiom. In her literary journals, Frances Cornford wrote, 'I long to write in the stresses of my natural speaking voice though I think I only occasionally succeed in doing this.'[21] In 1935 Valentine Ackland observed to Julius Lipton:

> I am still uncertain how to write poetry as it has to be written. Whether to carry on ... for the present, trusting that (as has happened before) the difficulty of reading a new style will wear off ... or whether to make a partial return to the old, simpler forms – renouncing the pleasures of inverting words and phrases; of using three-syllabled words; of using semi-scientific words; of assonance and rhyme. But we need something really *hard*. Not noisy and bombastic ... but definite and deliberately reasonable, well-devised and musical.[22]

Kathleen Raine's long poem 'Fata Morgana' which was published in *New Verse* and several anthologies registers the paradox which dogged most writers that her poetry was a poor substitute for social action:

> Books, idle books, and hours, unfruitful hours,
> Weigh on my genius and lay waste my will,
> ...
> But I, who have no words, nor heart, nor name,
> Can still suppose how it would feel to march
> Guided by stars along the roads of Spain
> Because of what I learn, but cannot teach.[23]

Kathleen Raine's poems were published as much as anyone's during the 1930s

---

20   Laura Riding, 'An Enquiry', *New Verse*, No. 11, October 1934: 5.
21   Cornford, 'Lunchtime Talk at Foyles', *Literary Papers of Frances Cornford,* Mss 58386 (London: British Library, Department of Manuscripts).
22   Valentine Ackland, letter to Julius Lipton, 1935, Wendy Mulford, *This Narrow Place: Sylvia Townsend Warner and Valentine Ackland – Life, Letters and Politics 1930–1951* (London: Pandora, 1988), 207.
23   Kathleen Raine, 'Fata Morgana', *New Verse*, No. 25, May 1937: 79.

although she was not politically motivated. I am not discussing her work in more detail because she has renounced her early poetry and is antagonistic to being read as a 'woman poet'. Although she claims that she is 'as good as any woman poet who's written in the English Language',[24] she articulates the unresolved contradictions of most twentieth-century women, between her denunciation of the 'woman poet' as a valid category – one should be 'a poet, pure and simple'[25] – and her claims that 'men and women are different'.[26]

Political Lyricism[27]

In her review of *Women's Poetry of the 1930s*, the contemporary poet Kate Clanchy observed that the poems which deal with the private life were better than those which attempted a public register, because women were 'out it the backfield, singing an entirely different tune'.[28] The problem with this conclusion is that it continues to devalue women in relation to an elusive and mythologised 'Audenesque' and to polarise private and public with the associated polarities of the feminine and masculine, domestic and political. Valentine Ackland, Sylvia Townsend Warner, Naomi Mitchison, Nancy Cunard, Winifred Holtby and Stevie Smith are central thirties' poets because they grappled with representing their commitment to social change without writing propaganda. They negotiated between the revolution of the word of high modernism and polemical doctrinaire poetry. Winifred Holtby suffered a lifelong quarrel between the artist and social reformer in her[29] whereas Sylvia Townsend Warner reconciled the tension in her 'discovery that the pen could be used as a sword'.[30]

The political engagement of women has been ironed out by literary historians and sometimes by their biographers. Clare Harman softens the commitment of Sylvia Townsend Warner and Valentine Ackland by

---

24 Kathleen Raine, 'A Passion for Poetry', interview with Naim Attallab, *Guardian*, 23 March 1993, Section 2: 23.
25 Kathleen Raine, letter to Jane Dowson, 29 August 1992.
26 Kathleen Raine, 'A Passion for Poetry'.
27 There is a shortened version of this and the next section in Jane Dowson, 'Women Poets and the Political Voice', in Mary Joannou (ed.), *Women Writers of the 1930s: Gender, Politics and History* (Edinburgh University Press, 1999), 46–62.
28 Kate Clanchy, 'Loud hailers and currant rolls', review of *Women's Poetry of the 1930s*, ed. Jane Dowson, *Independent* 3 February 1996.
29 Vera Brittain, *Testament of Friendship: the Story of Winifred Holtby* (London, Virago 1980), 87.
30 Sylvia Townsend Warner, 'The Way By Which I Have Come', *The Countryman*, XIX, No. 2, 1939: 475.

concentrating on their relationship and on their minor political differences or vicissitudes. The journalism of these and others registers their concern for social equalities. Vera Brittain frequently took up issues such as the awarding of degrees for men and women.[31] She, with Amabel Williams Ellis and Storm Jameson responded to the arrests of unemployed demonstrators in a letter 'Silencing the Unemployed' printed in *Time and Tide*. They opposed the views expressed in the House of Commons that the unemployed might be demonstrating 'for the fun of things':

> Can it be that the Government are so anxious to silence them because it would rather not hear too much of what it feels like to try to feed a child on 2s a week? It is with considerable disquiet that we see a National Government attempting to suppress the views of any body of its subjects and especially that section which has fewest opportunities of making itself articulate.[32]

They do not challenge the stereotype of the inarticulate working class but their promotion of democratic ideals was characteristically unrelenting. Winifred Holtby also combated social and sexual oppression, stating:

> I want there to be no more wars: I want people to recognise the human claims of negroes and Jews and women and all oppressed and humiliated creatures. I want a sort of bloodless revolution.[33]

She tackled bureaucracy and injustice in her novels, journalism and critical books. She was an influential feminist who opposed the liberal tendencies of the 'New Feminism'[34] and lectured on women's rights and pacifism. During the 1920s, she had spent three months in central Europe and went to South Africa to fight for civil liberty. In the 1930s she became director of *Time and Tide*, and accompanied Lady Rhondda to France and Germany in order to meet up with the Six Point Group which was working with the Equal Rights International for an international equal rights treaty. Holtby does not articulate

---

31 Vera Brittain, 'The University Idea', *Time and Tide*, 28 February 1931: 243.
32 Vera Brittain, Amabel Williams Ellis and Storm Jameson, 'Silencing the Unemployed', *Time and Tide* 31 December 1932. Amabel Williams Ellis was one of the editors of *Left Review*.
33 Winifred Holtby, letter to her mother, 1933, *A Feminist Companion to English Literature*, ed. Blain et al. (London, Batsford, 1990), 35.
34 The 'New Feminism' is explained by Rosalind Delmar in 'Afterword', Vera Brittain, *Testament of Friendship*, 449–53. See also, Winifred Holtby, 'Feminism Divided', *Time and Tide* 26 July 1926, in which she accuses the New Feminists of digressing from the goal of equality in legislation which must precede all other reforms, and for being divisive.

her politics in her poems although it is difficult to be conclusive since she destroyed most of them.

During the 1930s, Nancy Cunard became mythologised as a rebel for her 'almost frenetic involvement in social and political affairs'.[35] Her articles appeared in *Left Review* and the publication of her bold treatise *Black Man and White Ladyship* (1931) was a controversial attack on the prejudices of the British aristocracy: 'How come, white man, is the rest of the world to be reformed in your dreary and decadent image?'[36] *Negro: an anthology* (1934) was an eight hundred page 'record of the struggles and achievements, the persecutions and the revolts against them, of the Negro people'; it consisted of writings and photographs which documented various phases of Negro life.[37] Her two visits to Harlem in 1931 and 1932 to research for the anthology apparently provoked 'outrageous lies, fantastic inventions and gross libels' in the American press.[38] She became frustrated with the way in which everything was translated into a sex scandal which discredited her enterprise. Nancy Cunard is alleged to have instigated the letter from Paris addressed to 'To the Writers and Poets of England, Scotland, Ireland and Wales', requesting a statement of their position regarding the Spanish Civil War. The replies were published by *Left Review*, in 1937, as 'Authors Take Sides on the Spanish War'[39] and sold a good three thousand copies. She travelled to America, Moscow and Geneva between 1930 and 1935 to fight for the cause of the dispossessed. In 1936 she went to help the republicans in Spain and in 1939 to give aid to the Spanish refugees; she continued to write articles on Spain for *The Manchester Guardian*. On her second visit to Barcelona, she was appalled to find 'hunger everywhere' and started a food campaign through the *Manchester Guardian*, *News Chronicle* and *Daily Herald*.[40] Through her political activities, Nancy Cunard became a good friend of Sylvia Townsend Warner.

Sylvia Townsend Warner and Valentine Ackland similarly worked for democracy. After the Reichstag Fire Trial in Germany caught their attention in 1933, they became tireless in their activities connected with the British Communist Party; they subscribed to the *Daily Worker* and joined the Left

---

35   Hugh Ford (ed.), *Nancy Cunard: Brave Poet, Indomitable Rebel 1896–1965* (Philadelphia: Chilton Book Company, 1968), 37.

36   Nancy Cunard, 'Black Man and White Ladyship', Ford, 103–9.

37   Nancy Cunard, Introduction to *Negro: an anthology*, ed. Cunard, 1934 (New York: Frederick Ungar Publishing Co., 1970).

38   Ford, 114–21.

39   See Valentine Cunningham, Introduction, *The Penguin Book of Spanish Civil War Verse* (Harmondsworth, Penguin, 1980), 50.

40   See 'The Refugees at Perpignan, Miss Cunard's Appeal', Ford, 196.

Book Club.[41] In 1935, they joined the Communist Party and went to the Congress of Writers in Paris, which was also attended by Winifred Holtby, Storm Jameson and Naomi Mitchison. In 1939, they went to the United States for the 3rd American Writers Congress in New York, to consider the loss of democracy in Europe and returned when war broke out. Warner became an executive committee member of the Association of Writers for Intellectual Liberty. In 1936, she went as a British delegate to the International Peace Congress in Brussels, organised by the Communist Party, and in 1937 to the Congress of the International Association in Defence of Culture in Madrid and Valencia. The Association aimed for an international exchange of literature and to fight against war, fascism and 'everything that menaces culture'.[42] At home in Dorset she was a founder member of the local Readers and Writers Group which was affiliated to the Left Book Club and later became secretary to the Dorset Peace Council. In September 1936, Sylvia Townsend Warner and Valentine Ackland responded to an article by Nancy Cunard, published in the *Daily Worker* and *News Chronicle*, appealing for volunteers to help the Spanish Republicans. They gave assistance to the Red Cross Unit in Barcelona. On returning to England, Valentine Ackland intended to drive a lorry from London to Valencia but was too unwell to go. In 1937, she worked voluntarily at Tythrop House, near Thame, a home for Spanish Refugee children. Warner 'wrote as much as anybody did about the war'[43] and, like Nancy Cunard's, her letters and notebooks are evidence of her admiration for the determination and spirit of the people of Barcelona. Her anti-fascist articles were published in *Time and Tide* and *Left Review*. As Branson and Heinemann indicate, 'Why Warner and others like her were against the British government is clear from the pages of *Left Review*'. Although Sylvia Townsend Warner and Valentine Ackland found that *Left Review* was inappropriately dominated by poets 'from Oxbridge or Chelsea or Bloomsbury', it was an outlet for their poems, fiction, and journalism. Ackland also reviewed books on the Spanish Civil War and wrote a series of articles called 'Country Dealings' which exposed the deprived conditions of the rural poor. Sylvia Townsend Warner's concern for the exploitation of the rural poor is dramatised in her long satirical narrative poem *Opus 7* (1931).

Naomi Mitchison and Winifred Holtby were known as anti-fascist writers

---

41 Left Book Club was founded by Victor Gollancz and its political books reached a wide readership. It was a centre for political artists. See Noreen Branson and Margot Heinemann, *Britain in the Nineteen Thirties* (St Albans: Panther, 1973), 299.

42 Declaration of the Association of Writers in Defence of Culture, *Left Review*, Vol. 1, No. 11, August 1935: 462.

43 Valentine Cunningham (ed.), *Spanish Front: Writers on the Civil War* (New York: Oxford University Press, 1986), xxxii.

involved in *Left Review*.[44] Naomi Mitchison was committed to active politics and went to Vienna in 1934 to provide aid to the social democrats after the killings and violations by the government. She aimed to promote socialist and feminist ideals through journalism and other non-fictional writing and through the women's, peace and labour movements. She joined the Labour Party in 1930 and stood as Labour candidate for the Scottish Universities parliamentary seat in 1935. At the onset of the Second World War, she settled in a house at Carradale, Kintyre and introduced her political ideals into the feudal traditions of the small Scottish Community. Margaret Cole with her husband Douglas were among the 'labourite' friends of the Mitchisons. Jill Benton describes the Mitchisons' home in Hammersmith during the 1920s and 1930s as a 'class melting pot', where working class neighbours mixed with their social circle of politicians and artists.[45]

The Spanish Civil War

For all writers, the Spanish Civil War most clearly posed the opportunity and difficulty of negotiating between propaganda and imaginative art. As Barbara Brothers observes, however, its poetry has not been viewed as 'real literature':

> Literary histories of the Spanish Civil War proclaim themselves as part social history – the literature not real literature – and part literary history … Modernist canon controls the script of literary history even when the subject is not aesthetics. In the narrative of Spanish Civil War writing, women become an emblem, bibliographic entry, or footnote.[46]

The poetry written by these women could be undermined as mere propaganda or autobiography, but one way of appreciating the imaginative aspect of the poetry is to compare it with their journalism and essays, such as Sylvia Townsend Warner's article 'Barcelona', written for *Left Review* after her first visit to help the Republican Medical Services.[47] Warner's best poems combine her skills as a narrator and observer. 'El Heroe' depicts the unseen death of the unknown soldier:

> The mountain wind arising
> Keened all night for woe;

---

44   Branson and Heinemann, 299.
45   Jill Benton, *Naomi Mitchison: a biography* (London: Pandora, 1990), 38–9.
46   Brothers, 350.
47   Warner, 'Barcelona', *Left Review*, Vol. 2, December 1936: 812.

Midnight laid on his face
A handkerchief of snow;
Dawn came with a handful
Of woodland flowers to strow;
Like mourners through the hills
The freshets began to flow.[48]

Interestingly, one stanza was omitted from the typescript which Warner prepared for *Collected Poems*:

And the western sky was flushed
With the setting sun when a shot
Rang out, and he fell to the ground
With a bullet through his head.

As Barbara Brothers puts it, Warner's poems, 'do not romanticise or sentimentalise the soldier. Her poems are written in the context of suffering and unheroic battlefield conditions that the world war one poets, such as Wilfred Owen, pictured for those who remained at home'.[49] This is also applicable to 'Port Bou' the monologue of a young dying soldier:

I have usurped the breath
of the rose plucked for the bridal,
I am the odour of the wreath
that is held out for heroes[50]

Here, Warner acts as both poet and journalist in relating the smells, tastes and sounds of Spain for those not there. The accelerated heart beat rhythm contrasts with images of stasis to reconstruct the sense of anticipation which was in tension with the inactivity. This tension was recorded by many writers. She does not seem to know how to end the poem; presumably closure would be inappropriate, so there is a rousing call for 'those who fight for Spain!' In her lecture 'Women as Writers' Warner explained the importance of 'immediacy' which should be freed from the author's 'anxious presence'.[51] In 'Journey to Barcelona' she succeeds in achieving 'immediacy' through first-hand narration: 'the train took us by / We debated if it were mountainside we saw or cloud'.

---

48 Warner 'El Heroe', Dowson, 153–4.
49 Brothers, 358. The stanza of 'El Heroe' omitted from the typescript is printed in Sylvia Townsend Warner, *Collected Poems* (Manchester: Carcanet, 1982), 276.
50 Warner, 'Port Bou', Dowson, 154.
51 Warner, 'Women as Writers', *Collected Poems* 1982, 265–70.

She mirrors the pallid landscape and the dwellings 'like hempen shrouds' with the lifelessness of the peasants who are under the shadow of death: 'Pale is that country like a country of bone.' The last line, however, is a polemical call for the communist cause: 'Rain for the red cloud, come to Spain.' 'Waiting at Cerbere' more successfully combines the eyes of the journalist and the poet while 'Benicasim' pulls together her observations of waiting, stillness, heat, salt air, the rugged landscape and the numbed inhabitants.[52]

Warner's two most militant poems, 'Red Front' and 'In This Midwinter', are not included in her *Collected Poems* or *Selected Poems*. 'Red Front' was printed in *Left Review*, 1935,[53] and, as Clare Harman records

> [It was] read as a declamation in Battersea late in 1935 and again in Whitechapel in 1936 (Sylvia was not able to attend); with its worker-memorable chorus in common time, it harks back to the Great War, the war promoted as the one to end all wars, and takes an overview of the whole period, using the image of 'the saddest wine that ever was pressed in France' for the war's legacy.[54]

In 'Red Front' Warner draws upon the associations of the French Revolution to cultivate the sense of horror in those looking at the war. Its anachronistic vocabulary like 'mire' and 'blight' sits oddly with the rousing refrain:

> Comrade, are you mired enough,
> Sad enough, tired enough –
> Hush! – to march with us tonight
> Through the mist and through the blight?
> Can the knitted heart sustain
> The long Northeaster of In Vain,
> The whining, whining wind unbinding? –
>   Red! Red![55]

Barbara Brothers observes that the direct call to action:

> offends the sensibilities of poetry readers taught to disdain didacticism ... Yet the history and experience evoked by the surface details, her imagery and allusions, evoke the suffering and deprivation of the poor whom those in power in the government and in the church use to serve themselves. As Warner expresses the situation, revolution is necessary because the human costs of not fighting

---

52 Warner, 'Waiting at Cerbere', *Collected Poems* 1982, 36.
53 Warner, 'Red Front', *Left Review*, Vol. 1, April, 1935: 255–6.
54 Claire Harman, *Sylvia Townsend Warner: A Biography* (London: Minerva, 1985), 147.
55 Warner, 'Red Front'.

are greater than the price the people would pay through taking up arms and
waging war to claim power over their own lives.[56]

'In This Midwinter' is similarly didactic but more imaginative. This is the
third and last stanza:

> In this midwinter, comrade, a child certainly
> This midnight midwifes. Tougher than God or beast man yet
> Envoy on envoy aims to persuade futurity.
> To those new eyes we bear our lantern's well-met.
> Not lamb nor Lenin, maybe, but to co-heir of earth, comrade,
> Plight we darkling our lantern's friendly assurance.[57]

There is no hint of gender distinction in Warner's war writing, partly because
she echoes Thomas Hardy and the first world war poets and partly perhaps
because the Marxist emphasis on collective not individual identity superseded
gendered imperatives. She is depicting men and women, old and young, *in
extremis*, where hegemonic government, not gender, is the site of struggle.

The speakers in Valentine Ackland's war poems like 'Communist Poem
1935' are also the genderless voices of republican supporters. 'Instructions
for England' is unashamed polemic while an uncollected poem on ageing, 'I
crack like a machine gun', printed in *Left Review*, demonstrates Ackland's
intention to create what she called 'hard' poetry.[58] 'Winter', another
uncollected poem which was published in *Left Review* in 1936, expresses and
invokes support for the Spanish Republicans without forgoing lyricism. The
first person plural, which blends private lyric with public rhetoric, constructs
a collective consciousness:

> Then the word moves in us and we stir in our bed,
> Clotted together in misery, hungry and time-besotted,
> The drag of time on our hands and on nerves the nag,
> Then we whisper together and the word we say is red.
>
> Red and angry as the sun will be when it rises,
> As their furnace-fires we kindle, as the fury which burns us,
> The word unspoken in mind, soon to be spoken and heard,
> Over screech of sirens when morning comes and the red sun rises.[59]

---

56 Brothers, 58.
57 Warner, 'In This Midwinter', *Left Review*, Vol. 1, June 1935: 101.
58 Valentine Ackland, 'I crack like machine gun', *Left Review*, Vol. 3, 1937: 416.
59 Ackland, 'Winter', *Left Review*, Vol. 2, March 1936: 250.

'Winter' represents Ackland's conscious search for a voice within traditional forms; it also illustrates her preference for lyrical and descriptive modes which made it difficult for her to harness her political engagement to her creative writing. In the thirties, however, her poems were published in the *London Mercury* and *Left Review*.

Like Sylvia Townsend Warner and Valentine Ackland, Nancy Cunard also fuelled much of her political anger into journalism, but her poem 'To Eat Today' is a strikingly successful dramatisation of a Spanish peasant family ravaged by the civil war. The strong rhythms, shocking images and dialogue between the oppressors and the oppressed construct a kind of filmic realism but Cunard cannot resist the didactic note in addressing the fascists, 'is the mark worth the bomb?'[60] Initially, she went to Spain as a journalist but became engaged by the republican cause, 'Spain took hold of me entirely'.[61] She worked for the League of Nations and provided money towards a mobile exhibition which would raise awareness about the victims of the Spanish war. At the end of the war she assisted refugees in Southern France and obtained the release of the Spanish poet Caesar Arconada, who, with others, lived in her home in Réanville. In a letter to Nan Freen in 1963 she wrote, 'I have so many poems written on Spain that I wonder if they, in their different years, during and after, could not be done up into a volume.'[62] The volume was never completed.

Nancy Cunard's unusual 'Sonnet in Five Languages' is printed with her explanatory notes in Valentine Cunningham's anthology, *The Penguin Book of Spanish Civil War Verse* (1980). The anthology also reproduces some of her translations, such as Pablo Neruda's 'Almeria', which provided another outlet for her hostility to upper class complacency:

> Yes, a dish for the lot of you, the rich of the whole earth,
> Ambassadors, ministers, guests in abominable assembly,
> Aristocrats, landowners, writers labelled *neutrality*,
> Ladies of tea-room and of divan ease –
> A dish of destruction, befouled with the blood of the poor,
> Every noon, every week, for ever and ever from now on,
> Before you, a dishful of blood – Almeria – for ever.[63]

---

60 Nancy Cunard, 'To Eat Today', Dowson, 53.
61 Ford, Foreword, 1968.
62 Ford, 173–4.
63 Cunard, tr. of 'Almeria' by Pablo Neruda, Cunningham 1980, 379–80.

Cunningham also includes Warner's translations of the poets Francis Fuentes, Julio D. Guillén, Felix Paredes, and José Herrera Petere. Petere's 'El dia que no vendra', which commemorates the fall of Madrid, is translated with Warner's characteristic blend of the choric and demotic:

> Day of metal and of masses –
> All the Fascist drums foretold it,
> All the parrot voices hailed it.
> Not tomorrow? Well, the next day,
> Wednesday perhaps, or Thursday
> (All are one to Radio Burgos).[64]

The rhythmic beat and strong rhetoric may have influenced Warner's own poems like 'Red Front'. Valentine Ackland's translation of a poem by Louis Aragon, 'Waltz', was published in *Left Review,* but is not included by Cunningham.[65] These translations epitomise the way in which women assumed a male poet's identity in writing war poems because there was no tradition of women's war poetry.

Cultural Warfare

Just as Valentine Ackland's subjects in 'Communist Poem, 1935' are universal comrades, so considerations of gender seem to be suspended in addressing class differentials in Britain. In party politics women were presumed to be honorary men.[66] Warner assumes the persona of a rebellious male civilian in 'Some Make This Answer', published in *Left Review*, February 1936:

> But from other brows than yours I have felt a stronger
> Voltage of death, walking among my fellow men
> Have seen the free and the fine wasted with cold and hunger,
> Diseased, maddened, death-in-life doomed, and the ten
> Thousand this death can brag have reckoned against your thousand.
> Shoddy king of terrors, you impress me no longer.[67]

---

64   Warner, tr. 'El dia que no vendra', by José Herrera Petere, Cunningham 1980, 291–3.

65   Louis Aragon, 'Waltz', *Left Review*, Vol. 1, October 1934: 3–5.

66   Ackland, 'Communist Poem, 1935', *Left Review*, Vol. 1, July 1935: 430; Dowson 1996, 32.

67   Warner, 'Some Make This Answer', *Left Review*, Vol. 2, February 1936: 214; Dowson 1996, 155–6.

Warner's vehement opposition to bureaucratic fudging of unjust systems is dramatised into the rhetorical assertiveness of the speaker. 'Song for a Street Song' also looks at collective rather than individual experiences. It represents the break-up of local communities caused by war:

> War is near,
> And freedom in muck of warfare maimed and defiled
> Is a bitterer hazard than loss of mate or child.
> There's the sting
> When the drums go rub-a-dub!
> There's the rub[68]

Warner's poems often conflate the literary and popular by combining conversational with formal registers. Although her diction is stilted in places, she was obviously developing a more natural voice which was at it freest in the Spanish Civil War poems. Her difficulty in negotiating the interface of the didactic and aesthetic is further illuminated by the easier lyricism of her love poems which are unencumbered by the impulse for propaganda.

Naomi Mitchison was unashamed in her feminist and socialist drives and successfully reproduced conversational registers. 'To Some Young Communists From An Older Socialist', which was printed in *New Verse*, January 1933, registers her interest in building bridges between communism and socialism. The rift between old socialism and the intellectual socialism of the younger generation is strikingly similar to Britain's Old and New Labour movements of the 1990s:

> Look, our car's luggage of high violent hopes is only socks and vests:
> Kick them away, careless, marching, you and your mates.
>
> We who were young once in that war time, we are now not young but apart,
> Living with photos of friends, dead at Ypres or Menin,
> Remembering little of lies or truth perhaps defended;
> We were hit then in the head, but now, hopeless, in the heart.[69]

The voice is 'Audenesque' in blending personal and public registers. Naomi Mitchison's *The Alban Goes Out*, a long allegorical narrative poem about sea fishermen, which was allegedly read aloud to the local fishers in the evenings

---

68 Warner, 'Song for a Street Song', Dowson 1996, 156–7.
69 Naomi Mitchison, 'To Some Young Communists From An Older Socialist', Dowson 1996, 76–7.

indicates her ability to represent and reach the 'masses'. A shorter poem, 'Eviction in the Hebrides', printed in'*Left Review* in 1937, expresses her anti-colonialism.[70]

Stevie Smith distanced herself from Naomi Mitchison's politics in a letter to Denis Johnson, 1937: 'more talkie from Naomi Mitchison, and she's got world problems on the brain too ... but if she thinks she is going to rope me in to the Haldane-communismus gang she is mistaken.'[71] Stevie Smith would have been more opposed to what she called the 'groupismus' of party politics than to Mitchison's socialist principles. Her novels *Novel on Yellow Wallpaper* (1936) and *Over the Frontier* (1938) deal with war but she tends to focus on cosmic evils in terms of the microcosm of individual relations. The major enemy for her was totalitarianism which would produce mediocrity; state control and organised religion were to be feared for being over tidy and stifling free expression. In 'Sterilisation', dated 21 October 1937, she mimics the grand narratives of Literature, Science, History and the Church while simultaneously recognising the need to foster genius:

> And soon all our minds will be flat as a pancake,
> With no room for genius exaltation or heartache.
>
> And our children and theirs will preen, smirk and chatter,
> With not even the sense to ask what is the matter.[72]

The tone is playful but she is serious in her championing of intellectual liberty and exposing the reader's assumptions concerning cultural norms. It is easy to dismiss Stevie Smith's challenge to patriotism, patriarchy and colonialism in 'Happy Dogs of England' as sheer nonsense, but she parodies the hymn tune 'O happy band of pilgrims' and offsets it with demotic prose:

> O happy dogs of England
> Bark well as well you may
> If you lived anywhere else
> You would not be so gay.[73]

70 Mitchison, 'Eviction in the Hebrides', *Left Review*, Vol. 3, No. 1, February 1937: 20.

71 Stevie Smith, letter to Denis Johnson, 10 June 1937, *Me Again: The Uncollected Writings of Stevie Smith* (London, Virago, 1981), 259.

72 Smith, 'Sterilisation', Dowson, 143.

73 Smith, 'Happy Dogs of England', *Stevie Smith: A Selection*, ed. Hermione Lee (London: Faber, 1983), 65.

As here, Stevie Smith relentlessly undermines the assumed superiority of high class accents which construct the rhetoric of institutionalised power. 'Souvenir de Monsieur Poop' is one of several swipes at the literary establishment which made it so difficult for her to get her poems published and properly reviewed:

> I am the self-appointed guardian of English Literature,
> I believe tremendously in the significance of age;
> I believe that a writer is wise at 50,
> Ten years wiser at 60, at 70 a sage.
> I believe that juniors are lively, to be encouraged with discretion and snubbed,
> I believe also that they are bouncing, communistic, ill mannered and, of course, young.[74]

Stevie Smith was a prolific poet during the 1930s – eighteen out of the sixty-two uncollected poems in *Me Again: The Uncollected Writings of Stevie Smith* (1981) were dated the 1930s – but not published until David Garnett risked printing some of her poems in the *New Statesman* in 1936. There was sufficient response to these to convince Jonathan Cape to produce *A Good Time Was Had By All* in 1937 and *Tender Only to One* in 1938. In many ways, Stevie Smith was ahead of her time: the irreverence of her literary referentiality, the indiscernible shifts between parody and pastiche and the disregard for conventional distinctions between disciplines or cultures, smack of postmodern practice. At the beginning of *Novel on Yellow Paper* (1936) she suggests that the opposition between prose and poetry is a false construction of literary tradition: 'Oh talking voice that is so sweet, how hold you alive in captivity, how point you with commas, semi-colons, dashes, and pauses and paragraphs?'[75] This statement can be read as women's confinement in patriarchal symbolic discourses which Dorothy Richardson and Virginia Woolf consciously fractured in their stream-of-consciousness narratives.

Stevie Smith's deceptively playful aesthetics are symptoms of her hostility to pretentiousness, particularly the pretensions of the upper classes towards high culture. Her essay 'Private Views', printed in the *New Statesman and Nation*, 7 May 1938, almost imperceptibly mocks the viewers at the Royal Academy exhibition of classic art – 'The summer show of the Royal Academy is a beautiful national institution'[76] – and her poem 'Salon D'Automne' reduces the claims of modern artists to male voyeurism:

74 Smith, 'Souvenir de Monsieur Poop', *Collected Poems* (London: Allen Lane, 1985), 137–8.
75 Smith, *Novel on Yellow Paper*, *Selections*, 34.
76 Smith, 'Private Views', *Me Again*, 130–33.

This is the Slap school of art,
It would be nice
To smack them
Slap, slap, slap,
That would be nice.
It is possible
One might tire of smacking them[77]

'Lord Barrenstock' is typical of several poems where a caricature is both reinforced and turned on its head. The baron is a 'seducer of a hundred little boys' who has wronged people through cheating them of their status and property. He also fiddles his gains at the stock exchange with intolerable indifference. Controversially, the poem explores the *response* to such a man as much as his wrongdoings: ''Tis not for these unsocial acts not these/I wet my pen.'[78] In 'The Bishops of the Church of England',[79] 'Major Macroo' and 'Lord Mope' Stevie Smith maintains the comi-tragic tone of 'Lord Barrenstock' but is more vitriolic:

What shall we say of this curious young man?
Scion of aristocracy sycophant of eld
Sitting at the feet of the old men because they are old
Warming his shivering behind at their gutted flame ...
Brace up oh bunny heart, that man's no sage[80]

'Major Hawkaby Cole Macroo' has a 'patient Griselda of a wife with a heart of gold' who does not complain about his boyfriends:

And she loved him and felt that he needed her and waited
And waited and never became exasperated
...
Such men as these, such selfish cruel men
Hurting what most they love what most loves them,
Never make mistake when it comes to choosing a woman
To cherish them and be neglected and not think it inhuman.[81]

---

77 Smith, 'Salon D'Automne', 1938, *Me Again*, 130–33; Dowson, 144–5.
78 Smith, 'Lord Barrenstock', *CP*: 69.
79 Smith, 'The Bishops of the Church of England', *CP*: 96.
80 Smith, 'Lord Mope', *CP*: 58.
81 Smith, 'Major Macroo', *CP*: 72.

Although rarely as direct in the language of feminist awareness, Stevie Smith's satires on self-appointed, oppressive and arrogant individuals oppose the patriarchal assumptions and systems which they represent. They can also be projections of her father who ran off to sea. 'Father for a Fool'[82] offsets the child's innocent suffering against the irresponsible parent who lost all his money and shot himself. Chillingly, the tragic tale is set to the carefree tune of 'Girls and Boys Come out to Play'. Martin Pumphrey points out this strategy of depicting the messy world of adults through children's eyes:

> Smith's poetry not only draws on children's culture for its form and content but knowingly exploits the interrogative play signal to challenge conventional literary and cultural frames and unsettle the reader's assumptions about the relationship with the text.[83]

Stevie Smith's irreverence towards those whose status was conventionally unquestioned stretches to war heroes in poems like 'Private Means is Dead' (originally entitled 'Chaps') and 'The Lads of the Village'. In the latter poem she is undermining the poetry of war (and implicitly those who market and consume it) for aestheticising pain rather than war'*per se*, but it was daring during a period where war sensitivities were still acute:

> Oh sing no more: Away with folly of commanders.
> This will not make a better song upon the field of Flanders,
> Or upon any field of experience where pain makes patterns the poets slanders.[84]

Here, the nonchalant air of anti-realism is a typical defence against going over the line of social conventions, particularly concerning what may or may not be talked about. Like other thirties poets, Stevie Smith wrote about the new developments on the edge of towns and cities, but unlike them she is more critical of social snobbery than the stereotyped uniformity of suburbia and its inhabitants. In 'The Suburban Classes' she exposes the manipulation of those who play upon the proverbial conformity of the lower middle class mind: 'There is far too much of the suburban classes / Spiritually not geographically speaking. They're asses.'[85]

---

82 Smith, 'Father for a Fool', *Selections*, 69.
83 Martin Pumphrey, 'Play, fantasy and strange laughter: Stevie Smith's uncomfortable poetry', *Critical Quarterly* 28. 3, Autumn 1986: 87.
84 Smith, 'Private Means is Dead', *CP*: 74; 'The Lads of the Village', *CP*: 142.
85 Smith, 'The Suburban Classes', *CP*: 26.

Again and again the reconstructed voice of the powerful is the object under scrutiny. Stevie Smith's association between voice and status is reflected in her reference to 'A lot of highclass people with irritating voices' in a letter to John Hayward.[86] Her treatment of the working class was similar to her treatment of the suburban classes, not patronising but giving dignity to unsung heroes of prosaic routines, like 'Alfred the Great':

> Honour and magnify this man of men
> Who keeps a wife and seven children on £2.10
> Paid weekly in an envelope
> And yet has never abandoned hope.[87]

In this rather oblique way, her poems are classic 'thirties poems' because they depict the class struggle and interweave personal with public registers. Stevie Smith's poetry can qualify as 'Audenesque' in aiming for a community of shared assumptions between the poet and the audience and in positioning the speaker on the same rung as the listeners. She did not refer directly to political events but shot her arrows under the cover of fictionalising them into her portraits of social oppressors and victims with unrelenting psychological realism. The authority of her writing derives from this persistent transgression of conventional frontiers. In her investigations of desire and social taboos, Stevie Smith frequently drew upon the new language of psychology, most directly in the poems with titles like 'Egocentric' and 'Analysand' and in her characteristic poems on death like 'Goodnight' and 'When I awake'.[88] Ultimately, Stevie Smith's politics are in her rejections of stereotype and her disregard for the discourses of power, whether of bureaucracy, royalty, aristocracy or academia; by disrupting familiar syntactical or formal structures, she challenges their associated assumptions and cultural authority.

Women, Home and Marriage

So far, my analysis of women's poems concerning the Spanish Civil War and class politics has been directed at the argument that women were not 'out on the backfields singing an entirely different tune'. Their shifting between formal and conversational idioms, their manipulation of narrative and ballad forms

---

86   Smith, letter to John Hayward, 24 April, 1942, *Me Again*, 283.
87   Smith, 'Alfred the Great', *CP*: 19.
88   Smith, 'Egocentric', *CP*: 18; 'Analysand', *CP*: 54; 'Goodnight', *Me Again*, 245; 'When I Awake', *Me Again*, 232.

and their ironic stance towards the discourses of power are typically 'Audenesque'. At the same time, 'Audenesque' is too limiting for the more radical poems. The 'Audenesque' also had no room for the treatment of gender issues, apart from homosexuality. The woman-centred poetry is a valuable record in this period of changing concepts of gender. Between 1928 and 1934 there were twelve law reforms concerning the rights and protection of women and children, which meant that issues concerning women's roles and women's rights were dominant in parliament, literature and ordinary discourses. Contemporaneous journalism and fiction suggest that most women had a complex relationship with these changes. For the woman poet, her sensitivity to the suppression of women was at odds with her avoidance of the 'poetess' association. Nevertheless, some women's poetry did tackle gender politics but often indirectly and never in a confessional or polemical mode.

Martin Pumphrey believes that although Stevie Smith 'is not a writer who can easily be recruited as a feminist', she connects to 'other women writers whose poetic strategies have been directed not towards the construction of an authoritative and consistent poetic persona or self but towards disruption, discontinuity and indirection' which are 'strategies of (covert) resistance to the silencing or muting experienced by women within mainstream culture'.[89] A later poem, 'Miss Snooks, Poetess' shows her to be clearly sensitive to the silencing and stereotyping of women poets:

> Miss Snooks was really awfully nice
> And never wrote a poem
> That was not really awfully nice
> And fitted to a woman.[90]

For Stevie Smith, feminism and socialism, never articulated as such, were parallel impulses rooted in a liberal temperament which sided with the underdog. There are assertive women of the moneyed classes, like the mother-in-law in 'Octopus', but sympathy is directed towards ordinary women like Sally Soo, who, vainly waiting for the fulfilment of empty promises, are often the casualties of man's freedom to choose.[91] Typically, however, Stevie Smith's treatment is dialectical and her attitude to organised feminism was characteristically liberal:

---

89   Pumphrey, 87.
90   Smith, 'Miss Snooks, Poetess', *Me Again*, 226.
91   Smith, 'Octopus' and 'The Word', Dowson 1996, 148, 147.

Dear Female heart, I am sorry for you,
You must suffer, that is all that you can do.
But if you like, in common with the rest of the human race,
You may also look most absurd with a miserable face.[92]

Naomi Mitchison, however, was an active feminist who tried to reconcile her socialist and feminist ideologies. During the 1920s she had helped to found the North Kensington clinic which undertook birth control and abortions. She belonged to the Women's National League; she lectured for the World Sexual Reform League which was aimed at educated career women; she published an essay 'Breaking Up the Home' which criticised the nuclear family as incompatible with work for women. She was commissioned by Faber to write *Comments on Birth Control* in 1930, and published *We Have Been Warned,* a novel 'about my own times' (1933), *The Moral Basis of Politics* (1938), *The Blood of the Martyrs* (1939), a modern political parable, and *The Kingdom of Heaven* (1939). During the 1930s, she, like others, became disillusioned with socialist communism, partly because of its disinterest in women's emancipation. In 1930, in *We Have Been Warned*, she had stated her belief that women would gain less than men under socialism and she found that her socialist colleagues, including her husband Dick who followed a career with the Labour Party, were not active in prioritising women's issues above general social problems, particularly unemployment. The impulse for freedom which strained against the reins of convention is the subtext of many of her poems. She and her husband practised an open marriage but 'Dick and Colin at the Salmon Nets', printed in *Time and Tide*, questions whether the traditional roles which separate men and women are based on essential differences:

How can I, being a woman, write all that down?
How can I see the quiet pushing salmon against the net?
How can I see behind the sticks and pipe-smoke, the intent frown,
And the things speech cannot help with on which man's heart is set?

Must we be apart always, you watching the salmon nets, you in the rain,
Thinking of love or politics or what I don't know.[93]

Here, as in 'Woman Alone', published in *Time and Tide* 7 December 1935, which depicts a woman going through the motions of lovemaking, Mitchison

---

92 Smith, 'Dear Female Heart', *CP*: 130.
93 Mitchison, 'Dick and Colin at the Salmon Nets', *Time and Tide* 25 February 1933; Dowson 1996, 81.

depicts psychological separateness, but the mood in 'Dick and Colin at the Salmon Nets' is more wistful.[94] Instead of triumphalistic independence, there is a resignation to the apparent inevitability that men will congregate with men and that women must remain indoors 'with the children and books'. It echoes Mitchison's assertion in 1930 that feminism's battles had not been won: 'Apparently, all the feminist battles are gained, or almost all. Actually nothing is settled, and the question of baby or not baby is at the bottom of almost everything.'[95]

After 1928, when all women over twenty-one had the vote, they were obliged to be thankful for their new equality of status. Women who were married had to be grateful for a mate when men were scarce but they resented having to give up work for marriage especially since many had experienced work and equal pay during the First World War. The sense of, impulse towards and fear of change which dogged educated women is frequently recorded. Ellen Wilkinson, a Labour MP, addressed the anxieties which could produce reactionary sentiments: 'Whether we like it or not, the old family life is changing just as are so many other things. And while we sometimes speak of the good old days, that is only because we are comfortably far away from them.'[96]

A series in the *Listener*, 'The Present Crisis of Marriage', called it 'the most debatable question of our time'. In a broadcast talk, 'Can Men and Women Really be Equal?', Ellen Wilkinson argued that new employment opportunities could only be enjoyed by single women: 'Today there is an ever-increasing number of married women who are wondering whether they really are pulling their weight in the world's work; whether the talk of the modern equality does not in fact, cover up dependence and not a little futility.'[97] On the other hand, single women without an income had no alternative to dependence on their parents for the rest of their lives. This grim prospect was expressed by Winifred Holtby in a letter to *Time and Tide* in 1932, which responded to the conventional views of a 'Mrs Case':

> [I am] an unmarried woman of thirty four whose parents live in a small provincial
> town … I am an ex-guide patrol leader; I have done that nursing and training

---

94   Mitchison, 'Woman Alone', *Time and Tide* 7 December 1935. Dowson 1996, 81.
95   Mitchison, *All Change Here* (1930), 52. See Benton, 72.
96   Ellen Wilkinson, 'Can Men and Women be Really Equal?', *The Listener*, 2 April 1930: 587–8. Ellen Wilkinson (1891–1947) became Labour MP for Middlesborough and Jarrow in 1924 and Minister for Education in 1945. She was admired by Winifred Holtby. See Vera Brittain, *Testament of Friendship*, 420.
97   Ellen Wilkinson, 587.

mentioned by Mrs Case; I have, I believe, the usual domestic accomplishments of plain sewing and invalid cookery. I have been a school manager, taught in Sunday School and have been secretary of several voluntary associations. It is out of intimate personal experience that I write, when I say that I have never yet met an unmarried woman of over thirty who leads from free choice the life of a 'daughter at home' as the most desirable vocation in the world. Either she is waiting in hopes of marriage, or she has abandoned hope and is resigned. As the life-work of a civilised adult, I find resignation inadequate.[98]

Holtby identified two classes of unmarried women: one who had been trained but were workless; the other group had not been trained except for a good time in a rich world of tennis-dancing, hunting, and the like but who would later regret their choice. Winifred Holtby was an 'Old Feminist' who believed that equality in legislation must remain central to women's activism whereas the 'New Feminists' began to champion women's issues such as childcare and birth control. In *Left Review* Naomi Mitchison's review of Winifred Holtby's book, *Women and a Changing Society*, was titled 'The Reluctant Feminists':

Women like Winifred Holtby and myself who are – well, between thirty and forty – have gone through the interesting experience of finding our deepest ideas and principles being conditioned by the economic position of the section of society to which we belong. We started before the war as good little bourgeois feminists, determined to beat, or at least to equal, men at their own game, which appeared to us at the time to be on the whole, 'the professions'. The war came and gave us our chance; we took it. During the boom time, the professions swung open to women and this reflected in our attitude of mind. We ceased to be militant feminists, ceased to regard men as enemies, we were doing so well that we did not feel the hand of ownership pressing upon us. We had earned our incomes, praise, and a good deal of freedom. But when the slump came, the professions began to squeeze us; capitalism could no longer afford itself the pleasant amusement of a class of unowned women.[99]

Mitchison expressed the divided sympathies towards women's emancipation which were common in this period and epitomised in a broadcast debate, 'Aren't Women Bored with Emancipation?' between Rose MacCaulay and E.

---

98 Winifred Holtby, 'Tea-Table Sitters', letter to *Time and Tide* 31 December 1932: 1437. She is responding to a letter by Mrs Cardew and Mrs Case.

99 Mitchison, 'The Reluctant Feminists', review of *Women and a Changing Society*, by Winifred Holtby (London: Bodley Head, 1934), *Left Review*, December 1934: 93; Benton 96–7.

Arnot Robinson. Robinson argued that women's innate orientation towards people not things and their 'spiritual dependence' meant that their new opportunities for independence and leisure were a burden, whereas MacCaulay argued that women's burdens were still mundane chores. In the course of the debate, Robinson cited the 1931 census figures for the employment of women: aged 18–21, over seventy-eight per cent; aged 21–25, sixty-five per cent and aged 25–34, thirty-five per cent. She interpreted the drop in employment at the marriageable age as evidence that women were bored with work and took the first chance of giving it up.[100] As MacCaulay replied, and as Mitchison and Holtby stated, this was not so, but it was difficult for women to complain when unemployment figures were high and there was much propaganda concerning the romanticised prewar model of family life. The married and financially comfortable woman was counted as being particularly lucky, but the growing centrality of the home brought pressures to find satisfaction within the family circle which was secure but stultifying. Many of the woman-centred poems written or published in the thirties record women's sense of change and of no change. Divided sympathies are evoked in poetry through dramatic monologues which allow for the dialectical representation of social constraints.

Holtby's interest in constructed gender roles, 'Beauty the Lovers Gift', printed in *Time and Tide* 8 July 1933, dramatises the dual expectations for women to be like ornaments and companions:

> Have I not thanked you well for your gift of beauty?
> See! I acknowledge it. I am your work of art.
> You modelled this gold, this rose and this pearl to suit ye.
> Is it my fault, if you say that I have no heart?
>
> Did you teach my tongue to be kind and my fingers tender?
> Did you ask me to spill my sweetness to quench your flame?
> You cried to my lips, 'Be red!' to my hands, 'Be slender!'
> They have obeyed. You have only yourself to blame.[101]

Taken collectively, thirties woman-centred poetry constitutes a body of writing which opposed the growing influence of popular romance caused by the influx of Hollywood Films, Mills and Boon novels and women's weeklies. As intellectuals, the poets may have been dissociating themselves from popular

---

100 E. Arnot Robinson and Rose MacCaulay, 'Are Women Bored with Emancipation?', *Listener*, 13 November: 35.
101 Holtby, 'Beauty the Lovers Gift', Dowson, 66–7.

culture but also challenging the influential myths of these popular romances and of literary fictions. The poems present a grim choice between loneliness within marriage or isolation without it. Sylvia Lynd's 'The Solitary' hauntingly evokes the emptiness of the unmarried woman in a society which centralises the marriage ideal:

> None stood with her the caverned dark to share,
> While the leaves whispered softly leaf to leaf
> Of lip pressed close to lip. This was her grief.
>
> And ah, she cried, That I must live alone –
> The song unsung, the blank uncarven stone,
> The jewel lost forever in the well,
> News that the runner, dying, did not tell.
> I am a plough whose share is red with rust,
> I am a harp whose gold is grey with dust,
> I am a wisdom that no man will heed,
> I am a garden that no hand will weed,
> I am a ruined house, a disused way,
> Silence, forgetfulness and dull decay –
> Ah, what false steward took and set aside
> This talent from love's treasury? she cried.[102]

Not all poems about women alone were as pitiful. Sometimes, the single woman was depicted as having a mental freedom which seemed enviable to the married one.[103] 'Seaside Cottage', an uncollected poem by Sylvia Townsend Warner printed in *Time and Tide* and the *Egoist,* expressed the mental confinement of the housewife. The through-the-window perspective is a literal device which punctuates the myth of domestic bliss. This is the entire poem because it is still uncollected:

> Oh how perplexed
> With this now and that next
> And hounding 'tother yet to do
> I double life-time through!
> Of every hour the prey,
> With never time to turn and stand at bay
> On the pursuing day.

---

102 Naomi Mitchison, 'Woman Alone'; Sylvia Lynd, 'The Solitary'; Dowson,81,60.
103 See for example, Ackland, 'The Lonely Woman', Dowson, 36.

The kitchen mock
Of every stationary crock,
My thoughts, besmirched with toil and swink
Drain greasy down the sink;
Nor banned with envy, dare
Wander through windowpane to where
White clouds idle on air.

Yet if my rage
Should smite away the cage
If from the sea a wind should come
And shout my jailors dumb,
This heart that bangs on bone
Tossed to the firmament of being alone,
Would sink me like a stone.[104]

The view of the cottage may be idyllic to the outsider, but to the women indoors the kitchen was a prison of overwork and confinement. It is not one of Warner's best but records the sentiments of many poems published in the journals. Like 'Seaside Cottage', 'Woman at Home', an uncollected poem from *Time and Tide*, both articulates and conceals a frustration which is barely presentable:

Is there not one side of her nature repressed?
Has she not longed, ached, craved for something for years?
Truth is: other minds have subjected hers
Incessantly! Incessantly!
Vainly has she striven (alas! in dreams) for release.
Will she get it – one day?
Her hand trembles as she carries the soup …
…
Oh! She is half-mad tonight,
The woman at home![105]

The repetitions, ellipses and gaps are important to the text in depicting what was unspoken and unspeakable. There was no available language model and the mother/housewife would have felt guilty about expressing rebellion. As Alison Light suggests, 'Just how unquiet the depths were beneath the apparently unruffled surface of sensible and quiescent women living between

---

104 Warner, 'Seaside Cottage, *Time and Tide* 12 August 1933: 960.
105 Vere Arnot, 'Woman at Home', *Time and Tide* 11 July 1936; Dowson, 186–7.

the wars can be gauged from the success of Daphne DuMaurier's 1938 bestseller, *Rebecca*.'[106] The woman-at-home's private monologue connects to writings like *The Diary of a Provincial Lady* by E.M. Delafield or Jan Struther's *Mrs Miniver*, both of which were published in serial form in *Time and Tide*.[107] Like these, the best poems evoke mixed feelings. Frances Cornford's popular 'Ode on the Whole Duty of Parents' is more disturbing when read in conjunction with her journals:

> constant ill health, exhaustion to be skilfully dodged ... just keeping my head above water ... mostly the sense of my being is a strain – hushed anxiety, depression, guilt, not keeping going as if in a beleaguered city.[108]

The 'unquiet depths' are also documented in Anna Wickham's 'Fragment of an Autobiography' which has been drawn upon in the previous section, 'Female Modernists':

> It is the fourth of March, 1935 ... 29 years attempting to order the house. For 25 years of my misery, it has been my passionate preoccupation ... the shades of the prison house began to close in on me. My husband ... from being my devoted lover seemed to become my enemy and my judge.[109]

Women poets writing in the thirties never depicted marriage as straightforward or happy. One way of survival was through silence. When 'Poor Maria' in Stevie Smith's 'Marriage, I think' spoke her mind she frightened off her husband:

> Better that she had kept her thoughts on a chain,
> For now she's alone again and all in pain;
> She sighs for the man that went and the thoughts that stay
> To trouble her dreams by night and her dreams by day.[110]

---

106 Alison Light, *Forever England: Femininity, Literature and Conservatism Between the Wars* (London: Routledge, 1991), 13.

107 During the 1930s, Jan Struther wrote columns describing the fictional life of a 'Mrs Miniver' which were turned into a best-seller and a Hollywood film. Her poems were printed in *The Spectator*, *The London Mercury* and *The Best Poetry* anthologies. E.M. Delafield, *The Diary of a Provincial Lady*, 1930 (London, Virago, 1984).

108 Frances Cornford, Journal 1934, Mss 58390, *Literary Papers*.

109 Anna Wickham, 'Fragment of an Autobiography', *The Writings of Anna Wickham: Free Woman and Poet*, ed. R.D. Smith (London: Virago, 1984), 45.

110 Smith, 'Marriage I think', *Me Again*, 216; Dowson, 147.

The collision between unspoken frustration or desire and women's official symbolised discourse is represented in the frequent not-waving-but-drowning motif. Like Stevie Smith above, most poets tended to fictionalise or dramatise internal conflicts concerning women's identity and roles through monologue and dialogue. Winifred Holtby's uncollected poem, 'Boats in the Bay' printed in *Time and Tide*, is an unsettling portrait of unspoken misery:

> I will take my trouble and drop it into the water
> It is heavy as stone and smooth as a sea-washed pebble.
> It will sink under the sea, and the happy people
> Will row over it quietly, ruffling the clear water
> Little dark boats like midges, skimming silently
> Will pass backwards and forwards, the girls singing;
> They will never know that they have sailed above sorrow.
> Sink heavily and lie still, lie still my trouble.[111]

Apart from Anne Ridler's 'The Letter', a verse epistle to her husband, there is no love poetry, except for the lesbian lyrics between Sylvia Townsend Warner and Valentine Ackland and by Vita Sackville-West. Being a woman was clearly a complex issue for all writers and particularly the lesbian as was demonstrated in the furore surrounding the publication of Radclyffe Hall's *The Well of Loneliness* in 1928. The disjunction between unarticulated expression, that is the semiotic, and the official symbolic formulation is most clearly manifested in the coded love poems between Sylvia Townsend Warner and Valentine Ackland, published in their combined volume *Whether a Dove or a Seagull* in 1934.[112] These lyrics indicate the double restraints of the lesbian existence under the guise of traditional form and the gender neutral pronouns. In Ackland's quasi-sonnet, 'What must we do if we cannot do this', the 'this' is the love which dare not speak its name – 'our tightened cord, our secret tether' – and in 'Drawing You Heavy with Sleep', Sylvia Townsend Warner plays with the complexities of female identity. The metaphors of fluidity and liquidity are paradigmatic representations of female sexuality:[113]

---

111 Holtby, 'Boats in the Bay', *Time and Tide* 18 February 1933; Dowson, 67.

112 Sylvia Townsend Warner with Valentine Ackland, *Whether a Dove or a Seagull* (New York: Viking, 1933) is out of print. Some poems are reproduced in Warner's *Collected Poems* and in Dowson 1996.

113 Jan Montefiore, *Feminism and Poetry* (London: Pandora, 1987), 158.

Heavy with sleep and with sleep pliable
You rolled at a touch towards me. Your arm fell
Across me as a river throws
An arm of flood across meadows.[114]

The representation of female desire was brave in a cultural climate which expected women, particularly poets, to conform to the conservative expectations of sexless femininity.

---

114 Dowson, 157.

Chapter Eight

Conclusion: The Legacy of Modernism

Throughout the twentieth century, the elevated status of modernism and its implicit or explicit gendering as male, have prevented poets from identifying themselves as women, from associating themselves with one another and from establishing a separate tradition. In the introduction to their anthology of Victorian women's poetry (1995), Angela Leighton and Margaret Reynolds hold modernism responsible for the disappearance of most of the poets in Elizabeth Sharp's anthology *Women's Voices* (1887). As they point out, the impulse of literary women was to deny, not to recover, a female lineage: 'partly because of the experiments of modernism, partly because of a new feminist sensibility, partly because of a critical value placed on the dry, intellectual, the dispassionate, early twentieth-century writers, readers and critics, were embarrassed by their Victorian grandmothers'.[1] I have not, however, intended to endorse the concept that nineteenth-century writers like Christina Rossetti and Elizabeth Barrett Browning espoused the feminine ideal. Revisionary criticism'has unlocked their resistance to the tropes of feminised sentimentality. Instead, I have suggested that early twentieth-century suffragism, the First World War and new legislation concerning women's rights changed women's consciousness and provided them with unprecedented opportunities. Women poets became a significant public presence. Their publishing initiatives and literary criticism were part of their new autonomy which was often threatening to a patriarchal literary establishment and perplexing to their male colleagues. Individually, however, they often invited respect. I arranged the chapters loosely chronologically but there is no tidy historical progression. In 1915, Anna Wickham was more overtly feminist and stylistically versatile than Frances Cornford in 1934.

In drawing an inclusive map of women's poetry, I have needed to challenge the supremacy of high modernism but at the same time to identify the ways in which women participated in its movements. In Britain, the avant-garde was associated with the Sitwells, particularly Edith, and imagism was identified with H.D. and Amy Lowell. Laura Riding, with Robert Graves, was the first to conceptualise the term 'modernist poetry'. Other American modernists were

---

1   Angela Leighton and Margaret Reynolds (eds), *Victorian Women Poets: An Anthology* (Oxford: Blackwell, 1985), xxxiii.

influential through the intellectual international network largely maintained by the little magazines. Apart from Edna St Vincent Millay, the 'female modernists' had little recognition, presumably because of the woman-centred subject matter, the assertive voices and difficulty in classifying their work. As Clare Hanson states, however, the significant relationship between women and modernism can be estimated in retrospect:

> One might suggest, for example, that the initial impetus from modernism came in fact from women writers, so that to talk of a female version of modernism – implying a secondary position for women – is misleading. One might suggest rather that modernism as we have been taught it is a male parasite on a body of experience and a way of seeing pioneered by women.[2]

Modernism has not just made a blind spot in Britain. In discussing 'the collapse of poetic modernism as a coherent aesthetic' on recent American poetry, David Kellogg maintains, 'Only recently has the academy begun to rediscover the varieties of poetry produced in the early part of this century, a poetry previously stabilised, and then left for dead, under the normative sign of modernism.'[3] The process of reinstatement, however, requires a refiguring of received histories from the vantage point of contemporary criticism. As Cheryl Walker points out in revaluing Edna St Vincent Millay, current cultural theories provide the terminology to articulate new reading positions:

> But what about the canon? Does the presence or absence of Edna St. Vincent Millay signal major differences in our understanding of who can be a part of the canon? Some years ago, let us say in Lionel Trilling's time, no modern women poets except for Marianne Moore were recognized as among the greats. Now a lot more women are taken seriously. Even more than Edna Millay, Gertrude Stein has come to seem an important literary (instead of simply cultural) figure. I would suggest, however, that Stein could not occupy this position were it nor for critical and cultural postmodernism and the popularity of gay and lesbian studies. It is not that we have suddenly come to see what was always valuable about her work. It is rather that, given our present literary values, we can make Stein into a representative figure.[4]

---

2   Clare Hanson, *The Gender of Modernism*, ed. Bonnie Kime Scott (Bloomington and Indianapolis: Indiana University Press, 1990), 303.

3   David Kellogg, 'Literary History and the Problem of Oppositional Practices in Contemporary Poetry', *Cultural Critique* 32 (Winter 1995–96): 153–4.

4   Cheryl Walker, 'Anti-modern, Modern and Post-modern Edna St. Vincent Millay: Contexts of Revaluation', in Margaret Dickie and Thomas Travisano (eds), *Gendered Modernisms: American Women Poets and Their Readers* (Philadelphia: University of Pennsylvania Press, 1996), 186.

Contemporary feminist criticism provides ways of investigating the poems as women-centred texts and as indicating a specifically female aesthetic. It is, however, futile to seek for a wholly distinct female language because, as has been illustrated, women wished to be freed from the negative mythologies of the feminine poetess. Instead, they negotiated with male-associated forms, metres and symbols. There is, however, a lingering tendency to privilege the experimentalists because poets who have not ostensibly fractured poetic forms have appeared chained by patriarchal literary tradition. In *Women: a cultural review* (1990), Wendy Mulford suggests that formal adventurousness is definable, preferable and the property of America: 'Why the work produced by women writing in the British Isles should be less formally adventurous [than in America] is the subject of a book waiting to be written.'[5] Gilbert and Gubar blame this kind of language-based modernism for depriving twentieth-century women of positive role models:

> As the modernist aesthetic was gradually institutionalised during the first half of the century, therefore, the accomplishments of Millay and Moore came to seem increasingly marginal, so much so that younger women who might have turned to them as heartening examples were often surprisingly ambivalent towards these important precursors. Traditional 'poetesses' like Millay had been defined as offensively emotional and anachronistic; ostensible innovators like Moore were seen as precious and recherché.[6]

As argued here, modernism's rhetoric of clear-cut oppositions between realist and anti-realist or between experimental and sentimental leave no place for poets like Millay – and to her can be added Charlotte Mew, May Sinclair, Sylvia Townsend Warner, Anna Wickham and others who are hard to classify.

Reductive binary oppositions also restrict subsequent generations. In 'Contemporary Women's Poetry: experimentalism and the expressive voice', Clair Wills indicates that the pervasive exaggeration of high modernist domination and the narrow conception of modernist radicalism continue to inhibit women from harnessing the expressive mode to their concerns or creativity:

---

5   Wendy Mulford, 'Curved, Odd ... Irregular. A Vision of Contemporary Poetry by Women', *Women: a cultural review* 1. 3 (Winter 1990): 261.

6   Sandra Gilbert and Susan Gubar, *No Man's Land: The Place Of The Woman Writer In The Twentieth Century. Vol. 3. Letters to the Front* (New Haven: Yale University Press, 1994), 74.

In modernist or experimental poetry, unlike its counterpart, language is not the means of representation but the object of representation itself.

There is plenty to argue about even in the distinction as I have presented it, [between experimental poetry and formally conservative poetic practices], yet the division of poetry into formally conservative and radical forms becomes more loaded in the context of poetry by women (or the poetry of marginalised groups in society). Can the formal disruption of representational norms act as the ground for a radical gender politics? ... As many critics have argued, the formal dynamics of modernism were predicated to some extent on a denial of sentimental or sensational 'feminine' forms. Indeed, the current resurgence of interest in Gertrude Stein (for example) may be symptomatic of the way that the contemporary debate is modelled on the earlier one. Feminist and experimental writers look to her as representative of the avant-garde attack on representational norms, and as an example of woman's response to patriarchal language. Standing outside mainstream modernism, she appears to hold together the female and the experimental, as is evidenced by the domesticity of 'Tender Buttons', or the sexuality of 'Lifting Belly'.[7]

As has been indicated, this holding together of the female and experimental is the cohering aesthetic of avant-garde, female modernist and thirties poets. The urgent goals for revisionary critics should be to emphasise the interface between anti-realist and representational writing and to provide strong models of women poets. As Carol Rumens comments on the recovery of women's poetry of the 1930s, 'What matters is to make audible the range of different voices, partly in the interests of historical accuracy, but not least so that female genius, when its next time comes, has a natural order in which to take its place. Minor poets may, of course, turn out to be major in the estimation of another age (and vice versa).'[8]

In order for women writers and critics to overcome the negative affiliation with each other, I have pluralised modernism and presented the significance of women as modernist poets. Some stylistic links are possible but the main coherence is their differing negotiations with their gendered subjectivity. They defined themselves in opposition to the feminine ideal with which they were confronted in the ideologies of First World War recruiting propaganda and the disparaging vocabulary of literary criticism. The over-riding impression of individuality and diversity also counteracts the myth of essentialist femininity.

---

7   Clair Wills, 'Contemporary Women's Poetry: experimentation and the expressive voice', *Critical Quarterly* 36. 3 (Autumn 1994): 35–52.

8   Carol Rumens, 'Smithwelby', review of *Women's Poetry of the 1930s*, ed. Jane Dowson, *Poetry Review* 85. 4, Winter 95/6: 23–4.

Bibliography

Primary Works

Djuna Barnes

The Book of Repulsive Women: 8 Rhythms and 5 Drawings, 1915, Los Angeles: Sun & Moon Press, 1994.
Ladies Almanack, 1928, New York: Harper and Row, 1972.

Vera Brittain

Verses of a VAD, London: Macdonald, 1916.
Poems of the War and After, London: Gollancz.

May Wedderburn Cannan

In War Time, Oxford: Blackwell, 1917.
The Splendid Days, Oxford: Blackwell, 1919.
The House of Hope, London: Milford, 1923.
Tears of War, ed. Charlotte Fyffe, London: Cavalier, 2000.

Margaret Postgate Cole

Poems, London: Allen and Unwin, 1918.

Frances Cornford

Poems, London: The Priory Press, 1910.
Death and the Princess: A Morality, Cambridge: Bowes and Bowes, 1912.
Spring Morning, London: The Poetry Bookshop, 1915.
Different Days, London: Hogarth Press, 1928.
Mountains and Molehills, illustrated by Gwen Raverat, Cambridge: Cambridge University Press, 1934.
Travelling Home and Other Poems, illustrated by Christopher Cornford, London: Cresset Press, 1948.
Collected Poems, London: Cresset Press, 1954.
On a Calm Shore, London: Cresset Press, 1960.

Frances Cornford: Selected Poems, ed. Jane Dowson, foreword by Hugh Cornford, London: Enitharmon, 1996.

Nancy Cunard

Outlaws, London: Elkin Mathews, 1921.
Sublunary, London: Hodder and Stoughton, 1923.
Parallax, London: Hogarth Press, 1925.
Poems (Two) 1925, London: Aquila Press, 1930.
Negro: an anthology (ed.), 1934, New York: Frederick Ungar Publishing Co., 1970.
Rélève into Marquis, Derby: The Grasshopper Press, 1944.
Poems for France (ed.), London: La France Libre, 1944.
Poèmes à la France (ed.), Paris: Pierre Seghers, 1949.
Sonnets on Spain (unpublished), 1958.

Elizabeth Daryush

Verses, Oxford: Blackwell, 1917.
Sonnets from Hafaz and Other Verses, London: Milford, 1921.
Verses, Oxford: Oxford University Press, 1930.
Verses: Second Book, Oxford: Oxford University Press, 1932.
Verses: Third Book, Oxford: Oxford University Press, 1933.
Verses: Fourth Book, Oxford: Oxford University Press, 1934.
Poems, London: Macmillan, 1935.
The Last Man and Other Verses, Oxford: Oxford University Press, 1936.
Verses: Sixth Book, Oxford: Oxford University Press, 1938.
Selected Poems, ed. Yvor Winters, New York: Swallow Press, 1948.
Verses: Seventh Book, ed. Roy Fuller, Manchester: Carcanet, 1971.
Selected Poems: Verses I–VI, Manchester: Carcanet, 1972.
Collected Poems, ed. Donald Davie, Manchester: Carcanet, 1976.

Eva Gore-Booth

Broken Glory, London: Maunsel, 1918.
The Shepherd of Eternity and Other Poems, London: Longmans, 1925.
Poems of Eva Gore-Booth, London: Longmans, 1929.
Selected Poems of Eva Gore-Booth, London: Longmans, 1933.

H.D.

Sea Garden, 1916, London: St James Press and New York: St Martin's Press, 1975.
Hymen, London: The Egoist Press and New York: Henry Holt & Co. 1921.

Heliodora and Other Poems, London: Jonathan Cape and Boston: Houghton Mifflin, 1924.

Collected Poems of H.D., 1925, New York: Boni & Liveright, 1940.

Helen in Egypt, New York: Grove Press, 1961, Manchester: Carcanet Press, 1985.

Hermetic Definition, New York: New Directions and Manchester: Carcanet, 1972.

Trilogy, New York: New Directions and Manchester: Carcanet, 1973.

H.D. *Collected Poems 1912–1944*, ed. Louis L. Martz, New York: New Directions, 1983.

Amy Lowell

A Dome of Many Coloured Glass, Boston: Houghton Mifflin, 1912.

Sword Blades and Poppy Seed, London and New York: Macmillan, 1914.

Men, Women and Ghosts, London and New York: Macmillan, 1916.

Can Grande's Castle, London and New York: Macmillan, 1918; Oxford: Blackwell, 1920.

Pictures of the Floating World, Boston: Houghton Mifflin, 1919.

Legends, Boston: Houghton Mifflin, 1921.

Fir-Flower Tablets, Poems translated from the Chinese, London: Constable, 1922.

What's O'Clock, Boston: Houghton Mifflin, 1925.

East Wind, Boston: Houghton Mifflin, 1926.

Ballads for Sale, Boston: Houghton Mifflin, 1927.

Selected Poems of Amy Lowell, ed. J.L. Lowes, Boston: Houghton Mifflin, 1928.

The Complete Poetical Works of Amy Lowell, Boston: Houghton Mifflin, 1955.

A Shard of Silence: Selected Poems of Amy Lowell, ed. G.R. Ruihley, New York: Twayne Publishers, 1957.

Mina Loy

Lunar Baedecker [sic], Paris: Contact Publishing Co., 1923.

Lunar Baedeker & Timetables, North Carolina: Jonathan Williams, Highlands, 1958.

The Lost Lunar Baedeker, 1982, ed. Roger Conover, Manchester: Carcanet, 1997.

Sylvia Lynd

The Thrush and the Jay: Poems and Prose Sketches, London: Constable and Co., 1916.

The Goldfinches: Poem, London: R. Cobden-Sanderson, 1920.

Selected Poems, London: Ernest Benn, 1928.

The Yellow Placard: Poems, London: Victor Gollancz, 1931.

The Enemies: Poems, London: Dent, 1934.

Collected Poems, London: Macmillan, 1945.

Charlotte Mew

The Farmer's Bride, London: The Poetry Bookshop, 1916.
The Farmer's Bride, new edition with 11 new poems, London: The Poetry Bookshop, 1921.
The Rambling Sailor, London: The Poetry Bookshop, 1929.
Collected Poems, London: Duckworth, 1953.
Charlotte Mew: Collected Poems and Prose, ed. Val Warner, Manchester: Carcanet, 1981.
Charlotte Mew: Collected Poems and Selected Prose, ed. Val Warner, Manchester: Carcanet, 1997.

Alice Meynell

Later Poems, London and New York: John Lane, 1910.
Poems, London: John Lane, 1911.
Poems, London: Burns and Oates, 1913.
Ten Poems 1913–1915, privately printed, 1915.
A Father of Women and Other Poems, London: Burns and Oates, 1917.
Poems, London: Burns, Oates and Washbourne, 1921.
The Last Poems of Alice Meynell, London: Burns, Oates and Washbourne, 1923.
Selected Poems of Alice Meynell, London: Nonesuch, 1930.
The Poems of Alice Meynell, complete edition, 1923, Oxford: Oxford University Press, 1940.

Edna St Vincent Millay

Renascence and Other Poems, New York: Mitchell Kennerley, 1918.
Second April, New York: Mitchell Kennerley, 1921.
A Few Figs from Thistles: poems and sonnets, New York and London: Harper and Brothers, 1921.
The Ballad of the Harp Weaver, New York: Frank Shay, 1922.
Poems, London: Martin Secker, 1923.
The Harp Weaver and Other Poems, New York and London: Harper and Brothers, 1923.
The Harp Weaver, London: Martin Secker, 1924.
Renascence and Other Poems, New York: Harper and Brothers, 1925.
The Buck in the Snow and Other Poems, New York and London: Harper and Brothers, 1928.
Fatal Interview: Sonnets, New York and London: Harper and Brothers and London: Hamish Hamilton, 1931.

Wine from these Grapes, New York and London: Harper and Brothers; London: Hamish Hamilton, 1934.

Conversations at Midnight, New York and London: Harper and Brothers; London: Hamish Hamilton, 1937.

Collected Lyrics, New York and London: Harper and Brothers, 1939.

Huntsman, What Quarry?, New York and London: Harper and Brothers; London: Hamish Hamilton, 1939.

Make Bright the Arrows, New York and London: Harper and Brothers, 1940.

'*There are No Islands any More*', *Lines Written in Passion and in Deep Concern for England, France and my own Country*, New York and London: Harper and Brothers, 1940.

Lyrics and Sonnets, New York: Editions for the Armed Services, 1941.

Collected Sonnets, New York and London: Harper and Brothers, 1941.

Mine the Harvest. A Collection of New Poems, New York: Harper, 1954.

Collected Poems, New York and London: Harper and Brothers, 1956.

Collected Lyrics of Edna St Vincent Millay, New York: Harper and Row, 1962.

Edna St Vincent Millay: Selected Poems, ed. Colin Falck, Manchester: Carcanet, 1992.

Marianne Moore

Poems, London: Egoist Press, 1921.

Observations, New York: The Dial Press, 1924.

Selected Poems, introduction by T.S. Eliot, New York: Macmillan; London: Faber & Faber, 1935.

The Pangolin and Other Verse, London: The Brendin Publishing Company, 1936.

What Are Years?, New York: Macmillan, 1941.

Nevertheless, New York: Macmillan, 1944.

Collected Poems, New York: Macmillan; London: Faber & Faber, 1951.

The Fables of La Fontaine, trans., New York: Viking, 1954.

Like a Bulwark, New York: Viking, 1956.

O to Be a Dragon, New York: Viking, 1959.

The Arctic Ox, London: Faber & Faber, 1964.

The Complete Poems of Marianne Moore, 1967, London: Faber & Faber, 1968.

Unfinished Poems by Marianne Moore, Philadelphia: The Philip H. and A.S.W. Rosenbach Foundation, 1972.

Marianne Moore: Collected Poems, London: Faber, 1981.

Dorothy Parker

Enough Rope, New York: Boni & Liveright, 1926.

Sunset Gun, New York: Boni & Liveright, 1928.

Death of Taxes and Other Poems, New York: Viking, 1931.

Not so Deep as a Well: *Collected Poems of Dorothy Parker*, London: Hamish Hamilton, 1937.

Ruth Pitter

First Poems, London: Cecil Palmer, 1920.
First and Second Poems 1912–25, preface by Hilaire Belloc, London: Sheed and Ward, 1927.
Persephone in Hades, privately printed, 1931.
A Mad Lady's Garland, London: Cresset; New York: Macmillan, 1934.
A Trophy of Arms: Poems 1926–1935, preface by James Stephens, London: Cresset; New York: Macmillan, 1936.
The Spirit Watches, London: Cresset and New York: Macmillan, 1939.
The Rude Potato, Illustrated by Roger Furse, London: Cresset, 1941.
The Bridge: Poems 1939–1944, London: Cresset and New York: Macmillan, 1945.
Pitter On Cats, London: Cresset, 1946.
Urania, London: Cresset, 1951.
The Ermine: Poems 1942–1952, London: Cresset, 1953.
Still By Choice, London: Cresset, 1966.
Poems 1926–1966, London: Barrie and Rockliff, 1968.
Ruth Pitter: Collected Poems, New York: Macmillan, 1969.
End of Drought, London: Barrie and Jenkins, 1975.
A Heaven to Find, London: Enitharmon, 1987.
Collected Poems, introduced by Elizabeth Jennings, London: Enitharmon, 1996.

Jessie Pope

Jessie Pope's War Poems, London: Grant Richards Ltd., 1915.
More War Poems, London: Grant Richards Ltd., 1915.
Simple Rhymes for Stirring Times, London: Pearson, 1916.
Hits and Misses, London: Grant Richards Ltd., 1920.

Laura (Riding) Jackson

The Close Chaplet, London: Hogarth and New York: Adelphi, 1926.
Poems: A Joking Word, London: Cape, 1930.
Twenty Poems Less, Paris: Hours Press, 1930.
Laura and Francisca, Deya: Seizin Press, 1931.
Poet: A Lying Word, London: Arthur Barker, 1933.
The Life of the Dead, London: Arthur Barker, 1933.
Collected Poems, London: Cassell and New York: Random House, 1938.
Selected Poems: In Five Sets, London: Faber & Faber, 1970.

The Poems of Laura Riding, new edition of *Collected Poems* 1938, Manchester: Carcanet, 1980.
First Awakenings: The Early Poems, ed. Elizabeth Friedmann, Alan J. Clark and Robert Nye, Manchester: Carcanet, 1992.
A Selection of the Poems of Laura Riding, ed. Robert Nye, Manchester: Carcanet, 1994.

Margaret Sackville

The Pageant of War, London: Simpkin, 1916.

Vita Sackville-West

Poems of West and East, London: Bodley Head, 1917.
Orchard and Vineyard, London: Bodley Head, 1921.
The Land, London: Heinemann, 1926.
The King's Daughter, London: Hogarth, 1929.
Sissinghurst, London: Hogarth, 1931.
Invitation to Cast out Care, London: Faber, 1931.
Rilke, trans., London: Hogarth, 1931.
Collected Poems, London: Hogarth, 1933.
Solitude, London: Hogarth, 1938.
Selected Poems, London: Hogarth, 1941.
The Garden, London: Michael Joseph, 1946.
Sissinghurst, London: Hogarth, 1964.

May Sinclair

Nakiketa and Other Poems (pseudonym 'Julian Sinclair'), privately printed, 1886.
The Dark Night, London: Jonathan Cape, 1924.

Edith Sitwell

Clowns' Houses, Oxford: Blackwell, 1918.
Mother and Other Poems, Oxford: Blackwell, 1918.
The Wooden Pegasus, Oxford: Blackwell, 1920.
Bucolic Comedies, London: Duckworth, 1923.
The Sleeping Beauty, London: Duckworth, 1924.
Troy Park, London: Duckworth, 1925.
Rustic Elegies, London: Duckworth, 1927.
Gold Coast Customs, London: Duckworth, 1929.

Collected Poems, London: Duckworth, 1930.
Five Variations on a Theme, London: Duckworth, 1933.
Selected Poems, London: Duckworth, 1936.
Poems New and Old, London: Faber, 1940.
Street Songs, London: Macmillan, 1943.
Green Song and Other Poems, London: Macmillan, 1944.
The Song of the Cold, London: Macmillan, 1945.
The Shadow of Cain, London: John Lehmann, 1947.
The Canticle of the Rose: Selected Poems 1920–1947, London: Macmillan, 1949.
Façade and Other Poems 1920–1935, London: Duckworth, 1950.
Selected Poems, Harmondsworth: Penguin, 1952.
Gardens and Astronomers: New Poems, London: Macmillan, 1953.
Collected Poems, 1957, London: Macmillan, 1961.
The Outcasts, London: Macmillan, 1962.
Selected Poems, London: Macmillan, 1965.
Collected Poems, repr., London: Macmillan, 1982.

Stevie Smith

A Good Time Was Had By All, London: Cape, 1937.
Tender Only to One, London: Cape, 1938.
Mother, What is Man?, London: Cape, 1942.
Harold's Leap, London: Cape, 1950.
Not Waving but Drowning, London: Cape, 1957.
Some are More Human than Others: A Sketch-book, London: Gabberbocchus, 1958.
Selected Poems, London: Longmans, 1962.
The Frog Prince, London: Longmans, 1966.
Two in One, London: Longmans, 1971.
Scorpion and Other Poems, London: Longmans, 1972.
Collected Poems, London: Allen Lane, 1975.
Selected Poems, Harmondsworth: Penguin, 1978.
Me Again: The Uncollected Writings of Stevie Smith, London: Virago, 1981.
Stevie Smith: A Selection, ed. Hermione Lee, London: Faber, 1983.

Gertrude Stein

Tender Buttons, 1914, New York: Haskell House, 1982.
Stanzas in Meditation and Other Poems 1929–1933, New Haven: Yale University Press, 1967.
Bee time Vine and Other Pieces 1913–1927, 1953, New York: Books for Libraries Press, 1969.

The Yale Gertrude Stein, ed. Richard Kostelanez, New Haven: Yale University Press, 1980.
Selected Writing of Gertrude Stein, New York: Vintage Books, 1990.
A Stein Reader, ed. Ulla E. Dydo, Illinois: Northwestern University Press, 1993.

Iris Tree

Lamplight and Starlight, New York: Boni and Liveright, 1919.
Poems, decorated by Curtis Moffat, London and New York: John Lane, 1920.
The Traveller and Other Poems, New York: Boni and Liveright, 1927.
The Marsh Picnic, introduction by John Betjeman, Cambridge: Rampant Lions Press, 1966.

Katherine Tynan

New Poems, London: Sidgwick & Jackson, 1911.
Flower of Youth: Poems in War Time, London: Sidgwick & Jackson, 1915.
The Holy War, London: Sidgwick & Jackson, 1916.
Late Songs, London: Sidgwick & Jackson, 1917.
Collected Poems, London: Macmillan, 1930.
Augustan Books of Poetry, ed., London: Ernest Benn, 1931.

Sylvia Townsend Warner

The Espalier, London: Chatto & Windus, 1925.
Time Importuned, London: Chatto & Windus, 1928.
Opus 7, London: Chatto & Windus, 1931.
Rainbow, New York: Alfred A. Knopf, 1932.
Whether a Dove or a Seagull, with Valentine Ackland, New York: Viking, 1933.
Boxwood, London: Chatto & Windus, 1960.
King Duffus and Other Poems, London and Wells: Clare, Son & Co. Ltd., 1968.
Twelve Poems, London: Chatto & Windus, 1980.
Collected Poems, Manchester: Carcanet, 1982.
Selected Poems, Manchester: Carcanet, 1985.

Dorothy Wellesley

Poems, London: privately printed, 1920.
Genesis: An Impression, London: Heinemann, 1926.
Deserted House: A Poem Sequence, London: Hogarth, 1930.
Poems of Ten Years, London: Macmillan, 1934.

Selections from the Poems of Dorothy Wellesley, London: Macmillan, 1936.
The Last Planet and Other Poems, London: Hogarth, 1942.
Desert Wells: New Poems, London: Michael Joseph, 1946.
Selections from the Poems of Dorothy Wellesley, London: Williams and Norgate, 1948.
Rhymes for Middle Years, London: Barrie, 1954.
Early Light: The Collected Poems of Dorothy Wellesley, London: Hart Davis, 1955.

Anna Wickham

Songs (pseudonym 'John Oland'), London: privately printed, 1911.
The Contemplative Quarry, London: The Poetry Bookshop, 1915.
The Man with a Hammer, London: Grant Richards, 1916.
The Little Old House, London: The Poetry Bookshop, 1921.
Anna Wickham, Richards Shilling Selections, London: Richards Press, 1936.
Selected Poems, London: Chatto & Windus, 1971.
The Writings of Anna Wickham: Free Woman and Poet, ed. R.D. Smith, London: Virago, 1984.

Elinor Wylie

Nets to Catch the Wind, New York: Alfred A. Knopf, 1921.
Black Armour: a book of poems, London: Martin Secker, 1927.
Trivial Breath, New York and London: Alfred A. Knopf, 1928.
Angels and earthly Creatures, New York: Alfred A. Knopf, 1929.
Birthday Sonnet, New York: Random House.
Collected Poems, New York: Alfred A. Knopf, 1932.

Anthologies of Women's Poetry

Adcock, Fleur (ed.), *The Faber Book of 20th Century Women's Poetry*, London: Faber, 1987.
Bax, Clifford and Meum Stewart (eds), *The Distaff Muse: An Anthology of Poetry written by Women*, London: Hollis and Carter, 1949.
Brereton, Frederick (ed.), *An Anthology of Women's Poems*, London: Collins, 1930.
Dowson, Jane (ed.), *Women's Poetry of the 1930s: A Critical Anthology*, London: Routledge, 1996.
Kaplan, Cora, *Salt and Bitter and Good: Three Centuries of English and American Women Poets*, New York: Paddington Press, 1975.
Reilly, Catherine (ed.), *Scars upon my Heart: Women's Poetry and Verse of the First World War*, London: Virago, 1981.
Squire, J.C. (ed.), *A Book of Women's Verse*, Oxford: Clarendon, 1921.

General Anthologies of the Period

Bolt, Sidney (ed.), *Poetry of the 1920s*, London: Longman, 1967.

Cunningham, Valentine (ed.), *The Penguin Book of Spanish Civil War Verse*, Harmondsworth: Penguin, 1980.

Day Lewis, C. and L.A.G. Strong (eds), *A New Anthology of Modern Verse 1920–40*, London: Methuen, 1941.

Eliot, T.S. (ed.), *The Little Book of Modern Verse*, 1934, new edition ed. Anne Ridler, London: Faber, 1941.

Grigson, Geoffrey (ed.), *Poetry of the Present: An Anthology of the Thirties and After*, London: Phoenix House, 1949.

————, *New Verse: An Anthology*, London: Faber, 1939.

Larkin, Philip (ed.), *The Oxford Book of Twentieth-Century English Verse*, London: Oxford University Press, 1973.

Lowell, Amy, with Louis Untermeyer (eds), *A Miscellany of American Poetry*, New York: Alfred Harcourt, 1917.

———— (ed.), *A Miscellany of American Poetry Vol. II*, Boston: Houghton Mifflin Company, 1918.

Marsh, Eddie (ed.), *Georgian Poetry*, London: The Poetry Bookshop, annually 1912–22.

Monro, Alida and Harold (eds), *Recent Poetry 1923–1933*, London: Gerald Howe & Co.; London: The Poetry Bookshop, 1933.

Monro, Harold (ed.), *Twentieth-Century Poetry*, 1929, revised and enlarged by Alida Monro, London: Chatto & Windus, 1933.

Moult, Thomas (ed.), *The Best Poetry*, London: Jonathan Cape, annual publication.

Murphy, Gwendolen (ed.), *The Modern Poet: An Anthology*, London: Sidgwick & Jackson, 1938.

Poems of Today, compiled by The English Association, London: Sidgwick and Jackson, annual publication.

Poetry of Today: A Quarterly 'Extra' of the Poetry Review, London: Erskine MacDonald Ltd., 1926.

Pryce Jones, Alan (ed.), *Georgian Poetry*, London: Edward Hulton, 1959.

Reeves, James (ed.), *Georgian Poetry*, London: Penguin, 1962.

Roberts, Michael (ed.), *The Faber Book of Modern Verse*, 1936, revised edition with supplement by Anne Ridler, 1951, London: Faber, 1954.

Some Imagist Poets: An Anthology, Vols. I–III, ed. Amy Lowell, Boston: Houghton Mifflin Company, 1915–17, New York: Kraus Reprint, 1969.

Spender, Stephen and John Lehmann, *Poems for Spain*, London: The Hogarth Press, 1939.

Wheels, Oxford: Blackwell, 1916–21, Liechtenstein: Kraus Reprint, 1972.

Wollman, Maurice (ed.), *Modern Poetry 1922–34*, London: Macmillan, 1934.

————, *Poems of 20 Years: An Anthology 1918–1938*, London: Macmillan, 1938.

Yeats, W.B. ed. *The Oxford Book of Modern Verse 1892–1935*, Oxford: Oxford University Press, 1936.

Periodicals of the Period

Adelphi, ed. John Middleton Murry, London: n.p., June 1923–June 1927.

Bookman (became *American Review*), New York, February 1895–March 1933.

Contact. An American Quarterly Review, ed. William Carlos Williams and Robert McAlmon, New York: December 1920–June 1923, New York: Kraus Reprint, 1967.

Criterion, ed. T.S. Eliot, 1919–39 (*New Criterion* from 1926), London: Faber, 1967.

Dial, 1880–1929, ed. Scofield Thayer (from 1920), then Marianne Moore (from 1925), New York: Dial Press.

Egoist, ed. Dora Marsden (formerly *New Freewoman*.) London, 1914–19, New York: Kraus Reprint, 1967.

Freewoman: A Weekly Feminist Review, ed. Dora Marsden, London: 23 November 1911–10 October 1912.

Left Review, ed. Montagu Slater, Amabel Williams, T.H. Wintringham, Vols 1–3, London: Collets Bookshop, 1934–38.

Listener, London: British Broadcasting Corporation, 1929–.

Little Review, ed. Margaret Anderson with Jane Heap, Chicago, New York and Paris: 1914–29, New York: Kraus Reprint, 1967.

New Adelphi (*New Series*, formerly *Adelphi*), ed. John Middleton Murry, London, 1927–31.

New Age, ed. O.R. Orage, London, October 1894–April 1938.

New Freewoman (formerly *Freewoman*; became *Egoist*), ed. Dora Marsden, London: 1913–1914, New York: Kraus Reprint, 1967.

New Oxford Poetry, ed. A.W. Sandford, Oxford, Blackwell, 1936–37.

New Statesman and Nation, London: The Statesman and Nation Publishing Company Ltd. 1931–57.

New Verse, ed. Geoffrey Grigson, 1933–39, New York, Klauss Reprint Corporation, 1966.

New Writing, ed. John Lehmann, London, Lawrence & Wishart, 1936–39.

New Writing, New Series Autumn, ed. John Lehman, Christopher Isherwood, Stephen Spender, London, Lawrence & Wishart, 1938–39.

Oxford Poetry, ed. Richard Goodman, Oxford, Blackwell, 1929–32.

Poetry: A Magazine of Verse, ed. Harriet Monroe, Chicago, 1912–35, New York: AMS Reprint, 1966.

Poetry Review, The Poetry Society, London: The Saint Catherine Press, 1909–.

Scrutiny, A Quarterly Review, ed. D.W. Harding, L.C. Knights, F.R. Leavis, Denys Thompson, Cambridge, Cambridge University Press, 1932–39.

Time and Tide, Cheshire: Europress Limited, 1920–76.

Times Literary Supplement, London, weekly publication.
Twentieth Century Verse, ed. Julian Symons, 1937–39.

Secondary Works

Ackland, Valentine, *For Sylvia: An Honest Account*, London: Chatto & Windus, 1985.
Anand, Mulk Raj, *Conversations in Bloomsbury*, London: Wildwood House, 1981.
Armstrong, Isobel, *Victorian Poetry*, London: Routledge, 1993.
Auden, W.H., *The English Auden: Poems, Essays and Dramatic Writings 1927–1939*, ed. Edward Mendelson, London: Faber and Faber, 1977.
Bakhtin, M.M., 'Rabelais and His World', 1965, *The Bakhtin Reader: Selected Writings of Bakhtin, Medvedev, Voloshinov*, ed. Pam Morris, London: Edward Arnold, 1994, 195–244.
Beach, Sylvia, *Shakespeare and Company*, London: Faber and Faber, 1960.
Bell, Anne Olivier (ed.), *A Moment's Liberty: The Shorter Diary.Virginia Woolf*, London: Hogarth Press, 1990.
Bell, Kathleen, 'Mew, T.S. Eliot and Modernism', Bertram, q.v., 13–24.
Bell, Michael (ed.), *The Context of English Literature: 1900–30*, London: Methuen, 1980.
Bell, Quentin, *Bloomsbury*, London: Weidenfeld and Nicolson, 1968.
Benstock, Shari, *Women of the Left Bank: Paris 1900–1940*, London: Virago, 1987.
Benton, Jill, *Naomi Mitchison: A Biography*, London: Pandora, 1990.
Bergonzi, Bernard, *The Myth of Modernism and Twentieth-Century Literature*, London: Harvester, 1986.
Berry, Paul, *Testament of a Generation: The Journalism of Vera Brittain and Winifred Holtby*, London: Virago, 1985.
Bertram, Vicki (ed.), *Kicking Daffodils – Twentieth-Century Women Poets*, Edinburgh: Edinburgh University Press, 1997.
Blackburn, John (ed.), *Hardy to Heaney: Twentieth-Century Prose. Introductions and Explanations*, Edinburgh: Oliver & Boyd, 1986.
Blain, Virginia, Paulina Clements and Isobel Grundy (eds), *A Feminist Companion to English Literature*, London: Batsford, 1990.
Blasing, Mutlin Konuk, *American Poetry: The Rhetoric of its Forms*, New Haven and London: Yale University Press, 1987.
Bloom, Clive (ed.), *Literature and Culture in Modern Britain. Vol. 1. 1900–1929*, Essex: Longman, 1993.
Bloom, Clive and Brian Docherty (eds), *American Poetry: The Modernist Ideal*, Basingstoke: Macmillan, 1995.
Boland, Eavan, 'Letter to a Young Woman Poet', *PN Review* 118, 24.2, November/December 1997: 16–21.

Boland, Eavan, 'The Woman Poet: Her Dilemma', *The American Poetry Review* 16. Jan/February 1987: 17–20.

———, *Object Lessons: The Life of the Woman and the Poet in Our Time*, Manchester: Carcanet, 1995.

Boll, Theophilus, E.M., *Miss May Sinclair: Novelist. A Biographical and Critical Introduction*, New Jersey: Associated University Presses, 1973.

Boulton, James T. and James Robertson (eds), *The Letters of D.H. Lawrence*, Vol. 3, Cambridge: Cambridge University Press, 1984.

Bowers, Jane Palatini, *Gertrude Stein*, Basingstoke: Macmillan, 1993.

Bradbrook, Muriel, *Women and Literature 1979–1982: Collected Papers of Muriel Bradbrook*, Sussex: Harvester, 1982.

Branson, Noreen and Margot Heinemann, *Britain in the Nineteen Thirties*, St Albans: Panther, 1973.

Brittain, Vera, 'America Tackles the Marriage Problem', *Time and Tide* 18 December 1925.

———, 'The University Idea', *Time and Tide* 28 February 1931: 243.

———, Amabel Williams Ellis and Storm Jameson, 'Silencing the Unemployed', *Time and Tide* 31 December 1932.

———, *Testament of Experience: An Autobiographical Story of the Years 1925–1950*, London: Virago, 1979.

———, *Testament of Friendship: the Story of Winifred Holtby*, London: Virago, 1980.

Broe, Mary Lynn and Angela Ingram (eds), *Women's Writing in Exile*, Chapel Hill: University of Carolina Press, 1989.

Brooke, Rupert, *Collected Poems*, 1932, London: Sidgwick and Jackson, 1974.

Brooks, Cleanth, *Modern Poetry and the Tradition*, London: Poetry London, 1948.

Brothers, Barbara, 'Against the Grain: Sylvia Townsend Warner and the Spanish Civil War', in Broe and Ingram, op. cit., 350–66.

Bruzzi, Zira, 'The Fiery Moment: H.D. and the Eleusinian Landscape of English Modernism', *Agenda* 25, Vol. 3–4, Autumn/Winter 1987: 97–112.

Bryher, Winifred, *Amy Lowell: A Critical Appreciation*, London: Eyre and Spottiswoode, 1918.

Buck, Claire, *H.D. and Freud: Bisexuality and a Feminine Discourse*, Hemel Hempstead: Harvester Wheatsheaf, 1991.

Bullough, Geoffrey, *The Trend of Modern Poetry*, 1934, London and Edinburgh: Oliver and Boyd, 1941.

Burke, Carolyn, *Becoming Modern: The Life of Mina Loy*, New York: Farrar, Straus, Giroux, 1996.

Byers, Margaret, 'Cautious Vision: Recent Poetry by Women', *British Poetry since 1960*, ed. Michael Schmidt, Manchester: Carcanet, 1972, 74–84.

Caesar, Adrian, *Dividing Lines: Poetry, Class and Ideology in the 1930s*, Manchester: Manchester University Press, 1991.

Carey, John, *The Intellectuals and the Masses*, London: Faber, 1992.

Carter, R. (ed.), *Thirties Poets: 'The Auden Group'*, London: Macmillan, 1984.

Caws, Mary Ann, *Women of Bloomsbury: Virginia, Vanessa and Carrington*, New York: Routledge, 1990.

Chevalier, Tracy (ed.), *Contemporary Poets*, 5th edn, London: St James Press, 1991.

Chisholm, Dianne, 'Pornopoeia, the Modernist Canon, and the Cultural Capital of Sexual Literacy: The Case of H.D.', in Dickie and Travisano, q.v., 69–96.

Clanchy, Kate, 'Loud Hailers and Currant Rolls', review of *Women's Poetry of the 1930s*, ed. Jane Dowson, *The Independent*, 3 February 1996.

Clark, Kenneth, 'On the Development of Miss Sitwell's Latest Style', *Horizon* July 1947: 7–17.

Clark, Suzanne, '*Jouissance* and the Sentimental Daughter: Edna St Vincent Millay', in Dickie and Travisano, q.v., 143–69.

———, *Sentimental Modernism: Women Writers and The Revolution of The Word*, Bloomington and Indianapolis: Indiana University Press, 1991.

Coffman, Stanley K., *Imagism: a Chapter in the History of Modern Poetry*, New York: Octagon Books, 1972.

Cole, Margaret, *Growing Up into Revolution*, London: Longmans, 1949.

Corbett, David Peters, *The Modernity of English Art 1914–30*, Manchester: Manchester University Press, 1997.

Cornford, Frances, *Literary Papers of Frances Cornford*, London, British Library, Department of Manuscripts.

Costello, Bonnie, Celeste Goodridge and Christanne Miller (eds), *The Selected Letters of Marianne Moore*, London: Faber, 1998.

Cunard, Nancy, *These Were the Hours: memories of my Hours Press Réanville and Paris 1928–1931*, London and Amsterdam: Walter Lowenfels, 1969.

Cunningham, Valentine (ed.), *Spanish Front: Writers on the Civil War*, New York: Oxford University Press, 1986.

———, *British Writers of the Thirties*, Oxford: Oxford University Press, 1988.

Day, Gary and Brian Docherty (eds), *British Poetry 1900–1950: Aspects of Tradition*, Basingstoke: Macmillan, 1995.

Day, Gary and Gina Wisker, 'Recuperating and Revaluing: Edith Sitwell and Charlotte Mew', in Day and Docherty, op. cit., 65–80.

Day Lewis, C. 'English Writers and a People's Front', *Left Review*, Vol. 2, October 1936: 671–4.

De Salvo, Louise and Mitchell A. Leaska (eds), *The Letters of Virginia Woolf and Vita Sackville-West*, London: Hutchinson, 1984.

De Sola Pinto, Vivian, *Crisis in English Poetry 1880–1940*, 1951, London: Hutchinson, 1967.

Deutsch, Babette, *This Modern Poetry*, London: Faber, 1936.

Dickie, Margaret, 'Recovering the Repression in Stein's Erotic Poetry', in Dickie and Travisano, q.v., 3–25.

Dickie, Margaret and Thomas Travisano (eds), *Gendered Modernisms: American Women Poets and Their Readers*, Philadelphia: University of Pennsylvania Press, 1996.

Dodsworth, Martin, 'Marianne Moore', in Hamilton, q.v., 1968: 125–33.

Dowson, Jane, 'The Importance of Frances Cornford', *The Charleston Magazine* 9, Spring/Summer 1994: 10–14.

———, 'Women Poets and the Political Voice', in Joannou, q.v., 46–62.

DuPlessis, Rachel Blau, *H.D.: the Career of that Struggle*, Sussex: Harvester, 1986.

Easthope, Anthony, *Contemporary Poetry meets Modern Theory*, Hemel Hempstead: Harvester Wheatsheaf, 1991.

Eldridge Miller, Jane, *Rebel Women: Feminism, Modernism and the Edwardian Novel*, London: Virago, 1994.

Eliot, T.S. as 'Apteryx', 'Observations', *Egoist* V, May 1918: 69–70.

Eliot, Valerie (ed.), *The Letters of T.S. Eliot: Vol. 1. 1898–1922*, London: Faber, 1988.

Empson, William, *Seven Types of Ambiguity*, London: Chatto & Windus, 1930.

Engle, Paul and Cecil Day Lewis, 'Modern Poetry–English and American', *The Listener* 15 May 1935: 852–4.

Faulkner, Peter (ed.), *A Modernist Reader: Modernism in England 1910–1930*, London: Batsford, 1986.

Featherstone, Simon, *War Poetry: An Introductory Reader*, London: Routledge, 1995.

Fielding, Daphne, *The Rainbow Picnic – A Portrait of Iris Tree*, London: Methuen, 1974.

Fitzgerald, Penelope, *Charlotte Mew & Her Friends*, 1974, London: Collins, 1984.

Flint, Kate, 'Public Antics, Private Angst', review of *His Arms Are Full Of Broken Things*, by P.B. Parris, *The Guardian* 6 March 1997.

Ford, Hugh (ed.), *Nancy Cunard: Brave Poet, Indomitable Rebel 1896–1965*, Philadelphia: Chilton Book Company, 1968.

Fraser, P.M. (ed.), *The Waves of Autolycus: Selected Literary Essays of Alice Meynell*, Oxford: Oxford University Press, 1965.

Fussell, Paul, *The Great War and Modern Memory*, 1975, London: Oxford University Press, 1977.

Gee, Maggie, 'Inside the Prickly Poet', review of *His Arms Are Full Of Broken Things* by P.B. Parris, *Daily Telegraph* 1 March 1997.

Gilbert, Sandra and Susan Gubar, *No Man's Land: The Place Of The Woman Writer In The Twentieth Century. Vol. 1. The War of The Words*, New Haven: Yale University Press, 1988.

———, *No Man's Land: The Place Of The Woman Writer In The Twentieth Century. Vol. 2. Sexchanges*, New Haven: Yale University Press, 1989.

———, *No Man's Land: The Place Of The Woman Writer In The Twentieth Century. Vol. 3. Letters to the Front*, New Haven: Yale University Press, 1994.

Gilkes, Martin, *A Key to Modern English Poetry*, 1937, London: Blackie & Son, 1948.

Glendinning, Victoria, *Edith Sitwell: A Unicorn Among Lions*, London: Weidenfeld and Nicolson, 1981.

Glendinning, Victoria, *Vita: The Life of Vita Sackville-West*, London: Weidenfeld & Nicolson, 1983.

Goldman, Dorothy, Jane Gledhill and Judith Hattaway, *Women Writers and the Great War*, New York: Twayne Publishers, 1995.

Goody, Alex, review of *The Lost Lunar Baedeker*, by Mina Loy, *PN Review* 120, 24.4, March/April 1998: 62–3.

Grant, Joy, *Harold Monro and the Poetry Bookshop*, London: Routledge & Kegan Paul, 1967.

Graves, Robert, *Goodbye to all That*, 1929, Harmondsworth: Penguin, 1979.

Gray, Richard, *American Poetry of the Twentieth-Century*, London: Longman, 1990.

Greene, Richard (ed.), *Selected Letters of Edith Sitwell*, London: Virago, 1997.

Greer, Germaine, *Slipshod Sibyls: Recognition, Rejection and the Woman Poet*, New York: Viking Press, 1995.

Gregson, Ian, *Contemporary Poetry and Postmodernism: Dialogue and Estrangement*, Basingstoke: Macmillan, 1996.

Gross, John (ed.), *The Modern Movement*, London: Harvill, 1992.

Hamilton, Ian (ed.), *The Modern Poet: Essays from 'The Review'*, London: Macdonald & Co., 1968.

———, *The Oxford Companion to Twentieth-Century Poetry*, Oxford: Oxford University Press, 1994.

Hanscombe, Gillian and Virginia Smyers, *Writing for their Lives: The Modernist Women 1910–1940*, London: The Women's Press, 1987.

Harman, Claire (ed.), *The Diaries of Sylvia Townsend Warner*, London: Chatto & Windus, 1994.

———, *Sylvia Townsend Warner: A Biography*, London: Minerva, 1985.

———, 'I'd Rather have Tea with the Birds', review of *Charlotte Mew and Her Friends*, by Penelope Fitzgerald, *PN Review* 11.6, 1985: 60–1.

Herring, Phillip, *Djuna: The Life and Work of Djuna Barnes*, New York: Viking, 1996.

Heuving, Jeanne, 'Laura Riding Jackson's "Really New" Poem', Dickie and Travisano pp.192–213.

Hobsbaum, Philip, 'Modernism. "The Road not Taken"', in Martin and Furbank, q.v., 12–8.

———, *Tradition and Experiment in English Poetry*, Basingstoke: Macmillan, 1979.

Hoffman, Frederick J. and Charles Allen, *The Little Magazines*, New Jersey: Princeton University Press, 1946.

Holland, Matt, 'Anna Wickham: Fettered Woman, Free Spirit', *Poetry Review* 78.2, 1988: 44–5.

Holtby, Winifred, 'Feminism Divided', *Time and Tide* 26 July, 1926.

———, 'Tea-Table Sitters', letter to *Time and Tide* 31 December, 1932: 1437.

———, *Letters to a Friend*, London: Collins, 1937.

Homans, Margaret, *Women Writing and Poetic Identity*, New Jersey: Princeton University Press, 1980.

Howe, Stephen (ed.), *Lines of Dissent: Writing for The New Statesman 1913–1988*, London: Verso, 1988.

Irigaray, Luce, *This Sex Which Is Not One*, trans. Catherine Porter with Carolyn Burke, New York: Cornell University Press, 1985.

Joannou, Maroula, *'Ladies, Please Don't Smash those Windows': Women's Writing, Feminist Consciousness and Social Change 1918–1938*, Oxford: Berg, 1995.

Jones, Peter, *An Introduction to Fifty American Poets*, London: Pan Books, 1979.

Juhasz, Suzanne, *Naked and Fiery Forms: Modern American Poetry by Women, A New Tradition*, London and New York: Harper and Row, 1976.

Jump, Harriet Devine (ed.), *Diverse Voices: Essays on Twentieth-Century Women Writers in English*, Sussex: Harvester Wheatsheaf, 1991.

Kaplan, Cora, 'Language and Gender', in Deborah Cameron (ed.), *Feminist Critique of Language*, London: Routledge, 1990, 57–69.

Kellogg, David, 'Literary History and the Problem of Oppositional Practices in Contemporary Poetry', *Cultural Critique* 32, Winter 1995–96: 153–86.

Kemp, Sandra, '"But how Describe a World Seen without a Self?" Feminism, Fiction and Modernism', *Critical Quarterly* 32.1, Spring 1990: 99–118.

Kenner, Hugh, *The Pound Era*, London: Faber, 1972.

Kermode, Frank, 'First Pitch', review of *The Selected Letters of Marianne Moore*, ed. Costello, Goodridge and Miller, *London Review of Books* 16 April 1998: 15–16.

Khan, Nosheen, *Women's Poetry of the First World War*, London: Harvester Wheatsheaf, 1988.

Kouidis, Virginia M., *Mina Loy: American Modernist Poet*, Louisiana State University Press and London: Baton Rouge, 1980.

Laity, Cassandra, 'H.D., Modernism, and the Transgressive Sexualities of Decadent-Romantic Platonism', in Dickie and Travisano, op. cit., 45–68.

Leavis, F.R., *New Bearings in English Poetry*, 1932, London: Chatto & Windus, 1979.

Lehmann, John and Derek Parker (eds), *Edith Sitwell: Selected Letters*, Basingstoke: Macmillan, 1970.

Leighton, Angela, *Victorian Women Poets: Writing Against the Heart*, Hemel Hempstead: Harvester Wheatsheaf, 1992.

Leighton, Angela and Margaret Reynolds (eds), *Victorian Women Poets: an anthology*, Oxford: Blackwell, 1985.

Lewis, Jane, *Women in England 1870–1950: Sexual Division and Social Change*, Bloomington: Indiana University Press, 1984.

Light, Alison, *Forever England: Femininity, Literature and Conservatism between the Wars*, London: Routledge, 1991.

Loeffelholz, Mary, 'History as Conjugation: Stein's *Stanzas in Meditation* and the Literary History of the Modernist Long Poem', in Dickie and Travisano, op. cit., 26–42.

Lowell, Amy, *Six French Poets*, London & New York: Macmillan, 1915.

Lowell, Amy, *Tendencies in Modern American Poetry*, 1917, Oxford: Blackwell, 1922.

———, *John Keats*, Boston: Houghton Mifflin, 1925.

———, *Poets and Poetry* (essays), Boston: Houghton Mifflin, 1930.

Lucas, John, 'Making the 1920s New', *Poetry Review* Winter 1993/4: 21–6.

——— (ed.), *Writing and Radicalism*, London: Longman, 1996.

———, 'The 1920s: radicals to the right and to the left', Lucas, ed. 1996, pp.178–200.

———, *The Radical Twenties*, Nottingham: Five Leaves, 1997.

Macbeam, E. 'Poetry and the Woman: The Creative Power', *Time and Tide* 9 June, 1922: 545.

Macdougall, Allan Ross (ed.), *Letters of Edna St Vincent Millay*, New York: Grosset and Dunlap, 1952.

Marsland, Elizabeth A., *The Nation's Cause: French, English and German Poetry of the First World War*, London: Routledge, 1991.

Martin, Anne, 'Aspects of British and American Feminism', *Time and Tide* 21 and 28 March 1924: 268, 292.

Martin, Graham and P.N. Furbank (eds), *Twentieth-Century Poetry: critical essays and documents*, Buckingham: Open University Press, 1975.

Maxwell, William (ed.), *The Letters of Sylvia Townsend Warner*, London: Chatto & Windus, 1982.

McGuiness, Patrick, 'Robert Graves, Modernism and the "Poetic Body"', *PN Review* January/February 1996: 16–22.

Miller, Cristanne, *Marianne Moore: Questions of Authority*, Cambridge, Massachusetts: Harvard University Press, 1995.

Minogue, Sally, 'Prescriptions and Proscriptions: Feminist Criticism and Contemporary Poetry', in Sally Minogue (ed.), *Problems for Feminist Criticism*, London: Routledge, 1990, 179–236.

Mitchison, Naomi, *All Change Here: Girlhood and Marriage*, London: Bodley Head, 1975.

Monro, Harold, *Some Contemporary Poets*, London: Simpkins & Marshall, 1920.

Monroe, Harriet, *A Poet's Life: Seventy Years in a Changing World*, New York: The Macmillan Company, 1938.

Montefiore, Jan, *Feminism and Poetry: Language, Experience, Identity in Women's Writing*, London: Pandora, 1987.

Monteith, Moira (ed.), *Women's Writing: A Challenge to Theory*, Sussex: Harvester, 1986.

Moody, A.D., 'H.D. Imagiste: An Elemental Mind', *Agenda* 25.3–4, Autumn/Winter 1987: 77–86.

Moore, Marianne, *Predilections*, 1931, New York: Viking, 1955.

Mott, Frank Luther, *A History of American Magazines. Vol. V: Sketches of Twenty One Magazines 1905–1930*, Cambridge, Massachusetts: Harvard University Press, 1968.

Mulford, Wendy, *This Narrow Place: Sylvia Townsend Warner and Valentine Ackland – Life, Letters and Politics 1930–1951*, London: Pandora, 1988.

———, 'Curved, Odd … Irregular. A Vision of Contemporary Poetry by Women', *Women: A Cultural Review* 1.3, Winter 1990: 261–74.

Murphy, Francis (ed.), *Uncollected Essays and Reviews of Yvor Winters*, 1973, London: Allen and Lane, 1974.

Nicolson, Nigel (ed.), *The Question of Things Happening: The Letters of Virginia Woolf. Vol. 2. 1912–1922*, London: Hogarth, 1976.

——— (ed.), *A Change of Perspective: The Letters of Virginia Woolf. Vol. 3 1924–1928*, London: Hogarth, 1977.

———, *Portrait of a Marriage*, 1973, Basingstoke: Macmillan, 1980.

——— (ed.), *Vita and Harold: The Letters of Vita Sackville-West and Harold Nicolson 1910–1962*, London: Weidenfeld & Nicolson, 1992.

Ostriker, Alicia, *Stealing the Language: The Emergence of Women's Poetry in America*, London: The Women's Press, 1987.

Ouditt, Sharon, *Fighting Forces: Writing Women, Identity and Ideology in the First World War*, London: Routledge, 1994.

Paige, D.D. (ed.), *The Selected Letters of Ezra Pound 1907–1941*, New York: New Directions, 1950.

Palatini Bowers, Jane, *Gertrude Stein*, Basingstoke: Macmillan, 1993.

Parris, P.B., *His Arms are Full of Broken Things*, New York: Viking, 1996.

Pearson, John, *Facades: Edith, Osbert and Sacheverell Sitwell*, Basingstoke: Macmillan, 1978.

Perkins, David, *A History of Modern Poetry. Vol. 1. From The 1890s to the High Modernist Mode*, Cambridge, Massachusetts: Harvard University Press, 1976.

———, *A History of Modern Poetry. Vol. 2. From the 1920s to the Present Day*, Cambridge, Massachusetts: Harvard University Press, 1976.

Plain, Gill, 'Great Expectations: Rehabilitating the Recalcitrant War Poets', *Feminist Review* 51, Autumn 1995: 41–65.

PN Review 23, 8.3, 1981, special edition on Sylvia Townsend Warner.

Powell Ward, John, *The English Line: Poetry of the Unpoetic from Wordsworth to Larkin*, Basingstoke: Macmillan, 1991.

Press, John, *A Map of English Verse*, Oxford: Oxford University Press, 1969.

Pumphrey, Martin, 'Play, Fantasy and Strange Laughter: Stevie Smith's Uncomfortable Poetry', *Critical Quarterly* 28.3, Autumn 1986: 85–96.

Raitt, Suzanne, *Vita and Virginia: The Work and Friendship of Vita Sackville-West and Virginia Woolf*, Oxford: Oxford University Press, 1993.

———, 'Charlotte Mew and May Sinclair: A Love Song', *Critical Quarterly* 37.3, Autumn 1995: 3–17.

Ransom, John Crowe, 'The Poet as Woman', *The World's Body*, Ransom, 1938, New York: Kennikat Press, 1964, 76–110.

Rattenbury, Arnold, 'Literature, Lying and Sober Truth: Attitudes to the Work of Patrick Hamilton and Sylvia Townsend Warner', in Lucas, op. cit., 1996, 201–44.

Raverat, Gwen, *Period Piece: A Cambridge Childhood*, London: Faber, 1952.

Rhondda, Lady Margaret, *This Was My World*, Basingstoke: Macmillan, 1933.

Rich, Adrienne, *Blood, Bread and Poetry: Selected Prose 1979–1985*, London: Virago, 1987.

Richards, I.A., *Practical Criticism*, 1929, London: Routledge & Kegan Paul, 1982.

Riding, Laura and Robert Graves, *A Survey of Modernist Poetry*, London: Heinemann, 1927.

———, *Contemporaries and Snobs*, Frome and London: Butler and Tanner, 1928.

——— with Robert Graves, *A Pamphlet against Anthologies*, London: Jonathan Cape, 1928.

———, 'An Enquiry', *New Verse* 11, October 1934: 2–5.

——— with Harry Kemp, *The Left Heresy in Literature and Life*, London: Methuen, 1939.

(Riding) Jackson, Laura, *The Telling*, New York: Harper and Row, 1972.

———, *The Word 'Woman' and Other Related Writings*, ed. Elizabeth Friedman and Alan J. Clark, New York: Persea, 1993.

——— and Schuyler B. Jackson, *Rational Meaning: A New Foundation for the Definition of Words and Supplementary Essays*, ed. William Harmon, introduction by Charles Bernstein, University Press of Virginia, 1997.

Roberts, Michael, 'American Poetry', *The Listener* 22 August 1934: 335–6.

Rogers, Timothy (ed.), *Georgian Poetry: The Critical Heritage*, London: Routledge & Kegan Paul, 1977.

Rose, Jacqueline, *Why War? – Psychoanalysis, Politics, and the Return to Melanie Klein*, Oxford: Blackwell, 1993.

———, review of *Virginia Woolf*, by Hermione Lee, London: Chatto 1996, *London Review of Books* 23 January 1997: 3–7.

Ross, Robert H., *The Georgian Revolt: Rise and Fall of the Poetic Ideal*, London: Faber, 1967.

Rumens, Carol, 'Smithwelby', review of *Women's Poetry of the 1930s*, by Jane Dowson, *Poetry Review* 85.4, Winter 95/6: 23–4.

Russell, Arthur (ed.), *Ruth Pitter: Homage to a Poet*, London: n.p. 1969.

Salter, Elizabeth and Allanah Harper, *Edith Sitwell: Fire of the Mind*, 1956, London: Michael Joseph, 1976.

Schenck, Celeste M., 'Exiled by Genre: Modernism, Canonicity, and the Politics of Exclusion', in Broe and Ingram, op. cit., 225–50.

Schlack, Beverley Ann, 'The Poetess of Poets: Alice Meynell Rediscovered', *Women's Studies* 7, 1989: 111–26.

Schmidt, Michael, *Introduction to 50 Modern British Poets*, London: Pan, 1979.

Schulze, Robin Gail, '"The Frigate Pelican"'s Progress: Marianne Moore's Multiple Versions and Modernist Practice', in Dickie and Travisano, op. cit., 117–42.

Schweik, Susan, 'Writing War Poetry like a Woman', *Critical Inquiry* 13, Spring 1987: 532–56.

Scott, Bonnie Kime (ed.), *The Gender of Modernism*, Indianapolis: Indiana University Press, 1990.

———, *Refiguring Modernism. Vol. 1: The Women of 1928*, Bloomington and Indianapolis: Indiana University Press, 1995.

Scully, James (ed.), *Modern Poets on Modern Poetry*, London: Collins, 1966.

Seymour-Smith, Martin (ed.), *Who's Who in 20th Century English Literature*, London: Weidenfeld and Nicolson, 1976.

Shils, Edward and Carmen Blacker (eds), *Cambridge Women: Twelve Portraits*, Cambridge: Cambridge University Press, 1996.

Silkin, John, *The Penguin Book of First World War Poetry*, 1979, Harmondsworth: Penguin, 1981.

Sinclair, May, *The Divine Fire*, London: Constable & Co. 1904.

———, *A Journal of Impressions in Belgium*, London: Hutchinson, 1915.

Sisson, C.H., *An Assessment of English Poetry 1900–1950*, 1971, Manchester: Carcanet, 1981.

Sitwell, Edith, *Poetry and Criticism*, London: Hogarth, 1925.

———, 'Some Observations on Women's Poetry', *Vogue* (London) 65.5, March 1925: 117–18.

———, review of *The Farmer's Bride* and *The Rambling Sailor*, by Charlotte Mew, *The Criterion* IX.34, October 1929: 130–34.

———, *The English Eccentrics*, London: Faber, 1933.

———, *Aspects of Modern Poetry*, London: Duckworth, 1934.

———, *A Poet's Notebook*, London: Macmillan, 1943.

———, *Taken Care Of: An Autobiography*, London: Hutchinson, 1965.

Smith, Stan, *The Origins of Modernism*, Sussex: Harvester Wheatsheaf, 1994.

Smulders, Sharon, 'Feminism, Pacifism and the Ethics of War; the Politics and Poetics of Alice Meynell's War Verse', *English Literature in Transition* 36.2, 1993: 159–77.

Southworth, James (ed.), *More Modern American Poetry*, Oxford: Blackwell, 1954.

Spalding, Frances, *Stevie Smith: A Critical Biography*, London: Faber, 1988.

Spender, Dale, *Women of Ideas and What Men Have Done to Them: From A. Behn to A. Rich*, London: Ark, 1983.

Spender, Stephen, 'Poetry and Revolution', *New Country*, March 1933.

———, *The Thirties and After: Poetry, Politics People 1933–1975*, London: Collins/Fontana, 1978.

Stansky, Peter, *In or About December 1910: Studies in Cultural History*, Cambridge, Massachusetts: Harvard University Press, 1996.

Stapleton, Laurence, *Marianne Moore: The Poet's Advance*, New Jersey: Princeton University Press, 1978.

Stauder, Ellen Keck, 'On Mina Loy', review of *Becoming Modern: The Life of Mina Loy*, by Carolyn Burke, and *The Lost Lunar Baedeker*, ed. Roger Conover, *Modernism/Modernity* 4. 3, The Johns Hopkins University Press, 1997: 141–59.

Steele, Timothy, *Missing Measures: Modern Poetry and the Revolt against Meter*, Fayetteville Arkansas and London: University of Arkansas Press, 1990.

Stein, Gertrude, *The Making of Americans*, 1925, London: Peter Owen, 1968.

——, *The Autobiography of Alice B. Toklas*, 1933, Harmondsworth: Penguin, 1986.

——, *Look at Me Now and Here I am. Writings and Lectures 1909–45*, 1941, ed. Patricia Meyerowitz, Harmondsworth: Penguin, 1971.

Steinman, Lisa M., 'Marianne Moore and Literary Tradition', in Dickie and Travisano, op. cit., 97–116.

Stephen, G.W., 'The War Poets: Time for a New View?', *Agenda* 22, 3–4, Autumn/Winter, 1985: 144–51.

Stevenson, Anne, 'Some Notes on Women and Tradition', *PN Review* 87, 19.1, September/October 1992: 29–32.

Swinnerton, Frank, *The Georgian Literary Scene*, 1938, London: Dent, 1946.

Symons, Julian, 'How Wide is the Atlantic? or Do you believe in America?', *Twentieth-Century Verse* 12–13, special edition on American poetry, September/October 1938: 80–84.

——, 'Miss Edith Sitwell have and had and heard', *The London Magazine*, IV.8, November 1964: 63.

——, *The Thirties: A Dream Revolved*, London: Faber, 1975.

——, *Makers of the New: The Revolution in Literature 1912–1939*, London: Andre Deutsch, 1987.

Thacker, Andrew, 'Amy Lowell and H.D.: The Other Imagists', *Women: A Cultural Review* 4. 1, Spring 1993: 49–59.

Thompson, Tierl (ed.), *Dear Girl – The Diaries and Letters of Two Working Women 1897–1917*, London: The Woman's Press, 1967.

Thurley, Geoffrey, *The Ironic Harvest: English Poetry in the Twentieth Century*, London: Arnold, 1974.

Thwaite, Anthony, *Twentieth-Century English Poetry*, London: Heinemann, 1978.

Tylee, Claire, *The Great War and Women's Consciousness: Images of Militarism and Womanhood in Women's Writings 1914–1964*, Basingstoke: Macmillan, 1990.

Untermeyer, Louis, *Modern British Poetry*, New York: Harcourt, 1925.

Walker, Cheryl, 'Anti-modern, Modern and Post-modern Edna St Vincent Millay: Contexts of Revaluation', in Dickie and Travisano, op. cit., 170–90.

Waller, Philip and John Rowett, *Chronology of the 20th Century*, Oxford: Helicon, 1995.

Walsh, Jeffrey, 'Alternative "Modernists": Robert Graves and Laura Riding', in Day and Docherty, op. cit., 131–50.

Walter, George, 'Loose Women and Lonely Lambs: The Rise and Fall of Georgian Poetry', in Day and Docherty, op. cit., 14–36.

Warner, Sylvia Townsend, 'The Way By Which I Have Come', *The Countryman* XIX. 2, 1939: 472–86.

Warner, Val, 'New Light on Charlotte Mew', *PN Review*, 24.2, 1997: 43–7.

Wellesley, Dorothy, *Far Have I Travelled*, London: James Barrie, 1952.

—— (ed.), *Letters on Poetry from W.B. Yeats to Dorothy Wellesely*, 1940, new edition, ed. Kathleen Raine, Oxford: Oxford University Press, 1964.

West, Rebecca, 'Women Poets', review of *An Anthology of Women's Verse*, ed. J.C. Squire, *The Bookman*, May 1921: 92–3.

Whitehead, John, *Hardy to Larkin: Seven English Poets*, Shropshire: Hearthstone Publication, 1995.

Wilkinson, Ellen, 'Can Men and Women be Really Equal?', *The Listener* 2 April 1930: 587–8.

Williams, Ellen, *Harriet Monroe & the Poetry Renaissance: The First 10 Years of Poetry 1912–1922*, Urbana: University of Illinois Press, 1977.

Williams, John, *Twentieth-Century British Poetry: A Critical Introduction*, London: Edward Arnold, 1987.

Williams, Raymond, *Culture and Society 1780–1950*, London: Chatto & Windus, 1958.

Willis, Patricia (ed.), *The Complete Prose of Marianne Moore*, London: Faber and Faber, 1987.

——, *Marianne Moore: Woman and Poet*, National Poetry Foundation, 1990.

Wills, Claire, 'Contemporary Women's Poetry: Experimentation and the Expressive Voice', *Critical Quarterly* 36.3, Autumn 1994: 35–52.

Winters, Yvor, 'A Woman With a Hammer', review of *The Contemporary Quarry* and *The Man With a Hammer*, by Anna Wickham, in Francis Murphy, op. cit., 11–12.

——, 'Robert Bridges and Elizabeth Daryush', *American Review* VIII.3, 1936–73: 353–67, reprinted in Francis Murphy, op. cit., 271–83.

Wittig, Monig, *The Straight Mind and Other Essays*, London: Harvester, 1992.

Woolf, Virginia, *Orlando*, 1928, ed. Rachel Bowlby, Oxford: Oxford University Press, 1998.

——, *A Room of One's Own*, 1929, London: Granada, 1977.

——, *Three Guineas*, London: Hogarth Press, 1938.

——, *Collected Essays*, Vol. 2, London: Hogarth Press, 1966.

——, *A Woman's Essays*, Harmondsworth: Penguin, 1992.

Wright, Anne, *Literature of Crisis: 1910–1922*, Basingstoke: Macmillan, 1984.

Yorke, Liz, *Impertinent Voices: Subversive Strategies in Contemporary Women's Poetry*, London: Routledge, 1991.

Zytaruk, George J. and James Boulton (eds), *The Letters of D.H. Lawrence*, Vol. 2, June 1913–October 1916, Cambridge: Cambridge University Press, 1981.

Manuscript Papers

Journals and Literary Papers of Frances Cornford, London: British Library, Department of manuscripts.

Letters from Frances Cornford to Gilbert Murray, Gilbert Murray Papers, Oxford: Bodleian Library.

Letters from Frances Cornford to Virginia Woolf 1923–26, Sx. Ms. 18. MHL, (VW), Brighton: University of Sussex Library.

Unnamed articles

'An Anthology of American Verse', review of *Modern American Poets*, ed. Conrad Aiken, *TLS* 2 November 1922: 703.

'Dame Edith Sitwell: Poetess of Elaborate Style and Originality', Obituary, *Times* 10 December 1964: 12.

'Elizabeth Daryush', Obituary, *Times* 9 April 1977: 14g.

'England's Jealousy of America: The Need for Frankness', *Time and Tide* 1 February 1929: 104–5.

'Feminism in England and America', *Time and Tide* 9 July 1926: 616.

'Georgian Poetry', review of *Georgian Poetry 1916–17*, *TLS* 27 December 1917: 646.

'Georgian Poets', review of *Georgian Poetry 1920–22*, *TLS* 11 January 1923: 24.

'Interview with Edith Sitwell', *Sunday Times* 8 September 1957.

'Miss Victoria Sackville-West: Novelist and Poet', Obituary, *Times* 4 June, 1962: 19.

'On the Threshold', review of *The Gift*, by Margaret Cecilia Furse, London: Constable, *Three Days*, by Rose Macaulay, London: Constable and *The Splendid Days*, by May Wedderburn Cannan, Oxford: Blackwell, *TLS* 13 November 1919: 647.

'Poetesses', review of *A Book of Women's Verse*, ed. J.C. Squire, *TLS* 24 November 1921: 267.

'The Art of Anthology', leading article, *TLS* 1 February 1923: 65.

'The Poetry of Women', review of *The House*, by Gladys Mary Hazel, Oxford: Blackwell, *Poems of Motherhood*, by Dorothea Still, Oxford: Blackwell and *The Verse Book of a Homely Woman*, by Fay Inchfawn, *Girl's Own Paper* and *Woman's Magazine*, *TLS* 9 December 1920: 810.

'Women Poets', *Poetry Review* May 1912: 199–202.

Index